PRAISE FROM THE FIRST EDITION OF
MAKING STRATEGY WORK

"I truly believe that if General Motors had incorporated Dr. Hrebiniak's proposals at any time over the past 15 to 20 years, the picture of General Motors today would be extremely different."

—**James P. Powers**, Strategic Planning,
General Motors Corporation (Ret.)

"I am a big Larry Hrebiniak fan. In his book he offers a comprehensive, disciplined process model for making strategy work in the real world. All of us owe him our thanks."

—**Ken Blanchard**, Coauthor of
The One Minute Manager and *The Secret*

"Strategy is the starting point, but without implementing actions, even the best laid plans remain just that. In *Making Strategy Work*, Hrebiniak provides a powerful and persuasive field manual for execution by laying out the logic, order, and essence of the strategic decisions that must follow."

—**Michael Useem**, Professor of Management and Director of the Center for Leadership and Change at the Wharton School, University of Pennsylvania

"Terrific...I have read all the 'handbooks,' 'guides to,' and 'roadmaps,' but in this book Larry has create the world's first Strategy Implementation GPS...spot on."

—**Gordon Peters**, founding Chairman, CEO,
Institute for Management Studies

Making Strategy Work

Making Strategy Work

Leading Effective Execution and Change

Second Edition

Lawrence G. Hrebiniak

Vice President, Publisher: Tim Moore
Associate Publisher and Director of Marketing: Amy Neidlinger
Executive Editor: Jeanne Glasser
Operations Specialist: Jodi Kemper
Marketing Manager: Megan Graue
Cover Designer: Chuti Prasertsith
Managing Editor: Kristy Hart
Senior Project Editor: Lori Lyons
Copy Editor: Geneil Breeze
Proofreader: Sarah Kearns
Indexer: Lisa Stumpf
Senior Compositor: Gloria Schurick
Manufacturing Buyer: Dan Uhrig

FT Press offers excellent discounts on this book when ordered in quantity for bulk purchases or special sales. For more information, please contact U.S. Corporate and Government Sales, 1-800-382-3419, corpsales@pearsontechgroup.com. For sales outside the U.S., please contact International Sales at international@pearsoned.com.

Printed in the United States of America

First Printing June 2013

ISBN-10: 0-13-309257-7
ISBN-13: 978-0-13-309257-8

Pearson Education LTD.
Pearson Education Australia PTY, Limited.
Pearson Education Singapore, Pte. Ltd.
Pearson Education Asia, Ltd.
Pearson Education Canada, Ltd.
Pearson Educación de Mexico, S.A. de C.V.
Pearson Education—Japan
Pearson Education Malaysia, Pte. Ltd.

Library of Congress Control Number: 2013935246

DEDICATION

In memory of Donna, who left us much too soon,
but who still lives in pleasant memories.

CONTENTS AT A GLANCE

TABLE OF CONTENTS

ABOUT THE AUTHOR

Lawrence G. Hrebiniak, Ph.D., has emeritus status at the University of Pennsylvania. Professor Hrebiniak was a member of the faculty of the Department of Management of The Wharton School for 36 years, where he taught courses in strategic management in the Wharton M.B.A. and Executive Education Programs. He still is very active in the Wharton Executive Education arena, teaching and working with managers in the area of strategy implementation or execution.

Dr. Hrebiniak held managerial positions in the automobile industry prior to entering academia, which provided him with valuable real-world experience. He is a past President of the Organization Theory Division of the Academy of Management. For more than two years he was one of a handful of Wharton faculty members providing commentaries on the *Wharton Management Report*, a TV program on the Financial News Network.

Professor Hrebiniak's most notable research of late has been in the area of strategy execution. He has consulted with or participated in executive development work with scores of companies, profit and not-for-profit alike, both inside and outside the U.S. He facilitated many of Jack Welch's legendary "Work-Outs." Based on his research and experience with strategy implementation, he developed integrated processes that help make strategy work in different organizations, across different industry settings. He is still active as a researcher and consultant.

Dr. Hrebiniak has authored seven books and numerous professional articles. This book, the second edition of the best-selling *Making Strategy Work*, reflects his experience as a manager, consultant, and educator in creating a culture of execution and facilitator of the execution process in complex organizations.

Introduction to the Second Edition

This book continues a critical, needed focus on strategy execution or implementation in complex organizations. Since the original publication of *Making Strategy Work* in 2005, increasing numbers of managers have come to realize the importance of execution for effective performance and competitive advantage. These managers supported and validated the original facts and findings in the research underlying this book and, more importantly, provided valuable feedback that has strengthened the new edition of *Making Strategy Work*.

The original version of this book differentiated itself in important ways:

- It was empirically based, building on the insights and experiences of managers involved in the difficult task of strategy execution, as well as my research and consulting work in this area. No armchair musings or war stories here; rather, the book reflected the views of practicing managers and their actual experiences with a challenging management task.

- It was action or decision oriented, with an eye to actual outcomes or results. It suggested ways to attain the results promised by sometimes lofty strategic plans.

- It presented an integrated approach to execution. It showed how key factors are interdependent and how they work together to achieve desired strategic and operating outcomes.

- It melded theory and real-world practices in a useful way. Execution deals with decisions that must pass muster in the real world of management, and *Making Strategy Work* responded to this important need.

The second edition of *Making Strategy Work* continues the tradition and trajectory laid out in the original work. It adds new, up-to-date examples, while retaining the critical theoretical underpinnings and practical insights of the first edition. The best of the old is retained, while adding new and useful knowledge about strategy execution.

Along the lines of new and useful knowledge is the addition of Part II, "Applications." This section applies the insights of the basic model and approach to execution to situations that managers suggested needed additional coverage. Part II of the revised edition of *Making Strategy Work* includes four chapters, the last three of which are new:

- Chapter 10, "Making Mergers and Acquisitions Work"
- Chapter 11, "Making Global Strategy Work"
- Chapter 12, "Executing Strategy in Service Organizations"
- Chapter 13, "Project Management and Strategy Execution"

Part II adds much to the original discussion of *Making Strategy Work*. It provides additional fuel for thought and insight into strategy execution in the settings analyzed, which represents a new and exciting contribution of the revised look. Every effort has been made in the new edition of *Making Strategy Work* to retain the best of the old while adding new and valuable information. The road to effective execution and organizational performance is a challenging one, full of potholes and obstacles. This book is intended to help managers in all organizations—for-profit, not-for-profit, product-based, and service-oriented—identify and cope with challenges as they become more adept at making strategy work.

ACKNOWLEDGMENTS

As usual, there are people whose help was invaluable in making this project work, and I would like to recognize their contributions. Cecilia Atoo of Wharton's Management Department did amazing work on this project. She again was a multitasking stalwart as she typed, created tables and figures, and met all sorts of demands made by me and the editorial staff of the publisher. Jeanne Levine was a knowledgeable editor with an ability to make suggestions in a nice, clear, and helpful way. Lori Lyons and other members of Pearson's editorial staff did an efficient job, for which I am grateful. Special thanks are due to Laura Marmar for her artistic bent and amazing ability to offer constructive ideas. I still consider her both my muse and practical helper. Finally, as always, there is my son, Justin, who not only is family, but is also a good friend who is there when I require some encouragement and need to talk to a buddy. Thanks to all.

Introduction to the First Edition

This book focuses on a critical management issue: making strategy work or executing strategy effectively.

Theories and advice about the requisites of good planning and strategy formulation abound in management literature. A vast array of planning models and techniques has been paraded before managers over the years, and managers for the most part understand them and know how to use them effectively.

The problem with poor performance typically is not with planning, but with doing. That is, strategies often aren't implemented successfully. Making strategy work is more difficult than strategy making. Sound plans flounder or die because of a lack of execution know-how. This book focuses on execution—the processes, decisions, and actions needed to make strategy work.

What differentiates this book from others, beyond its emphasis on a critical management need? I'm excited about the present approach to execution for the six following reasons.

LEARNING FROM EXPERIENCE

This book is based on data. It borrows from the experiences of hundreds of managers actually involved in strategy execution. There are multiple sources of data, which ensures complete coverage of execution-related issues. This book doesn't rely on the armchair musings of a few people relating unconnected anecdotes; it is based on real-world execution experiences, problems, and solutions—including mine over the last two decades.

WHAT YOU NEED TO LEAD

The focus of the book is on the knowledge, skills, and capabilities managers need to lead execution efforts. Its content is action- and results-oriented.

Most organizations recruit, train, and retain good managers; they are staffed by good people—even great people. Most managers are motivated and qualified people who want to perform well.

Even good people, however, can be hampered by poor incentives, controls, organizational structures, and company policies or operating procedures that inhibit their ability to execute and get things done. Even great leaders, in top management positions, will fail if they're not well versed in the conditions that affect execution success. Managers need to understand what makes strategy work. Intuition and personality simply aren't sufficient, given such a complex task. This book focuses on this knowledge and the capabilities and insights leaders need for execution success.

THE BIG PICTURE

In this book, I develop a unifying, integrated approach to execution. I focus on the big picture, as well as the nitty-gritty of the execution process and methods. I spell out a logical approach to execution and the relationships among key execution decisions.

This book not only identifies these key factors and their relationships, but also goes into detail on each of the factors needed for execution success. It provides an important, integrated approach to execution and dissects the approach to focus on its key elements, actions, or decisions. This book then provides both an overview of the execution process and an in-depth reference manual for key aspects of this process.

EFFECTIVE CHANGE MANAGEMENT

Leading successful execution efforts usually demands the effective management of change, and this book integrates important change-management issues into its treatment of execution.

This book discusses power, influence, and resistance to change. It focuses on real and practical change-related issues—such as whether to implement execution related changes quickly, all at once, or in a more deliberate and sequential fashion over time. I tell you why "speed kills" and explain how large, complex changes can severely hurt execution outcomes. I focus on the details of cultural change and the organizational power structure, and how they can be used to make strategy work.

APPLYING WHAT YOU LEARN

This book practices what it preaches. The final chapter shows how to apply the logic, insights, and practical advice of preceding chapters to a real, huge, and pervasive problem: Making mergers and acquisitions (M&A) work.

M&A strategies often flounder or fail; my last chapter explains why this is the case and how to increase the success of M&A efforts by applying the book's approach to execution. I also highlight the utility of the book's advice and guidelines when trying to make M&A efforts successful. I feel it is only fitting and proper to end an execution book on a positive and useful note—by showing how practical execution can be in confronting an important and pervasive real-world issue and how it can save management a lot of time, effort, and money.

THE BOTTOM LINE

Sixth and finally, the reasons above—taken together—distinguish this book significantly from other recent works, such as Bossidy and Charan's *Execution* (Crown Business, 2002). This book covers more of the important factors and decisions related to successful execution. It offers an empirically based, integrative, complete approach to making strategy work and focuses more extensively on managing change than other publications dealing with implementation.

The bottom line is that my book greatly adds to and follows logically Bossidy and Charan's *Execution*. It is an important and necessary addition to the toolkit of managers looking to execute strategy and change effectively.

ON A FINAL NOTE

Leading execution and change to make strategy work is a difficult and formidable task. For the six reasons I have listed, I believe this task can be made more logical, manageable, and successful by the present book's approach and insights.

A FEW THANKS

An undertaking such as the present one is challenging and difficult because of its complexity. I alone assume responsibility for the book's content, its interpretation of data and facts, and its conclusions. Still, while the ultimate responsibility is mine, there are a number of people who helped me in my task, and I would like to recognize them for their contributions. Brian Smith of the Gartner Research Group helped immensely with the creation of the online research survey and contributed important technical support. Cecilia Atoo of Wharton was a real stalwart as she typed the manuscript, created figures and tables, and otherwise helped meet my demands and those of the copyeditors. Many thanks are due to my editor, Tim Moore, as well as Russ Hall and others at Pearson Prentice Hall who helped me develop the manuscript into its present form. The anonymous reviewers who provided valuable feedback and suggestions for improving the manuscript also deserve recognition for their efforts. Finally, special thanks are due to my son, Justin, and my muse, Laura, whose encouragement, friendship, and support were constant sources of motivation to me.

Key Factors in Strategy Execution

Creating an Integrated Approach to Making Strategy Work

Strategic planning or "strategy making" is difficult. It demands time and attention paid to industry forces, competitors' actions, and organizational capabilities and investments. Planning involves positioning decisions and steps to differentiate the organization in significant ways and then protecting its position from competitive challenges and risks. Strategy formulation is no easy task.

As difficult as strategy making is, making strategy work is even more difficult and challenging. There are tremendous obstacles to effective strategy execution or implementation. Some of the obstacles or hurdles arise from the conditions or demands of the execution process, including the following:

- The need to get many more people involved in execution than were involved in planning
- The longer time frames associated with the process of strategy implementation and the resultant probability that competitive forces or conditions will change over time
- The existence of many factors or variables that can affect execution results or success, and the need to handle them effectively to achieve desired outcomes

A related challenge is the high interdependence among execution-related decisions and actions. Changing one factor can affect needed changes in other factors or variables—a situation that clearly demands an integrative process or approach to making strategy work.

Part I of this edition of *Making Strategy Work* presents the key issues involved in strategy execution or implementation. It discusses the key decisions and actions of the execution process, including those emanating from: the demands strategy places on the organization; the role of organizational structure and the coordination requirements associated with it; the need for clear responsibility and accountability in execution decisions; the need to define effective incentives and controls; and the importance of managing change, including culture change, to achieve successful execution outcomes.

A major differentiating aspect of the current approach to making strategy work is the development and use of an integrative model that ties together key decisions and actions. It is not sufficient to mention key variables or factors in the process of strategy implementation—it is imperative to focus as well on the interdependence of these factors and how their interaction affects overall execution outcomes. Making strategy work is a complex task, and only an integrative model or approach can handle this complexity effectively.

Part I of this book presents an integrated approach to strategy execution or implementation. It shows the flow of key decisions and actions as well as the interactions between or among them. It contains the essence or *raison d'être* of the strategy execution process. Its goal is to improve understanding of this process, including the key variables involved, obstacles to the process, how key variables interact to produce execution outcomes, and how the management of change is vital to the success of any approach to making strategy work. Let's turn now to this interesting and challenging task.

Strategy Execution Is the Key

Introduction

In 2013, eight years after the publication of *Making Strategy Work*, the strategic implementation problems organizations face are remarkably similar to those reported by managers in 2005. The obstacles to effective strategy execution are still real and formidable. While strategic planning or strategy making is difficult and challenging, as always, it's still obvious that managers feel more than ever that the successful implementation of strategy is more problematic than the formulation of a chosen strategy and even more important for organizational performance. It is still clear and notable that making strategy *work* is more difficult and challenging than making or creating strategy.

If, indeed, there is a notable change in 2013, it's that the execution of strategy is receiving more attention than it did a decade or so ago. Managers realize more than ever that execution is a key to strategic success and that the obstacles to implementation are real and demand managerial time and attention. Despite this insight, however, the road to successful execution is still bumpy and full of potholes, suggesting that managers haven't come fully to grasp with what contributes to making strategy work. Let's note what these challenging issues were in 2005 and why they still set the tone for this book and underlie the present treatment of what's needed to make strategy work. Looking at the past and present clearly shows that the challenges to execution were and still are real, salient, and worthy of attention.

More than two decades ago, I was working with the Organizational Effectiveness Group in AT&T's new Consumer Products division, a business created after the court-mandated breakup and reorganization of the company. I remember one particular day that made an impression on me that would last for years.

I was talking to Randy Tobias, the head of the division. I had met Randy while doing some work for Illinois Bell, and here we were talking about his division's strategic issues and challenges. Randy later moved into the chairman's office at AT&T and then became a successful CEO of Eli Lilly, but his comments that day years ago were the ones that affected me most.[i]

Here was a new business thrust headlong into the competitive arena. Competition was new to AT&T at the time. Competitive strategy for the business was nonexistent, and Tobias was laboring to create that elusive original plan. He focused on products, competitors, industry forces, and how to position the new division in the marketplace. He handled expectations and demands from corporate as he forged a plan for the business and helped position it in the AT&T portfolio. He created a strategic plan where previously there had been none, a Herculean task and one well done at the time.

On that day, I recall asking Randy what was the biggest strategic challenge confronting the business. I expected that his answer would deal with the problem of strategy formulation or some competitive threat facing the division. His answer surprised me.

He said that strategy formulation, while extremely challenging and difficult, was not what concerned him the most. It was not the planning that worried him. It was something even bigger and more problematic.

It was the execution of strategy that concerned him above all else. Making the plan work would be an even bigger challenge than creating the plan. Execution was the key to competitive success, but it would take some doing.

I, of course, sought further clarification and elaboration. I can't remember all of his points in response to my many questions, but here are some of the execution challenges he raised that day, referring to his own organization. He mentioned the following:

- The culture of the organization and how it was not appropriate for the challenges ahead
- Incentives and how people have been rewarded for seniority or "getting older," not for performance or competitive achievement
- The need to overcome problems with traditional functional "silos" in the organization's structure
- The challenges inherent in managing change as the division adapted to new competitive conditions

This was the first elaboration of execution-related problems I had ever heard, and the message has stayed with me over the years. This early experience has been repeated countless times in many other organizations. A number of critical insights have stayed with me as I've dealt with execution- or implementation-related programs in many different organizations. It became clear to me that day and over the years that: Execution is a key to success.

EXECUTION IS A KEY TO SUCCESS

Execution clearly is a key to success, but it is no easy task. Here was a company back then with an ingrained culture and structure, a set way of doing things. For AT&T to adapt to its new competitive environment, major changes would be necessary, and those changes would be no simple cakewalk. Obviously, developing a competitive strategy wouldn't be easy, but the massive challenges confronting the company made it clear to me early on that: Making strategy work is more difficult than strategy making.

MAKING STRATEGY WORK IS MORE DIFFICULT THAN THE TASK OF STRATEGY MAKING

Execution represents a disciplined process or a logical set of connected activities that enables an organization to take a strategy and make it work. Without a careful, planned approach to execution, strategic goals cannot be attained. Developing such a logical approach, however, represents a formidable challenge to management.

Even with careful development of an execution plan at the business level, execution success is not guaranteed. Tobias' strategic and execution plans for the Consumer Products division were well thought out. Yet troubles plagued the division's progress. Why? The problem was with the entire AT&T corporation. The company was about to go through a huge metamorphosis that it simply was not equipped to deal with and make work. Execution plans at the business level founder or fail if they don't receive corporate support. AT&T was, at the time, a slow-moving behemoth in which change was vehemently resisted. Well-prepared and logical plans at the Consumer Products business level were hampered by a poor corporate culture. Tobias' insights and potentially effective execution actions were blunted by corporate inertia and incompetence. A host of factors, including politics, inertia, and resistance to change, routinely can get in the way of execution success.

In the years since this first encounter with strategy execution or implementation, I have worked with numerous managers and many organizations from different and diverse industries, I've worked with many different companies or organizations—large and small, service organizations and nonprofits, government agencies—and the message has remained entirely consistent and clear: The execution of strategy is vital to company or organizational performance, but pulling it off successfully is a huge challenge and difficult task.

One striking aspect of all this, even in the present, is that managers apparently still don't know a great deal about the execution of strategy. It is still seen as a major problem and challenge.

Management literature has focused over the years primarily on parading new ideas on planning, strategy formulation, and so on in front of eager readers, but it has sorely neglected execution. Granted, planning is important. Granted, people are waking up to the challenge and are beginning to take execution seriously.

Still, it is obvious that the execution of strategy is not nearly as clear and understood as the formulation of strategy and other management issues. Much more is known about planning than doing, about strategy making than making strategy work.

An obvious question that presents itself is: Is execution really worth the effort? Is execution or implementation truly worth managerial time and attention?

Consider some relatively recent comprehensive studies of what contributes to company success.[ii] In one study of 160 companies over a five-year period, success was strongly correlated, among other things, with an ability to execute flawlessly. Factors such as culture, organizational structure, and aspects of operational execution were found to be vital to company success, with success measured by total return to shareholders. Focusing on execution, the study found, is definitely worthwhile, leading to increased profitability.

Another, more recent study of CEO abilities and the effects on company performance is even more striking in its findings.[iii] The authors of the research published in 2012 found, shockingly, that CEOs who were good listeners, team builders, or great communicators did not lead successful companies. What was most significant were the top manager's execution and organizational skills. Managers who focused on details, the integration of long-term and short-term goals and performance metrics, and analytical thoroughness were the ones leading successful companies. Coordination and follow-through were more important than being an enthusiastic colleague. The people or social skills, one can infer, can add to the top manager's execution prowess, but they alone are insufficient to guarantee company success.

This and other studies suggest that the market wants top management to fill an organizational role more than a social one.[iv] What's desired from leaders is a relentless and even mind-numbing focus on execution and incremental changes in performance. Charisma and charm help, but the delivery of performance metrics and the ability to execute a plan are what really counts. The methodical manager whose relentless focus is on execution and the organizational design capabilities supporting it is the man of the hour. Making strategy work is the mark of the successful CEO and his or her staff.

Other recent works have added their support to these studies' findings that execution is important for strategic success, even if their approach and analysis are less rigorous and complete.[v] These works then, in total, support the view I've held for years: A focus on execution pays dividends.

A FOCUS ON MAKING STRATEGY WORK PAYS MAJOR DIVIDENDS

Despite its importance, execution is often handled poorly by many organizations. There still are countless cases of good plans going awry because of substandard execution efforts. This raises some important questions.

If execution is central to success, why don't more organizations develop a disciplined approach to it? Why don't companies spend time developing and perfecting processes that help them achieve important strategic outcomes? Why can't more companies execute or implement strategies well and reap the benefits of those efforts?

The simple answer, again, is that execution is extremely difficult. There are formidable roadblocks or hurdles that get in the way of the execution process and seriously injure the implementation of strategy. The road to successful execution is full of potholes that must be negotiated for execution success. This was the message two decades ago, and it still is true today.

Let's identify some of the problems or hurdles affecting implementation. Let's then focus on confronting the obstacles and solving the problems in subsequent chapters of this book.

MANAGERS ARE TRAINED TO PLAN, NOT EXECUTE

One basic problem is that managers know more about strategy formulation than implementation. They are trained to plan, not execute plans.

In most MBA programs I've looked at, students learn a great deal about strategy formulation and functional planning. Core courses typically hone in on competitive strategy, marketing strategy, financial strategy, and so on. The number of courses in most core programs that deal exclusively with execution or implementation? Usually none. Execution is most certainly touched on in a couple of the courses, but not in a dedicated, elaborate, purposeful way. Emphasis clearly is on conceptual work, primarily planning, and not on doing. At Wharton, there is at least an elective on strategy implementation, but this is not typical of many other MBA programs. Even if things are beginning to change, the emphasis still is squarely on planning, not execution.

Added to the lack of training in execution is the fact that strategy and planning in most business schools are taught in "silos," by departments or disciplines, and execution suffers further. The view that marketing strategy, financial strategy, HR strategy, and so on is the only "right" approach is deleterious to the integrative view demanded by execution.

It appears, then, that many MBA programs (undergrad, too, for that matter) are marked by an emphasis on developing strategies, not executing them. Bright graduates are well versed in strategy and planning, with only a passing exposure to execution. Extrapolating this into the real world suggests that many managers have rich conceptual backgrounds and training in planning but not in "doing." IF this is true—if managers are trained to plan, not to execute—then the successful execution of strategy becomes less likely and more problematic. Execution is learned in the "school of hard knocks," and the pathways to successful results are likely fraught with mistakes and frustrations.

It also follows logically that managers who know something about strategy execution very likely have the advantage over their counterparts who don't.

If managers in one company are better versed in the ways of execution than managers in a competitor organization, isn't it logical to assume, all other things being equal, that the former company may enjoy a competitive advantage over the latter, given the differences in knowledge or capabilities? This certainly seems to be the message in the studies cited previously. The benefits of effective execution include competitive advantage and higher returns to shareholders, so having knowledge in this area would clearly seem to be worthwhile and beneficial to the organization.

LET THE "GRUNTS" HANDLE EXECUTION

Another problem is that some C-level and other top-level managers actually believe that strategy execution or implementation is "below them," something best left to lower-level employees. Indeed, the heading of this section comes from an actual quote from a high-level manager.

I was working on implementation programs at GM, under the auspices of Corporate Strategic Planning. In the course of my work, I encountered many competent and dedicated managers. However, I also ran across a few who had a jaundiced view of execution. As one of these managers explained:

> "Top management rightfully worries about planning and strategy formulation. Great care must be taken to develop sound plans. If planning is done well, management then can turn the plans over to the grunts whose job it is to make sure things get done and the work of the planners doesn't go to waste."

What a picture of the planning and execution process! The planners (the "smart" people) develop plans that the "grunts" (not quite as smart) simply have to follow through on and make work. "Doing" obviously involves less ability and intelligence than "planning," a perception of managerial work that clearly demeans the execution process.

The prevailing view here is that one group of managers does innovative, challenging work (planning) and then "hands off the ball" to lower levels for execution. If things go awry and strategic plans are not successful (which often is the case), the problem is placed squarely at the feet of the "doers," who somehow screwed up and couldn't implement a perfectly sound and viable plan. The doers fumbled the ball despite the planners' well-designed plays.

Every organization, of course, has some separation of planning and doing, of formulation and execution. However, when such a separation becomes dysfunctional—when planners see themselves as the smart people and treat the doers as "grunts"—there clearly will be execution problems. When the "elite" plan and see execution as something below them, detracting from their dignity as top managers, the successful implementation of strategy obviously is in jeopardy.

The truth is that all managers are "grunts" when it comes to strategy execution. From the CEO on down, sound execution demands that managers roll up their sleeves and pitch in to make a difference. The content and focus of what they do may vary between top and middle management. Nonetheless, execution demands commitment to and a passion for results, regardless of management level.

Another way of saying this is that execution demands ownership at all levels of management. From C-level managers on down, people must commit to and own the processes and actions central to effective execution. Ownership of execution and the change processes vital to execution are necessary for success. Change is impossible without commitment to the decisions and actions that define strategy execution.

The execution of strategy is not a trivial part of managerial work; it defines the essence of that work. Execution is a key responsibility of all managers, not something that "others" do or worry about.

PLANNING AND EXECUTION ARE INTERDEPENDENT

Even though, in reality, there may be a separation of planning and execution tasks, the two are highly interdependent. Planning affects execution. The execution of strategy, in turn, affects changes to strategy and planning over time. This relationship between planning and doing suggests two critical points to keep in mind.

Successful strategic outcomes are best achieved when those responsible for execution are also part of the planning or formulation process. The greater the interaction between "doers" and "planners," or the greater the overlap of the two processes or tasks, the higher the probability of execution success.

The real and difficult question, of course, is how to get the "doers" involved in the planning process. Top managers who formulate strategy cannot talk to or seek advice from thousands of lower-level personnel spread out around the globe. So, how do the planners pool the doers and get them involved?

Methods can be used to foster interaction and knowledge sharing, and these are discussed in greater detail later in this chapter. These methods include meetings and direct contact (e.g., GE's "Work-Outs," strategic management meetings with representatives of key businesses and functional areas) and the use of surveys. The latter involves the collection of data from key managers whose commitment to execution is vital. E-mails collected from a sample of managers worldwide can provide valuable information for planners and increase the commitment of the doers to chosen plans of action. The task is to derive ways to reach out to the doers in some way to get them involved in the process of strategic thinking and planning.

A related point is that strategic success demands a "simultaneous" view of planning and doing. Managers must be thinking about execution even as they are formulating plans. Execution is not something to "worry about later." All execution decisions and actions, of course, cannot be taken at once. Execution issues or problem areas must be anticipated, however, as part of a "big picture" dealing with planning and doing. Formulating and executing are parts of an integrated, strategic management approach. This dual or simultaneous view is important but difficult to achieve, and it presents a challenge to effective execution.

The methods used to foster interaction and knowledge sharing just mentioned can help to foster this simultaneous view of planning and doing. A survey instrument or questionnaire collected from a sample of managers globally can raise issues related to competitive strategy. However, it can also generate thoughts and opinions about what resources or capabilities are needed to make the strategy work. Generating a strategic "wish list" is helpful; creating a realistic view of implementation needs or requirements simultaneously aids by attaching priorities to that wish list and identifying which strategic thrusts are most likely to succeed.

Randy Tobias had this simultaneous view of planning and doing. Even as he was formulating a new competitive strategy for his AT&T division, he was anticipating execution challenges. Competitive strategy formulation wasn't seen as occurring in a planning vacuum, isolated from execution issues. Central to the success of strategy was the early identification and appreciation of execution-related factors whose impact on strategic success was judged to be formidable. Execution worries couldn't be put off; they were part and parcel of the planning function.

In contrast, top management at a stumbling Lucent Technologies never had this simultaneous view of planning and execution.

When it was spun off from AT&T, the communications, software, and data networking giant looked like a sure bet to succeed. It had the fabled Bell Labs in its fold. It was ready to hit the ground running and formulate winning competitive strategies. Even as the soaring technology market of the late 1990s helped Lucent and other companies, however, it couldn't entirely mask or eliminate Lucent's problems.

One of the biggest problems was that management didn't anticipate critical execution obstacles as they were formulating strategy. Its parent, Ma Bell, had become bureaucratic and slow moving, and Lucent took this culture with it when it was spun off. The culture didn't serve the company well in a highly competitive, rapidly changing telecom environment, a problem that was not foreseen. An unwieldy organizational structure, too, was ignored during Lucent's early attempts at strategy development, and it soon became a liability when it came to such matters as product development and time to market. More agile competitors beat Lucent to market, signaling problems with Lucent's ability to pull off its newly developed strategies.

One thing lacking at Lucent was top management's having a simultaneous view of planning and doing. The planning phase ignored critical execution issues related to culture, structure, and people. The results of this neglect were extremely negative, only magnified by the market downturns that followed the Lucent spinoff.

There are many examples of poor simultaneous thinking. I've seen companies change or tweak strategies, only to find that they lack the capabilities down the line to pull them off. A charge against Avon Products, Inc., in light of its years of poor performance, was that it changed its strategic course and didn't see the problems that would materialize because of it. The company slowly, but inexorably, moved away from its core approach of direct selling and tried to be more like the big "beauty" companies, like P&G and L'Oreal. The move was problematic because top management and the board didn't see that their direct selling model, their capabilities, especially in sales, and their culture would get in the way of such a move. The lack of forward-oriented, simultaneous thinking led to troubles that at first were unforeseen.

In April 2012, the Avon board announced that Sherilyn McCoy would be Avon's new CEO after 30 years at J&J. Can she improve Avon's performance? She'll need to focus on Avon's core business and capabilities and make decisions driven by both a strategic and short-term point of view. She'll virtually have to act as both a CEO and COO, with a simultaneous view of needed quick actions and the long-term implications of those same actions. Also needed is a handling of organizational culture that supports a move focusing on returning to the company's lost core capabilities. This, of course, will not be an easy task.

EXECUTION TAKES LONGER THAN FORMULATION

The execution of strategy usually takes longer than the formulation of strategy. Whereas planning may take weeks or months, the implementation of strategy usually plays out over a much longer period of time. The longer time frame can make it harder for managers to focus on and control the execution process, as many things, some unforeseen, can materialize and challenge managers' attention.

I recently was involved in the planning and execution of strategy with a medium-size company whose headquarters is close to Philadelphia. The company is really a division of a larger corporation, but it enjoyed autonomy and flexibility as it was formulating a strategy in 2010 for implementation in 2011 and a few years thereafter.

The plan involved the expansion of most strategic business units (SBUs) into Europe. Questions about strategy dealt with which products to push, where, and how, with emphasis on cost position or differentiation. Implementation issues dealt with the organizational structure (for example, centralization versus decentralization in foreign markets), coordination requirements of capabilities and units, and talent acquisition to support the expansion.

For present purposes, the point is that the planning stage was much shorter and controllable than the implementation or execution stage. Working with the top management of the business and SBU managers at home and abroad, the strategy was laid out nicely in just a couple of months. The execution of the plan, however, was projected to require, at minimum, two to three years. The longer time frame for implementation clearly would increase the difficulty of execution efforts. Why is this true?

Steps taken to execute a strategy take place over time, and many factors, including some unanticipated, come into play. Interest rates may change, competitors don't behave the way they're supposed to (competitors can be notoriously "unfair" at times, not playing by our "rules"!), customers' needs change, and key personnel leave the company. The outcomes of changes in strategy and execution methods cannot always be easily determined because of "noise" or uncontrolled events. This obviously increases the difficulty of execution efforts.

The longer time frame puts pressure on managers dealing with execution. Long-term needs must be translated into short-term objectives. Controls must be set up to provide feedback and keep management abreast of external "shocks" and changes. The process of execution must be dynamic and adaptive, responding to and compensating for unanticipated events. This presents a real challenge to managers and increases the difficulty of strategy execution.

When the DaimlerChrysler merger was consummated, many believed that the landmark deal would create the world's preeminent carmaker. Execution, however, was extremely difficult, and the years after the merger saw many new problems unfold. The company faced one crisis after another, including two bouts of heavy losses in the Chrysler division, a series of losses in commercial vehicles, and huge problems with failed investments in an attempted turnaround at debt-burdened Mitsubishi Motors.[vi] Serious culture clashes also materialized between the top-down, formal German culture versus the more informal and decentralized U.S. company. The merger was doomed; what looked good at the outset turned into a catastrophe. The long time frame for execution, coupled with a lack of simultaneous thinking, led to major problems and disaster. Problems and issues originally unanticipated and not discussed popped up as formidable barriers to the effective execution of strategy.

Another example is the case of J.C. Penney. After years of poor performance at the embattled company, Ron Johnson was appointed CEO and charged with the responsibility of turning things around. In 2012, he promised significant change, committing to doing for Penney what he had done previously for Apple stores.

Some changes were done quickly, for example, a new three-tiered pricing structure and limitation on the number of expensive major advertising promotions. But other elements of strategy execution inevitably will take time. Johnson faces the need to reinvent 1,100 retail stores, many of which aren't very attractive. This is an old chain—110 years old—and many changes will come slowly. Doing too many things at once can create confusion and perhaps resistance to needed change. Care must be taken to recognize that some aspects of reinventing the department store chain are best done over time with careful preparation and thought. It also must be recognized, however, that the long time frame devoted to execution can breed some of its own problems. Johnson indeed faces challenges as he tries to turn around the lumbering giant.

Execution always takes time and places pressure on management for results. But the longer time needed for execution also increases the likelihood of additional unforeseen problems or challenges cropping up, which further increases the pressure on managers responsible for execution results. The process of execution is always difficult and sometimes quarrelsome, with problems only exacerbated by the longer time frame and uncertainty usually associated with execution.

EXECUTION IS A PROCESS, NOT AN ACTION OR STEP

A point just made is critical and should be repeated: Execution is a process. It is not the result of a single decision or action. It is the result of a series of integrated decisions or actions over time.

This helps explain why sound execution confers competitive advantage. Firms will try to benchmark a successful execution of strategy. However, if execution involves a series of internally consistent, integrated activities, activity systems, or processes, imitation will be extremely difficult, if not impossible.[vii]

Southwest Airlines, for example, does many things differently than the few larger, long-established airlines. It has no baggage transfer, serves no meals, uses one type of airplane (reducing training and maintenance costs), and incents fast turnaround at the gate. It has developed capabilities and created a host of activities to support its low-cost strategy. Other airlines are hard pressed to copy it, as they're already doing everything Southwest isn't. They're committed to different routines and methods. Copying Southwest's execution activities, in total, would involve difficult trade-offs, markedly different tasks, and major changes, which complicates the problem of developing and integrating new execution processes or activities. This is not to say that competitors absolutely cannot copy Southwest; indeed, other low-cost upstarts and traditional airlines are putting increasing competitive pressure on Southwest. This is simply arguing that such imitation is extremely hard to do when the potential imitators have already committed to routines and activities that Southwest or other low-cost carriers aren't committed to or doing.

Execution is a process that demands a great deal of attention to make it work. Execution is not a single decision or action. Managers who seek a quick solution to execution problems will surely fail in attempts at making strategy work. Faster is not always better!

EXECUTION INVOLVES MORE PEOPLE THAN STRATEGY FORMULATION

In addition to being played out over longer periods of time, strategy implementation always involves more people than strategy formulation. This presents additional problems. Communication down the organization or across different functions becomes a challenge. Making sure that incentives throughout the organization support strategy execution efforts becomes a necessity and, potentially, a problem. Linking strategic objectives with the day-to-day objectives and concerns of personnel at different organizational levels and locations becomes a legitimate but challenging task. The larger the number of people involved, the greater the challenge of effective strategy execution.

I once was involved in a strategic planning project with a well-known bank. Another project I wasn't directly involved in had previously recommended a new program to increase the number of retail customers who used certain profitable products and services. A strategy was articulated and a plan of execution developed to educate key personnel and to set goals consistent with the new thrust. Branch managers and others dealing with customers were brought in to corporate for training and to create widespread enthusiasm for the program.

After a few months, the data revealed that not much had changed. It clearly was business as usual, with no change in the outcomes being targeted by the new program. The bank decided to do a brief survey to canvas customers and branch personnel in contact with customers to determine reactions to the program and see where modifications could be made.

The results were shocking, as you've probably guessed. Few people knew about the program. Some tellers and branch personnel did mention that they had heard about "something new," but nothing different was introduced to their daily routines. A few said that the new program was probably just a rumor, as nothing substantial had ever been implemented. Others suggested that rumors were always circulating, and they never knew what was real or bogus.

Communication and follow-through for the new program were obviously inadequate, but the bank admittedly faced a daunting task. It was a big bank. It had many employees at the branch level. Educating them and changing their behaviors was made extremely difficult by the bank's size. Decentralized branch operations ensured that problems were always "popping up" in the field, challenging employees' attention and making it difficult to introduce new ideas from corporate to a large group of employees.

In this example, the number of people who needed to be involved in the implementation of a new program presented a major challenge to the bank management. One can easily imagine the communications problems in even larger, geographically dispersed companies such as GM, IBM, GE, Exxon, Nestle, Citicorp, and ABB. The number of people involved, added to the longer time frames generally associated with strategy execution, clearly creates problems when trying to make strategy work.

ADDITIONAL CHALLENGES AND OBSTACLES TO SUCCESSFUL EXECUTION

The issues previously noted are serious, potentially impeding execution. Yet there are still other challenges and obstacles to the successful implementation of strategy. These need to be identified and confronted if execution is to succeed.

To find out what problems managers routinely encounter in the execution of strategy, I developed two research projects to provide some answers. My goal was to learn about execution from those most qualified to give me the scoop—managers actually dealing with strategy execution. I could have relied solely on my own consulting experiences. I felt, however, that a more widespread approach—surveys directed toward many practicing managers—would yield additional positive results and useful insights into execution issues.

WHARTON-GARTNER SURVEY AND EXECUTIVE EDUCATION DATA COLLECTION

The first survey was a joint project involving the Gartner Group, Inc., a well-known research organization, and me, a Wharton professor. The purpose of the research, from the Gartner introduction, was as follows:

> "To gain a clear understanding of challenges faced by managers as they make decisions and take actions to execute their company's strategy to gain competitive advantage."

The research instrument was a short online survey sent to 1,000 individuals on the Gartner E-Panel database. The targeted sample comprised managers who reported that they were involved in strategy formulation and execution. Complete usable responses were received from a sample of 243 individuals, a return rate that is more than sufficient for this type of research. In addition, the survey collected responses to open-ended questions to provide additional data, including explanations of items covered in the survey instrument. A copy of the overall Wharton-Gartner survey can be found in the appendix of this book.

There were 12 items on the survey dealing with obstacles to the strategy-execution process. They focused on conditions that affect execution and were originally developed in conjunction with a long-running Wharton Executive Development Program on strategy implementation.

Using the 12 items to gather opinions over a large number of executive education programs provided me with responses from a sample of 200 managers. They provided a ranking of the items' impact on strategy execution. Open-ended responses to questions about execution issues, problems, and opportunities were also collected over time, providing additional valuable data. Coupled with the data collected in the Wharton-Gartner Survey using the same 12 items, I had complete responses from 443 managers involved in strategy execution who told me about their execution problems and their solutions to them.

In subsequent Wharton Executive Development Programs and consulting engagements after this data collection and publication of *Making Strategy Work* in 2005, I was able to gain additional insight into execution problems and difficulties. I held formal and informal discussions during the executive programs and while working with companies in the period from 2005 to the present, asking managers what the data were actually saying or implying. I asked managers why, in their opinion, people responded the way they did. "What are the survey data telling us about execution problems or issues?" was the predominant question.

These discussions forced managers to read between the lines and interpret the formal data. They also enabled me to probe into what could be done to overcome the obstacles and achieve successful execution outcomes. Insights were collected, then, not only on the sources of execution problems but their solutions as well.

The surveys and follow-up discussions provided data right from "the horse's mouth." These were not idiosyncratic data, the opinions or observations of a few managers or CEOs who, against all odds, "did it their way." The number of managers providing answers, coupled with an emphasis on real problems and solutions, added a strong sense of relevance to the opinions gathered about strategy execution.

What insights did these additional discussions, interviews, and analyses reveal? What did managers say about execution problems and how do their opinions affect the topics and issues that this revised book addresses to further the cause of more successful strategy execution programs?

THE RESULTS: OBSTACLES TO SUCCESSFUL STRATEGY EXECUTION

Table 1.1 summarizes the main points that emerged from the original research and that managers discussed and analyzed in the period 2005 to the present. Taken together, the data suggest clearly why the execution of strategy is such a difficult task, one that deserves dedicated managerial attention.

The importance of managing change to enable effective strategy execution comes across from the data immediately.

Table 1.1 Obstacles to Effective Strategy Execution

1. Inability to manage change effectively and overcome resistance to change
2. A poor or vague strategy
3. Not having guidelines or a model to guide strategy-execution efforts
4. Trying to execute a strategy that conflicts with the existing power structure
5. Poor or inadequate information sharing between individuals or business units responsible for strategy execution
6. Unclear communication of responsibility or accountability for execution decisions or actions
7. Lack of feelings of ownership of a strategy or of execution steps or plans among key employees
8. Lack of understanding of the role of organizational structure and design in the execution process

Inability to manage change effectively clearly was seen as injurious to strategy-execution efforts. Managers cited the fact that execution or implementation often involved new methods or approaches—new structures, incentives, coordination methods, controls and information sharing—and that managers often resisted these changes, preferring to operate as they always had. Resistance to change, then, had to be confronted and overcome to achieve positive execution results.

Although culture was not mentioned explicitly in the item, the discussions with managers placed culture at the core of many change-related problems. To many of the respondents, "change" and" "culture change" were synonymous. To other managers, culture change was a subset of change management that doesn't always come into play, but when it does, always deserves additional, separate attention. Suffice it to say presently that handling change effectively, including culture change, is central to effective execution attempts, and discussions in later chapters address this issue.

Another change-related issue raised by managers dealt with the speed of change when implementing new aspects of the execution process. Should managers do everything quickly, at once, or focus on slower, more deliberate change activities? This is an important issue that only arose in discussions because managers read between the lines and raised important issues derived from their own experience but not addressed directly by the data in the survey instruments.

Trying to execute a strategy that conflicts with the prevailing power structure clearly is doomed to failure according to the managers surveyed. Confronting those with influence at different organizational levels who disagree with an execution plan surely will have unhappy results in most cases. The underlying question in need of attention deals with the use and support of the power structure. How does one gain influence or use the power structure to foster and aid strategy execution efforts? This issue certainly requires explication later in the book.

Poor sharing of information or poor knowledge transfer and unclear responsibility and accountability also can doom strategy-execution attempts. These items suggest that attempts at coordination or integration across organizational units can suffer if unclear responsibilities and poor sharing of vital information needed for execution is the rule. This makes sense because complex strategies often demand cooperation, effective coordination, and information sharing. Not achieving the requisite knowledge transfer and integration certainly cannot help the execution of these strategies.

These items also raise the issue of why managers are motivated *not* to share knowledge or accept responsibility for execution decisions and actions. Whether this is caused, in part, by poor information-sharing resources or poor communication about who exactly is accountable for critical action items and decisions is an issue in need of additional discussion in later chapters.

Having a poor or vague strategy certainly detracts from implementation or execution success. Discussions with managers revealed a number of underlying problems. First, a poor strategy creates uncertainty about how the organization plans to compete and, consequently, how to execute the weak or unclear plan. Second, an unclear or poor strategy fosters problems as to what skills or capabilities a company must invest in and develop to make strategy work. Third, managers stressed that the uncertainties and problems mentioned detract from managers' confidence about their ability to compete successfully against foes in the market whose plans and approaches to execution are more clear, certain, and attuned to the prevalent market and competitive conditions. A lack of confidence and distrust of approaches to strategy and the resources and capabilities surrounding it can only lead to poor performance according to the managers interviewed in this research.

Another a issue that came up repeatedly is the need for a model or plan to guide execution efforts. What should the flow of decisions and activities look like? What is the logic that underlies sound approaches to execution? If execution is to be a solid, controlled effort and not a haphazard or idiosyncratic approach to making strategy work, what should this effort look like? This is an important issue in need of attention.

Many managers, especially those in higher-level positions, raised questions about the role and impact of organizational structure in the implementation or execution process. While managers responded to the survey, saying that structure was important, many admitted in discussions that they didn't quite know why! They wanted more information about the choice of structure, the costs and benefits of different structural options, how often and why structure should be changed, and whether structure was helpful for, or a hindrance to, strategy execution efforts. The lack of knowledge about structure was surprising, but it did suggest clearly the need to cover the topic in greater detail.

There were also consistent mentions of issues around communication, buy-in, incentives, and controls in the best approaches to strategy execution. Table 1.1 makes no direct mention of incentives, for example, but managers constantly raised this issue in the discussions subsequent to the original research and data collection. Their interest and comments suggest strongly that incentives are implied in a number of areas in Table 1.1, even if not explicitly mentioned. The incentives to cooperate, share knowledge, accept responsibility, and support change programs are vital to execution success. Incentives, like communication and buy-in, must be an integral part of execution-related programs.

One other critical issue was raised fairly frequently by managers in the discussions of execution that took place in the time from the original survey research in 2005 to the present. Like the issue of incentives, which underlies much of what is being said in Table 1.1, so too this additional issue is a vital force affecting execution success or failure.

The issue is: Leadership and the need to create an execution-based culture in the organization.

Discussions with managers and executives constantly mentioned the issues of sound leadership and its connection to building an organizational culture based strongly on execution success. Their thoughts closely mirrored those in the 2012 study by Kaplan, Klebanov, and Sorensen cited previously. Successful leaders, it was emphasized, focus on the "details" of integrating strategy and short-term, operational goals. They create a culture based on performance, with incentives to support operational excellence. They demand the acceptance of responsibility and clear accountability in the process of goal attainment. Having leaders with charm, charisma, or social skills helps, but alone these characteristics don't create the performing organization. It's the focus on execution and results that matters.

The need for leadership that creates a climate of effective performance, then, is a critical ingredient in the quest to make strategy work. Leadership in some general sense may be important, but leadership in the more specific role of creating a widespread culture of execution based on clear performance standards, accountability, and a concern with integrating long- and short-term objectives clearly is the key to success.

The phenomenon of leadership and its relation to an execution-based culture is implied by the survey results in Table 1.1. This concept appears in various forms and places later in the book, as we flesh out the conditions for making strategy work.

EXECUTION OUTCOMES

The survey research, coupled with data derived from years of working with managers in the period after 2005, provides strong evidence of what are seen to be the outcomes of both good and poor execution. Focusing first on the positive, Table 1.2 summarizes the positive outcomes most commonly attributed to sound execution processes. Interesting, too, is the fact that managers linked the benefits to the possible attainment of competitive advantage. Solid execution, that is, can lead not only to more effective performance against an organization's own goals, but also to significantly better performance against others in the same industry or market space.

Table 1.2 Benefits of Sound Execution: Possible Contributions to Competitive Advantage

- Lower costs
- Faster response to customers and markets
- Appropriate structures, incentives, and controls: Focusing attention on the right strategic and operating issues
- More effective and efficient coordination
- Clear responsibility and accountability
- Effective management of human resources
- Increased ability to manage change and adapt to external shocks

The benefits in Table 1.2 are self-explanatory. The one that perhaps needs some clarification is the third one noted on structures, incentives, and controls. Managers, in effect, are saying that an emphasis on strategy, supported by an appropriate structure, set of incentives, and control mechanisms, increases managerial focus on the right things, strategically and operationally, and facilitates change and adaptation. The process might be shown as follows:

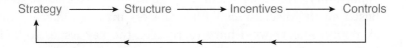

Strategy ⟶ Structure ⟶ Incentives ⟶ Controls

Organizational structure and incentives support a chosen strategy, and effective controls provide feedback about performance, allowing the organization to adapt and retain its market or customer focus. The process is ongoing, allowing the organization to focus on learning in a continuous cycle of performance, evaluation, learning, and adaptation. More will be said in subsequent chapters about the relationship among these factors and how they affect performance, adaptation, and making strategy work.

Managers in the original surveys and in the post-survey discussions identified some of the results of poor execution. In addition to "not achieving desired execution outcomes or objectives," managers noted a few additional results of poor execution methods as being highly problematic. These include the following:

- Employees don't understand how their jobs contribute to important execution outcomes.
- Time and money are wasted because of inefficiency or bureaucracy in the execution process.
- Execution decisions take too long to make.
- The company reacts slowly or inappropriately to competitive pressures.

These are not trivial issues. Execution problems can cost the organization dearly. Time and money are wasted, and a company can face serious competitive setbacks because of an inability to respond to market or customer demands. Execution problems must be addressed, but which ones and in what order?

THE EXECUTION CHALLENGE

Table 1.1 previously listed eight areas of obstacles or challenges to strategy execution. Or, to put it positively, there are eight areas of opportunity: Handling them well guarantees execution success. Based on the discussions with managers involved in the strategy execution interviews, I have rearranged the key issues to include the points raised by the managers and to present a logical approach to development of a process for making strategy work. Emphasis, that is, is on a logical flow of execution steps or activities.

Inability to manage change effectively, for example, was shown in Table 1.1 to be the largest obstacle to the effective execution of strategy. But logically something must precede change attempts. Decisions and actions must have been taken and new factors introduced before change can occur. In effect, there must be something to change before change can occur.

Keeping this in mind resulted in a plan for the flow of material that follows. Again, the emphasis is on a logical, step-by-step approach to the decisions vital to making strategy work. The areas relating to successful strategy execution are as follows:

1. Developing a model to guide execution decisions or actions
2. Understanding how the creation of strategy affects the execution of strategy
3. Developing organizational structures that support strategic objectives and foster information sharing, coordination, and clear accountability
4. Creating and using incentives to support strategy execution processes and decisions
5. Developing effective controls and feedback mechanisms to enable the organization to assess performance and adapt to changing conditions
6. Understanding an organization's power or influence structure and using it for execution success
7. Knowing how to create an execution-supportive culture
8. Exercising execution- biased leadership
9. Managing change effectively, including culture change

HAVING A MODEL OR GUIDELINES FOR EXECUTION

Managers need a logical model to guide execution actions.

Without guidelines, execution becomes a helter-skelter affair. Without guidance, individuals do the things they think are important, often resulting in uncoordinated, divergent, even conflicting decisions and actions. Without the benefit of a logical approach, execution suffers or fails because managers don't know what steps to take and when to take them. Having a model or roadmap positively affects execution success.

STRATEGY IS THE PRIMARY DRIVER

It all begins with strategy. Execution cannot occur until one has something to execute. Bad strategy begets poor execution and poor outcomes, so it's important to focus first on a sound strategy.

Good people are important for execution. It is vital to get the "right people on the bus, the wrong people off the bus," so to speak. But it's also important to know where the bus is going and why. Strategy is critical. It drives the development of capabilities and which people with what skills sit in what seats on the bus. If one substitutes "jet airplane" for "bus" above—given today's high-flying, competitive markets—the importance of strategy, direction, and the requisite critical skills and capabilities necessary for success are emphasized even more.

Strategy defines the arena (customers, markets, technologies, products, logistics) in which the execution game is played. Execution is an empty effort without the guidance of strategy and short-term objectives related to strategy. What aspects of strategy and planning impact execution outcomes the most is a critical question that needs answering. Another critical question deals with the relationship between corporate- and business-level strategies and how their interaction affects execution outcomes.

CHOOSING AN ORGANIZATIONAL STRUCTURE

Structural choice must support an organization's strategy. Different structural forms have different benefits (and costs), and these must be matched with a chosen strategy. A strategic emphasis on becoming a low-cost producer, for example, logically demands a structure that fosters or enables low cost, for example, via standardization, repetition, and volume of services performed by structural units. The need is to understand the demands or needs of a given strategy and choose a structure that best meets the requisite demands.

COORDINATION AND INFORMATION SHARING

Knowing how to achieve coordination and information sharing in complex, geographically dispersed organizations is important to execution success. Yet managers are often motivated *not* to share information or work with their colleagues to coordinate activities and achieve strategic and short-term goals. Why? The answer to this question is vital to the successful execution of strategy.

CLEAR RESPONSIBILITY AND ACCOUNTABILITY

This is one of the most important prerequisites for successful execution, as basic as it sounds. Managers must know who's doing what, when, and why, as well as who's accountable for key steps in the execution process. Without clear responsibility and accountability, execution programs go nowhere. Knowing how to achieve this clarity is central to execution success.

THE POWER STRUCTURE

Execution programs that contradict the power or influence structure of an organization are doomed to failure. But what affects power or influence? Power is more than individual personality or position. Power reflects strategy, structure, and critical dependencies on capabilities and scarce resources. Knowing what power is and how to create and use influence can spell the difference between execution success and failure.

INCENTIVES, CONTROLS, FEEDBACK, AND ADAPTATION

Strategy execution processes support organizational change and adaptation. Effective incentives are at the forefront of this support. Incentives tell people what's important. They fuel motivation and point managers in the right direction for strategy execution. Incentives support both strategic and short-term objectives, and successful execution and change would be impossible without them.

Making strategy work also requires feedback about organizational performance and then using that information to fine-tune strategy, objectives, and the execution process itself. There is an emergent aspect of strategy and execution, as organizations learn and adapt to environmental changes over time. Adaptation and change depend on effective execution methods.

As important as controls and feedback are, they often don't work. Control processes fail. They don't identify and confront the brutal facts underlying poor performance. Adaptation is haphazard or incomplete. Understanding how to manage feedback, strategy reviews, and change is vital to the success of strategy execution.

THE RIGHT CULTURE

Organizations must develop execution-supportive cultures. Execution demands a culture of achievement, discipline, and ownership. But developing or changing culture is no easy task. Rock climbing, whitewater rafting, paint-gun battles, and other activities with the management team are fun. They rarely, however, produce lasting cultural change. Knowing what does affect cultural change is central to execution success.

LEADERSHIP

Leadership must be execution-biased. It must drive the organization to execution success. It must motivate ownership of and commitment to the execution process.

Leadership affects how organizations respond to all of the preceding execution challenges. It is always at least implied when discussing what actions or decisions are necessary to make strategy work. A complete analysis of execution steps and decisions usually defines what good leadership is and how it affects execution success, directly or indirectly.

MANAGING CHANGE

Execution or strategy implementation often involves change. Not handling change well spells disaster for execution efforts.

Managing change means much more than keeping people happy and reducing resistance to new ideas and methods. It also means knowing the tactics or steps needed to manage the execution process over time. Do managers implement change sequentially, bit by bit, or do they do everything at once, biting the bullet and implementing change in one fell swoop? The wrong answer can seriously hamper or kill execution efforts. Knowing how to manage the execution process and related changes over time is important for execution success.

****

These are the issues that impact the success or failure of strategy-execution efforts. Coupled with the issues previously mentioned (longer time frames, involvement of many people, and so on), these are the areas that present formidable obstacles to successful execution if they are not handled properly. They also present opportunities for competitive advantage if they are understood and managed well.

The last words, "managed well," hold the key to success. Knowing the obstacles or potential opportunities is necessary but not sufficient. The real issue is how to deal with them to generate positive execution results. The major significant point or thrust of this chapter is that execution is not managed well in many organizations. The remainder of this book is dedicated to correcting this woeful situation.

APPLICATIONS AND SPECIAL TOPICS

This edition of *Making Strategy Work* expands the applications section significantly. The critical issues for successful execution just noted can be applied to real-world issues and problems that enhance the value and utility of the present approach to strategy execution. While examples from different types of organizations and industries appear throughout the book, a more dedicated approach to making strategy work is offered in a new and expanded applications section. The topics are

- **Making mergers and acquisitions work.** This chapter appeared in the original edition of this book but is updated in the current revision.

- **Strategy execution in service organizations.** This new chapter also includes discussion of government service agencies or organization, as well as not-for-profit organizations. Many managers requested that this chapter be added to the revision of this book.

- **Making global strategy work.** A more in-depth analysis of global execution issues is offered in this new chapter. Again, managers asked for this coverage of execution in the global arena.

- **Project management and strategy execution.** This new chapter presents an overview of a useful tool for the ongoing management of the execution process. It represents the application of a well-known tool to the strategy implementation challenge.

THE NEXT STEP: DEVELOPING A LOGICAL APPROACH TO EXECUTION DECISIONS AND ACTIONS

So where and how does one begin to confront the issues just noted? Which execution problems or opportunities should managers consider first? What decisions or actions come later? Why? Can an approach to strategy execution be developed to guide managers through the maze of obstacles and problematic issues just identified?

The next chapter begins to tackle these questions. It presents an overview, a conceptual framework to guide execution decisions and actions. Managers need such a model because they routinely face a bewildering set of decisions about a host of strategic and operating problems, including those dealing with execution. They need guidelines, a "roadmap" to steer them logically to execution success.

Priorities are also needed. Tackling too many execution decisions or actions at once will surely create problems. "When everything is important, then nothing is important," is a clear but simple way of expressing the issue. Priorities must be set and a logical order to execution actions adequately defined if execution is to succeed.

Having a model, finally, also facilitates a "simultaneous" view of planning and doing. All execution actions cannot be taken at once; some must precede others logically. A good overview or model, however, provides a "big picture" that enables managers to see and anticipate execution problems. Execution is not something that others should worry about later. Planning requires anticipating early on what must be done to make strategy work.

Development of a logical overview is a step that has been ignored by practitioners, academics, and management consultants alike. Execution problems or issues typically have been handled separately or in an ad-hoc fashion, supported by a few anecdotes or case studies. This is not sufficient. Execution is too complex to be approached without guidelines or a roadmap.

Managers cannot act in a helter-skelter fashion when executing strategy. They can't focus one day on organizational structure, the next on culture, and then on to "good people," only to find out that strategy is vague or severely flawed. They need guidelines, a way to see and approach execution and the logical order of the key variables involved. A roadmap is needed to guide them through the minefields of bad execution decisions and actions. Managers require a "big picture" as well as an understanding of the "nitty-gritty," the key elements that comprise the big picture.

The next chapter tackles the essential task of providing this overview by showing the order and logic of key execution decisions. It also begins to confront the obstacles identified in this chapter as it lays out this sequence of decisions or actions. These decisions and actions simultaneously define the areas needing additional attention in later chapters of this book. Having a model of execution is vital to making strategy work, so let's take this important and necessary step.

SUMMARY

- Execution is a key to strategic success. Most managers, however, know a lot more about strategy formulation than execution. They know much more about "planning" than "doing," which causes major problems with making strategy work.

- Strategy execution is difficult but worthy of management's attention across all levels of an organization. All managers bear responsibility for successful execution. It is not just a lower-level task.

- Part of the difficulty of execution is due to the obstacles or impediments to it. These include the longer time frames needed for execution; the need for involvement of many people in the execution process; poor or vague strategy; conflicts with the organizational power structure; poor or inadequate sharing of information; a lack of understanding of organizational structure, including information sharing and coordination methods; unclear responsibility and accountability in the execution process; and an inability to manage change, including cultural change.

- Knowing execution hazards (opportunities) is necessary but not sufficient. For successful execution to occur, managers need a model or a set of guidelines outlining the entire process and relationships among key decisions or actions. A "roadmap" is needed to help with the order of execution decisions as managers confront obstacles and take advantage of opportunities.

■ This overview of execution is vital to success and is developed in the next chapter. Subsequent chapters can borrow from this model and focus more specifically on aspects of it to achieve positive execution results.

ENDNOTES

i. For those interested in an informative memoir about Randy Tobias' career, his many experiences (especially as CEO of Eli Lilly), and his views on effective leadership, I suggest you read *Put the Moose on the Table* by Randall Tobias with Todd Tobias, Indiana Press, 2003.

ii. William Joyce, Nitin Nohria, and Bruce Roberson, *What (Really) Works,* Harper Business, 2003.

iii. Steven Kaplan, Mark Klebanov, and Morten Sorensen, "Which CEO Characteristics and Abilities Matter," Swedish Institute for Financial Research Conference on the Economics of the Private Equity Market, New Orleans, 2008. A version of this paper was also published in May, 2012, in the *Journal of Finance*.

iv. David Brooks, "In Praise of Dullness," *The New York Times*, May 18, 2008.

v. See Jim Collins, *Good to Great*, Harper Business, 2001; Larry Bossidy and Ram Charan, *Execution*, Crown Business, 2002; and Amir Hartman, *Ruthless Execution*, Prentice Hall, 2004.

vi. "Daimler CEO Defends Strategy, Reign," *The Wall Street Journal*, May 6, 2004.

vii. For a good discussion of how a series of integrated activities, activity systems, or processes thwarts imitation and leads to competitive advantage, see Michael Porter's "What Is Strategy?" in the *Harvard Business Review*, November-December, 1996.

2

Overview and Model: Making Strategy Work

Introduction

Chapter 1 emphasized the fact that strategy execution is extremely difficult. It also argued that most managers know much more about planning or strategy making than about "doing" or making strategy work.

There are many obstacles to execution that, taken together, present a formidable challenge and contribute to poor execution, as the preceding chapter indicated. One of these is that managers often suffer from not having a conceptual framework or a model to guide execution efforts.

The lack of a model, blueprint, or template to shape execution decisions or actions is a major obstacle to making strategy work. Managers need a roadmap to guide execution. "Tell us what to do, when, and in what order," is the request. Without a guide or model, execution efforts simply cannot proceed in a logical way. Without a model, it is difficult to develop a sound plan of execution.

Managers often told me after the original data collection and research that they thirst for a good blueprint for execution. They also told me that anecdotes or "war stories" aren't enough. Stories and anecdotes about execution are always interesting, and they sometimes hold implications for the practice of management. Yet stories and anecdotes alone simply cannot explain the complex issues affecting the execution of strategy that were identified in the preceding chapter. Making strategy work requires more than a handful of managerial sound bites. It requires a template to guide thought and effort in a logical, systematic way.

The purpose of this chapter is to provide a conceptual framework or model of the strategy-execution process. The goal of this chapter is twofold. First, it provides a guide to execution, a "big-picture" view showing how key decisions and actions relate to each other in a logical way. Chapter 1 identified the key issues or challenges that affect execution. Rather than immediately handling each of the issues separately, as if each were totally independent of the others, the intention presently is to show first how the issues are interdependent—how they relate to each other—and how they come together to define a coordinated approach to execution. This is an important first step in attacking the complexities involved in making strategy work.

Second, this chapter identifies the critical topics or factors that will be considered in detail in subsequent chapters. Presenting a logical overview of execution is the present goal, with the needed details coming later.

Before presenting this blueprint or model, it is necessary to emphasize two points relating to its use.

COMMON VERSUS UNIQUE EXECUTION SOLUTIONS

The first point is that the guide to execution that follows can be applied across the board in virtually all organizations and industry settings. It is meant to provide a useful overview of execution decisions and actions to help management in all kinds of businesses or organizations.

The model presents an approach that identifies common critical execution issues that, if ignored, will lead to execution difficulties. This alone is valuable. This "25,000-foot view" offers an important integrative perspective to help the reader understand the logic of the entire execution process as it plays out consistently in different organizations.

It is also necessary to note, however, that the importance of specific decisions or actions in the model can vary from organization to organization or from industry to industry. Each strategy and its demands are in some way unique, given such factors as company culture, history, competition, growth patterns, competencies, and previous successes and failures. Consequently, different organizations may need to place emphasis on different parts of a common roadmap at a given point in time. Execution problems and solutions can vary, even among organizations using the same model or set of guidelines.

An important issue that has arisen repeatedly since the initial publication of *Making Strategy Work* is whether a general model of execution applies equally well to service organizations or even government agencies and organizations. Are service organizations like manufacturing companies or is execution somehow different? Will the advice and recommendations in this revised work hold sway with managers in the service or government sector?

The short answer is "yes," with some slight modification. The material on execution can be used by a president of a university, the head of a health services organization, or the CEO of a large or small company. Service companies need to formulate strategy and then focus on structure, coordination, incentives, change management, and so on, to make the strategy work. The basic execution issues and problems must be confronted; service organizations aren't immune to execution challenges.

Truth be told, some service organizations or government agencies may pose additional issues or problems challenging effective execution. The questions or concerns raised by managers after publication of the previous edition of this book has resulted in a new chapter dealing with these issues, problems, or questions. For now, it simply can be stated that the model of execution developed presently indeed does have validity for service companies. The differences or added challenges are noted in the new chapter, but the relevance of the execution overview is clearly strong. Additional service examples are used throughout the book to stress and validate this point.

In brief, differences in industry or type of organization in no way negate the value of the general model and its execution guidelines. The model provides the structure, the "menu," that identifies key execution decisions or actions that all organizations must confront and handle. That the importance of certain decisions and actions varies among organizations or industries at any point in time in no way detracts from the importance of the menu and its overview of execution needs. The menu lists the choices that managers must analyze as they face and solve their execution problems.

A NEED FOR ACTION

The execution of strategy takes place in the real world of management. It is concerned not only with questions of "why" but also of "how." Managers are rewarded for "doing" as well as "knowing," "snowball throwing" as well as "snowball making."[i] This places the constraint of "action" on any approach to executing strategy, if it is to be useful.

For an approach to be action oriented, it must emphasize variables that can be manipulated or changed. Effective managerial action assumes that key variables are under a manager's control; without this, there is nothing to manage. It is important to lay out an approach to execution that focuses as much as possible on measurable, manipulable factors and that has a direct relation to managerial action and decision-making.

To be action oriented, a model must also be prescriptive. It must tell us what should be done, when, why, and in what order. A model is action oriented and useful if it identifies how execution decisions should logically be made.

In the real world, aberrations from a logical model can always be found. As is emphasized in Chapter 4, for example, strategy should logically affect the choice of organizational structure. Structure, that is, should reflect and be consistent with the strategy an organization is pursuing.

Does structure always follow strategy logically in the real world? Do certain structural units or divisions occasionally become so powerful that they reverse the model and drive the choice of strategy? The answers, of course, are "no" and "yes," respectively.

But aberrations from a model do not negate it or its usefulness. It still is important to know what should be done, when, why, and in what order.

A good model helps us understand why and where aberrations actually occur so that corrections or changes can be made. In the preceding example, structure affected strategy because of the influence of a "powerful" unit. Power, that is, can affect execution, with good and bad results. It is vital, then, to understand power and include its effects when using the model. The existence of power does not negate the validity or usefulness of the model. Aberrations from the template must be explained, but they certainly don't destroy its basic logic or utility.

This chapter can now turn to an overview of strategy execution. It addresses many of the obstacles and concerns noted in Chapter 1 as it develops a logical, action-oriented approach to execution. These obstacles and concerns are analyzed separately and in depth in later chapters. The purpose presently is to show how they relate to each other in the execution process.

A MODEL OF STRATEGY EXECUTION

Figure 2.1 presents a model of the strategy-execution process.[ii] This is the same model developed in the earlier edition of *Making Strategy Work*. Managers have since discussed its strengths and utility as a guideline for execution decisions and actions, so it again provides an early overview of the process of strategy execution. Additional examples are provided to flesh out the model more completely and another element is added to it below, but the model still has merit as a guiding document. It still has utility as a vehicle to spark discussion about strategy execution. A few general observations are in order before getting into its details.

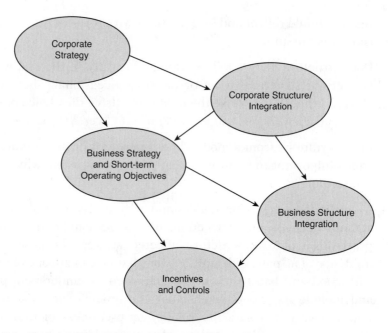

Figure 2.1 Executing Strategy: Key Decisions and Actions

First, strategy is important. Managers in the surveys and subsequent discussion groups mentioned in Chapter 1 identified "poor or vague strategy" as a major impediment to sound execution. A clear, focused strategy is necessary for effective execution.[iii] One cannot talk of execution without focusing first on sound strategy formulation. Strategy formulation and execution are separate, identifiable activities or processes. Yet they are highly interdependent. Good planning aids the execution process. Similarly, poor planning begets poor implementation.

Some managers may disagree and argue that good execution can compensate for bad strategy or poor planning. My experience, however, generally proves otherwise. Executing bad strategy is usually a losing proposition. Poor planning usually steers the execution process into troubled waters that become increasingly difficult to navigate. It should not be surprising, then, that Figure 2.1 includes corporate and business strategy formulation in an overview of strategy execution.

Second, Figure 2.1 shows that there is a logical flow of execution decisions or actions. The arrows in the figure show this flow. Incentives, for example, are last in the model because they must be. Incentives cannot be set until prior decisions about strategy, short-term objectives, coordination requirements, and structure are made. Logically, incentives must reward and reinforce the right decisions, which must clearly precede the development of those incentives. Similarly, corporate strategy is of paramount importance. If the strategy of a business unit is inconsistent with (or contradictory to) corporate strategy, the latter must prevail. The dog should wag its tail, not vice versa.

The arrows, then, show a logical order to execution decisions. They show which decisions precede others when executing strategy. They do not suggest a unilateral, downward-only flow of communication or a lack of participation. As is stressed often in later chapters, execution involves participation and communication up and down the organization, as well as lateral flows of information and coordination across operating units.

Third, there are feedback loops in the model, though they are not obvious. The "controls" portion of the model comprises feedback and change. Execution is a dynamic, adaptive process, leading to organizational learning. For learning and change to occur, feedback about performance against strategic and short-term objectives is necessary. It must come from managers at all levels: from the C-level suites, from regional or district offices, and from people dealing with customers or walking around on the production floor.

An effective model of execution emphasizes both action and reaction. It must be dynamic, allowing for feedback and adaptation. The present model is not static by any means, a notion I wish to stress strongly at the outset.

CORPORATE STRATEGY

The model in Figure 2.1 begins with corporate strategy. GE, Asea Brown Boveri (ABB), Citicorp, Merck, J&J, Becton Dickinson, and most other companies have corporate strategies, and their many businesses also formulate strategy in a search for competitive advantage in their respective industries. The University of Pennsylvania has a "corporate" planning function, while its colleges or "businesses" create plans to deal with their own competitive settings.

Corporate strategy is concerned with the entire organization, focusing on such areas as portfolio management, diversification, and resource allocations across the businesses or operating units that make up the total enterprise. In a corporation, the levels of strategy and associated tasks would look like the following:

Level	Examples of Issues or Tasks
Corporate strategy	■ Portfolio management
	■ Diversifications, including vertical integration
	■ Resource allocations across businesses
Business, divisional, or SBU strategy	■ Which products and services to offer
	■ How to compete
	■ Achieving competitive advantage in an industry
Strategy within businesses	■ How to differentiate the firm in a given market
	■ Functional plans

In a bank or similar service organization, there is a corporate level and shared functions, just as there are businesses, strategic business units (SBUs), or service areas focusing on different markets or customers. The commercial credit, retail credit, or private banking/trust areas of a large bank represent examples of these different business areas or market foci. Similarly, the corporate level of the University of Pennsylvania manages a portfolio of "businesses" (colleges) with different customer foci and areas of expertise. This book simply uses the terms "corporate" and "business" strategy. The former refers to or reflects decisions for the total enterprise, decisions or actions that cut across businesses (divisions, colleges, SBUs), whereas the latter represents strategy for the businesses and major operating units within them.

The present model, again, begins logically with corporate strategy. At this level, decisions are made as to what businesses or industries should make up the corporate portfolio. Diversification via acquisition adds organizations to the portfolio, and divestitures eliminate them. Vertical integration typically increases not only the number of companies in the portfolio, but also the number of industries in which the corporation operates or competes. Corporate choices clearly affect the number of operating companies or units in the organization.

Corporate strategists also must decide how to allocate resources across the businesses or operating units, given differences in competitive conditions and growth possibilities across industries. This resource allocation or investment process is critical because it affects strategy execution at both the corporate and business levels.

What decisions or actions affect the execution and success of corporate strategy? Figure 2.1 and the preceding discussion suggest that there are two key areas to focus on when executing corporate strategy: corporate structure and business strategy. Let's consider each in turn.

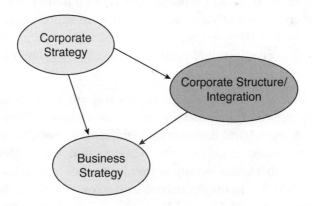

CORPORATE STRATEGY AND STRUCTURE

Corporate structure, the second element in the model, refers to the organizational units created in response to the demands of corporate strategy. Organizational structure depicts the major pieces or operating units that make up the entire enterprise. Figure 2.1 indicates that the creation of organizational structure is important to the execution of corporate strategy. What is the logic here?

To answer the question, consider the case of diversification as a corporate growth strategy. Mergers and acquisitions (M&A) are a big business. In 2003, $1.2 trillion in mergers were consummated by investment banks. After 2003, M&A activity continued its upward pace until the 2008 financial collapse worldwide, but signs are that M&A deals will soon return to pre-crisis levels. In 2010 and 2011, U.S. activity in M&A increased significantly, with the first quarter in 2011 increasing nearly 117.3 percent over the first quarter of 2010. Global activity in the same period topped $800 billion. The cash buildup in major corporations in the United States and the low interest rates since 2008 suggest that cash burning a hole in companies' pockets will soon find its way into M&A activity.[iv] Nearly seven of ten executives in one survey expected their companies to make at least one acquisition in 2012, up significantly from prior years, while another study shows top management's desire to expand globally via the M&A route in 2012.[v]

The sad truth is that corporate M&As often don't work, and a large number are actually marked by a drop in shareholder value. The execution of M&A strategy is often rife with problems that detract from the organizational performance. What accounts for this poor showing?

Consider the example of related diversification in the banking industry, where acquisitions and consolidation occur routinely. Bank A buys Bank B, the stated goal usually being increased size, market penetration, and the benefits that follow logically from scale, such as the synergies or economies generally associated with scale. There are numerous examples: PNC-RBC Bank (2012); Capital One-ING Direct (2011); M&T-Wilmington Trust (2011); PNC-National City (2008); Wells Fargo-Wachovia (2008); Bank of America-Merrill Lynch (2008), and so on. Predictably, the goals of these combinations include cost reductions, elimination of redundancies, scale economies related to size, and better customer service.

To achieve synergies and scale economies, the banks often must be melded into one organization. Duplications must be eliminated. One marketing group, smaller than the combined groups of the separate banks, is expected to do the same work much more effi-ciently. Similarly, elimination of some bank branches can make the structure leaner and less costly, but with the same capacity to service the market. Finally, one set of back-room operations can replace the original two separate operations, doing the same work with larger scale and resultant efficiencies.

To execute the bank's strategy of related diversification, then, structural change is necessary. Execution of corporate strategy relies in part on the appropriate structure to support it. The fail-ure of so many mergers in banking and other industries to deliver on their promises suggests that these structural changes simply haven't been done well. To be sure, other factors come into play when explaining poor performance, such as the premium prices paid for acquisitions. Still, given the nature of this form of diversi-fication, structural change is vital, and poor decisions here lead to poor performance. Structure does affect the execution of corpo-rate strategy.

Consider next a strategy of vertical integration. One company buys another company that has proven its worth in a competitive industry. The purchase could result in backward integration (buy-ing a supplier) or forward integration (expansion into distribution or retail to sell a product). The result is that a company controls the end product and either its component parts or its distribution. Making this strategy work is often a challenging task.

An actual case still receiving a some attention years later is Disney's acquisition of ABC. This was a case of forward integra-tion, as a content producer (movies, animated features) bought a TV station to control distribution for its product. The acquisition seemed to make sense: Content that lacks distribution is virtually worthless, but a distribution capability is nothing if access to solid content is missing. The acquisition of ABC by Disney thus seemed like a good marriage of content and distribution.

But what comes next? What is needed to execute the vertical-integration strategy? One important decision deals with organiza-tional structure. Corporate can leave its acquisition as a separate, independent profit center, or it can meld it into an existing division or function. The former choice lets the acquired company continue to function as it did before as a viable force in its own industry. The latter makes it a captive unit, part of a functional area or existing business.

Disney faced a tough structural choice after it bought ABC. Should it meld it tightly into the Disney structure, exert control, and increase its say over how ABC operates? If so, ABC might be seen as a pawn of Disney, which would upset ABC's management and perhaps drive away other content producers.

On the other hand, letting ABC function independently as a profit center might mean that ABC could reject Disney's content, especially "dogs," movies or shows that Disney would try to foist on ABC because no other networks or cable stations were interested. Also, as an independent, ABC could show programming that conflicts with Disney's wholesome, family orientation, thus hurting its corporate image.

What should Disney or any other corporation do under similar circumstances? What form should the structure take? The answer depends on corporate strategy and its attendant goals. What the acquirer hopes to achieve from vertical integration drives the structural position of the acquired company. A desire for cost controls or synergies would lead to more control and structural integration of an acquisition. A need for an effective presence and growth in a different competitive market would opt for decentralization and an independent profit center.

Consider next a report in 2012 about vertical integration in the tech industry where the strategy is becoming as common as in manufacturing.[vi] Google acquired Motorola Mobility to manufacture smartphones and television set-top boxes; Oracle bought Sun Microsystems to integrate hardware and software; Microsoft makes software, but also hardware for its Xbox products; Sony tried to meld hardware and software, but hasn't yet succeeded fully.

There are other examples, but the point is that vertical integration in the tech industry is proving to be a difficult strategy to implement. There are many reasons for this, but, for present purposes, suffice it to say that structural issues represent one set of factors adding to the difficulty. Hardware and software require different competencies and capabilities in areas like manufacturing and procurement. Trying to integrate two businesses structurally when they are very different can be difficult. Keeping the businesses separate results in some of the control problems noted previously in the Disney case.

These examples raise the age-old issue of centralization and decentralization of organizational structure. Over time, the corporation creates or acquires the businesses that make up and define the organization. Some corporate acquisitions become relatively independent, decentralized units competing in different industries. Yet there may be activities or functions that cut across different businesses that allow for centralization, reduced duplication of resources, and the scale economies so often sought by corporate strategists. Different businesses must be sufficiently independent to respond quickly to market demands, competitors' actions, and customer needs. Yet they can't be so independent as to create an unnecessary duplication of resources and destroy all chances for synergies or scale economies across businesses. The corporation, then, must create the right balance of centralization and decentralization to execute its strategy and achieve its strategic goals.

Looking at the real world provides countless examples of trying to achieve this structural balance. GE, GM, J&J, Microsoft, ABB, Citicorp, Merck, Corning Glass, GlaxoSmithKline, and so on, are characterized by corporate-level shared resources that define the "corporate center." Simultaneously, they are decentralized around business units that compete in different industries, product markets, or geographical areas, usually with large amounts of autonomy and local control in a decentralized structure. Similarly, universities are marked by decentralized units (colleges) but have centralized staff functions such as HR that service all colleges to avoid duplication and generate cost savings.

The trick, again, is to create balance between centralization and decentralization. Each has benefits and costs, as Chapter 4 enumerates fully. Most organizations are marked by both forms of structure; the need is to avoid excessive imbalance where the emphasis on one negates or constrains the benefits of the other.

How a company is organized clearly depends on and is related to corporate strategy. Structure is important to the execution of corporate strategy, a point fleshed out in greater detail in Chapter 4.

NEED FOR INTEGRATION

The integration component of corporate structure noted in Figure 2.1 refers to the methods used to achieve coordination across the units comprising organizational structure.

Decisions about structure result in different units focusing on different tasks or specialties. To achieve a unity of effort and combine the activities of these diverse units, formal attention to integrative methods or mechanisms is needed. Business processes that coordinate corporate and business activities or focus on coordination of corporate center functions with business operations are included under the heading of structural integration.

Consider, again, the vertical integration case. To make the strategy of vertical integration work, processes and methods are needed to coordinate the flows of work and materials between supplier and user divisions within the company. Transfer pricing mechanisms must be developed to facilitate internal buy-and-sell transactions. Methods to facilitate information sharing and knowledge transfer also must be developed to facilitate coordination and cooperation. These processes and mechanisms are part of the integration function noted in Figure 2.1.

Consider, too, the case of the global organization. Central to the success of many global strategies is effective integration or coordination. Citibank must coordinate programs and services to its multinational customers worldwide. Work directed toward these large global players must be coordinated across countries or regions. Yet the services performed globally cannot violate local regulations or norms or ignore local economic problems and opportunities. Processes of integration are needed worldwide to deal with this complexity and achieve a strong competitive position.

Asea Brown Boveri (ABB) competes globally in many different businesses with many different companies that make up the corporation. A critical task challenging its global approach is the integration of a strategy across many regions or countries. To execute strategy, heavy investments are made in its IT system ("Abacus"), global managers, and a worldwide matrix organization in an attempt to facilitate the needed integration. Integration across structural units and geography is vital to making ABB's strategy work.

The methods of achieving structural integration or coordination are handled in Chapter 5. These are important topics that need additional exposition. Recall from Chapter 1 that managers surveyed mentioned the importance of sharing information and coordination mechanisms for execution success. In fact, in the interviews and discussions conducted after publication of *Making Strategy Work*, managers said emphatically that the structural integration required for sound execution is a vital concern and a formidable execution obstacle if not done well. Consequently, detailed attention is devoted to these and related structural issues in Chapters 4 and 5. For now, the point of the examples in this overview of execution is to stress that:

> *Corporate strategy affects the choice of organizational structure. Alternatively, organizational structure is important to the execution of corporate strategy. To execute strategy effectively, managers must make sound decisions about structure and develop methods or processes to achieve the needed integration of structural units.*

Business Strategy and the Execution of Corporate Strategy

Figure 2.1 shows that businesses, divisions, or SBUs must create strategies of their own, and this represents the next element of the model. At the business level, strategy is focused on products, services, and how to compete in a given industry. Emphasis is on industry analysis and industry forces external to the organization as the business attempts to position itself for competitive advantage. Attention is also paid to internal resources and capabilities as the business tries to create skills and competencies that differentiate it from competitors. In essence, business strategy deals with how to compete and gain advantage in a given market, and much has already been written on the topic.

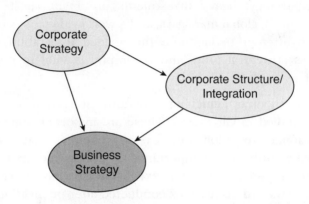

What I want to stress presently in our model of strategy execution is that business strategy is important to the execution of corporate strategy.

Business strategy is important in its own right because it helps achieve competitive advantage and profitability for the business unit and, ultimately, the entire organization. But business strategy is also important to the execution of corporate strategy, a role not often assigned to it by those interested in execution. Indeed, business strategy and corporate strategy are interdependent; each affects and is affected by the other.

Consider the corporate portfolio strategies developed by the Boston Consulting Group (BCG), GE, Novartis, and others and the familiar terms that have been generated by these approaches: "cash cows," "stars," "pillar" companies, "dogs," and so on. These are familiar names given to business units in a corporate portfolio, *but they also describe the role the businesses must play to successfully implement the corporate strategy.*

"Cash cows" in the BCG matrix, for example, generate cash. Corporate "milks" them and uses their cash to feed and grow other business units, such as "stars" with growth potential. Corporate needs the "cash cows" to grow parts of its portfolio, consistent with its strategy. What would happen if "cash cows" did not meet corporate expectations? What if they fail to produce the requisite cash nourishment for the internal funding of growth and acquisition? Clearly, funds would have to come from elsewhere; otherwise, corporate strategy could not be executed successfully.

The point is that business-level strategy is vital to the success of corporate strategy. Business strategies are important to the successful execution of corporate plans and the attainment of corporate goals. Similarly, corporate and business strategies must be integrated effectively to achieve desired levels of company performance. Chapter 3 expands upon and clarifies these important points. Suffice it to say for now, given the purpose of this chapter's overview, that:

> *Business strategy is essential to the successful execution of corporate strategy. Corporate planning assigns roles and goals to business units, the performance of which affects the execution of corporate strategy. Poor strategic performance at the business level detracts from corporate's ability to achieve its strategic aims, while good performance helps make corporate strategy work.*

EXECUTING BUSINESS STRATEGY

The focus in the model thus far has been on the execution or implementation of corporate strategy via choices of organizational structure and the contribution of business-level strategies. We now can begin looking more closely at the execution of business strategies.

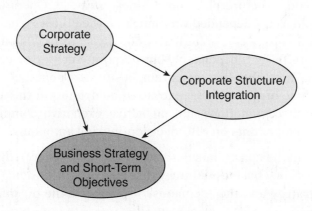

As Figure 2.1 shows, business strategy is affected or constrained by corporate strategy and corporate structure. Even independent, standalone businesses can be constrained somewhat by prior decisions about corporate strategy and structure. The development of business strategy, while dependent primarily on industry forces and business capabilities, will reflect these constraints.

Business strategy is constrained and affected first by resource allocations and the demands of corporate strategy. Resources are allocated to businesses as a function of their role in the corporate portfolio, as emphasized previously. If businesses don't meet corporate expectations in terms of performance, it follows logically that their resource allocations will suffer. These allocations (or lack thereof) clearly will affect a business' ability to execute its future strategies. Even relatively independent businesses are constrained by corporate demands for profitability and contributions to the overall company.

Business strategy is also constrained by prior corporate decisions about organizational structure, as Figure 2.1 shows. Centralization of structural units (such as R&D) constrains a business because it doesn't control needed resources locally, but must rely on a corporate function located elsewhere in the organization. The business is dependent on the centralized resource without control over it, which affects decision-making. Still, though faced with this structural constraint, businesses must formulate and execute strategies to contribute to organizational performance.

There are many examples of the constraints that corporate strategy and structure place on business strategy. Operating units in the old AT&T depended very much on the processes and outcomes of Bell Labs, a corporate R&D unit. Divisions or companies within GE are fairly independent, but corporate center or central functional area activities constrain businesses nonetheless. Even in J&J, one of the most decentralized companies in the world, a few centralized functions and an active executive committee place some constraints on SBU decision-making autonomy.

Beyond the constraints posed by the corporate level, there are two aspects of a business strategy that affect its execution: (1) the type of strategy and the "demands" it places on the organization, and

(2) the need to translate strategy into short-term, measurable objectives. Handling these issues well will drive execution success.

"DEMANDS" OF BUSINESS STRATEGY

Business strategy creates "demands" that must be satisfied to ensure successful execution. Cost-leadership or low-cost strategies, for example, create demands on organizational investments, resources, and capabilities that are vital to achieving low-cost status. Capital investments in technology and manufacturing are required to drive down the variable cost of goods sold or services rendered. Demands for standardized products and high production volume must be met to achieve economies of scale and scope, whether making dishwashers or selling term insurance. Incentives must be developed that reward cost reductions; otherwise, people will not perform consistent with the demands of the low-cost strategy.

On April 30, 2012, Delta Airlines shocked its industry and Wall Street by announcing it would buy a refinery complex in Trainer, Pennsylvania, just outside Philadelphia, to produce jet fuel. This is significant, as Delta would be the first U.S. airline to enter the refinery business. The announced goal is to reduce the carrier's jet-fuel costs by $300 million.[vii]

This attempt at backward integration for cost containment faces challenges to successful execution. Heavy investment will be needed to prepare the faculty to produce the required levels of fuel to achieve the lofty cost savings. Refining obviously is a different business than running an airline, so questions regarding the new facility's independence and role in the corporate structure are bound to arise. Delta is jumping into a particularly challenged market, with high price volatility. Market forces may challenge Delta's ability to achieve the low-cost position it seeks. Work will be needed to meet the demands of a low-cost strategy, including the volume requirements, standardization, and scale economies necessary to make the strategy work. These demands will be significant, posing challenges to Delta.

Consider, too, the remarkable run that Walmart has had for years in the area of cost reduction. Emphasis has been on volume and quick turnover, with little investment in inventory. Investment in information technologies ensured superior inventory control. These investments also created dependencies among suppliers for up-to-date sales and customer information, which increased Walmart's power over them. Reward systems have focused on reducing "shrinkage" and lowering other costs. Sales and advertising expenses have been benchmarked against the industry, with resulting costs always below industry average. Investments in warehousing have reduced logistical costs. Walmart, in effect, has invested money and energy into creating capabilities and activities that support its low-cost strategy and, in total, are difficult for competitors to imitate.

Nucor provides another good example in an unattractive steel industry. Nucor's investments clearly support its strategy. It invested in new steel-making technologies to control costs and quality. It also made a ton of investments in its people, developing HR policies and incentive plans that differentiate it in a stodgy industry and make imitation by larger, slower competitors difficult.

The key point here is that strategies demand certain investments and the development of organizational capabilities or resources if successful execution is to result. And different strategies demand different investments and the development of different capabilities. Chapter 3 goes into more detail on these points. For now , suffice it to say that:

> *Business strategy creates demands for organizational investments in technology, people, and capabilities. These investments must be made and the appropriate skills developed to successfully execute a business strategy.*

INTEGRATING STRATEGY AND SHORT-TERM OPERATING OBJECTIVES

To execute business strategy, Figure 2.1 also indicates that strategic plans and objectives must be translated into short-term operating objectives. Long-term goals must generate short-term metrics, measures of performance that relate logically to the business plan.

Most managers in complex organizations face and deal with local, short-term issues. The focus is on what's needed daily, weekly, monthly, or quarterly, as managers confront the usual problems and opportunities associated with customers, competitors, and employees. It is impossible, even at the highest levels of a business, to manage effectively armed only with a strategic plan. Key issues, elements, and needs of the business strategy must be translated into shorter-term objectives and action plans, and this translation process is an integral and vital part of the execution of strategy. Short-term thinking is okay if it's tied to long-term, strategic thinking.

Because the translation of strategy into short-term operating objectives is so important to the execution of business strategy, it must be controlled and orchestrated. Without this control, managers and workers at mid- and lower-level positions may be focusing on the wrong things. A differentiation strategy based, in part, on improved customer service will fail if short-term concerns focus primarily on cost and the avoidance of additional expenses, including those related to customer service. Similarly, if business strategies are changing and adapting to industry forces over time, execution of the new strategies will suffer if short-term objectives and performance metrics don't change and continue to emphasize decisions, actions, and measures "we've always had or relied on in the past." A business simply must ensure that everyday objectives and performance metrics are consistent with its strategic goals and plans.

As basic as this point is—that strategy must be translated into short-term metrics—this translation is often incomplete or faulty. Short-term objectives or metrics in use often are not related logically to business strategy.

As a follow-up exercise to my Wharton executive program on executing strategy, top managers, responding to a challenge from me, have occasionally gone back to their companies and had managers below them ask their subordinates two simple, related questions: "What activities and objectives do you routinely pursue (in your department, unit, and so on), and what business strategy do these activities and objectives support?" The answers are often surprising, I've been told, with people down through the organization unaware of how everyday objectives, activities, or performance metrics relate to business strategy. There are even cases in which everyday activities and efforts are inconsistent with business strategy, placing successful execution in jeopardy.

How does a business achieve the needed consistency? To integrate strategic and short-term objectives, an effort with some formality must be developed and employed. Part of an organization's routines or standard management practices must focus on this integration. Short-term objectives and performance metrics must be tied to strategy formally, not left to chance or haphazard practices. Integrating long- and short-term objectives is important for the effective execution of strategy and, thus, must be taken seriously.

A number of methodologies related to management-by-objectives programs or their offshoots, such as the Balanced Scorecard or Enterprise Performance Management Systems, exist to help managers integrate long- and short-term business objectives.[viii] How these programs aid this integration is presented in greater detail in Chapter 3. For now, the present position and emphasis can be summarized as follows:

> *Business strategy must be translated into short-term operating objectives or metrics to execute the strategy. To achieve strategic objectives, an organization must develop short-term, measurable objectives that relate logically to, and are consistent with, business strategy and how the organization plans to compete.*

Business Structure and Integration

Figure 2.1 shows next that business structure is also important to the execution of business strategy.

Much of the theory and practice in the area of organizational design has been devoted to business structure, the next component of our overview. This design work has focused primarily on the structure of businesses and the coordination of work across units within the business. This stream of work has provided us with valuable insights into these aspects of organizational design and need not be reviewed exhaustively here.

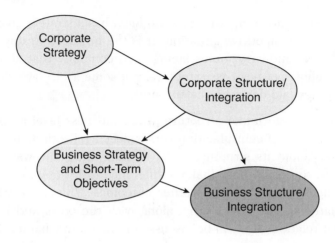

Figure 2.1 shows the place of business structure in the execution of strategy. First, similar to the case at the corporate level, strategy again drives the choice of structure. Business-level strategy and its logical offshoots—short-term operating objectives—affect the choice of business structure.

In a sense, it is necessary now to talk about organizational "designs" or "structures." Different businesses in the same company can face very different competitive situations and thus have a need for different structures. Imposing the same structure on all businesses or divisions simply because they are part of the same organization is not a logical and appropriate way to determine structure. Corporate should avoid this execution error at all costs. Figure 2.1 does show that corporate structure can constrain business structure. To reiterate an example used previously, a centralized R&D unit creates a dependency on the corporate unit and affects coordination between businesses and the corporate staff. Still, this is a vastly different situation than corporate imposing the same structure on all its businesses. Business structure should reflect, and be driven primarily by, the nature of business strategy.

GE Capital and Jet Engines represent two different divisions or product areas under the GE umbrella. Both are dependent somewhat on centralized functions and staff. To argue, however, that both should be structured in the same way because they both, after all, are GE companies would be a major mistake. Both companies are in totally different industries, and both face different industry and competitive forces. Each has a strategy to cope with its own competitive situation. It is the business strategy and the different industry forces facing each company that should drive the choice of business structure, not some arbitrary rule for consistency laid down by the corporate level.

Issues raised under structure at the business level again include the degree of centralization versus decentralization, as a business must adopt its structure to its strategy the same way corporate does. Structure does make a difference to business performance. It does affect costs and other outcomes. The strategy-structure relationship, consequently, along with the costs and benefits of that relationship, will be discussed in depth in Chapter 4.

Integration again comes into play at the business level, just as it did at the corporate level. Once again, structure defines the major functions or operating units that make up the business. Once more, the issue is one of coordination or integration, as businesses develop processes or methods of achieving lateral coordination across these major operating units or functions.

In geographically dispersed businesses, managing across organizational units is of paramount importance. Coordinating work flows, transferring relevant knowledge effectively from one part of the business to another, and achieving integration so as to meet business objectives are necessary ingredients for successful performance. A focus on knowledge transfer, information sharing, and effective integration or coordination is vitally important, as the survey data and discussions with managers showed convincingly.

Consider a large consulting company such as McKinsey. Clearly, one of its needs for continued effectiveness is the transfer of knowledge and information sharing across offices around the world. Helping clients in one location or industry demands the sharing of information about previously developed processes and methods from other locations and industries. Managing across specialized areas of expertise and transferring knowledge effectively are absolutely essential to the execution of McKinsey's service-based strategy.

Size and geographical dispersion are not the only challenges to effective communication and coordination. Different units and functional areas within a business are often characterized by differences in goals, perceptions, and time frames for action. They often have very different cultures. Conflicts often occur across functions such as marketing, production, and R&D because of these differences in goals and perceptions, as every practicing manager knows. Integration of these diverse, differentiated units ("silos") to achieve superordinate goals is certainly a challenging task, but it is central to the successful execution of business strategy.

A large university has different colleges or strategic units in its portfolio. University programs directed toward social or economic goals—improving minority businesses, mental health outreach programs, small business development centers, training for health care jobs—often involve integration of effort across colleges or research centers. Different colleges may be characterized by different customers, goals, and decision processes, but common or superordinate goals demand effective communication, coordination, and management to achieve university-wide programs and outreach potential.

Effective communication, coordination, and knowledge sharing are important for effective strategy execution. These issues are confronted in detail in Chapter 5. For now, suffice it to say that:

> *Lateral communication and managing across organizational boundaries are important to successful strategy execution. Transferring knowledge and achieving coordination across operating units within a business are vital to strategic success. Information sharing and integration methods can increase the flexibility of structure and the organization's ability to respond to execution-related problems.*

INCENTIVES AND CONTROLS

The picture of strategy execution is not yet complete because the creation of strategy, objectives, structure, and coordinating mechanisms is not sufficient to ensure that individuals will adapt their own goals to those of the organization. Some method of obtaining individual and organizational goal congruence is required. Prior decisions and actions can be negated by a lack of commitment among individuals charged with execution. Execution suffers if people are rewarded for doing the "wrong" things. Execution fails when no one has skin in the game.

Feedback on performance is also needed so that the organization can evaluate whether the "right" things are indeed being accomplished in the strategy-execution process. Feedback is absolutely essential to organizational change or adaptation over time.

In essence, what is required is the careful development of incentives and controls, the last component of the model in Figure 2.1.

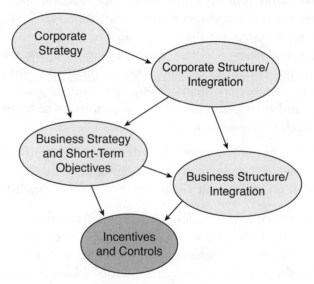

Incentives and controls are together in Figure 2.1 because they represent the "flip sides" of decisions and actions concerned with performance. On one hand, incentives motivate or guide performance; on the other, controls provide feedback about whether desired performance outcomes are being attained. Controls allow for the revision of incentives and other execution-related factors if desired goals are not being met.

INCENTIVES

Incentives must reinforce strategic and short-term objectives. Individual and group rewards are an important aspect of strategy execution because they control performance with respect to desired strategic and short-term outcomes. It truly is critical that the organization rewards the "right things," including previously defined strategic and short-term objectives.

Organizations always seem to be grappling with the right incentives to facilitate strategy execution. For example, more and more CEOs can be seen striking deals that tie pay to performance. James Rogers, CEO of Duke Energy, had a nice compensation package in 2010 based on company performance, with a significant portion of his compensation paid in company stock. GE CEO Jeffrey Immelt is paid in "performance share units," which will become stock shares if performance measures related to cash flow and shareholder value are met. A Wall Street survey of CEO compensation conducted by the Hay Group revealed clear evidence that companies like Disney, HP, Boeing, Avon, Caterpillar, Citigroup, Motorola, and many others tied top managers' incentives like stock awards to company performance.[ix] The intention, of course, is to forge a concern with long-term, strategic performance that leads to increased shareholder value.

Many companies are beginning to question "related-party transactions" that pose the risk of "conflicts between a company official's two roles: representative of the shareholder and an individual seeking to get the best deal for himself.[x] This is the "agency" problem revisited, the concern being that managers' rewards should be tied to the right things, including shareholder value and other strategic and short-term objectives.

In addition to reinforcing attention to desired objectives, the model in Figure 2.1 also indicates that incentives must support key elements of business structure. In a matrix organization, for example, incentives must support the two-boss or multiple-boss structure. If only one boss controls rewards, the "grid" or dual nature of the matrix structure is compromised, even destroyed. Similarly, incentives that reward only individual performance will have deleterious effects on the effectiveness of group- or team-based approaches to integration or coordination.

Incentives, then, are central to any plan of execution. They tell people what's important and what to emphasize. Thorndike's age-old law of effect definitely is still salient: Behavior that is reinforced tends to be repeated.[xi] Successful execution requires that incentives reward the right things.

CONTROLS

Controls round out the final element of our model in Figure 2.1. Controls represent a feedback loop. They provide information about the achievement of objectives that derive from strategy and other aspects of our model of execution. This feedback is important because strategy execution is an adaptive process. Managers rarely get everything right; fine-tuning of plans, objectives, and implementation methods is more often the rule than the exception.

Ineffective market and customer surveillance, poor information about organizational performance, and a company's inability or reluctance to act on feedback received from the marketplace surely spell disaster for strategy-execution efforts. Without good controls in place, effective change and adaptation are not possible. Recall that the data presented in Chapter 1 showed emphatically that the ability to manage change is an extremely critical execution need. Change is not possible, however, if feedback mechanisms do not exist. The market surveillance and information flows back to the organization upon measurement of performance are critical for change and adaptation. Thus, the final element of the present model, treated in depth in Chapter 6, stresses that:

Incentives must support the key aspects of the strategy-execution model. They must reinforce the "right" things if execution is to succeed. Controls, in turn, must provide timely and valid feedback about organizational performance so that change and adaptation become part and parcel of the execution effort.

ANOTHER VIEW OF THE MODEL OF STRATEGY EXECUTION

In the years following publication of *Making Strategy Work*, managers I worked or consulted with suggested additions to the model of Figure 2.1. Figure 2.2 presents one addition to the model based on these managers' views. The flow diagram in the new figure retains all of what's been discussed thus far but adds another element that's only implied in Figure 2.1. The new element is "project management."

Figure 2.1 is still the principle model driving analysis of execution and discussion for the remainder of this book; it shows the critical decisions and actions needed to make strategy work. Figure 2.2 retains the key aspects of the original figure, but adds a piece to it. The inclusion of project management simply adds a tool or process that can be applied to support strategy execution decisions. Project management, that is, supports the basic model and approach, and doesn't change or replace parts of it in any way.

Figure 2.2 begins with a focus on business strategy. It shows that strategy makes "demands" on the business in terms of the skills, capabilities, or resources needed to support and execute the strategy. It also shows that strategy must be translated into short-term objectives or metrics tied to strategic performance.

The demands of strategy and the short-term operating objectives, along with strategy itself, affect the choice of organizational structure and process. Organization supports the objectives and requirements that strategy needs for success. These objectives and demands are, in turn, supported by incentives designed to motivate behavior consistent with the actions, decisions, and goals of effective strategy execution. Controls ensure that the right things are being done and provide feedback to enable the organization to adapt to changing conditions and tweak execution efforts accordingly. These points are clearly a summary or synthesis of the key elements of Figure 2.1.

What many managers suggested is the addition of project management. The logic is straightforward. Care has been taken to flesh out strategy, objectives, structure, process, and the incentives to support key execution needs. These steps are critical, but one additional step is required: actually doing the work and moving things along. The "devil is in the details," and project management focuses on the details. The project management function targets coordination. It is action oriented and concerned with making everything work and performing efficiently and effectively.

The addition of a project management concept and function only adds to and solidifies the model of Figure 2.1. Managers who used the ideas and concepts presented in *Making Strategy Work* made a strong case for the project management addition to add a stronger sense of action and trajectory to the critical decisions and steps needed to foster effective strategy execution. The original model of Figure 2.1 certainly implied this thrust of action, detail, and continuous movement toward execution-related milestones, but the addition of project management in Figure 2.2 formalizes and makes more explicit what previously had only been implicit. Figure 2.1 is still the working model for execution, and subsequent chapters consider its elements and contributions to making strategy work in a step-by-step manner. Figure 2.2 simply refines and adds to the basic model with the addition of the project management tool or process.

A brief overview of the essential elements of sound project management is provided in a chapter in the "Applications" part of this book. This is a significant addition, stretching the needed emphasis on coordination and action in the execution process.

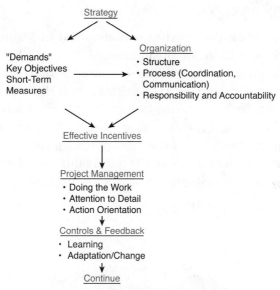

Figure 2.2   Successful Execution: An Overview of Making Strategy Work

---

CONTEXT OF EXECUTION DECISIONS

The model of strategy execution lays out the major elements or stages in the process and focus on the logical connections and order among them. It identifies the broad areas that demand management attention and decisions if execution is to succeed. The task in later chapters is to flesh out the key issues or decisions inherent in each of the elements or stages of the model presented.

However, the overview requires one more step to make it complete and useful. Managers' opinions about execution problems noted in Chapter 1 suggest that an additional set of factors must be considered when trying to make strategy work: namely, the context within which execution decisions and actions take place.

THE EXECUTION CONTEXT

The execution decisions or actions noted in Figures 2.1 and 2.2 take place within an organizational or environmental context. This context is important because it can affect execution processes and outcomes. Consistent with the views discussed in Chapter 1, four contextual factors deserve attention when explaining the success of the execution decisions and actions just considered in the models: (1) the change management context, (2) the culture of the organization, (3) the organizational power structure, and (4) the leadership context (see Figure 2.3).

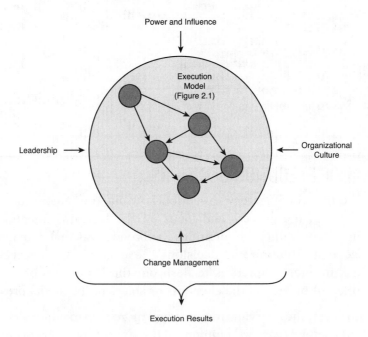

Figure 2.3　Context of Execution Decisions

The four items are not independent; they relate to one another in many ways. The four areas—power, culture, change, and leadership—clearly affect and are affected by each other. One can safely argue that, when all four are in sync, the prognosis for execution success is positive. Yet, for purposes of analysis and understanding, each is important enough to deserve separate attention. Managers must understand each of the four well before they can understand their interdependence and interactive effects.

MANAGING CHANGE

Much attention has been devoted to managing change in organizations. Strategy execution, of course, often involves change. Execution may demand changes in job responsibilities, organizational structure, coordination methods, people, incentives, or controls. These changes may be vital to the success of execution outcomes.

Yet we know that individuals often resist change. They may not buy into the execution program. They might actually try to sabotage the changes and cause execution-related efforts to fail. Managing change effectively, then, is obviously an important ingredient in making strategy work.

Despite its importance, there are vast differences in organizational capabilities when it comes to managing change. Some companies do it well, while others' attempts at major changes are absolute disasters. Cultural change is especially difficult, often challenging or negating execution efforts.

That the ability to manage change well is a hallmark of successful execution is only reinforced strongly by the present data. Managers in the surveys and interviews discussed in Chapter 1 reported that problems with change management constitute the single biggest threat to successful strategy execution. This clearly is an extremely important topic, and it is treated in depth in Chapter 7.

CULTURE

A great deal has been written about organizational culture and rightfully so, for culture affects much of what goes on (and doesn't go on) in organizations. Culture can affect the problems or opportunities managers actually notice or focus on. Culture helps define the performance outcomes held dear by organizational members. Culture defines how work gets done, what rewards are valued, how mistakes or errors are treated, and what management styles are appropriate. Subcultures within organizations or across operating units certainly affect attempts at lateral communication and coordination. Figure 2.3 shows the impact of culture, an important context factor affecting execution.

Perhaps, most importantly, culture reflects and affects the drive and ownership that individuals feel for execution-related goals and activities. When managers are committed to execution success and they feel ownership of the means to successful outcomes, the prognosis for making strategy work is most positive.

Culture, admittedly, is a "soft" variable, hard to measure and put your hands around. Still, we all know it when we see it. I have worked in companies in the same industry whose cultures were light years apart. Though focused on the same markets and customers, the companies' methods, managerial styles, rewards, and control processes were quite different. The companies had "different feels" to them. Managers acted differently. The cultures were divergent, and they affected how work was done, including how strategy was executed.

Some companies are just "loaded" with culture that one can immediately discern. In my work with Microsoft, GE, J&J, and Centocor, the culture was clearly felt in a short period of time. One could easily see the drive, results orientation, ownership, and commitment to task and coworkers. One could see how people aimed high, trying to improve performance and achieve innovation.

Organizational culture affects the execution of strategy. Inappropriate cultures must be changed if they don't support execution efforts. But change is difficult to achieve, as was just mentioned. Consequently, Chapter 8 is devoted to the critical topic of managing culture and change.

THE ORGANIZATIONAL POWER STRUCTURE

Power is social influence, the ability to influence others to do something. Power usually can be described in terms of dependency.

If an individual or unit within an organization solves the critical problems facing an organization or is able to control important scarce resources, the dependency of others results in power dif-ferences. The individual or unit relied upon can exercise social influence. One such exercise among top managers is the formula-tion of strategy. Those in power identify external needs or oppor-tunities, define new markets and customers, and determine company direction. Power, then, affects the creation of strategic plans and goals.

Power differences don't only affect the formulation of strategy; they also affect key execution decisions and outcomes. Those in power decide on resource allocations to individuals and organiza-tional units that affect execution efforts. If those in power resist or don't support an execution plan, the success of the plan clearly is jeopardized.

Power is social influence, and that influence can materialize in dif-ferent ways. Managers can influence others directly, relying on hierarchy or position. They can influence others indirectly by "persuading" them via reliance on expertise or logic to act in a cer-tain way. However it's done, power and the exercise of influence clearly can affect execution.

Power thus is an important contextual factor in the execution of strategy, as Figure 2.3 indicates. Chapter 1 notes that understand-ing the power structure was rated by managers as an important ingredient in the execution process. Understanding and using the power structure effectively can greatly increase the probability of success of strategy execution efforts. Consequently, a chapter is devoted to this important topic (Chapter 9).

THE LEADERSHIP CLIMATE

People are vital to execution success. Clearly, their motivations, capabilities, commitments, and ability to create and follow through on plans of action affect the success of execution efforts.

Among the characteristics or qualities of people who have received a great deal of attention is leadership. Recent popular books have played up the importance of leadership for the execution of strat-egy.[xii] They have consistently stressed the characteristics of great leaders, including their personality traits (quiet, self-effacing, and demanding) and ability to choose and motivate followers.

I, too, argue that leadership is critical to the successful execution of strategy (see Figure 2.3). My focus, however, concentrates more on the context of leadership than on the actions of a few individuals. I'm concerned with the climate created by leaders at all levels of an organization (not just the top) that affects strategy execution. How leaders create this climate or context is the critical issue here.

It is important to focus on the climate that leaders create. The responses from managers reported in Chapter 1 emphasized the central role of the leadership climate. My own experiences reinforce the notion that it is important to focus on the reactions of followers to the context or climate that leaders create. Most managers up and down the organization, after all, are both leaders and followers. They create and react to climate, which again suggests its role in execution.

Leadership, of course, is pervasive. It affects or reflects a host of things, including the management of change, culture, and the exercise of power or influence. The importance of leadership for execution is duly expanded upon and emphasized, although a separate chapter is not dedicated to the topic. The need for effective leadership, in effect, is discussed or implied in every chapter of this book.

NEED FOR A DISCIPLINED APPROACH

My argument in this chapter has been that a disciplined approach to execution is needed to make strategy work. A reliance on a few sound bytes, anecdotes, or stories is not sufficient. Chapter 1 revealed the complexity and difficulty of the strategy-execution process and the obstacles it confronts. Only an integrated, disciplined approach can cut through this complexity and achieve execution success.

Managers need to see the "big picture," an overview of key decisions or actions that, in total, represent a template, model, or guide to effective execution. They must understand the contextual forces that affect the workings of this model. Decisions about structure, incentives, coordination, and controls, after all, do not occur in a vacuum. They take place in a setting or climate that itself can affect execution outcomes.

Managers responsible for making strategy work must keep a model like the one discussed in this chapter firmly in mind. Having such a model allows one to take a disciplined approach to the execution task. It lays out the order and logic of execution decisions and action. With such an approach, one can see the variables essential to the development of a solid execution plan.

The overview in this chapter identified the decisions and actions that need additional attention and analysis, as each is central to execution success. So, let's start looking more specifically and in greater detail at the topics suggested in this chapter.

SUMMARY

This chapter presented an overview of the strategy-execution process. It emphasizes the following:

- Strategy execution is difficult and is not easily explained by managerial sound bytes or the idiosyncrasies of a few successful managers.

- A logical model and a disciplined approach are needed to understand the strategy-execution process. Emphasis must be on what to do, when, why, and in what order. This chapter initiates this logical overview of strategy execution. No model is perfect or all-inclusive, of course. Still, managers interested in execution must start somewhere. They need a blueprint for analysis and action. The reasons why execution succeeds or fails can only be understood by having a benchmark against which to analyze execution decisions and actions.

- The key ingredients defining strategy execution include decisions about strategy, structure, coordination, information sharing, incentives, and controls. These decisions take place within an organizational context, aspects of which include power, culture, leadership, and the ability to manage change. An understanding of the interactions among key execution decisions and contextual forces is necessary to understand how to make strategy work.

■ Subsequent chapters consider components of the execution model and organizational context in greater detail. Having provided the big picture or overview in this chapter, additional attention can now turn to specific topics or factors and how they affect execution.

ENDNOTES

i. The terms "snowball making" and "snowball throwing" are used in McKinsey and Company to denote conceptual planning and knowledge creation ("snowball making") and the application of the knowledge to solving client problems and generating revenues ("snowball throwing"). I personally don't know if the terms are still in use, but my McKinsey informants assure me that these were actual descriptive terms used for years in the consulting giant.

ii. An earlier version of this model can be found in L. G. Hrebiniak and W. F. Joyce's *Implementing Strategy*, Macmillan, 1984.

iii. See, for example, William Joyce, Nitin Nohria, and Bruce Roberson's *What (Really) Works*, Harper Business, 2003.

iv. See *The Merger & Acquisitions Review*, 5th ed., September, 2011; *Money Morning's Quarterly Outlook*, April 2011.

v. "KPMG-Wharton Survey Indicates Boost for M&A Activity in 2012," *PR Newswire*, February 28, 2012; "M&A Activity Seen Increasing After Slow Start in 2012," Reuters, March 22, 2012; Bank of America, Merrill Lynch, "M&A Activity, Outlook Asia, 2012."

vi. "Vertical Integration Works, for Apple—But It Won't for Everyone," *Knowledge@Wharton*, March 14, 2012.

vii. "Delta to Buy Refinery in Effort to Lower Jet-Fuel Costs." *The Wall Street Journal*, May 1, 2012; "A Personal Trainer for Delta Air," *WSJ*, May 2, 2012.

viii. See, for example, Robert Kaplan and David Norton's *The Balanced Scorecard*, Harvard Business School Press, 1996.

ix.   The Wall Street Journal Survey of CEO Compensation, *WSJ*, October 12, 2009.

x.   "Many Companies Report Transactions with Top Officers," *The Wall Street Journal*, December 29, 2003.

xi.   Edward Thorndike, *The Elements of Psychology*, A. G. Seiler, 1905.

xii.   Jim Collins, *Good to Great*, Harper Business, 2001; M. Useem, *Leading Up*, Crown Business, 2001; Warren Bennis, *On Becoming a Leader*, Basic Books, 2009; James MacGregor Burns, *Leadership*, Harper Collins, 2010; Peter Drucker, *The Effective Executive*, Collins, 2006.

3

The Path to Successful Execution: Good Strategy Comes First

Introduction

It all begins with strategy.

It is impossible to discuss execution until one has something to execute. Central to the model of execution presented in Chapter 2 is strategy, at both the corporate and business levels. Strategy is the driving force, the first essential ingredient in the execution process.

That strategy is so important and fundamental to execution efforts should hardly be surprising. Logically, it follows that poor inputs to the execution process result in poor outputs. Execution outcomes can be hurt severely by problems that arise from faulty strategy formulation or poor strategy. It is vital to eliminate as many problems as possible in the strategy-formulation stage, as they will surely emerge to haunt, test, even destroy the execution process.

There is another direct connection between strategy and execution: A sound, successful strategy can create conditions and outcomes that make execution easier. A company whose strategy achieves increased market share and a resultant increase in power over suppliers, for example, may find execution of its strategy to be a bit easier because of its market share and the newfound power over suppliers. Strategy, indeed, can create conditions that facilitate execution.

There is a connection between planning and doing. The purpose of this chapter is to clarify this link and show how strategy creation affects strategy execution.

IS THE IMPACT OF STRATEGY OVERRATED?

The major obstacles to execution noted in Chapter 1 included poor or vague strategy as a significant barrier to effective execution. Managers indicated that lack of a sound strategy often causes major difficulties. Their point was that bad strategy begets poor execution. Of course, even good strategies can suffer from poor execution plans and processes. But bad or ill-conceived strategies virtually guarantee poor results, despite execution efforts.

Strategy clearly is important to the managers who provided their views on execution in this research. Still, some argue that strategy may not be the first critical step to competitive success. Jim Collins, for example, in a book that still appears in 2013 on some best seller lists, tells us that strategy did not "separate the good-to-great companies from the comparison companies" in his research.[i] Both sets of organizations had well-defined strategies, he asserts, so strategy didn't account for greatness.

Yet his own examples contradict his point. Nucor's strategy, for instance, couldn't have been more different than that of Bethlehem Steel. Nucor was a first mover, the initial adopter of the thin slab casting process for producing flat-rolled steel developed by SMS in Germany. Nucor had highly developed technological capabilities, including the ability to construct new mills and then run them efficiently. It was entrepreneurial, willing to take technical and financial risks. Its HR policies, flat organizational structure, meritocracy based on performance, and ample at-risk reward structure supported its strategy and clearly differentiated it in the steel industry.

Did Bethlehem, the counterpart company to Nucor in Collins' work, also have a solid, well-defined strategy? Hardly, in my opinion. For years it was a slow mover, turtle-like in adopting the new technologies of integrated Japanese and European steel makers. A low-cost strategy wasn't supported at all by its HR policies, a tall, bureaucratic organizational structure, or labor-management relations. Strategic inertia and risk avoidance allowed a nimble competitor like Nucor to outmaneuver it and become the most profitable, low-cost producer in the industry. Nucor's strategy and capabilities clearly made a difference.

Similarly, Gillette developed a differentiation strategy by investing in new, radical technology to support product innovation, while its competition didn't. Philip Morris recovered from a bad bout of diversification, including the Seven-Up acquisition debacle, better than its competition. Its strategic focus on food (Kraft/General Foods/Nabisco) and economies of scope in brand management and other functional areas gave it a competitive edge. Pitney Bowes followed a disciplined strategy of related diversification and its counterpart didn't, fueling its successful performance.

Collins' examples clearly seem to support a case for the importance of strategy in helping to make companies great, not a lack of importance. His argument to the contrary is mystifying at best. Coupled with the opinions of managers in this research regarding poor strategy being a significant barrier to execution, the impact of strategy as a critical variable for organizational performance is only reinforced. The importance of a sound strategy cannot be overrated.

Returning to the impact of strategy on execution, the main focus here, it can be said unequivocally that:

> *Bad strategy begets poor execution. Ill-conceived strategies virtually guarantee poor execution outcomes. A sound strategy can actually facilitate effective implementation. Execution truly does begin with a good strategy.*

But what are "good" and "bad" strategies? What characterizes "good" planning and differentiates it from "bad" planning? Most managers know quite a bit about strategy and planning and far less about execution, a point emphasized previously. So, the present purpose isn't to teach good planning or to repeat what most managers already know about competitive strategy.

The goal at present is to look at those elements or aspects of planning and strategy that cause the most problems for execution. With this in mind, let's emphasize four points or issues, critical aspects or properties of strategy and planning that affect subsequent efforts at execution and the success of those efforts. The four issues are as follows:

1. The need for sound planning and clear, focused strategies at both the corporate and business levels

2. The vital importance of integrating corporate and business strategies and conducting strategy reviews

3. The need to define and communicate clearly the key operational components of strategy and the measurement of execution results

4. The importance of understanding the "demands" of strategy, their effects on the development of organizational resources and capabilities, and the impact of the resources and capabilities on execution

ISSUE #1: THE NEED FOR SOUND PLANNING AND A CLEAR, FOCUSED STRATEGY

This is not a book about strategy formulation; the focus is on executing strategy and making strategic plans work. Nonetheless, a focus on formulation and the development of clear strategies is necessary because of the impact on execution outcomes. This is true for both corporate and business planning, especially in the latter case in which business strategy is so vital to the development and maintenance of competitive advantage.

CORPORATE-LEVEL PLANNING

Strategic planning at the corporate level is primarily involved with portfolio decisions and resource allocations across businesses. The former includes decisions about diversification and the array of industries in which the corporation feels comfortable competing. These components of corporate strategy, along with some of their key issues or questions, are noted in Table 3.1.

Table 3.1 Corporate Level Strategy

Key Components	Major Decisions or Issues
Portfolio analysis	Right "mix" of businesses
	Cash generators and cash users
	Positioning the company for growth
	Stable returns vs. risk-taking and high returns
	Eliminating "deadwood"
Diversification	Analysis of industry attractiveness
	Return on invested capital
	Integration of acquisitions
Resource allocations to businesses	Internal vs. external sources of investment capital
	Performance expectations of different businesses
	Review of business performance and future allocations of resources

The thrust of Table 3.1 is that corporate planners must make sound strategic and financial decisions to grow their company. Investments in new businesses must be preceded by a thorough analysis of the corporate portfolio, including the mix of cash generators and cash users. Decisions about diversifications should be made only after careful analysis of the attractiveness or profit potential of target industries. Resource allocations must take into account the levels of risk that corporate leaders and stakeholders can comfortably assume. Sound corporate strategic planning is vital to overall organizational performance.

Corporate strategy must be clear and sound. If corporate planning is poor or ill conceived, the effects on strategy execution and corporate and business performance are many and potentially fatal.

Resources won't be available or sufficient to sustain growth. The "right" business decisions can be thwarted or compromised by corporate mistakes. Needed resources won't be forthcoming for businesses that potentially could grow into stars in the corporate portfolio. Cash generators could be overtaxed or "milked" too extensively by corporate, seriously hampering future cash-generation capabilities. Diversifications could fail because of poor corporate planning, affecting the entire organization.

CORPORATE STRATEGY: SOME CORPORATE EXAMPLES, GOOD AND BAD

On April 10, 2012, Sony predicted it would suffer a major loss in the fiscal year ending on March 31, approximately $6.5 billion, the largest loss in its history. The company's core product areas—digital imaging, phones, gaming—were doing okay, but some products (such as televisions) were dragging the company down. The professed corporate strategy called for change, but it gave Sony, at best, a "blurry future."[ii]

The strategy wasn't clear and sound. It didn't address such issues as divestiture of nonperforming divisions or businesses. It talked instead of managed decline rather than concerted action. Divisions that were doing poorly would continue to employ resources or assets best allocated to other, more promising business areas. While Kazuo Hirai, Sony's head man, promised he would spin off companies and make major changes, his thrust wasn't clear and convincing. The company's corporate strategy was still unclear, creating uncertainty as to the company's ability to bounce back from its largest historical loss. Hopefully, in time, Sony's corporate strategy will become more clearly stated.

In April 2012, Wall Street analysts lit into P&G's CEO, Robert McDonald, because of the company's weak results. There always are multiple factors that affect results, but two issues that may be involved are corporate strategy and its execution.[iii]

First, there may be a strategic, product-mix issue. P&G has been focusing increasingly on higher-end products, for example, in beauty and cosmetics. This contrasts with its historical emphasis on "rack 'em, stack 'em, and sell 'em" products like Tide detergent that the company was known for. This new strategic thrust may mark a movement away from a commodity focus and toward a higher-end focus that could be new and problematic for P&G. This new thrust, coupled with a worldwide economy that's tough on certain luxury goods, could be responsible, in part, for P&G's poor performance.

Relatedly, the execution of this new corporate strategic thrust may be adding to the problem. Growing emerging markets globally are looking for the low-cost commodity products that P&G seems to be emphasizing less and less. Greater decentralization of structure and operations is likely needed to get close to these markets and cater to local needs and tastes, but P&G appears to have been weak in this regard. Its recent moves to relocate some businesses abroad could suggest that the company finally realizes the importance of getting close to customers and their needs. Structural change can aid execution-related attempts to reach markets with varying needs and customer demands.

More will be said in Chapters 4 and 11 about the importance of decentralized structures in strategy execution and getting close to customers in divergent markets. The present point is that corporate strategy and its emphasis on product areas in the corporate portfolio can significantly affect the performance of the portfolio. Corporate decisions about resource allocations can affect the success of business-level strategies and the attainment of corporate goals.

Avon products may share one of P&G's problems. One of its corporate strategy problems may be that Avon is straddling two worlds—direct selling and high-end beauty products—and such straddling usually leads to big troubles. Avon's traditional, core strength has been direct selling to busy housewives with a stable of tried-and-true basic, nonfancy products. Andrea Jung, former CEO, may have led the company astray in an attempt to recreate Avon as a retail powerhouse that could compete with L'Oreal and P&G. The company, however, doesn't have the resources, capabilities, and culture necessary to support this change in corporate strategy.[iv] There is a real link between strategy formulation and implementation requirements. Obviously, if true, the company, under new CEO, Sherilyn McCoy, faces a daunting task in 2013 and beyond as it tries to refocus on its corporate strengths and revitalize its direct sales model. Possible takeover attempts will only complicate McCoy's task immensely.

There are also apparent positive examples of corporate strategy and its impact on company performance, although the ultimate test of success may require years to judge. Consider, for example, the corporate strategy of vertical integration. Although it took some work and many resources, Microsoft's foray away from software into hardware and products like Xbox has been successful. It's been a costly and difficult vertical integration move, but one that seems to be paying off.

Microsoft's logic and success in introducing a Surface tablet in June 2012, however, may take a while to assess. This is clearly another case of vertical integration; the company that focused on software and then outsourced the hardware design and manufacture now has moved forward, producing its own hardware. Will the corporate strategy work? Only time will tell. Microsoft is now competing with its partners and PC makers who make or want to make their own tablets. Customers becoming competitors can present a challenge to Microsoft's strategy. Add this to its obvious competition with Apple's iPad and the future looks even more challenging. Again, time will tell.

Oracle's purchase of Sun Microsystems likewise seemingly represents a good integration of software and hardware, combining best-in-class enterprise software and mission-critical computing systems, according to Oracle CEO Larry Ellison. But Oracle's sales of Sun's products have been less than satisfactory to many managers and analysts. Some have labeled the acquisition a mistake, while others, including Ellison, are still arguing that the hardware business has a bright future with growth just around the corner. Again, time is needed to play out the corporate strategy and accurately judge the results.

IBM's transformation from a primarily hardware company to one emphasizing hardware and, especially, software and service, is a remarkable success story. The corporate decision-makers abandoned the commodity PC business and entered the consulting/software service area in a big way, showing how effective a vertical integration strategy can be. IBM effectively added a new company and strategic thrust to its portfolio of businesses, a move that presented new opportunities and strengthened the entire organization. This clearly is a positive example of corporate adaptation and the development of critical capabilities to facilitate execution.

Corporate diversification attempts provide good and bad examples of corporate strategy, often in the same company. In the 1990s for example, Lego expanded feverishly into "adjacent" industries—theme parks, television, watches, clothes—with poor results. The firm hit a brick wall, not one made of plastic pieces.[v] The decision to focus again on its roots, with a simpler corporate strategy, moved it back to its prior strong position. In 2013, Lego seems to have a solid business model, based on a core competence and strong set of capabilities. A corporate strategy of excessive diversification affected company performance negatively, but a return to its core business promises continued positive results.

Many other examples can be cited, but the ones offered make some key points:

- **Corporate strategy is important.** A poor, unfounded, or unclear strategy creates major problems for an organization.

- **Corporate strategy must be clear and sound.** Poor planning wastes resources and hurts execution plans and processes. Poor strategy begets poor execution and poor company performance.

Another point should be obvious from the previous examples and the decisions noted in Table 3.1; namely, that corporate strategy affects how businesses operate. Corporate resource allocations affect the execution of business strategies. Reviews of business performance and resource allocations by corporate personnel suggest an important control function that affects company direction. Sound corporate planning is essential to the integration of corporate and business plans. This integration of plans is vital to the successful execution of strategy at both the corporate and business levels.

In a following section, I return to the integration of corporate and business strategies because of its impact on successful execution. First, let's consider the importance of business planning and business strategy for subsequent efforts at execution.

BUSINESS STRATEGY

Good planning and sound strategy are also vital at the business level. Business strategy, too, must be focused and clear. The goal is to develop a strategy that leads to competitive advantage in an industry or market segment. Strategy formulation here depends upon a company's ability to understand its industry and competitors and to develop resources and capabilities that lead to a favorable competitive position.

Figure 3.1 shows the external and internal analyses needed to develop a sound business strategy and achieve competitive advantage. At the business level, it is absolutely essential that management perform an in-depth analysis of the following:

- Industry/market forces
- Competitors, actual and potential, including their strategies and capabilities
- The company's own resources and capabilities, including those that represent a distinctive or core competence

These analyses tell management what's possible or doable in terms of strategy development. Strategy formulation doesn't occur in a vacuum. An organization must match its capabilities with external opportunities and position itself accordingly to maximize its chances for competitive advantage.

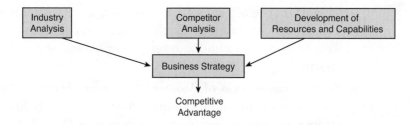

	Key Issues
Industry Analysis	• Size/Concentration of Industry • Number of Strategic Groups (Market Segments) within Industry • Power of Buyers or Customers • Power of Suppliers to Industry • Number of Substitute Products • Rivalry within Industry
Competitor Analysis	• Competitors' Resources and Capabilities • Competitors' Size and Market Power • Competitors' Strategies • Competitors' Previous Offensive and Defensive Moves
Resources and Capabilities	• Our Own Resources, Tangible and Intangible • Our Competitive Capabilities • Existence of a Core Competence – Do we have one? • Competitors' Resources and Capabilities

Figure 3.1   Business Strategy Formulation

The issues and analyses in Figure 3.1 have been presented and debated more than adequately in the management literature, most notably by Michael Porter.[vi] The point to emphasize presently is that business planning and business strategy and the conditions that affect industry position and competitive advantage can also affect the success of strategy execution. Here are some examples that I've observed over the years:

■ **Having market share often facilitates execution.** Market share or size can lead to power over suppliers or buyers if the latter groups become increasingly dependent on a company. Market share can compensate for inefficiencies elsewhere in the organization, such as in systems integration or channel support on the sell side. Having market share certainly is not a total panacea, but it generally is easier to execute strategies with market share and market power behind the execution efforts.

■ **Witness the success of Walmart.** Its power over suppliers has enabled it to execute its vaunted low-cost strategy for years. Or look at the success in the heydays of IBM, Dell, GM, and AT&T when they enjoyed similar market power. It simply is easier to make strategy work when market power is on your side. Pressuring a supplier for price concessions will work if the supplier is extremely dependent on your business. Having market share and market power obviously can support the execution of a business strategy.

■ **Entry barriers support strategy execution.** Market share is a formidable entry barrier, but there are others: capital requirements, brand or reputation, distribution channels, patented technologies or processes, service capabilities, customer relationships, and so on. High entry or mobility barriers keep others from entering a company's space and competing with its strategy and operations. High barriers to entry facilitate strategy execution for the protected organization. It is easier to execute a plan when others cannot easily copy what's being done. Like market share, entry barriers don't guarantee execution success. They can, however, insulate execution efforts from challenges, thereby providing support for execution activities.

■ **Executing a differentiation strategy in a competitive industry marked by increased commoditization is extremely difficult to do.** Commoditization is becoming increasingly prevalent in many industries. Indicators of the phenomenon include the following:

   a. A large number of substitute products

   b. Increased competition, almost always based on price

   c. Changes in key industry forces, for example, increases in customer power

    d. Technological "leveling," when new more efficient technologies are easily imitated, eliminating any machine-based or technical advantage a given organization has achieved

Global competition in a "flat world" supports and exacerbates these trends or challenges. It often results in a proliferation of substitute products and an emphasis on price as a competitive factor. Innovations are shared quickly, greatly reducing the benefits to any organization of its "creative destruction" or technological breakthroughs. Execution of a differentiation strategy, given many similar, lower-priced, substitute products, becomes extremely challenging at best.

The PC business provides a good example. Companies like HP and Dell made their reputations and decent profits in the PC business. The technical landscape has changed dramatically, however, posing new challenges. Many companies make PCs and the level of substitutability is high. Other products like smartphones and tablets are replacing many of the PCs' functions. Leo Apotheker, prior to his ouster as CEO of HP, recommended getting out of the PC business, which, he argued, had become hopelessly commoditized, but the company ignored his advice and is still struggling in a tough competitive marketplace.

Consider next, the interesting and more positive case of Publicis, one of the top two or three advertising holding companies in the world. Headquartered in Paris, it provides advertising and media services globally. In 2008, I and others at Wharton worked with Publicis as the company was facing new challenges.

The basic issue was that customers were questioning the value of traditional advertising. The industry was becoming commoditized. Substitute services and competition were growing, fueled by Internet-based media companies. Customers were saying that advertising sellers "were all alike," and their services were perfect substitutes, leading to customers' focus on price as the critical buy factor.

The strategy of Publicis was twofold: Meet the Internet challenge by acquiring and developing Internet capabilities, and make great efforts to differentiate itself in an increasingly commoditized market. In the latter case, the company strove to:

a. Define and provide value-added services.

b. Find or develop talent to provide the new services.

c. Develop metrics of effectiveness or value-added measures.

d. Become consultants to some customers, learning about their industries and competitive forces, so as to tailor advertising efforts better.

This differentiation attempt is still being played out, but it appears as if the company is having some success. Publicis beat analysts' forecasts, with revenue up 8.3 percent in 2010. In 2011, revenue again increased, 7.3 percent, and operating margin increased by 8.8 percent. Faced with increased competition and the threat of commoditization, Publicis worked diligently to differentiate itself by focusing on the customer and defining value-added services, a Herculean task that appears to be paying dividends.

Other companies have seen similar success in the face of commoditization, as shown by Nucor in the steel industry or Porsche or Audi in an increasingly competitive global automotive industry. But it normally is difficult to achieve and sustain differentiated products and services under these conditions. Execution simply is a more formidable challenge.

■ **Misreading major competitors' technological capabilities can doom a strategy premised on technological differentiation in the marketplace.** Microsoft, Sony, and Intel are keenly aware of the effects of imitation on the ability to execute a business strategy successfully over time. The more difficult the imitation, the greater the likelihood of execution success.

I was once told by a manager at Intel that imitation must be assumed, no matter how technologically advanced a new product is. The company goal is technological leadership, and even self-cannibalization is preferable to competitive incursions by imitating companies. All effort must be expended to maintain a differentiation edge.

■ **Easy imitation injures execution efforts.** The value of a competitive strategy at the business level is undermined by easy imitation. This point was mentioned in the preceding examples, but it is worth repeating. One measure of the worth of any strategy is the difficulty competitors have copying it. The greater the difficulty, the greater the ease and success of execution.

Actually, it can be stated with some force that easy imitation is the bane of effective execution. If the low-cost producer invests heavily in technology to reduce costs only to find that others can invest similarly, the result is a technological convergence and like organizational capabilities that will destroy the original company's cost edge. New entrants are challenging Southwest Airlines by copying the company's activities and modus operandi. The PC industry, as noted previously, is marked by increased competition because all players are increasingly alike due to the ready availability of technology and software from Microsoft, Intel, and others that levels the playing field, fosters imitation and convergence, and creates cutthroat competitive conditions.

■ **A company's assumption of a core competence when formulating strategy can lead to an execution disaster if the original critical assumption of a competence is wrong.** Quite frankly, I've been amazed by the number of companies I've worked with that assume a core competence and advantage over competitors. I recently asked a top-management team if their company enjoyed a distinctive or core competence and was told that "we have at least seven or eight, maybe more." In truth, given the conditions that spell out a distinctive or core competence,[vii] the company had none!

If strategy execution and success depended on these nonexistent capabilities, the company would certainly find itself in a troubled competitive position. The lack of clear core capabilities could be a source of confusion to employees trying to execute the flawed strategy. It could also be frustrating when the strategy reaps few or no benefits for the organization.

Strategy execution can be helped immensely by having distinctive capabilities that competitors cannot easily develop. A technological advantage (as with Microsoft and Intel) or a series of interconnected activities or business processes that are hard to duplicate (as with Walmart and Southwest Airlines) certainly can provide a strong competitive position. But assuming the impact and importance of these capabilities when they don't exist only leads to trouble and disappointment when trying to execute a flawed strategy.

- **Assuming that customers face high "switching costs" can lead to disaster if that assumption is invalid.** Strategy execution will definitely suffer, given such an erroneous assumption.

When Dell first came up with its "direct" model, selling high-end PCs directly to savvy, corporate customers and avoiding resellers and retailers, I was told by some managers that Dell's strategy wouldn't work. The assumption was that customers of other PC manufacturers faced high switching costs. This simply was not the case. Knowledgeable customers could easily switch to Dell.

The low switching costs enabled Dell to grab market share. The inability of IBM, HP, and Compaq to "go direct" and imitate Dell immediately due to commitment to a business model involving retailers and resellers clearly facilitated Dell's ability to execute its strategy. Trade-offs and channel conflicts reduced the ability to imitate Dell, paving the way for Dell's execution success.

- **Relying on a low-cost position to support price cuts can likewise be disastrous if competitors have more favorable cost positions and are in better position to sustain a price war.** Poor competitor intelligence can lead to poor decisions about competitors' capabilities and can make a strategy based on erroneous information impossible to execute successfully. Assuming a low-cost position that doesn't exist can spell strategic disaster for the executing company.

When Ryanair first entered the lucrative London-to-Dublin market, it came in as a carrier stuck between two strategies: low cost and a differentiated service provider such as Aer Lingus or British Air. It lowered prices, assuming that the other airlines wouldn't engage in a price war. Ryanair was wrong. British Air and especially Aer Lingus undercut its prices. Ryanair had miscalculated its competitors' capabilities and resolve not to give away a profitable route. Being stuck between two strategies and performing neither particularly well, it was driven literally to the brink of disaster and bankruptcy. It recovered by creating a more focused low-cost strategy and developing the capabilities and activities to execute it effectively.

Renault has been able to take the low-cost lead in Europe, a profitable niche that was surprising to many of its competitors. By focusing on low-cost cars in emerging markets, the company could easily expand to more developed markets where customers clamored for Renault's low-price product offerings. Renault enjoys a low-cost position in 2013 that it developed quietly, over the years and under the radar, and that competitors are already trying to imitate and match.

THE SERVICE BUSINESS

As mentioned earlier in Chapter 1, an important addition to this revised edition of *Making Strategy Work* is a new chapter on strategy execution in service organizations. Despite this in-depth coverage later in the book, it would be beneficial to question presently whether the strategic issues mentioned thus far apply equally well to service and product-based businesses. The resounding answer is that virtually all of the internal and external analysis (refer to Figure 3.1) needed to develop a sound business strategy and achieve competitive advantage are applicable, useful, and necessary for the success of service organizations.

The Ryanair and Publicis examples above show clearly that service companies act very much like product-based companies. Each had to perform in-depth industry and competitor analyses. Each had to develop or acquire the requisite skills or capabilities needed to execute a strategy successfully in the face of intense competitions and industry commoditization. Each developed goals and processes to support strategic choice. Publicis, especially, had to develop measures or metrics of value-added services in an industry where such measures hadn't existed or, at best, were implied, not defined.

Truth be told, not all service businesses are exactly like Ryanair or Publicis. Some nonprofits, professional service organizations, or government agencies are dissimilar in some ways, a point more fully explored later in Chapter 12. Law firms or physicians' practices, for example, act like product-based companies in many respects, but their high level of professionalization and desire for self-control present additional challenges to the process of strategy definition and execution. People-based professional organizations pose some problems that product-based companies do not, a point expanded upon later. Still, for present purposes, the indisputable point is that service organizations must do most, if not all, of the things product companies do to formulate and execute business strategies successfully.

A myriad of other examples exist, but the point should be clear: The key issues noted in Figure 3.1 must be carefully analyzed as part of strategy development. Sound business planning dictates that all relevant data must be analyzed in the strategy-formulation process. Less than thoughtful and thorough analysis can lead to "poor or vague strategy" or inadequate strategic planning, which can hinder or render useless strategy-execution efforts, as managers in the Wharton surveys emphasized. Execution is easier if, borrowing from the classic analysis of Chester Barnard years ago, an organization is pursuing "the right things."[viii] Execution is more difficult, if not impossible, if business strategy is unclear, unfocused, ill-founded, pursuing the "wrong things," or reading the competitive environment incorrectly.

In sum, sound planning and a good strategy are necessary ingredients for the successful execution of strategy. Whatever the strategy—low cost, product differentiation, innovative services—it will only work if it is "sharply defined, clearly communicated, and well understood by employees, customers, partners, and investors."[ix] In IT circles, a popular expression is "garbage in, garbage out." The same is basically true with strategy: Poor, ill-conceived plans breed poor results. Managers cannot execute an unclear, unfocused, or poorly created plan. Strategy drives or affects a great deal; it should be developed carefully.

ISSUE #2: THE IMPORTANCE OF INTEGRATING CORPORATE AND BUSINESS STRATEGIES

Corporate and business strategies must be consistent with and support each other. They must work together, not be in conflict. Achieving this integration or consistency has positive implications for strategy execution, at both corporate and business levels.

The need for consistency and balance of corporate and business strategy is clearly a condition suggested by the preceding discussion of sound planning and the model presented in Chapter 2. Yet my experience, and that of many managers in this research, suggests that this consistency between corporate and business strategies is occasionally elusive and difficult to come by. And inconsistency or conflicts in strategy breed execution problems. Consider just one example previously mentioned—that of portfolio analysis—to see what can go wrong and negatively affect the execution of strategy.

Table 3.2 lists some purposes or goals of portfolio models in strategic planning. These include resource allocations by corporate to its businesses or major operating units. A search for balance in the portfolio suggests that the proper mix of businesses—cash generators and cash users—helps to achieve internal financing and long-term growth. The approaches to portfolio analysis done by companies such as GE or consulting firms such as BCG or McKinsey & Co. highlight this quest for balance and a good mix of businesses.

Table 3.2   Consistency Between Corporate and Business Strategies: The Case of Portfolio Analysis

Purposes/Goals

Resource allocations/internal financing
Portfolio balance
Achieve growth and future profitability
Guide business strategy formulation
Set business performance objectives
Develop criteria for assessment of business performance

Needs or Conditions for Success

Adequate communication between corporate and businesses
Unambiguous role of businesses in the corporate portfolio
Clear, well-defined business strategies
Proper balance of centralization and decentralization of structure
Appropriate business-level incentives based upon measurable performance metrics

Portfolio analysis is also intended to guide strategy formulation at the business level. "Cash cows" or cash generators would likely pursue cost-leadership strategies to take full advantage of their market share and power to increase the flow of funds available for internal distribution or investment. Businesses tagged as high-growth prospects by corporate are likely to attempt to differentiate themselves in some inimitable way, such as via technology, brand, or product performance. Performance metrics can then be developed that are consistent with strategy at the business level, and corporate can use these criteria to measure and assess business performance. "Cash cows" can be evaluated on their cost savings. Differentiators can be evaluated against metrics that logically reflect their basis of differentiation, such as product performance.

So, what can go wrong? Table 3.2 suggests a number of potential problems.

THE ROLE OF THE BUSINESS IS UNCLEAR

Corporate assumes one role, the business another. Corporate treats the business like a "cash cow," but the business sees itself as a potential star that should receive an infusion of capital and not be "milked" dry. Poor planning at the business level doesn't paint a clear picture of business strategy and fails to convince corporate about the business' role in the portfolio.

Different perceptions or assumptions create conflict. A business wants capital to grow, add products, and increase R&D. But corporate sees it differently, treating it as a cash generator or cost center, denying the business the resources it feels it desperately needs. Tensions grow, and the inconsistency between corporate and business perceptions fuels conflict and negatively affects performance. The execution of strategy at both the corporate and business levels is severely compromised.

Before Ciba Geigy merged with Sandoz to form Novartis, it had a portfolio-planning problem with its pigments division. This division was classified as "core" or a cash cow, which affected a host of corporate decisions such as investment levels, return on investment required, and payback period for invested capital.

The high-performance pigment products within the division, however, did not behave as core, commodity-type products. They acted more like "pillar" or high-growth products, capable of generating high returns on investment. Managers in charge of the high-performance pigments bristled at being treated like a commodity division. They saw a different role for their business within Ciba's portfolio than corporate did, which led to both planning and execution difficulties. Managers at the corporate and business levels evaluated the portfolio differently, creating an inconsistent and problematic situation.

The role of the cash cow can also be observed in universities and service organizations. In the university, certain colleges or schools are cash cows (e.g., business schools) while others lose money for different reasons, including low enrollment. The cash cows are "milked" to support the other colleges or programs, creating a complete and strong university portfolio. Absent the cash-producing colleges, new and exciting (and expensive) opportunities elsewhere would go unfulfilled. If the cash-producing organization doesn't play its role effectively or if it actively rejects its status, the performance of the corporate portfolio would suffer.

INAPPROPRIATE PERFORMANCE METRICS

Because of different assumptions of the business' role, corporate may expect levels of performance (such as cash flows, return on assets) that the business cannot deliver. Poor communication and poor planning processes ensure that corporate and business people do not see eye to eye on key performance measures. The company wants more in terms of performance, but the business feels that those requests are unrealistic. Again, the potential for conflict is high, and the negative consequences for strategy execution are obvious.

A related problem is when corporate holds all businesses accountable for the same performance measures, even though the businesses are in different industries with different competitive conditions.

A good example comes from a company with mainly high-tech products that I'm currently involved with but cannot identify due to the company's insistence on confidentiality. Corporate had always looked to each business for the same profit growth and return on assets, despite varying competitive conditions across industries. Most businesses had achieved technological differentiation due to the reliability and performance of their products, and achieving the profit goal was no problem. In contrast, in one business manufacturing commodity products, with competition based primarily on price, the situation is different. Most of the other businesses face more favorable competitive conditions, making the profit goal more realistic. Still, the "different" division is being held accountable for the same goal as the other divisions, a situation that is unrealistic and conflict producing. It is easy to see how this could cause major problems between corporate and the business and affect the execution of strategy at both levels. Corporate is currently evaluating the wisdom of this approach in an attempt to eliminate a conflict-ridden situation.

BATTLES OVER RESOURCE ALLOCATIONS

In the cases mentioned previously, there clearly will be differences in resource allocations throughout the corporate portfolio. Some businesses will feel neglected in the allocation process, feeling that other businesses are receiving favorable, but inappropriate, treatment by corporate. Businesses may even feel that organizational structure is wrong, with way too much centralized control over scarce resources and not enough decentralized control with more resources entrusted to the business.

In the example just mentioned, the commodity business consistently couldn't make its profit bogey. Allocation of resources to it was negatively affected. It felt it was being cheated by corporate. It also felt that too much corporate control was negatively affecting its ability to respond to its market and competitive conditions. Corporate strategy and goals were and still are seen as inconsistent with business strategy and industry conditions. Tensions exist between the business leaders and corporate staff. Again, these issues are being addressed currently.

ASSESSMENTS OF BUSINESS PERFORMANCE CREATE ADDITIONAL PROBLEMS

If a business feels that it's been assigned an inappropriate strategy or role in the corporate portfolio, it follows that the business would see the assignment of performance objectives as invalid or unrealistic. From the corporate point of view, the business' performance rating would be low. The business, in turn, would feel it's been mistreated. If incentives such as pay, bonus, or future promotion are based on these "exaggerated" or "invalid" performance metrics, managers at the business level would feel mistreated and violated, causing further tension. The prognosis for future planning is bleak, as business people may feel the need to "lowball," "play games," "change corporate's expectations," or "prove them wrong," according to some managers in this situation I was able to interview.

The point is that there must be a logical consistency between corporate and business strategy. The latter is vital to the successful execution of the former. Corporate expects a certain level or type of performance of businesses in its portfolio. If the businesses see different strategic roles and different performance criteria, the execution of corporate strategy will be jeopardized. If businesses don't perform to corporate's expectations, resource allocations will be affected, thereby injuring the businesses' ability to execute competitive strategy.

The argument can be summarized by the following two statements:

- Corporate strategy can affect businesses' ability to execute strategy and achieve competitive advantage.

- Businesses' performance in the portfolio can affect the execution of corporate strategy, thereby affecting firm-wide performance.

Corporate and business strategies are interactive and interdependent. Resources given to (or withheld from) businesses affect their ability to execute strategy and achieve competitive advantage. The performance of businesses, in turn, affects the implementation of corporate strategy. Businesses' playing (or not playing) their assigned roles in the portfolio will impact the execution of corporate plans and the attainment of company-wide goals.

To avoid problems, adequate communication and interaction between corporate and businesses are absolutely essential. Agreement must be reached on the key elements listed in Table 3.2 to execute strategy successfully. Inconsistencies or conflicts between corporate and business strategies and businesses' roles in the corporate portfolio must be identified. Inability to do so will surely lead to execution mishaps that affect both business unit and company-wide performance. How can these problems be avoided?

THE STRATEGY REVIEW

One way to improve the requisite communication between corporate and businesses is through a strategy review. While the review is discussed again in Chapter 6 dealing with the control process, it should be mentioned in the present context.

Figure 3.2 depicts a simple graphic of the strategy review. It is a tool that has been used successfully in various forms by GE, Crown Holdings, Allied Signal, Boeing, and other well-known companies. The purpose of the review is fourfold:

1. To discuss the development of corporate and business strategies

2. To integrate strategy at both levels by clarifying roles, responsibilities, and goals for corporate and the businesses

3. To provide a forum for the review and evaluation of business performance

4. To allow for change and adaptation over time to keep strategy and performance metrics current and meaningful

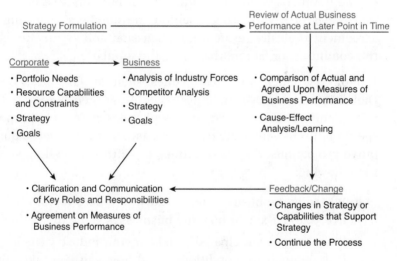

Figure 3.2 The Strategy Review

Basically, what does Figure 3.2 show? It shows, first, a high degree of communication between corporate and business levels. The position of a business within the corporate portfolio is analyzed, including its role or function in the corporate game plan. The support or value-added contribution that the corporate center can provide the businesses is discussed. Also communicated are the resource conditions and constraints under which businesses must perform.

Figure 3.2 shows, second, that agreement is reached on business strategy and operating goals. A business' responsibilities include industry and competitor analysis and the justification of its strategy, given the state of competitive industry conditions. Steps 1 and 2 include necessarily an analysis of past performance, as well as anticipation of future competitive, technological, and economic trends. Discussion between corporate and business leaders focuses on the business' analysis of industry forces and future competitive conditions to reach agreement on the business' strategy and goals.

The important issue here is to focus on the key competitive, technological, and economic conditions that affect business strategy. All too often, the focus of the corporate-business discussion is only on the numbers. Numbers are important but only to a point. The real issues deal with what's behind the numbers. Learning and agreement typically result from discussion and arguments about the conditions or factors that drive the numbers.

I like very much what companies such as GE, J&J, Becton Dickenson, and Crown Holdings try to do in their corporate-business planning sessions. Part of the planning process is purposely spent on discussion of the qualitative factors that underlie quantitative projections. Simple questions drive the discussion, such as the following:

- Where is the business now, and where does it want to be in five years? Explain how the business is going to get there.
- What are the anticipated trends in your industry (technological, competitive conditions), and how can you take advantage of them to improve your business?

Discussions of qualitative issues such as these don't necessarily create a panacea, but they do help the process of agreement. They help corporate and business managers get beyond the numbers and the "low-balling" or posturing that often accompanies an exclusive focus on numbers. Such discussions improve communication and both corporate's and businesses' abilities to see the other's constraints, opportunities, and point of view. The value of these discussions to planning and execution: priceless.

The figure shows, third, that the agreed-upon measures of business performance are used in the reviews of the business' actual performance. There can be no surprises. Corporate is forced to recognize differences in the competitive landscape across industries, allowing potentially for different performance metrics for each business. These metrics, in turn, become the criteria against which business performance is judged at a later date.

Finally, Figure 3.2 shows that the planning and review process is not only interactive but adaptive as well. Corporate and business strategies are reviewed to determine their continued relevance and feasibility, given changes in external conditions and internal capabilities. The strategy review focuses on the roles of the corporate level and the various businesses and how these roles must change over time.

The strategy review is an important step in integrating corporate- and business-level strategies. It helps to foster analysis, communication, and debate between the levels, ensuring that "good" plans are being executed by the organization. Without this clarification of the corporate-business relationship, execution efforts will suffer. My dealings with managers responsible for execution have constantly reinforced the need for a strategy review and the process of communication and interaction demanded by it.

Strategy execution cannot succeed without effective communication across levels of the organization. The strategy review helps accomplish this, in both product-based and service organizations.

ISSUE #3: THINKING SHORT TERM—THE NEED TO DEFINE AND COMMUNICATE THE OPERATIONAL COMPONENTS OF STRATEGY

The critical first ingredient in an execution plan is strategy. But most people in an organization can't manage armed only with a strategy. Something else is needed to guide daily, monthly, or quarterly performance because many managers operate of necessity in the short term. How do we reconcile and integrate long-term strategic aims with short-term operating plans and objectives?

To execute a strategy successfully, it must be translated into short-term operational metrics that (a) are related to long-term needs, (b) can be used to assess strategic performance, and help the organization achieve long-term strategic goals. Figure 3.3 shows a simplified picture of this translation process.

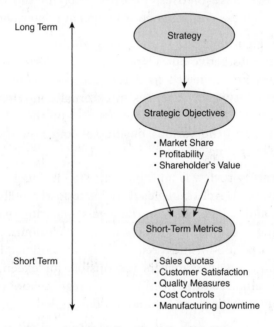

Figure 3.3   Translating Strategy into Short-Term Operating Objectives

Short-term operating objectives represent the grist of the strategic mill. Strategic plans are "ground" or refined into smaller, more manageable pieces, which become the operating criteria to guide short-term behavior. These short-term goals are "strategic" in that they are produced from and related to the long-term, strategic needs of the organization. To achieve long-term goals, it is necessary to manage the short term.

This last statement is important because it highlights a major misconception. Managers often believe that short-term thinking is bad. Emphasis on short-term objectives surely must breed long-term strategic problems. The popular mantra is that managers must become "strategic thinkers," virtually eschewing short-term performance measures.

Nothing could be further from the truth. Short-term operating objectives are vital to strategic performance if they reflect and are integrated with long-term strategic objectives. Execution will suffer if strategic needs are not translated properly into shorter-term metrics and communicated down the organization. If short-term objectives are not logically related to and consistent with strategic plans, the rift between short- and long-term needs will create problems.

INTEGRATING STRATEGIC AND SHORT-TERM OBJECTIVES

Much has been written over the years about the integration of the long and short terms. Early writers focused on management-by-objectives (MBO) programs. They talked about the translation of strategic needs to short-term objectives and the communication it required, but this integrative link never seemed to drive execution or implementation efforts.[x] MBO programs often came to be seen as paper-creating, bureaucratic burdens rather than facilitators of effective execution. Bill Joyce and I focused on the importance of "managing myopia" in two different publications, stressing the need to integrate long- and short-term objectives.[xi] Although I have had some success in forging this integrative link in companies I've worked with, the integration of long- and short-term metrics has not been achieved effectively in many other organizations I've known.

More recent attempts at this translation and communication process may be seeing greater success. The Balanced Scorecard, for example, provides a framework to translate strategy into operational terms.[xii] It helps to develop and communicate short-term objectives in the areas of financials, customer service, internal business processes, and learning and growth, and it attempts to link these objectives to company strategy and long-term goals. The success of the scorecard approach reported by Robert Kaplan and David Norton in a host of companies clearly suggests its impact on strategy execution and making strategy work.

To be sure, the Balanced Scorecard reiterates much of what previous work on the integration of long- and short-term needs espoused and discussed in detail. It is not, by any means, a brand-new thrust or invention in managerial thinking. Actually, one could easily argue that the Balanced Scorecard is simply a resurrection of MBO, with the added emphasis on translating strategy into four performance areas deemed important by its creators and many top managers. Still, it is useful in that it is very convincing about the importance of managing the short term well. It does offer a clear view on the needed integration of long- and short-term objectives. This serves to reinforce the message currently being discussed, namely the need to define and communicate the operational components of strategy if successful execution is to be achieved. To realize long-term goals, it is necessary to manage the short term well.

NEED FOR MEASURABLE OBJECTIVES

It is important to emphasize one final point: The operational aspects of strategic and short-term objectives mean that these objectives are measurable. They are useful for strategy execution if they measure important results. Strategy must be translated into metrics that are consistent with the strategy and measurable. Only then can the results of execution be adequately assessed. Without these useful metrics, successful evaluation of execution results is not possible.

To be sure, some managers will gripe about and resist a demand for measurability. Staff people or managers in not-for-profit organizations especially will argue vehemently that what they do is not measurable. I've heard lawyers in a number of companies insist that "you can't measure what lawyers do." I've worked with IT people who argue that their support services are not quantifiable. I've observed near rebellions in government organizations such as the FTC and Social Security Administration when managers tried to introduce zero-based budgeting and the use of clear, measurable objectives in planning and execution processes.

What can be done when confronting this type of resistance from staff managers or personnel in "soft," nonline functions? Here are some questions that can be used to facilitate the measurability of staff work. The questions come from various companies I've worked with, and I've seen them result in fruitful discussions of value-added and useful metrics of performance:

- If this unit or department were eliminated, what would change? What would be the impact on other units or departments in the company, and how, specifically, would this impact be felt or measured?

- Given two departments like mine, assume that one was highly effective and the other highly ineffective. How could you tell the two apart? With no one telling you who was effective and who was not, how could you identify and differentiate between the two departments?

- How do you, as an internal customer of my staff's services, evaluate what we do? What criteria do you use to judge or evaluate our performance?

Obviously, some jobs or functions are more difficult to measure than others. It may also be that people resist measurement and the accountability it implies. Still, simple questions such as the preceding can "break the ice" and help people see that they indeed are making valuable and measurable contributions to strategic and short-term goals. People can also be made to see that only things that are measurable can be improved or changed. Without measurement, there can be no useful assessment of the worth or contribution of a job or department to the execution of a chosen strategy.

The issue of measurability of performance is one often raised by managers in service companies, nonprofits, and government agencies. Strategies are more difficult to develop and assess, it is argued, thereby increasing the difficulty of creating strategic objectives and translating them into short-term performance metrics. Figure 3.3 is logical and valuable, but its utility in the organizations or agencies just mentioned is limited, the argument goes. Service organizations, nonprofits, and government agencies are "different," and they must be treated differently when it comes to this aspect of strategy execution.

These concerns and others are addressed in greater detail in a separate chapter later in the book. Suffice it to say at present that all organizations need to integrate the long and short terms and translate strategy into workable objectives. Managers in service organizations cannot hide behind a cloak of "nonmeasurability" for long;

competition for scarce resources and demands for accountability eventually ensure that the managers must prove the worth of their actions and decisions. Measurable objectives and performance metrics are required to show unequivocally what their contributions are. More is said later on this important point.

ISSUE #4: UNDERSTANDING THE "DEMANDS" OF STRATEGY AND SUCCESSFUL EXECUTION

The last point to emphasize is that strategy makes "demands" on the development of organizational skills, resources, and capabilities. To ignore these demands surely results in poor strategy execution and unfavorable performance.

I have long argued this position, that strategy demands the development of specific capabilities if the strategy is to succeed. In one study, Charles Snow and I examined the relationship between strategy and distinctive competence and its effect on organizational performance in 88 companies in four different industries.[xiii] The primary hypothesis was simple and straightforward: Companies that developed capabilities or competencies consistent with a chosen strategy would perform better than companies that hadn't achieved this fit between strategy and capabilities. Put another way, we were testing two related points:

1. Strategy demands investment in, and development of, specific capabilities or competencies.
2. Firms making such an investment perform better than companies in which the requisite capabilities are not developed.

The results of the studies were strong and consistent with expectations. The two points were clearly validated.

Companies that created capabilities to match their strategies outperformed their competitors, looking at return on assets. When the right capabilities or competencies weren't developed to support a strategy, execution suffered and performance outcomes were poor. The demands of strategy had to be met to achieve successful execution.

What are some examples of these demands, and how do they affect execution? Table 3.3 lists some of the demands for two generic strategies: low-cost producer and differentiation. I focus on these first because they are well-known approaches to competitive strategy. I've also been able to study companies with varying levels of success in executing these strategies and thus have developed some insights over the years into the factors that affect execution. Companies pursuing these two generic strategies do not always develop each and every item listed in Table 3.3. Still, the trend toward developing and "bundling" resources and capabilities consistent with the strategies has been obvious and striking to me over time.

Table 3.3   The "Demands" of Strategy

Low-Cost Producer	Differentiation
Capital investment in equipment, technology	Effective product engineering
Need for volume, standardization, and repetition	Sound R&D (emphasis on "D")
Focus on economies of scale and scope	Heavy emphasis on marketing and advertising
Development and use of appropriate accounting controls and methods	Concern with quality and quality assurance
	Reliance on intellectual property
Effective MIS or IT systems and processes	Organizational structures favoring effectiveness
Organizational structures favoring efficiency	Getting close to customers
Incentives and controls that support cost reduction	Incentives that support product/service differentiation

LOW-COST PRODUCER

To achieve this position in an industry or market segment, companies usually invest heavily in up-to-date equipment or technology to reduce costs. Computerized production controls and robotics, for example, reduce variable costs of production by replacing labor, a more expensive factor of production. This is readily seen in the automotive industry and other mass-production situations. In service industries, the same trend can be seen.

Airlines seek larger planes with fewer, more-fuel-efficient engines to reduce the operating cost per passenger mile. Even movie theaters invest in large, centrally located popcorn machines to serve all the theaters in their multiplex model.

The need under the low-cost strategy—indeed, the holy grail of sorts—is to achieve high volume, standardization, and repetition of work, for these lead invariably to economies of scale and scope, the basis of a low-cost position.

Standardization can lead to yet other decisions—such as a smaller or narrower product line—to help foster volume and large production runs in the quest for scale economies. Some large insurance companies specialize in term insurance, eschewing financial or estate planning and other more elaborate policies, to reduce and standardize product offerings and perform the same tasks over and over again.

Other investments are also suggested in Table 3.3 in companies' quest for a low-cost position. Effective and efficient IT or MIS systems are needed to provide up-to-date information about costs, production, shipments, and inventory. Accounting controls and methods are developed to provide valid information about variable costs in a timely manner. IT systems aid in knowledge transfer so that headway in cost reduction in one part of the organization can be understood and deployed in other, more remote parts of the company. Again, look at the success of companies such as Walmart that have made these IT investments.

Other changes also support the demands of the low-cost strategy. Organizational structure, for instance, must be consistent with strategy. Choice of structure usually focuses on functional structures to maximize repetition, volume, and economies related to scale and scope (see Chapter 4). Incentives are tied to cost reduction to support the strategy and "reward the right things" (see Chapter 6). Again, to achieve a low-cost position, decisions about investments, capabilities, and operations must support and be consistent with that strategy.

DIFFERENTIATION STRATEGIES

Table 3.3 notes the capabilities or decisions needed to support the differentiation strategy. For product companies, I've often found that companies invest heavily in R&D (emphasis on "D") and engineering to respond to customers' needs or demands and reconfigure products and services. Emphasis often is on quality, with programs and actions directed toward quality assurance.

Managers in companies pursuing differentiation strategies often talk of "getting close to customers," the manifestation of which takes many forms. "Getting close" may simply mean interviewing customers occasionally or conducting questionnaire surveys, or it might mean making customers part of internal business processes such as new product development or quality assurance programs. The emphasis on getting close to customers can similarly be seen in service organizations or service components of product-based companies. Banks, investment firms, advertising agencies, political parties, and restaurants routinely pool customers or involve them and other stakeholders in developing service approaches and quality assurance programs.

Virtually every company pursuing differentiation strategies in the marketplace relies heavily on marketing efforts. Marketing capabilities are usually developed internally, but even if they are outsourced, internal controls are developed to ensure effective execution of an overall marketing plan. Heavy advertising in targeted market segments usually is an integral part of the marketing efforts.

Organizational structure is designed around goals of effectiveness and performance rather than efficiency in the differentiating firm. While cost clearly comes into play at some point in every organization, the primary thrust is on customer satisfaction, product performance, service, market share, gross margins, and responding quickly to customer or market demands, rather than on pure cost issues. Logically, incentives are developed to support and reinforce these desired outcomes in companies pursuing differentiation strategies.

DEVELOPING THE RIGHT CAPABILITIES

Table 3.3 shows only a partial list of the resources and capabilities developed in response to the demands of a strategy. Still, hopefully one point is clear: The resources or capabilities needed to support and execute a strategy vary with the strategy employed.

What one invests in or nurtures in terms of organizational competencies clearly varies according to how one competes. Cost leadership demands a different set of skills or functional capabilities than the pursuit of a differentiation strategy. Two business units pursuing the two strategies noted in Table 3.3 should look and act very differently because of the requisite development of different resources and capabilities.

To execute strategy effectively, the right capabilities must be developed. The right capabilities, however, vary as a function of the type of strategy being pursued.

This discussion also suggests that caution must be exercised when changing strategies. Imagine a company that for years has pursued a differentiation strategy. Changing economic and competitive conditions over time (globalization, commoditization, and influx of new and larger competitors) dictate that the company must increasingly compete on price, emphasizing the need for a cost-based strategy.

But the company cannot simply or automatically convert to a cost-leadership mode: It has resources and capabilities that do not lend themselves to the execution of a low-cost strategy. For years, it has invested in and nurtured skills or competencies that support differentiation, and these competencies are not the ones that support a competitive strategy based on cost leadership. The company cannot simply expect or demand a change in strategy by fiat, as it doesn't have the appropriate skill set to do so.

Consider the case of Sun Microsystems. For many years, this Silicon Valley computer maker decided on a differentiation strategy to separate itself from the pack. It chose to ignore the standard chips and software that other computer makers routinely used. It chose instead to focus on its own high-powered custom inputs. Its machines, then, would be much more powerful—and expensive—than those of its competitors.

The gamble worked remarkably well for years. Sun became the provider of choice in certain market segments, such as servers that support Internet sites and powerful corporate computers. Customers paid more but clearly were happy with Sun's souped-up products. The attempt at differentiation and higher margins clearly was paying dividends.

Changes in the market and other suppliers' capabilities over time, however, soured Sun's prospects. "Standard" chips made by Intel and "standard" software by Microsoft matched the performance of Sun's souped-up, more expensive versions. Rival computer makers could provide the same powerful applications and solutions as Sun but at a much lower price. Standardization and commoditization of what had been powerful, differentiated components and computers in effect eliminated Sun's advantage and put it at a competitive disadvantage compared to lower-priced competitive products.

Sun's sales fell drastically as customers fled to rivals' product offerings. In October 2003, Sun's stock price had fallen to approximately $3.50, down from a split-adjusted high of about $65 in the fall of 2000.[xiv] Sun's CEO, Scott McNealy, finally let go of his persistent adherence to the higher-priced, differentiation strategy and decided that Sun had to change. It had to focus on standardized products and the low end of its market, a move that clearly challenged its long-held business model based on high-end, differentiated products.

The challenges facing Sun were obvious. Could Sun retain some ability to differentiate itself, consistent with its historical approach to the market? Could Sun become a low-cost producer of standardized products and still make money? Could its new strategy still allow it enough profit to focus on R&D and technology that heretofore had helped differentiate it from the competition? Competing in a new, low-end market segment in which experience and the appropriate capabilities were lacking surely presented many problems and few opportunities.

In 2010, some answers to these difficult questions were provided when Oracle bought Sun. Emphasis on new product development was continued, as Oracle and Sun engineers worked together to achieve new performance levels, for example, with the SPARC Super Cluster T4-4, in 2011, a system with Oracle Solaris that delivered ground-breaking performance, and an introduction of Java 7. The joint companies simultaneously worked on cost reduction in key areas, such as more efficient data centers and better server utilization. However, despite some focus on cost, the primary emphasis still seems to be on differentiation and product performance and not on a wholesale movement to a low-cost strategy. Movement to low cost would be difficult, as the companies don't seem to possess the capabilities to support this strategic move.

Questions still remain about the success of the Oracle-Sun acquisition. Can the combined company develop and hone the skills and capabilities needed for product and service differentiation, while also achieving some efficiency and cost reductions? Time will tell whether the company can pull off this strategy in a highly competitive marketplace.

A final point should be mentioned regarding a company's need to reduce its emphasis on differentiation and move to a low-cost strategy, a phenomenon not unheard of in industries that are becoming increasingly commoditized. To be sure, a company can meet the demands of a new, price-conscious market. It can acquire a competitor already well versed in cost-leadership skills. It can add a new division or business unit for the low-end market. It can create and develop a new structural unit internally with the requisite competencies for low-cost or price-based competition. It can buy or add the right capabilities.

What a company shouldn't do is try to pursue the new strategy with the old capabilities. If a company for years developed the skills or capabilities noted on the right side of Table 3.3, it would not have the skills and capabilities needed to compete on the left side of Table 3.3. The bulk of competencies developed for a strategy of differentiation are not fungible and easily applied to a new situation of cost leadership. Care must be taken to avoid setting up a "lose-lose" situation in which the failure of a new strategy is virtually guaranteed by failing to develop the requisite capabilities for success. Different strategies demand different capabilities; trying to execute a new strategy with old capabilities can only lead to major problems.

Can functions within a business pursue different goals or functional strategies, such as low cost in manufacturing and differentiation in marketing? Of course. Manufacturing, in fact, typically pursues a low-cost position, a normal quest for efficiency and lower variable costs. But that is not the issue here.

We're talking business strategy and how the entire company positions itself to compete. Manufacturing can pursue low cost. But if the company overall is attempting to differentiate its products and services, the right capabilities must be developed to support the differentiation strategy for successful execution to result. If the low-cost tactics of manufacturing injure the company's ability to attend to customers' needs or demands for product quality, then execution will suffer and corrective action must be taken. If manufacturing resists product development or product extensions that customers want because doing so is costly (stopping the line, retooling, experimentation), the interference with the differentiation strategy must be eliminated. The goals and operations of any functional area cannot be inconsistent with or injurious to business strategy. The demands of the differentiation strategy must be met.

THE DEMANDS OF GLOBAL STRATEGY

Let's mention one more example: the demands of global strategy. This is a hybrid of sorts, as global strategy certainly can include the low-cost and differentiation examples already discussed. Global strategy, however, does make additional demands on management to develop the right resources and capabilities to facilitate effective competition in world markets.

Consider briefly just one example: the coordinated global strategy. The key word here is "coordinated." Unlike the simple international presence of the multidomestic firm with independent operations in various countries, the coordinated global strategy is more complex.

Competitive advantage under a coordinated global strategy is derived, in large part, from the sharing and leveraging of skills or capabilities across country boundaries. Countries or regions may enjoy comparative advantages such as in labor costs or other factor prices. The trick is to leverage the low-cost position into competitive advantage elsewhere. Or a company may enjoy a technological capability in one part of the world that represents a core competence. Again, the need is to share and integrate the core competence across product lines and country boundaries.

It is clear that to execute a coordinated global strategy successfully methods directed to coordinating, sharing, and integrating knowledge and capabilities worldwide are critical for success. Communication and control across divisional and country boundaries are central to the successful execution of this global strategy.[xv]

The world is getting smaller and flatter, putting increased pressure on organizations to develop and execute sound strategies, including the coordinated global strategy. Because of its importance and in light of the many requests by managers after the original publication of *Making Strategy Work*, a separate new chapter is now devoted to this important topic. The new and expanded section on applications and special topics treats the issue of executing global strategies in detail.

A FINAL POINT

The value of a well-thought-out strategy to successful execution cannot be exaggerated. Care taken in strategy development at both the corporate and business levels, and in the integration of those strategic plans, will surely result in positive dividends for the organization.

A popular mantra among a handful of managers I've known is that "good execution can overcome bad strategy." In my experience, this is rarely the case. The typical result is that a poor strategy results in poor outcomes. Bad strategy can create major frustrations, as managers work long and hard hours in a futile attempt to execute that which is not executable. Hard work that produces no benefits is exasperating. Vague strategy and constant changes in strategy have the same frustrating results.

Managers who participated in the Wharton surveys and discussions were entirely correct when they argued that "poor or vague strategy" leads to execution problems. Attending to the four strategy-related issues noted in this chapter will reduce, if not entirely eliminate, these problems.

SUMMARY

A number of points in the present chapter relate to the success of a company's execution or implementation efforts:

- Strategy is the essential ingredient, the driving force behind execution efforts. Sound planning is essential, then, at both corporate and business-unit levels.

- It is vitally important to integrate corporate and business strategies. This means that effective communication is needed between levels, along with processes that enable decision-makers to reach agreement on strategies, goals, and performance metrics. The strategy review is one method of achieving this integration of corporate and business strategies.

- Long-term strategic needs of the organization must be translated into short-term operating objectives to successfully execute strategy. The short term is a key to successful execution; managers routinely spend a lot of time there. It is necessary to have short-term operating objectives that provide measures or metrics that can be used to evaluate execution plans and efforts.

- Finally, strategy makes demands on organizational resources and capabilities. Development of the appropriate skills and competencies is vital to the successful execution of strategy. Care must be exercised when changing strategy or pursuing different strategies simultaneously, as the skills and competencies needed will vary as a function of strategy pursued.

The focus in this book is on making strategy work. Toward this end, we considered the major obstacles to successful execution in Chapter 1. We've also begun to confront these obstacles. In Chapter 2, the vital importance of a model or template to guide execution decisions and actions was emphasized. In this chapter, key early elements of the model—corporate and business strategy—were discussed to show how the characteristics of strategy and sound planning affect execution outcomes. In Chapter 4, we turn to the next key element of our model or template—organizational structure and its impact on strategy execution.

ENDNOTES

i. Jim Collins, *Good to Great*, Harper Business, 2001, p. 10.

ii. "Back in Japanese Hands," *The Economist*, April 14, 2012.

iii. "Angry Analysts Scorch P&G CEO," *The Wall Street Journal*, April 27, 2012; See also "Has Procter and Gamble Made Some Bad Bets," Knowledge@wharton Today, April 30, 2012.

iv. "Changes Needed at Avon Are More Than Cosmetic," Knowledge@wharton, Strategy Management, April 25, 2012.

v. "Simplify and Repeat," *The Economist*, April 28, 2012.

vi. Michael Porter, *Competitive Strategy*, Free Press, 1980; "What is Strategy?" *Harvard Business Review*, November-December, 1996.

vii. See, for example, C. K. Prahalad and Gary Hamel, "The Core Competence of the Corporation," *Harvard Business Review*, May-June, 1990.

viii. Chester Barnard, *The Functions of the Executive*, Harvard University Press, 1938.

ix. William Joyce, Nitin Nohria, and Bruce Roberson, *What (Really) Works*, Harper Business, 2003, p. 16.

x. See, for example, Stephen Carroll and Henry Tosi, *Management by Objectives*, Macmillan, 1973.

xi. L. G. Hrebiniak and W. Joyce, *Implementing Strategy*, Macmillan, 1984; "The Strategic Importance of Managing Myopia," *Sloan Management Review*, Fall, 1984.

xii. Robert Kaplan and David Norton, *The Balanced Scorecard*, Harvard Business School Press, 1996.

xiii. Charles Snow and L. G. Hrebiniak, "Strategy, Distinctive Competence, and Organizational Performance," *Administrative Science Quarterly*, June 1980.

xiv. "Cloud Over Sun Microsystems: Plummeting Computer Prices," *The Wall Street Journal*, October 16, 2003.

xv. For an additional discussion of the problems and issues involved in executing different types of global strategy, see L. G. Hrebiniak, "Implementing Global Strategies," *European Journal of Management*, December, 1992.

4

Organizational Structure and Execution

Introduction

The model of execution outlined in Chapter 2 shows the central role played by organizational structure. Strategy affects structure, or alternatively, structure is important to the execution of strategy, at both corporate and business levels.

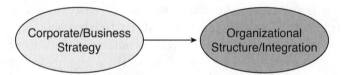

Despite its centrality, the role of structure in strategy execution is sometimes problematic. Managers who participated in the Wharton surveys and the subsequent discussions reported problems with structure in strategy execution. They argued that structure is often set up or changed for the wrong reasons. Design or redesign efforts are handled badly and, not infrequently, are frustrating or doomed to failure. Integration or coordination of diverse structural units is poor or incomplete. The link to strategy when changing structure is unclear or often simply missing. Managers reinforced poor interunit information sharing and unclear responsibility or accountability as major execution problems.

The purpose of this chapter is to clarify the role and impact of structure in strategy execution. The intent is not to try to summarize the massive volume of work already done on organizational design. Rather, the goal is to consider and clarify the handful of structural issues that are most important for making strategy work.

What are these issues? What are the biggest structural-related problems, challenges, or mistakes when executing strategy? Let's identify them by looking at a few examples.

THE CHALLENGE OF STRUCTURAL CHOICE

JOHNSON & JOHNSON

Consider the case of Johnson & Johnson (J&J). J&J has always been a decentralized company with a huge number of independent businesses or strategic business units (SBUs). It was long felt that decentralization fostered entrepreneurship, motivated managers to perform well in their own "small" companies, and allowed a closeness to the market and customers that was difficult to achieve in more centralized structural forms. Central staff was kept small, a further testimony to the company's preferred culture of decentralization and SBU autonomy. And J&J's outstanding performance over the years seemed to reinforce its belief in the benefits of decentralization and the smallness of companies in its portfolio.

There were and still are challenges to J&J's structure. One of these was the need for increased coordination across the independent business units. Increases in customer power (such as the rise of large HMOs in the hospital sales businesses) threatened the traditional autonomy and independence of decentralized SBUs serving these markets. Whereas the traditional model had numerous J&J companies selling different products (Tylenol, bandages, diagnostic equipment, and so on) to the same hospital, HMOs comprising many hospitals refused to deal with 10 or 20 different J&J companies when making purchases. They wanted to deal with one source representing all the J&J companies. They wanted J&J to perform the integration or coordination of purchases that individual hospitals previously were forced to do. These larger, more powerful buyers could force J&J to adopt a different operating structure.

Dealing with these new demands was a real challenge to J&J. The task was to coordinate work in areas that traditionally were the bailiwick of separate independent businesses. Increased centralization or corporate control was needed to affect the coordinated selling and delivery of products across units that traditionally had autonomy to do things in their own way. Care was needed so as not to confront and violate a company culture and operating structure premised on decentralization, independence, and local control.

That J&J successfully met this challenge with reengineering and restructuring (for example, a national sales group) says a great deal about its managerial capabilities. The task was not easy, however. Convincing independent SBU managers about the need for increased centralization of sorts, with more controls placed on autonomous units, was an important but delicate task. Changing structure, without threatening a structural "institution" of decentralization and autonomy in decision-making, clearly was a formidable challenge and difficult chore.

J&J's recent troubles involving one of its main businesses, McNeil Consumer products, draw attention to another aspect of organizational structure. A series of recalls of McNeil's products, including revered Tylenol-based products, raised issues about the division's quality control and response to customers' complaints. The Food and Drug Administration sent a warning letter to J&J on May 22, 2012, warning that it failed to respond adequately to complaints about K-Y Liquibeads between June 2010 and December 2011. Since September 2009, about 30 product recalls, most from McNeil, dealt with problems from Tylenol products to hip implants and some prescription drugs.[i]

These complaints and problems raise serious product-related issues that J&J must deal with and resolve. Our present attention, however, deals with organizational structure, not product integrity or performance. Could the excessive decentralization of J&J be contributing at all to these recent problems? This is an interesting and important question.

J&J's decentralization is seen by its managers as a critical contributor to company success. Decentralization, it is argued, creates autonomy, a clear focus on product and mission, and an ability to understand and respond to customers. But extreme decentralization may also create problems of oversight and control. Understanding and controlling approximately 240 SBUs is a daunting task that even the best of managers on J&J's executive committee may not be able to handle effectively. Excessive autonomy and a lack of control may possibly contribute to an SBU's enjoying free rein in its local decisions and actions. If local problems begin to brew, they conceivably could get very bad before the larger company was aware of them and their repercussions. The decentralized structure, while possessing many benefits, may indeed be contributing to J&J's problems. Structure clearly has benefits; under certain conditions, especially those marked by weak management controls, it can also create problems or challenges.

CITIBANK, ABB, AND OTHER LARGE GLOBAL PLAYERS

Consider, too, the structural needs and problems of large global players such as Citibank and Asea Brown Boveri (ABB). The issue of centralization and decentralization again comes into play. Global control demands centralization, as the need exists to focus on businesses worldwide and coordinate information flows and knowledge sharing across geographically dispersed units. There is a related need to create synergies or achieve economies of scale and scope, which again calls for centralization and corporate control over certain resources.

But global companies also need decentralization. Businesses must be able to respond to local needs and customer demands in a large, geographically dispersed company. Local autonomy is needed to cope with differences in economic conditions, laws, regulations, or aspects of culture that affect how business is done in different parts of the world.

Companies such as Citibank and ABB are forced to handle these and similar issues. They must create structural forms comprising corporate center staff and decentralized business units to handle global and local needs simultaneously. In both companies, a geographical organization exists side by side with a worldwide product- or service-based organization. Tensions between global and local controls must be handled, and a forum for resolving conflicts between overall company and local needs must be made operational. These and other issues have been and are being handled by Citibank, ABB, and other global players by using product- and geography-based organizations and matrix structures to achieve effective coordination and integrate global and local needs.

SERVICE ORGANIZATIONS AND NONPROFITS

Consider, finally, the large urban university, a type of service or nonprofit organization. It, too, has SBUs of sorts, as different colleges focus on different tasks, products, and customer groups. But the university also has outreach programs to aid inner-city residents and solve urban problems. Often these programs demand a multidisciplinary approach and coordination of work across autonomous colleges or research units, a situation that presents challenges or hurdles that must be overcome.

Achieving coordination and knowledge sharing is always difficult, but perhaps especially so in organizational units where professionals reign and feel their knowledge and intellectual property should rule. Colleges and academic departments within them vie for scarce resources and seek power in the larger university system, sometimes affecting cooperation or integration across units. Knowledge is a source of power or influence that some professional employees may share reluctantly. Defining responsibility or accountability in these organizations may be problematic, especially given the usual case of the existence of outcomes or metrics that aren't always amenable to easy measurement. Many of these structural and related issues are remarkably similar to those in for-profit organizations.

Similar structural problems exist in large government organizations. The U.S. intelligence community, for example, is marked by

15 to 64 agencies, organizations, or structural units, depending on who's counting.[ii] Each agency or unit is autonomous, much like the SBUs mentioned previously. The agencies compete against each other for budget, which often breeds a state of competition rather than cooperation. Unclear responsibilities and lines of authority (few, if any, exist) add to the problem of management and decision-making. Many "boxes" or structural units exist, with few "lines" connecting them formally. These government organizations, in effect, face similar problems of structure, coordination, cooperation, and accountability as their private-sector cousins.

THE CRITICAL STRUCTURAL ISSUES

What do these examples tell us about the structural issues that affect the execution of strategy? There are at least five issues suggested by them that deserve additional consideration. They are as follows:

1. **Measuring the impact of structure.** What are the costs versus benefits of different structural forms? How are the costs and benefits measured?

2. **Centralization versus decentralization.** What is the right balance, and what determines it? Included here is the size and role of the corporate center in organizations with both centralized and decentralized units.

3. **The relationship between strategy and structure.** What aspects or elements of strategy drive the choice of structure? How does structure affect the execution of a strategy?

4. **Achieving coordination and information sharing across organizational units.** Integration and knowledge sharing are important to execution, whether between corporate center staff and businesses or across decentralized geographical units of a company.

5. **Clarifying responsibility and accountability.** These basic structural definitions are necessary for effective execution. People must know who's responsible for what, when, and why, for execution to work.

The present model of execution uses two structural terms: organizational structure (corporate and business) and integration. The former is defined by boxes and lines. It shows the anatomy of an organization and how it groups and uses specialized resources, such as functions or divisions. The remainder of this chapter considers the first three items in the preceding list as elements of organizational structure and how structural choice depends on strategy.

Structural integration deals with the clarification of responsibilities and the mechanisms or management processes used to make the boxes and lines work. Processes of coordination or the integration of workflows between functional areas are examples of these operating mechanisms. Processes of knowledge transfer across organizational boundaries or units represent another example of structural integration. The last two structural issues in the preceding list, aspects of integration, are covered in Chapter 5. Other aspects of execution suggested by the preceding examples, such as managing change and culture, are handled in later chapters.

Let's now consider the first three organizational structural issues in the preceding list. The logic here is that, to understand the role of structure in strategy execution, it is necessary to do the following:

1. Understand the basics of structure, including its costs and benefits.

2. Apply the basics to make better decisions about centralization and decentralization.

3. Tie everything together by looking at the relationship between strategy and structure in the execution process.

Managers interviewed in the present research stated that basic aspects of structure are often misunderstood. Yet, they stressed, managers are sometimes reluctant to seek advice on basic issues. Consequently, I'll discuss the first two issues as precursors to the critical analysis of the third issue and let the reader pick and choose from among the facts or insights presented, as needed.

STRUCTURAL ISSUE #1: MEASURING COSTS AND BENEFITS OF STRUCTURE

How does structure affect actual costs or measurable benefits? What results can reasonably be expected from different organizational forms?

To answer these questions, let's go back to basics. Picture an organization in the very simple way suggested by the following diagram:

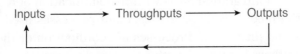

All organizations have inputs: raw materials, staff or employees, patients, financial resources, and so on. All have throughputs: processes or technologies that transform inputs into outputs. Manufacturing firms have mass-production equipment and robots. Hospitals employ different skill sets or techniques (surgery, lab tests, dietary regimes) when working on patients. Universities have "technologies" (Socratic dialogues, case teaching methods) to educate students. Finally, all organizations have outputs (cars, cured patients, educated MBA students).

Using this simple figure, it is possible to argue, first, that organizations can be structured around their throughputs—the processes, technologies, or skill sets (the "means") employed in converting inputs into outputs (the "ends"). The term "process specialization" can be used to emphasize this focus on throughputs or the common processes employed to generate organizational outputs.[iii]

Figure 4.1 shows the best-known example of process specialization—the common functional organization. Organization by throughput or process breaks the company into functions (manufacturing, R&D, marketing). As Table 4.1 shows, there are benefits and costs associated with the functional structure.

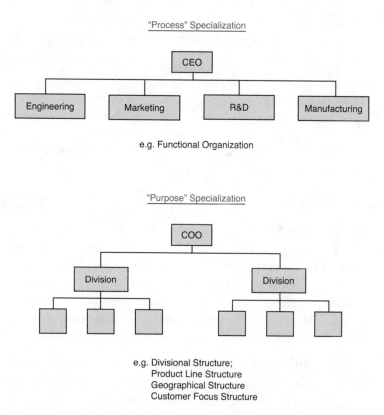

Figure 4.1 Organizational Structure: Process and Purpose Specialization

Table 4.1   Costs and Benefits of Process and Purposes Specialization

	Process Specialization/Functions	Purpose Specialization/Divisions
Benefits	■ Expertise of knowledge/a "critical mass"	■ Focus on customer, products, markets
	■ Economies of scale and scope/efficiency	■ Effectiveness
	■ Avoid duplication of scarce resources	■ Fewer coordination problems
	■ "Career" benefits	■ Quick response to industry change
Costs	■ Coordination costs	■ Duplication of scarce resources
	■ Functional myopia	■ Potential loss of economies/ efficiency
	■ "Distance" from customers of markets	■ Potential loss of control
	■ Loss of "big picture"	
	■ Bureaucracy	

The focus on expertise, with skilled engineers, scientists, or manufacturing managers working closely together, is a positive aspect. Groups of experts often form a "critical mass" that is needed for problem solving and innovation. A group of scientists working together in close proximity, with high levels of interaction and discussion, is more likely to discover something new than that same group split among a large number of separate divisions.

The repetition and standardization of work (such as doing lab tests in hospitals, assembly lines in manufacturing, engineers working on common problems, or insurance analysts working on and refining aspects of whole-life insurance) often lead to efficiency, economies of scale and scope. Duplication of resources is avoided, as personnel in a function can service many customers within the company.

Finally, there may be some "career" benefits when, for example, engineers work with engineers and know that their career path is through engineering. A handful of engineers reporting to a business manager in a small division in Tierra del Fuego may not see such a clear career ladder.

There are costs to the functional organization, as shown in Table 4.1. The most obvious are coordination costs. To service a customer or make a product, it is necessary to coordinate the many and diverse functions. The differences in goals and perceptions that mark different functions' views of work can exacerbate the problems of coordination and detract from a common goal such as customer service or high product quality. It simply is difficult to coordinate work among groups that hold differing views of what's important and what needs attention. Relatedly, the greater the number of diverse functions that need coordination, the more difficult the task and the higher the likelihood of problems.

Another way of looking at this is to talk about "functional myopia."[iv] Functional people get so wrapped up in their own technologies and views of the world that they lose sight of the "big picture." They lose contact with customers. R&D people get so involved in research, new technologies, and the long term that they totally ignore the "mundane" requests for product-line improvements now, in the near term. Science is more exciting and compelling than product revisions or customer demands. Functional myopia clearly exacerbates problems of coordination and unity of effort.

Finally, I've often heard the cry of "bureaucracy" by people who have trouble dealing with functional resistance to new ideas or the speeding up of work. Each function has its own rules and will follow them, the accusation goes, even if organizational work comes to a standstill.

Table 4.1 also shows the benefits and costs of what has been labeled "purpose" specialization. Purpose specialization simply means organization around "ends," or outputs, in contrast to the focus on "means," or throughputs, or the common functions of process specialization. For our purposes, think of "divisions" in organizations (see Figure 4.1). Strategic business units (SBUs) or product-line organizations also qualify as examples of this type of specialization, but let's focus on divisions to facilitate discussion. Divisional structures that focus on customers (Consumer Products Division), product lines (Mainframe Division), or geography (Asian or North American Division) are common examples of this form of organization.

As is seen in Table 4.1, the costs and benefits of purpose specialization or divisionalization are generally the opposite of those
shown under process specialization. Divisions can focus on customers, products, or geographical areas, increasing effectiveness.
A dedicated organizational structure allows for quick responses to
customer needs or industry changes. There are fewer coordination
problems. Even if divisions are organized functionally, the focus
derived from attention to one customer (the Government Products
Division), product (Mainframe Division), or geographical region
(the Asian Division) facilitates and enables coordination around a
common goal, customer, or output.

The costs of divisional structures include the duplication of scarce
resources. Each division head will argue for control over his or her
own resources, staff, or functional groups, leading potentially to
large amounts of costly duplication. Similarly, although the functional structure reinforces efficiency and scale economies, smaller
divisions may not be able to achieve or sustain these same efficiencies.

Finally, divisional or related forms (for example, SBUs) may
become so autonomous that the organization loses some control
over them. A strong focus on one market, customer, or technology
could result in decisions or behaviors inconsistent with larger
organizational goals or needs. Decentralization clearly has benefits
for the organization; excessive decentralization and autonomy,
however, may breed serious control or governance issues.

It is clear that the purpose/divisional form contributes to effectiveness or "doing the right things" (having the right products or
services, meeting customer needs quickly), whereas it may sometimes sacrifice efficiency or "doing things right" (low cost, scale
economies).[v] The process/functional form contributes heavily to
"doing things right" but potentially at the expense of "doing the
right things" because of the problems noted in Table 4.1.

The actual metrics that can be employed to measure the impact of
structure can be summarized under the headings of efficiency and
effectiveness.

Efficiency	Effectiveness
• Cost per (unit, patient, student)	• Market Share
• Economies of Scale	• Customer Satisfaction
• Duplication of Resources (Fixed costs, Costs of Staff)	• Revenue Growth
• Coordination Costs (# of people and time spent)	• Time to Market
	• Product Introductions

↓	↓
Functional Structure ("Doing Things Right")	Divisional Structure ("Doing the Right Things")

These prototypical organizational forms and metrics are basic. Still, keeping these basic ideas in mind, along with their costs and benefits, helps immensely when facing difficult structural decisions such as centralization versus decentralization of organizational structure or relating structure to strategy. Let's apply these basic ideas in the next section of this chapter, where we consider the choice between centralized and decentralized structures.

STRUCTURAL ISSUE #2: CENTRALIZATION VERSUS DECENTRALIZATION

"You're damned if you do and damned if you don't," lamented a CEO whose company I helped restructure. "If I ask corporate center people where resources should be, they answer 'here, naturally.' Ask the same question of my business heads, and of course, the answer is quite different. They want all resources in their businesses or divisions, not at corporate. As profit centers, they want total control of all functional staff. Corporate is seen as a hindrance, not a help."

This quote reflects a common problem in many organizations—where to put scarce resources or assets or how to organize to obtain maximum benefit from these resources. Should R&D or manufacturing be centralized and service all divisions or businesses, or should they be decentralized and under the control of managers who most directly need and use their capabilities? The quote shows that even today there obviously are mixed answers to this question.

Building on the preceding discussion of structural costs and benefits can help with decisions about the location of scarce resources. Should top management opt for the efficiencies of the functional structure, despite its coordination and other costs? Or should it choose to decentralize around product lines, customers, or geography to serve markets more effectively?

The simple answer is that structural choice depends on what is important to management in Table 4.1, strategically or operationally. Given competitive conditions, industry forces, and the company's strategy (see Issue #3 later in this chapter), choices are made between the different structural forms noted in Table 4.1.

Occasionally, the choice of structure is fairly straightforward, dictated by industry or competitive forces. Consider the example of Carrefour in France. Between 2000 and 2012, its share price plummeted about 70 percent. It lost business, especially to Leclerc, and some analysts actually believed that the company would be broken up and downsized. Why such dismal performance for such a well-known company?

One important issue was Carrefour's years of excessive structural centralization. Everything came from the top, the headquarters in Paris. The company sold the same things in every store, the product menu or mix being decided in Paris, not in local markets. In contrast, Leclerc's stores were heavily decentralized, with store managers having the power and ability to respond to local markets and quickly meet consumers' tastes and needs. Leclerc's managers were more nimble and free to adapt products and services as they saw fit. They were able to steal Carrefour's customers easily, given the ability to get close to the market and make decisions without corporate approval and without heated battles with centralized functional groups or experts.

The answer for Carrefour to avoid disaster was clear: Decentralization was definitely in order to stem the negative tide of lost sales and market share. A new CEO—Georges Plassat—took decisive action and moved authority down to the store managers who could now cater to local tastes. By early 2013, the move to decentralization was in full force, and it seems to be paying off. It is clear to many that this move is necessary and vital to

Carrefour's regaining its past industry position. The preference for decentralization in this case is fairly obvious, given the competitive conditions facing the company and its poor past performance record.

Complexity arises because most companies need and use both centralized and decentralized structures, and the need for one or the other isn't patently obvious to all concerned. The issue is how to think through the issue and create the right mix.

A Sequential Decision Process

To see the interplay between the need for efficiency and effectiveness in structural choices and understand better the mix of centralization and decentralization, consider the decision process suggested in Figure 4.2. At the corporate level, corporate center staff reports to the CEO, along with the COO, the top operations-oriented manager. The corporate center staff represents functions that service the entire company in the name of consistency of service across all businesses, such as legal, HR, or IT. Emphasis is on expertise, efficiency, and avoidance of duplication of key personnel. Corporate center staff thus represents process specialization and centralized company-wide functional support.

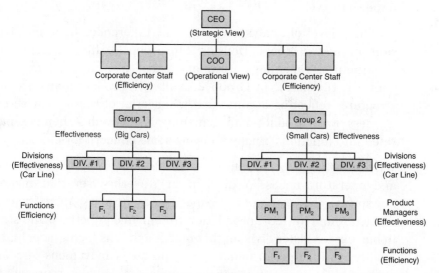

Figure 4.2 A Sequential Approach to Structural Decisions

Reporting to the COO are two groups, structural units representing clusters or group of divisions such as "big expensive cars" and
"small cheaper cars." The driver here is effectiveness, the assumption being that each group has its own particular strategic or operating needs that must be met. Each group may have different
customer demographics, strategies (such as differentiation vs. low
cost), and marketing approaches, and the structural separation
allows for the recognition of these important differences. The separation into groups could also reflect a size issue. The differentiated groups may represent a way to break down the product lines
into smaller, more manageable pieces to facilitate management
attention and decision-making.

Both groups are then broken up into divisions, representing a further emphasis on effectiveness. Each division (such as a car line)
has its own customers who express brand loyalty and whose
unique needs are met by divisional functions and personnel.
Cadillac within GM, for instance, has tried to differentiate itself as
a division catering to well-to-do customers who might otherwise
consider Lexus or Mercedes Benz cars as substitute products. The
Cadillac division has its own general manager to focus on the
unique strategic and operating needs of that brand of cars.
Emphasis is primarily on effectiveness, servicing the desired customer base well.

The next level of analysis shows some differences between divisions in the two groups. Division 2 in Group 1 exhibits a functional structure, reflecting a primary concern with efficiency. In
contrast, Division 2 in Group 2 exhibits a product-management
structure, reflecting a continued managerial concern with effectiveness. Each product-management unit in Group 2 then is separated into functions, finally showing some concern for efficiency.

Why the differences? Because each division has different strategic
and operating needs. A division in Weyerhaeuser that makes
newsprint, the commodity paper used in newspapers, needs
efficiency and low-cost production to remain competitive and stay
in business. A sister division that makes and sells high-grade, high-
quality, or high-performance paper products may focus less on
efficiency than on effectiveness, employing product representatives who get close to customers and tailor products to their needs.

The division selling a commodity product focuses earlier on efficiency than the latter division, whose main focus is on quality and customization of products. The commodity division has thin margins, making efficiency vital to survival. The latter division's margins are likely much higher because of its differentiated, customized products, giving it a bit more leeway on the cost side.

Large companies such as J&J, ABB, Corning Glass, Microsoft, Kraft, and GE likewise have numerous divisions or SBUs with varying strategic and operating needs. Some are organized primarily around efficiency concerns, while others are focused primarily on effectiveness, getting close to customers and markets. Divisions in the same company simply confront and solve different strategic and operating problems, giving rise to varying concerns with efficiency and effectiveness.

Decisions about structure, then, can be seen as a sequential process, a logical order of decisions that examines needs for efficiency and effectiveness at each descending level of organization. Corporate decides which staff should service all businesses (efficiency, centralization), which groups or divisions should be created to reflect varying market needs (effectiveness, decentralization), and which functional support groups should be in those groups or divisions rather than at corporate (decentralization). Group and division staff, in turn, decides which functions will service all product lines (centralization) and which functions are unique to each product line (decentralization). And so on. Decisions about centralization/decentralization occur between corporate and business levels and within businesses, reflecting a concern with efficiency and effectiveness and the performance measures previously listed.

Tall Versus Flat Organizations

The sequential decision process doesn't mean to imply that organizations need to be tall, with a lot of layers devoted to different needs or problems. The example in Figure 4.2 was used merely to show how decisions about structure may be made logically by looking at each adjacent level of organization. It is not intended to suggest that all organizations need a complex, tall structure. The sequential process certainly can also result in flat structures, which, to many managers, means faster decision-making, less bureaucracy, closeness to the customer or market, and greater flexibility of structure.

GE Capital

Consider for a moment the case of GE Capital. GE is a large, complex organization, marked by different sectors (high tech, service) and businesses within sectors. Traditionally, the business heads reported directly to the CEO. The head of GE Capital reported to Jack Welch for years and was responsible for all segments of the business in that financial services unit. The structure, very basically, looked like this:

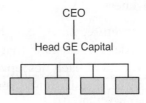

Business Areas

All communications about GE Capital business areas, strategy, functioning, earnings, and so on went through the head of the division or business unit. The CEO had only indirect access to the business areas within GE Capital, including consumer finance, insurance, commercial finance, and equipment management.

Over time, this structure created some problems. GE Capital grew immensely: By 2011, it had net income of $6.5 billion, almost $600 billion in assets, more than 50,000 employees, and over 180 million customers worldwide. While this growth was occurring, Jeffrey Immelt, GE's CEO and replacement for Jack Welch, felt that too much was going on in GE Capital's businesses that wasn't easily understood by management or external financial analysts. One article described GE Capital as a financial "black box" that acts as a huge private bank without adequate financial disclosure.[vi] Immelt felt that he didn't have enough contact with or control over what was happening within this black box, and he wanted more direct, unfiltered communication with business elements.

Accordingly, he changed the structure, flattening it. GE Capital was broken up into four separate businesses, which later morphed into five businesses: Commercial Lending and Leasing, Consumer Financing, Energy Financial Services, GE Capital Aviation Services, and GE Capital Real Estate. The businesses now report directly to Immelt, thereby flattening the structure while aiming to improve oversight, improve transparency, and streamline and speed up decisions in a complex business. Eliminating a level of management brings the performance effectiveness of the four businesses closer to top management scrutiny than had been the case.

Not everything was changed by Immelt's bold move. There still are common corporate functions within GE Capital serving all the businesses, such as risk management, capital markets, and tax and treasury. Reliance on the central functions still represents a quest for efficiency, consistency, and expertise that all businesses can tap into and use. The structural move flattening the organization, however, clearly is one driven primarily by. the CEO's perceived need to be closer to business performance while improving transparency, communication, and oversight. The new structure, eliminating a level, looks like this:

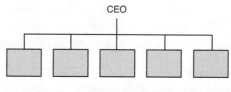

Five Businesses of GE Capital

Flatter structures clearly suggest benefits for organizations and management. They usually eliminate or reduce the problems associated with slow vertical communication. They result in greater decentralization and "job enlargement," as managers close to markets and customers assume more responsibility and make more decisions. They often are described as more "flexible" in their ability to respond more quickly to market changes than their taller counterparts. They increase control and improve transparency and accountability.

It must also be emphasized, however, that flat structures can fail to deliver. They are not an automatic panacea for structural woes.

In fact, flat organizational structures potentially create four highly related problems that must be handled for them to produce positive results. These problems are: (a) inertia, (b) inadequate expertise, individuals' not accepting responsibility for decision-making, and creation of lateral communication problems.

Inertia

Flattening an organization may scare some managers or disrupt their routines. Previously, nasty problems could be referred up the hierarchy to one's boss. Flat structures usually have larger spans of control, making such referrals difficult, thus forcing people to act or decide. Some may be reluctant to do things differently and may change slowly, if at all, negatively affecting problem-solving or decision-making.

Inadequate Expertise

For individuals to make the additional decisions required of them in flat organizations, an increase in expertise is usually necessary. Larger spans of control make it difficult to tap into a superior's knowledge. This means that lower-level managers must develop much of the expertise and knowledge that their bosses once controlled. They need the increased knowledge to make decisions and solve problems in a more decentralized setting.

If training and managerial education processes are lacking, the creation of new expertise suffers, as does the ability to solve problems in the flat organization. Flat structures demand greater knowledge and insight from managers and others responsible for more and more decisions over time. Without this expertise, they can actually create decision bottlenecks and poor results.

Not Accepting Responsibility

The inertia and inadequate expertise just discussed clearly can make people reluctant to accept responsibility for new, more complex decisions. Increased closeness to the market and customers, coupled with the "need for speed" and quick reaction to external threats and opportunities, demands that more responsibility be assumed by lower levels in flat structures. Not having the necessary tools and having a fear of failure or a feeling of inadequacy will work against the acceptance of new responsibilities, causing the organization a host of problems.

Lateral Communication Problems

Finally, flattening an organizational structure can create new, lateral communication problems. Let me use an actual example from a company I know well that went through a period in which it tried to "delayer" its structure, to use its term. In this case, results were far from happy and useful. In the words of one functional manager in a written critique of his new structure:[vii]

Spans of control increased tremendously due to the virtual elimination of an entire level. Of necessity, the company had to become more decentralized. Getting help from the boss is possible when span of control is one to seven; it's virtually impossible when span is one to forty-nine or some such ridiculous number.

Decentralization meant that we, this "group of forty-nine," had to communicate laterally with each other rather than go through our bosses as we did in the past. Only then did we realize that so many things were different across previously separate units. The beliefs, values, and operating principles were simply not the same due to past differences in goals, competition, and history of the units. One group talked about margins, contribution, real costs, and value-added measurements that were foreign to people in other units. Perceptions of profit varied, as different groups looked at different expenses to arrive at different net figures. One group mentioned customers' needs frequently, while another had never seen or talked to customers and, hence, couldn't care less about them. There literally was nothing in common to bind people who previously had different bosses and views of the world. A common outlook to help the restructuring was not present.

With so little in common, it was extremely difficult to communicate. I know it sounds unbelievable, being the same company and all that, but it's true. We couldn't talk to each other!

This is an extreme case, one clearly exaggerated by a disgruntled manager to make his point. Span of control never approached the huge number the manager referred to in his lament. Still, the problems he cites indeed did exist. The example helps make the point: Flat organizational structures have ample benefits if managers handle the problems of inertia, inadequate expertise, reluctance to accept responsibility, and new demands for lateral communication. Flat structures are not an automatic cure-all. They work, but they need adequate managerial attention.

The Corporate Center

The mix of centralization versus decentralization raises another structural issue that currently is receiving attention: the size and role of the corporate center.

The corporate staff's primary functions discussed thus far include efficiency, or economies of scale and scope, consistency of centralized support services across all businesses or operating divisions, and an avoidance of duplication of resources. Thus, legal or HR staffs are seen as providing the same consistent services to all businesses, regardless of their industries, technologies, or customer base.

These clearly represent important services with a definite value added. A staff of experts helps all businesses of divisions, thereby sharing expertise and avoiding duplications of effort. Recently, however, managers are telling me that they see an expanded role for the corporate center. They see additional tasks or services that can help strategy execution at both corporate and business levels. What are some aspects of this expanded role for the corporate center?

A number of tasks for an expanded corporate center have been suggested. Presently, I'll mention only three:

1. A strategic management function
2. An executive education function
3. "Centers of excellence" functions

Strategic Management Function

This group would advise the CEO and business leaders in a number of areas. Portfolio strategies could be reviewed to maximize strategic and financial goals. This group could help with benchmarking and the development of best practices in strategic planning, the management of information and information flows, and strategy-execution methods.

Developments at Crown Holdings a few years ago suggest this type of centralized function in a strategic management group. A corporate strategy group focuses not only on corporate issues but also integration of corporate and business strategy. An important objective is to create an interactive planning process, integrating both corporate and business unit plans. Processes also focus on integration across geographical regions as well as across businesses. Additionally, the group is charged with the task of identifying and understanding future trends in the industry that could affect business or geographical performance. Clearly, this unit is concerned with more than just efficiency or central support services. As a corporate center group, it is charged with a strategic, educational, and integrative role that affects company performance.

Another important task for this group is to facilitate the strategy review discussed in Chapter 3 and again in Chapter 6. This review is important for corporate-business interactions, the integrity of corporate portfolio models, and the metrics used to evaluate business performance, all of which affect strategy execution.

Executive Education Function

This group would concern itself with the continuing education of management. The knowledge and capabilities of top management are vital to the success of strategy formulation and execution and, ultimately, to a company's ability to achieve competitive advantage. This corporate center group would focus on executive development in generic areas—planning, incentive systems, marketing, leadership, managing change—as well as areas specific to success in a given industry—new product development, customer service, and competitor intelligence. The goal is to create an educational resource that can profoundly affect strategy execution and organizational performance over time.

Recent trends at Microsoft, UGI, GE, Aventis Behring, Publicis, and others indicate the development of an important executive education function. The growth, size, and increasing complexity facing the organizations suggest the need for such a centralized function. My work with many of their general managers and director-level people has been shaped and supported by a central group focusing on leadership and management development. Top managers in UGI Corporation who created UGI University correctly recognize that there are critical leadership and management capabilities that cut across the different businesses and consistently affect performance. The task of a new corporate center function in executive education and development is being directed toward these critical leadership and management skills.

More and more companies are creating internal "universities," corporate center groups involved in critical educational tasks. Indeed, by the end of 2011, there were more than 2000 corporate universities in the United States. The large range is due to nomenclature differences, as not all companies use the "university" label (most do). This number is greater than the number of actual universities conferring undergraduate degrees in the United States. Clearly, the executive education function is becoming an increasingly important task for the corporate center concept.

Centers of Excellence

In a program I did with Aventis Behring, management spoke often about "centers of excellence." Under this concept, emphasis was on groups responsible for industry-wide standards of performance in such areas as medical and regulatory systems, preclinical research, clinical quality control, and biometry and statistical services.

The goal of center formation at Aventis and elsewhere is to develop groups that create leading-edge knowledge and processes that result in better enterprise performance and industry leadership. A related goal is the attraction of highly qualified scientific and managerial staff, resources that can help the company innovate and achieve competitive advantage. The focus on leading-edge technology and attraction of the "brightest and best" scientific and management personnel is another step in ensuring that the organization has the requisite resources and capabilities to support strategy execution.

The "new" corporate center, then, would contain the typical functions found in a centralized structure, such as legal, HR, IT, and finance. However, it would also have additional value-added services such as those shown in Figure 4.3. Clearly, this expanded role can have a large impact on strategy-execution activities.

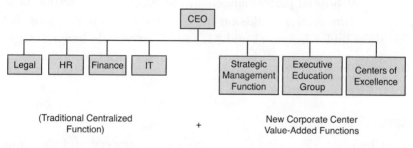

Figure 4.3 The Corporate Center

A final caveat is needed here. The new corporate center concept certainly seems to be attractive, offering critical value-added services to help the entire enterprise execute its strategy more effectively. Yet care must be taken when defining the center's role in strategy execution. The center does represent an increased emphasis on centralization of resources and capabilities. If successful execution depends more on the decentralization of businesses and the ability to react quickly and appropriately to customer or market needs, the corporate center concept might not contribute immediately to effective strategy implementation. The center might not respond quickly enough to the demands of managers facing local pressing problems.

The important issue to keep in mind is that both centralization and decentralization have costs and benefits. It is necessary to balance the emphasis on the two structural forms so as to attain the desired strategic and operating outcomes for the organization.

STRUCTURAL ISSUE #3: THE STRATEGY-STRUCTURE RELATIONSHIP AND EFFECTIVE EXECUTION

The previous two sections have already laid the basic groundwork for this issue. The basic elements of organizational structure and the costs and benefits of the structural forms suggest how structure might support strategy. This section takes the argument one step further, adding specificity to what has thus far been suggested. It takes a critical step in explaining how structure relates to organizational performance and the successful execution of strategy. This section builds on the foundation of the previous discussions under Issues #1 and #2, and shows clearly how strategy and structure are related and how alignment between them affects organizational performance.

The Demands of Strategy

Chapter 3 discussed the "demands" of strategy and their impact on resources and capabilities. The point then was that strategy demanded the development of certain skills, resources, or capabilities if successful execution was to occur. The latter resources include structure, which must reflect and respond to strategic demands. If structure doesn't reflect the demands of strategy, execution suffers. Let's look at some examples.

Low-Cost Strategy

Cost reduction and containment obviously are central to a cost-leadership or low-cost strategy. Commodity product or highly competitive industries usually are marked by price competition, with price as a "given" or constant. The fixed-price nature of these industries indicates that additional revenues cannot be gained by raising price and must come from lowered costs.

Organizational structure in these cases would favor the efficiencies and scale economies of centralized, functional forms. These forms are characterized by standardization, volume, and repetition, which foster efficiencies from economies of scale and scope. They also reduce unnecessary duplications of resources, further reducing costs. Thus, for the low-cost strategy:

Low-Cost Strategy ⟶ Centralized Functional Structures

• Commodity Products   • Efficiency, Economies of Scale and Scope

• Price Competition   • Standardization, Volume, and Repetition of Work

                              • Lack of Duplication of Scarce Resources

Focus Strategies

These strategies usually focus on the customer, geography, or product line. Organizational structure, in turn, reflects the critical focus, usually with emphasis on the divisional form or a similar type of decentralized structure.

Focus Strategy ⟶ Decentralized, Divisional Structure

• Focus on Customer,   • Dedicated Division and Staff
  Geography, or
  Product   • Focus on Object of Strategy (e.g. Consumer
                                Products and Government Products Divisions,
                                Mainframe and PC Divisions, Asian Division)

                              • Minimum Centralized Staff Needed to Support
                                Decentralized Operations

Even with the predominantly decentralized structure, there still may be some centralized staff to achieve efficiencies across the decentralized units. The primary emphasis, however, clearly is on decentralization.

Differentiation Strategies

The key question here deals with the type of differentiation intended or the product or customer characteristics important to differentiation, such as high end of market versus low-end products, "performance" products directed toward affluent buyers, and so on.

Using high-end (more expensive, higher quality, high performance) products versus low-end products as an example, the firm would opt for a structure with two businesses or divisions. The low-end division would likely pursue a low-cost strategy, whereas the high-end business would concern itself with satisfying its customers' needs for performance, quality, and "image." Each business would be relatively self-contained, as the resources or capabilities needed to pursue a low-cost strategy differ from those needed to pursue the high-end strategy (see Chapter 3).

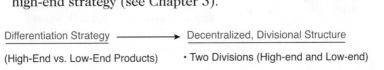

Differentiation Strategy ⟶ Decentralized, Divisional Structure

(High-End vs. Low-End Products)   • Two Divisions (High-end and Low-end)

• Self-Contained, with Different Resources and Capabilities

• Minimum Centralized Staff Needed to Support the Different Businesses

Simultaneous Pursuit of Two Strategies

The last example presents a common case: a company pursuing two or more strategies at once in a given industry. Care must be taken to develop for each strategy an appropriate structure and set of resources or capabilities to allow for successful execution. The divisional structure is ideal in this regard, in that it allows each business to focus on its own industry or market needs, as well as development of its own skills and resources. Using the simple case, again, of high-end and low-end products, we would have two separate divisions:

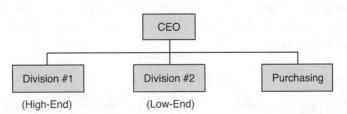

Having two separate, different, decentralized divisions, however, does not automatically rule out centralization and its attendant economies and related benefits. As the preceding figure shows, the two divisions, despite serving two different markets with diverse customer tastes and product characteristics, still can benefit from centralized purchasing. Economies of one-source, centralized buying can be achieved, despite the major strategic differences between the two divisions. A similar argument for centralized functions may be made in areas such as HR or legal, if the work done is identical across the different divisions based on customer or market.

An emphasis on decentralization is rarely total; the emphasis is usually relative. Some centralization may exist, even in highly decentralized organizations, consistent with the strategy being pursued and the resources required.

Global Strategy

Companies in global competition must often worry about focusing, at once, on both worldwide product or service lines and geographical differences in markets. They push products worldwide but also must adapt them, or their marketing and distribution, to local needs, tastes, and customer demographics. A common response here is the matrix structure that helps execute the coordinated global strategy. A "simultaneous" structure, with worldwide product and local geographical components, becomes the design of choice.

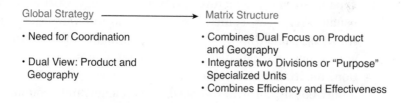

Global Strategy ⟶ Matrix Structure

- Need for Coordination
- Dual View: Product and Geography

- Combines Dual Focus on Product and Geography
- Integrates two Divisions or "Purpose" Specialized Units
- Combines Efficiency and Effectiveness

Because the matrix structure is primarily concerned with integration or coordination of diverse functions or units, a more in-depth discussion of it occurs in Chapter 5. Additional coverage of global strategies appears later in Chapter 11.

Strategic "Drivers" of Structural Choice

Let's try to synthesize this discussion of the impact of strategy on the choice of structure. Table 4.2 lists the four main strategic drivers of structural choice that are discussed or implied in this chapter. The first two can be summarized briefly, as they already have been clarified previously. Numbers 3 and 4, especially the latter, deserve additional, in-depth discussions.

Table 4.2 Strategic "Drivers" of Structural Choice

1. Type of strategy
    - a. Low-cost ⟶ Centralization, functional structure
    - b. Focus/differentiation ⟶ Decentralization, divisional structure
    - c. Coordinated global ⟶ Matrix organization

2. Need for efficiency/effectiveness
    - d. Efficiency ⟶ Centralization
    - e. Effectiveness ⟶ Decentralization

3. Market and technological relatedness
    - f. If both are high ⟶ Increased centralization
    - g. If both are low ⟶ Increased decentralization
    - h. If one is low and the other high ⟶ Mix of decentralization and centralization

4. Organizational size/growth
    - Growth/large size ⟶ Increased decentralization; reducing large organization to smaller, more manageable pieces
    - The global imperative ⟶ Adapting to global demands

1. **Type of strategy.** Structure varies with strategy. Cost leadership usually requires some reliance on a functional structure (process specialization) because of its ability to drive down costs and achieve various economies. The emphasis on standardization, repetition, and volume under this form of organization is totally consistent with the need for efficiency and economies of scale and scope that support the low-cost strategy.

In contrast, a focus or differentiation strategy usually requires some form of purpose specialization (divisions or SBU based on product line, geography, or customer; product- or project-management organizations) to provide the needed focus and attention to customer, geographical region, or product line.

A coordinated global strategy usually requires a simultaneous focus on worldwide businesses or product lines and different geographical regions or cultures. This typically results in a matrix structure that focuses on both dimensions (business, geography) at once when executing the strategy.

The main point in these examples is that structure is responding to the demands of strategy. Chapter 3 listed some demands of low-cost and differentiation strategies. To execute the strategies, these demands must be met. And one of these demands is selection on appropriate structure to support the chosen generic strategy. Centralized structures, for example, support low-cost strategies because they deliver on cost reduction. It's that simple and straightforward. Structure, with its costs and benefits, responds to and supports strategy, leading to execution success. Type of strategy drives the choice of structure and the desired attendant benefits.

2. **Need for efficiency/effectiveness as aspects of strategy.** The need for efficiency or effectiveness follows closely the previous discussion of type of strategy. The two are highly correlated, but the efficiency/effectiveness issue is well known and important and, accordingly, deserves separate mention.

Strategies may focus on efficiency or effectiveness in a quest to gain competitive advantage. The greater the need for efficiency, the greater usually is the reliance on centralization of structure and the cost controls inherent in it. The greater the need for effectiveness, the more likely it is that an organization will opt for a decentralized structure.

Cost-leadership strategies obviously need and rely on cost efficiencies, explaining again why centralized functional structures are critical for strategy execution and organizational success. When strategy focuses on effectiveness in serving different customers or geographical regions with a variety of products and services, emphasis will logically be on decentralization, with different divisional-type structures based on customer, geography, or product line.

A good recent example of centralization in an effort to reduce costs is provided by HP. The short-lived reign of CEO, Leo Apotheker, was marked by a desire to rid the company of its commodity PC business. When he was fired and replaced by new CEO, Meg Whitman, his strategic proposal to divest the PC business was not acted upon. Instead, Whitman took steps to attempt to increase efficiency.

CEO Whitman said in March 2011 that HP would combine its two biggest SBUs or business units—PCs and printers—and cut its workforce by about 30,000, a move to cut costs in its commodity-type product lines. HP also announced that it would centralize certain functions, such as marketing and public relations. This clearly is a move intended to increase efficiency. Whereas Apotheker pushed to refocus the company on some new services, for example, cloud computing services, Whitman is choosing, first, to focus on cost reduction in existing business areas. She wants to continue doing the same big things—HP's PC business is the largest in the world—but do them better.

In terms of Table 4.2, HP's thrust clearly focuses on the first two strategic drivers of structural choice. A strategy emphasizing low cost in existing businesses is executed via proposed staff reduction and increased centralization of certain key functional areas in a search for efficiency. This will be a tough strategic and operational row to hoe, but HP's intentions to give it a shot are clear.

There are also many examples of structural changes to increase effectiveness of companies' strategy and operations. Consider just a few recent examples. Netflix announced its desire to break into two businesses, DVD and Streaming (September 2011), arguing that the two are different businesses in need of different managerial attention.

Abbott Laboratories announced (October 2011) that it would split into two businesses, Pharmaceuticals and Medical Products because they serve different markets and are marked by different industry forces or conditions.

Tyco split into three companies (September 2011), arguing that ADT, Flow Control, and Commercial Fire and Security represent different businesses in need of separate and focused managerial attention.

Other recent examples at Kraft (Grocery and Global Snacks), Conoco Philips (Exploration and Production vs. Refining/ Marketing), Motorola (Motorola Mobility and Motorola Solutions), and so on mirror the previous efforts noted to identify and separate businesses because they are different, in need of specialized strategic and operational attention.

In terms of Table 4.2, these are clear moves to break out and decentralize different businesses in the quest for increased performance and organizational effectiveness. The strategies pursued can be labeled as differentiation or focus, with the decentralization of structure an important part of an execution plan to get closer to divergent markets and give them the managerial attention they deserve. Execution in these cases reflects decisions that the decentralized businesses are different, have different cost structures, and are in need of different marketing approaches to customers with specific, varying needs.

Some of these restructurings may also reflect size/growth changes and forays into global markets, points returned to later.

3. **Market and technological relatedness.** The degree of "relatedness" is an important strategic driver of structure. It was only implied in previous discussions, so it's important to spend a bit of time clarifying its role in structural choice.

A company may serve a variety of related or unrelated markets. Diversification strategies may focus on expansion into related or unrelated industries. High market relatedness simply means the same or similar customers, distribution channels, pricing, and demand elasticities. Unrelated markets denote differences on these same dimensions. Technological relatedness or unrelatedness refers to the use of the same versus different technologies, manufacturing processes, or "throughputs" that translate inputs into outputs.

Relatedness is important because the greater the degree of market and/or technological relatedness associated with a strategy, the higher the likelihood of centralization in organizational structure. The lower the relatedness, the higher the likelihood of decentralization.

If a company makes different products with the same manufacturing process and equipment, manufacturing will most likely be a centralized function, serving all product lines. If the markets for the products vary, necessitating product changes because of customer, cultural, or geographical differences in usage or taste, the marketing and distribution functions, and perhaps even manufacturing, will be decentralized, reflecting the need to tailor or modify products for the different markets. Great care must be taken when defining the degree of relatedness before choosing an appropriate structure. Poor or sloppy definition can result in structural choices that lead to execution problems.

This lesson was first driven home to me years ago. An entrepreneur named Howard Head founded a ski company that had amazing success. Its product was a metal ski—high end, high price, handmade, the "cheater," as it was dubbed, because it made people better skiers. At one point, it was suggested to Head that he enter the low end of the market to capitalize on his brand and extend his product line. A ski, after all, is just a ski, so he might as well saturate the entire market.

Head declined to enter the low-end market. Among the reasons to justify his decision, he considered what this discussion is focusing on currently—degree of market and technological relatedness. He pointed out that metal skis are made differently than cheaper plastic skis. The technology is different: a handmade product versus injection molding for the plastic ski, a technology Head knew nothing about.

The markets were also different or unrelated, given Head's competencies and marketing approach: a high-end, pricy product versus a low-end, cheap product; different elasticities of demand and profit margins; different distribution channels (ski-specialty shops vs. mass-market distribution in large retail discount stores); and different service capabilities (the ski pro vs. the discount-store clerk who sells fishing tackle and bowling balls as well as ski equipment).

There were other differences, but the point is clear: Though part of the same industry, the low-end and high-end ski markets were vastly different in terms of customers and technology. Entering an unrelated market would demand a different organization with different skills and capabilities. A strategy of unrelated diversification, even within the same industry, would demand a different technology and vastly different sales, distribution, and marketing. Head, of course, could have bought an existing company already in the low-end business, thereby immediately acquiring the needed capabilities and appropriate organizational structure, but he declined to do so. Better to "stick to one's knitting" and continue to do what one knows and does best, was his logical answer.

When Philip Morris, in pre-Altria days, bought Seven-Up, it entered an industry that in some respects was similar to tobacco and beer, its existing products at the time, but in many others was quite different. Some channels of distribution were the same. A sophisticated marketing group could service all industries, it was thought, perhaps achieving economies of scope.

But the industries were also very different. Tobacco and beer strategies had targeted men primarily, but soft drinks had a broader, more diverse market. Industry concentration was different, with Coke and Pepsi dominating the market with their brands and full array of products. Small players such as Seven-Up often "piggybacked" on Coke and Pepsi bottlers, making them dependent on and vulnerable before these giants. The soft-drink industry was basically different than the tobacco and beer industries.

Philip Morris' actions, however, suggested that it saw more elements of related diversification than others did. It treated the soft-drink industry as virtually the same as the tobacco and beer industries. It looked for economies of scale and scope in soft drinks that weren't easily attained. It didn't react effectively to an industry with different competitive forces, concentration, and customer demographics.

The Seven-Up venture failed, and Philip Morris sold the company at a loss. In part, the problem represented a misread of market relatedness and consequent mistakes in decisions about strategy and structure. Understanding the concepts of market and technological relatedness indeed are important to these choices and to strategic and execution success.

Consulting organizations are service companies that must be concerned with technological and market relatedness when planning and executing strategy. On one hand, data collection and analysis technologies, knowledge-sharing approaches, and management processes or technologies represent core skills that are useful and effective across many clients or industries. These common process technologies can be centralized, as they are similar or the same regardless of industry or client. On the other hand, industries and clients vary in their characteristics or needs. Distinctive demands by clients in different industries demand separate and dedicated attention. This explains why the consulting firm's structure is also marked by decentralized units that focus on industry or client, for example, health care, energy, manufacturing, professional organizations, education, government, and so on. The extent of the relatedness of markets and technology affects the choice of structure, resulting logically in both centralized and decentralized capabilities to meet clients' needs.

So, too, in the large hospital. The hospital has many technologies or capabilities that service all patients or clients, regardless of disease or injury (e.g., x-ray, dietary, lab work, etc.), and these can be centralized units or functions providing the same service for all customers. In contrast, certain patient or disease groups demand specialized attention or service or medical procedures that are not common across all patients or clients. This results in areas of specialty or medical focus that represent forms of decentralization serving different markets (e.g., pediatric vs. geriatric care, general hospitals vs. cancer centers). The relatedness or similarity of medical procedures or technologies and client groups determines the structure to a large degree.

In sum, the greater the market or technological relatedness across products or services, the higher the probability of centralization or sharing the same functions or capabilities. The greater the unrelatedness, the more likely it is to see decentralization of organizational units, as the following suggests:

a) High Market   and   High Technological   = Centralization
   Relatedness   Relatedness

   • Same Customers   • Same Manufacturing
   • Same Distribution   • Same Processes or
     Channels   Technologies
   • Same Pricing   • Use of Same Capabilities
   • Same Demand   or Skills
     Elasticities

b) Low Market   and   Low Technological   = Decentralization
   Relatedness   Relatedness

If either market or technological relatedness is high and the
other is low, then structure will be a combination of centralization and decentralization. To expand on the preceding examples, a high-end and low-end product company could have both
centralization (common functions) and decentralization (two
different divisions). The latter would reflect different customer
demographics, pricing, and distribution channels. The former
would reflect the need for efficiency and consistency of performance from a function (such as purchasing, manufacturing)
that services both high- and low-end products. A mixture of
market and technological relatedness will affect organization
structure (separate divisions vs. common functions) and its
degree of centralized versus decentralized decision-making.

c) A Mixture of Market and   =   A Mix of Centralization and
   Technological Relatedness   Decentralization
   (High and Low)

4. **Organizational growth, size, and the global imperative.** If a
   company's growth strategy works, organizational size can
   increase complexity and the difficulty of coordinating diverse
   organizational units. The usual response is to reduce large
   organizational size to smaller, more manageable units. This
   results in greater decentralization of structure.

   Size warrants at least a separate mention because of its independent impact on structure. Size often demands that big
   problems be factored into smaller, more manageable proportions and be handled by smaller structural units, resulting in
   decentralization. This results, for example, in regional offices
   within the United States, even when products and technologies
   are exactly the same across the country.

Following this logic, strategies that focus on growth—such as diversification and global expansion—usually create the need for increased decentralization over time. The effects of size are usually coupled with the effects of market and/or technological relatedness when diversifying or expanding globally, with increased size usually correlated with a larger number of unrelated markets. Global expansion typically results in product or service modifications to meet divergent customer or geographical needs and tastes and to reflect local capabilities or technological methods.

The mention of global strategy suggests a recent global expansion of sorts that represents more than the usual decentralization in response to unrelated markets and technologies. Recent global growth almost reflects a new kind of "global imperative," as noted in Table 4.2. Let's consider just a few examples.

P&G announced in the spring of 2011 that it's relocating the top executives of its global skin, cosmetics, and beauty-care unit from its Cincinnati headquarters to Singapore, a move that emphatically indicates the importance of Asia's growth market in beauty products.[viii] This isn't the normal move of setting up an SBU or division for local presence while maintaining the company headquarters where it's always been. This move represents a clear "symbolic break from P&G's centralized structure" and its concentration of decision-making in Cincinnati.[ix]

This obviously is more than a minor change in structure; it's a real break from centralization to a wholesale decentralization of top management talent, authority, and decision-making. Coupled with other P&G moves of business units abroad in recent years, the message is obvious: Global growth is critical to company success and drastic structural change is needed to get close to growth markets and execute a strategy that reflects both focus and differentiation components. Moving headquarters units to key growth areas reflects an alignment of structure to the demands of an evolving and important global strategy. Other factors may be at work—e.g., tax advantages of global decentralization—but clearly structural change is being implemented to focus on increased organizational effectiveness.

P&G isn't alone in this significant structural decentralization. In just 2011-2012 alone, a number of well-known companies made similar structural changes away from centralization to increased decentralization to reflect the importance of fast-growing global markets. A few well-known examples include GE's moving its x-ray operations to Beijing from Wisconsin; Halliburton's setting up a headquarters unit in Dubai, leaving Houston; and Rolls Royce moving its Global Marine headquarters to Singapore from London.[x]

These all are significant moves, showing a strong response to changing global conditions and the importance of emerging global markets. Table 4.2 suggests that response to this global imperative is an important aspect of organizations' responsibility to global growth with heavy investments in structural decentralization. Structure, indeed, does follow logically from strategy and the demands of strategic choice.

These four conditions or variables in Table 4.2, then, are the strategic "drivers" of structural choice. These are the factors that management must consider and analyze carefully as it ponders structural choice or structural change. An incomplete analysis of these factors can lead to major problems. Structure must respond to and be consistent with the demands of strategy if successful execution outcomes are to result.

SUMMARY

Four key conclusions or takeaways are suggested by the present chapter, beyond the basic point that structure is important to the execution of strategy:

1. The first is that structure affects real costs and benefits to an organization. Different ways of organizing affect outcomes. "Process" specialization or functional structures, for example, positively affect efficiency via standardization, repetition, high volume, and the economies that follow. This type of organization also avoids duplication of resources and efforts, which further reduces costs.

In contrast, "purpose" specialization (divisions, SBUs) loads on effectiveness by organizing around customers, products, or markets. Whereas process specialization enables the organization to "do things right," purpose specialization helps the firm "do the right things." Process specialization may occasionally work against effectiveness, while purpose specialization can increase costs, primarily due to duplication of resources.

2. The second key conclusion follows logically from the first: The right mix of centralization and decentralization must be attained to optimize both efficiency and effectiveness. Centralization results in efficiency and the creation of expertise, an organization-wide asset, resource, or capability. Decentralization results in getting close to customers or markets. Decentralized units must rely and draw on the expertise or knowledge of centralized resources, which can slow responses to customers and markets. Excessive decentralization, however, may injure overall company efficiency and result in a loss of central control and core competence. Again, a balance between centralized and decentralized resources must be achieved.

   Related to the discussion of centralization is the developing role of the corporate center. No longer just a way to achieve efficiency, a new corporate center concept focuses on adding value to an organization. By focusing on such areas or skills as executive education, strategic management, and worldwide centers of excellence, the corporate center's concerns and contributions far transcend those of basic efficiency and cost control.

3. This chapter also stressed that there are strategic drivers of structural choice. These include: (a) type of strategy (global, low-cost), (b) the need for efficiency or effectiveness, market and technological relatedness, and organizational size/growth. These issues, emanating from strategy and strategic analysis at both the corporate and business levels, affect the choice of structure. High market and technological relatedness, for example, usually argues for increased centralization, whereas low relatedness calls for increased decentralization.

Other examples of these "drivers" at work were provided in the chapter, explicating the relationship between strategy and structure. One such key driver was labeled the "global imperative." Growth of global emerging markets is becoming so important that companies are moving headquarters and operating units along with top managers to the new growth markets. These moves represent more than structural changes to increased decentralization; they often represent key symbolic breaks from centralization and the time-honored, routine ways of doing business. These moves represent structural change in response to strategy, but they also represent major culture change as organizations grow and focus on new markets.

4. Finally, the chapter suggests that a sequential process of analysis is useful when examining relationships between strategy and structure, as the following figure shows:

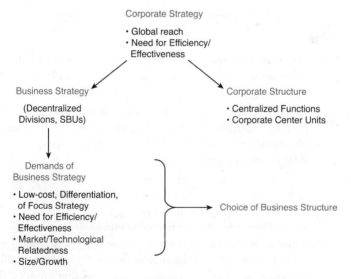

We see that corporate strategy is the lead driver as top management considers such factors as the organization's global reach and the relative need for efficiency and effectiveness. Strategy at this level includes a portfolio approach as decisions are made about what businesses to pursue and which ones to exit. These analyses fuel choice of corporate structure as decisions are made about centralization (centralized functions, corporate center units) and decentralization (business units and the resources they need to operate effectively). Each of the business units, in turn, creates or refines its strategy, which makes demands on the organization and defines the conditions (such as market and technological related-ness) that will drive structural choice at the business level.

Keep in mind that this process reflects a sequential logic. In most organizations, rarely are all of these analyses and decisions made from scratch, sequentially, in every planning cycle. Still, if, for example, strategy should change, this model provides a logical flow against which to consider the possibility of structural change, at both corporate and business levels.

This chapter looked at structure, the anatomy of the entire organ-ization. Attention can now turn to structural integration and how to coordinate the work of different organizational parts, the sub-stance of the next chapter.

ENDNOTES

i. "Johnson & Johnson Gets FDA Warning about K-Y Liquibeads Complaints and Other Issues." *The Washington Post*, May 30, 2012.

ii. See, for example, the Federation of American Scientists (FAS) list-ing of U. S. Intelligence and Security Agencies (go to www.fas.org/irp/official.html); see, too, an organization chart of the intelligence community, Carroll Publishing, Bethesda, Maryland, 2005 (www.carrollpub.com).

iii. Usage of the terms "process" and "purpose" specialization can first be found in the works of early management and organization theo-rists. For example, see the following: L. H. Gulick and L. Urwick (eds.), *Papers on the Science of Administration*, New York, 1937; James G. March and Herbert A. Simon, *Organizations*, John Wiley, 1958. Process specialization refers generally to a set of skills or processes (such as clerical, manufacturing) that are specialized, repeatable, and performed in the same or consistent ways. Purpose specialization refers to departmentation or ways to break up work into more focused tasks in smaller subunits of the organization.

iv. H. J. Leavitt, "Small Groups in Large Organizations," *Journal of Business*, 1955; *Managerial Psychology*, Chicago, 1958.

v. The description of efficiency as "doing things right" and effectiveness as "doing the right things" has been discussed or implied by managers and academics alike. Probably one of the earliest and most interesting discussions is by Chester Barnard in *The Functions of the Executive*, Harvard University Press, 1938.

vi. "GE Capital Is Split into Four Parts," *The Wall Street Journal*, July 29, 2002.

vii. The reorganization really didn't increase span of control to one to forty-nine, the number that would exist if an entire level was eliminated in the company doing the delayering. The manager's use of the large span in his example was meant to show an extreme case and his displeasure with it. The actual new span of control was more in the line of one to twenty, but the manager's concerns and perceived problems outlined in this chapter still were valid even at this smaller span ratio.

viii. "P&G Unit Bids Goodbye to Cincinnati, Hello to Asia," *The Wall Street Journal*, May 11, 2012; "P&G Beauty Chief Virginia Drosos to Step Down," *Fortune*, May 20, 2012.

ix. *Wall Street Journal*, Ibid.

x. *Wall Street Journal*, Ibid.

5

Managing Integration: Effective Coordination and Information Sharing

Introduction

Structure refers to the dissection or separation of the organization into operating units: divisions, functions, corporate center groups, and so on, as Chapter 4 just showed. This designation of form and function and the boxes and lines that depict it represent the anatomy of the organization, showing the separate parts and their positions, responsibilities, and relationships.

Creating a structure, however, is only half the story. For organizations to operate effectively, execute strategy, and achieve their goals, integration or coordination is also needed.

The work of diverse and separate organizational units must be coordinated to achieve desired results and a unity or consistency of effort. Structure shows the different parts of an organization and their separate capabilities. Integration or coordination of these parts or units and their capabilities is absolutely vital to the execution of a coherent, focused strategy.

To put it another way, structure paints a relatively static picture of the organization. To be sure, some dynamism and interaction are suggested by flat organizational structures or the "lines" that show relationships among units. One can envision the communication and interaction needed to get work done.

Still, the picture is incomplete. To make the organizational structure work to achieve strategic and short-term goals, we need to add "movement" to the static picture. Processes of integration and information sharing are needed to make the boxes and lines of organizational form come alive and accomplish something of value. Coordination processes are necessary for this vitality and interaction and, ultimately, the execution of strategy.

In the present model of strategy execution (see Chapter 2), strategy affects structure at both corporate and business levels. Structure contains two elements: organizational structure and structural integration.

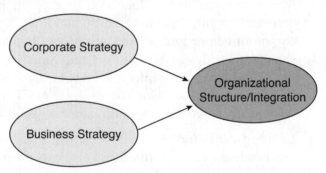

Structural integration provides the requisite coordination of structural parts and information flows among the parts. Creating the right structure is critical, as Chapter 4 stressed. But structural integration is also necessary for the success of execution. The obstacles to effective execution noted in the research surveys in Chapter 1 emphasized the negative consequences of poor integration and inadequate information sharing for execution success. Sharing information effectively and achieving coordination of important structural units are clearly vital to making strategy work.

THE IMPORTANCE OF INTEGRATION

To appreciate the importance of structural integration for execution and organizational performance, let's look at a few examples from some well-known companies.

BOEING

A number of years ago, Boeing merged its standalone space and military businesses.[i] The new business unit is called Integrated Defense Systems, with the emphasis on integration. Why the internal merger?

Boeing believes that bringing these diverse structural units together facilitates the sharing of expertise. Bringing different assets together helps achieve integration and makes it easier to develop coordinated programs and a focused strategy to give the company an advantage when competing for new military business. The goal is to bring different organizational pieces together so that customers don't have to deal with unconnected units. Customers desire integration, and the move is intended to provide it. That effective integration facilitates strategy execution is the operating assumption at Boeing.

HEWLETT-PACKARD

The same assumption regarding the importance of integration is supported by recent events at Hewlett-Packard.[ii] When Meg Whitman became CEO of HP In 2011, she saw a need to revamp the company's product line, especially the PC. Declining sales and chunky designs plagued over a dozen PC lines, and Whitman decided that something had to be done to make HP products look sleeker and more attractive, while also performing well.

Her intentions and actions became clear in 2012 when she reorganized the structure of the PC design team to achieve better integration and a more consistent look across products. HP computers, she found, were designed by different teams that had some independence, so the products looked different, with controls, buttons, and other elements varying from model to model. In response to this variability, Whitman centralized the design team around one key executive to achieve needed integration and come up with a common look and feel for PC products. The goal of the redesign clearly was one of coordination to create sleeker and more attractive products. Increased centralization and consolidation of team efforts were obviously aimed at improved integration and consistent results.

GENERAL MOTORS

In August, 2012, GM announced a reorganization that would centralize key functions, such as marketing, purchasing, and product development. The reported purpose, according to CEO Dan Akerson, is to attack the long-entrenched, decentralized regional authority that had created "fiefdoms" that militated against cooperation and a more nimble and efficient company.[iii] The logic is basic: Use centralized, global functions to improve communication and coordination across the splintered fiefdoms, as effective integration is the key to improved performance.

GM faces many hurdles in its announced plan, including a strong culture favoring decentralization that will likely resist the move to increased centralized control. Still, Akerson's implicit approach is clear in its logic: Effective integration is important to making strategy work. Knowledge sharing facilitates learning, efficient use of resources, and the execution of strategy. Results aren't always easy to attain, but the effort directed to increased integration can often pay dividends.

Whether GM can pull off its attempt to create a structure to facilitate the desired integration remains to be seen. The need for centralized control and integration may conflict with the long-used decentralization that allows better local market focus and quicker response to diverse customer needs, especially in the global arena. Centralization sometimes results in less nimble and slower response to regional needs, so the balance between centralized control to achieve integration and regional needs and adaptability will have to be handled carefully.

ROYAL DUTCH/SHELL GROUP

An interesting but unusual article in the March 12, 2004, *Wall Street Journal* proclaimed that Shell's structure was responsible, in part, for the company's overstatement of its reserves of oil and natural gas.[iv] How can structure "fuel" such overreporting of critical assets? How did the company misjudge its reserves so badly?

Shell's structure is based on a vast empire of independent operating units that, over time, found themselves under two different, but equal, holding companies. Both holding companies have separate boards and separate headquarters in The Hague and London, respectively. The companies and their units enjoy exceptional autonomy, including when estimating oil and gas reserves. They have the leeway to use their own geological methods and financial assumptions to project reserves, the cost of bringing them to market, and the profits that would accrue to the company. To project a unified position on oil and gas reserves and execute a focused, company-wide strategy at Shell, integration of the holding companies is absolutely essential. The problem is that integration apparently failed.

There is a committee of managing directors over the operating companies that was charged with the integration responsibility, but it didn't do its job. Outlandish forecasts of reserves and future profits from two holding companies competing with each other were never challenged, examined, and integrated. Aggressive reporting of separate, autonomous companies likely led to the exaggeration of oil and gas reserves. The failure of effective integration mechanisms allowed for mistakes. It also caused the company great embarrassment when it was forced to publicly announce the reduction of reserves on four separate occasions. Poor integration and an incentive system that rewarded overreporting of reserves were the major culprits in this unusual, but real, example. Effective integration is necessary for execution success, but it's not always easy to achieve.

LAW FIRMS AND INTEGRATION

In 2011, there were more than 60 mergers of domestic and international law firms, a 54 percent increase over 2010.[v] The promise of the mergers was larger firms that could increase efficiency and, with size and market power, weather the changing competitive forces in domestic and global markets. The mergers presented the companies with the wonderful opportunity to strengthen their brand and position themselves strategically in the market.

The increased size, power, and potential efficiency of the merged organizations were not enough to guarantee competitive success, however. What was also vitally needed was an emphasis on strategic communications and effective internal integration of the merged companies.[vi] A merger strategy places demands on the organizations joining forces to share knowledge, capabilities, and expertise, making integration plans or coordination processes vital to success. More will be said in Chapter 10 about integration in M&A activities. For present purposes, it's sufficient to note that, even in service organizations like large law firms, effective coordination across structural units is important for the successful execution of strategy.

These brief case examples indicate the importance of integration or coordination for making strategy work. The Wharton surveys also emphasized the contribution of integration to execution. Accordingly, the remainder of this chapter looks at the steps that must be taken to achieve effective coordination and information sharing. Its purpose is to consider those issues most central to execution.

What are the critical issues, topics, or steps managers must confront or take to achieve effective integration? What do the previous examples and the opinions of managers surveyed in this research tell us is necessary to help make strategy work? There are four such issues. Three are handled in this chapter and one in the following chapter. The issues are as follows:

1. How task interdependence affects the choice of methods to achieve effective integration or coordination.

2. How to foster information sharing, knowledge transfer, and communication among individuals or organizational units responsible for strategy execution.

3. How to clarify responsibility and accountability to ensure that the right tasks get done and are effectively integrated to execute a strategy.

4. How to develop incentives to support the dynamism and flexibility of an operating structure geared to effective integration.

The first issue, on interdependence, needs coverage because it defines the arena or setting within which integration or coordination takes place. The second and third issues are especially vital to making strategy work, according to managers in both the Wharton-Gartner and Wharton surveys. The fourth issue, dealing with incentives, is discussed in Chapter 6.

INTERDEPENDENCE AND COORDINATION METHODS

The first issue is one that I see popping up repeatedly in strategy-execution efforts. It is the definition of interdependence and the methods of coordination required by different kinds or types of interdependence.

This is an important issue. Managers use inappropriate or wrong integration methods, given the nature of the problem they are addressing. They "under-" or "overcoordinate," both of which can affect costs and execution results.

This issue may seem a bit "under the radar" to some, but mistakes here are real and affect performance. Managers may not use the word "interdependence" in their daily discussions, but they usually respond knowingly when I use the term and discuss its effects on coordination needs. So, let's see what's involved here and what affects execution.

TYPES OF INTERDEPENDENCE

Three important types of interdependence can be found in most organizations. I'll discuss them and add examples to show how they relate to organizational tasks and execution needs.[viii]

Pooled Interdependence

This represents a low level of interdependence and need for coordination. Consider the sales organization shown in Figure 5.1. It is a picture of pooled interdependence. Each district manager works in a separate geographical location. The territory could be part of a state, country, or global region, but each is relatively defined, self-contained, and independent. Each sales manager responds to the particular needs of his or her district. There is little need for active, ongoing communication or coordination across districts. This is a case in which "people work alone together." There is a low level of interdependence.

Figure 5.1   Example of Pooled Interdependence

Consider, too, the case of the prototypical conglomerate that, over time, expands and adds new companies to its portfolio. Though part of a "whole" (the corporate entity), each addition is relatively independent. Each does its own thing in different industries or markets. The subsidiaries and holdings of Berkshire Hathaway, Warren Buffett's noted conglomerate, numbered well over 100 in 2012 and clearly represent companies with low interdependence and little or no need to actively work together in a coordinated fashion. This is another case in which people or companies usually work alone together.

The word "together," of course, suggests some interdependence. If, for example, the bonus of each manager in Figure 5.1 is based, in part, on overall or corporate earnings as well as regional performance, interdependence is clear. One manager may perform outstandingly, but poor performance by the others obviously can detract from the high performer's rewards. Or in the case of the conglomerate, companies performing poorly can negatively affect cash flow and the resources available to the other companies.

Even pooled interdependence suggests, then, that people in an organization are in some ways in the same boat. It usually is a big boat, however, and there is ample room and distance between its passengers, necessitating little direct contact and coordination.

Sequential Interdependence

This is the next type, which is more complex than the pooled variety. Consider the case of vertical integration shown in Figure 5.2. In this example, the flow of work or materials is sequential. Work flows from "S," the supplier, to two end-user divisions. Semifinished goods also flow from End-User Division 1 to Division 2. The movement of product or service is unilateral or unidirectional.

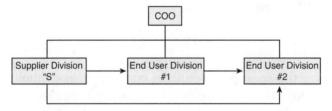

Figure 5.2   Vertical Integration: An Example of Sequential Interdependence

Comparing sequential to pooled interdependence reveals that the cost of failure is higher in the former. In a pooled case, each district office looks and acts like the following:

Each office does its own thing. A problem at A does not directly and immediately affect B or C. Routine communication and coordination across A, B, and C are not vital to ongoing operations.

Sequential interdependence is different and can be represented by the following illustration. Problems at A not only affect A, they also affect B and C directly and immediately. Poor materials from the supplier division have a direct, immediate impact on the end-user divisions shown in Figure 5.2.

In addition, communication and coordination laterally, across A, B, and C, clearly are essential to ensuring smooth flows of work. Managers in all three locations have something at stake under sequential interdependence. The operation of the overall system defined by the sequential chain is vital to each individually. So, communication and coordination laterally affect both the overall system of vertical integration and the parts of that system at work.

The greater complexity of sequential interdependence demands that this form be managed differently than the pooled variety. Methods of coordination and control are different. These differences in method are spelled out later. First, however, let's consider a third type of interdependence.

Reciprocal Interdependence

This is the most complex form and the most difficult to manage. Consider the representation in Figure 5.3. In this case, people in each function deal with people in all the other functions. A, a function, both affects and is affected by B, C, D, and E, other functions and a customer. One function can change the rules or affect much of what is done by the others at virtually any time.

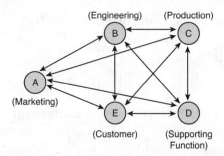

Figure 5.3 A Picture of Reciprocal Interdependence (New Product Development Team)

Coordination and control under reciprocal interdependence are difficult because many things are going on simultaneously. Planning is difficult because members of the network can change their positions or even veto the decisions of others without warning.

Think, for a moment, about the activities of a new product development team (see Figure 5.3). Think of how product development would look if it were approached in a sequential fashion. Someone from marketing, A, contacts a potential customer, E, and asks what she would like. The marketing manager brings the information to engineering, B, where product design must occur. Engineering's response is, "Sorry, there's no way we can design that." Marketing goes back to the customer and asks what else she would take. When the new request is brought to engineering, the response now is, "You must be kidding!"

By now, the marketing manager is throwing up his hands in frustration. "What can you design?" he finally demands from engineering. But when he brings what's possible to the potential customer, she is not at all interested. Back to the drawing board. And so on—back and forth.

At last, marketing, engineering, and the customer agree on a viable product. They finally can bring the specifications and the product requirements to production or another supporting function. Much to their chagrin, however, the production manager says, "Sorry, there's no way I can make something like this. With the pressure on me for volume and low-cost production, this product would kill me. Maybe next time."

Obviously, the production manager has affected engineering, marketing, and the customer. He has negated much of their effort. He is able to veto what others have spent a great deal of time pursuing. Assuming a sequential approach when reciprocal interdependence is the rule can lead to problems, as the new product development case just showed.

The reciprocal case is difficult. Under this form of interdependence, all are equals in the decision process, and any player can affect all the others. Each player is necessary to the solution of a problem, but no one player or subset of players is sufficient. High levels of cooperation and coordination are needed to make things work. Effective coordination is vital to strategy execution.

COORDINATION PROCESSES AND METHODS

How does the type of interdependence affect the methods or processes used for coordination or integration? Table 5.1 presents some of these methods. The table shows, first, that managing pooled interdependence is relatively easy. Standard operating procedures (SOPs) or rules govern all the independent individuals equally. (All district managers in Figure 5.1 report sales in the same way; all submit quarterly plans.) When problems or unusual cases pop up, the role of hierarchy becomes important—resolving disputes, handling exceptions, and so on. People work alone together but in the same or consistent ways.

Table 5.1 Types of Interdependence and Methods of Achieving Effective Coordination or Integration

Type of Interdependence	Level of Coordination Required	Methods of Achieving Coordination or Integration
Pooled	Low	Rules/SOPs/hierarchy
Sequential	High	Coordination by plan; managing the flow of work and information
		Scheduling/just-in-time inventory controls
		"Transfer" activities—e.g., transfer pricing, terms to facilitate "passing of the baton"
		Having "linking" or transition managers to facilitate the flows of work and information
		Appropriate incentives to motivate the effective flow of work and information
Reciprocal	Very high	Coordination by "mutual adjustment"
		Face-to-face integration or "managing by living together"
		Removing administrative and geographical barriers to face-to-face interaction
		Fostering communication, processes of agreement, and trust
		Appropriate incentives to work together and make joint decisions

Pooled interdependence does not generate the need for ongoing, active coordination. The SOPs used for control and coordination are consistent for all units, but few, if any, deal with integration across units. Similarly, reliance on hierarchy stresses mainly vertical communication, not lateral forms.

The task confronting managers under pooled interdependence is twofold: (a) ensuring that the SOPs, rules, or routines used for control are appropriate and consistent across all units, and (b) maintaining open communication channels vertically so that exceptions or problems can move up the hierarchy and be handled quickly and effectively. These tasks are basic and common to all organizations, but managers must monitor them carefully to ensure that they are functioning as designed.

Sequential interdependence, as Table 5.1 suggests, raises the cost of sound management. Managing cooperation is more complex, and more time and resources must be devoted to the task. SOPs and hierarchy still play a role, but other, more complex issues surface when focusing on coordination across the value chain, as in the case of vertical integration. Planning and scheduling are critical to smooth, predictable flows of work and materials. Poor planning or scheduling can lead to task interruptions and conflicts, which clearly detract from coordination, communication, and results.

Managing transactions and lateral transitions of work from unit to unit is central to sequential interdependence. Tasks and activities within units are important, but so are the linkages between adjoining work groups. Transfer pricing in the vertical integration example, for instance, is vital to effective linkages. Inappropriate pricing affects not only workflow but perceptions and cooperation as well.

Similarly, the quality of the products, services, or information being transferred affects perceptions and the viability of coordination. Consider the following comments made by a manager in a vertically integrated company:

> *I'm getting gouged price-wise by my own supplier, which happens to be a sister division in the same company. Nice, isn't it? He sells the good stuff on the outside and sends me the rest, the junk. Why do I have to deal with this?*

The same issue of quality holds for the transfer of information needed to support a line organization or facilitate decision-making. Poor information or information sharing affects cooperation, coordination, and results.

The managerial task when strategy creates sequential interdependence is primarily one of ensuring the smooth flow of transactions and information laterally across the value chain, as Table 5.1 shows. The focus must be on linking mechanisms—including people—to act as integrators and facilitate the movement of work and information from one unit to the next in the sequential chain. Appropriate incentives must also be developed to ensure that one division is not motivated to "sell the junk" to a sister division while selling the "good stuff" on the outside.

With reciprocal interdependence, coordination and control are extremely difficult to manage. Under this type, the other forms of interdependence also exist, so many of the previously identified problems are again important. But there are also new obstacles, as Table 5.1 shows, along with new methods of achieving coordination or integration.

The need for coordination and information sharing is very high, as all the members in the network affect and are affected by all the other members. All have something at stake. One person under reciprocal interdependence can negate the work of others, even after significant amounts of time and effort have been expended.

Because of the impact of any one member, coordination greatly relies on face-to-face interaction. Coordination and control are by "mutual adjustment" or, as a manager once expressed it to me, "managing by living together."

In the case of the new product development team introduced earlier, problem definition and solution ideally should be done together, with all team members, even customers, participating simultaneously. All individuals should be "locked up together," with no one leaving until agreement is reached on critical aspects of the new product. Working alone together clearly is ruled out in this case.

But managing by living together is not always easy. Key team players involved in complex tasks related to strategy execution might be spread out geographically or "administratively." They might be all over the company, country, or world, in different functions or divisions, and even at different hierarchical levels. Getting them together and ensuring communication, agreement, and cooperation can be difficult.

Still, reciprocal interdependence demands that the attempt be made. Getting people together via telecommunications technologies (such as teleconferences and interactive video telecommunication sessions) is possible, of course, given advances in technological capabilities. But managers tell me that this alone is not sufficient. They tell me that, under reciprocal interdependence, individuals must meet occasionally face to face. While expensive, managers say that getting commitment to courses of action needed to make strategy work absolutely demands face-to-face interaction. As one vice president of marketing and product development in a recent Wharton executive program stated:

> *When I need the support of engineering or production, and that support is vital to my plan's success, I want to look directly into the eyes of my colleagues when I ask for help. I'll know if they're serious or lying. I'll see whether their promised support is for real or if they're BSing me or putting me off. Believe me, I'll know.*

Another example of the need for face-to-face interaction comes from Jeffrey Immelt, GE's chairman and CEO. Immelt spends a great deal of time on the road. Meeting with GE managers, customers, and shareholders face to face, he has stated that "seeing people in person is a big part of how you drive any change process." [viii] New strategies, operating plans, and methods of coordination take on new and important meaning when discussed face to face.

These individuals' stance on face-to-face interaction is certainly clear. It also has a ring of logic and practicality to it that can't easily be denied. Enough managers I've known agree with these statements that I feel there must be some truth to them. Face-to-face interaction can add immensely to the effectiveness of coordination and management of change, especially when strategy results in reciprocal interdependence.

Finally, the role of incentives is important. The managerial task is to make sure that the individuals or units bound together under reciprocal interdependence are motivated to work together. Team-based incentives may be needed to prevent individuals from going off and doing their own thing and hurting group performance. The need for joint decisions demands this focus on appropriate, team-performance-based incentives. (Incentives are discussed further in Chapter 6.)

THE GE "WORK OUT"

Does all this make sense? Should managers worry about defining interdependence before designing coordination or integration mechanisms? I think so, obviously. But let me focus on GE for a while and use the well-known example of Jack Welch's "Work Out" to bolster and support my claims. "Work Out" was based on a simple concept—generate ideas about how to improve company performance and then execute those ideas—but it had far-reaching positive results.

I spent a significant amount of time as a "Work Out" consultant for GE's Aerospace Division before it was sold. I enjoyed my "Work Out" experience and felt it was tremendously effective in solving problems and furthering GE's goals. I felt that it worked extremely well as a vehicle to capture ideas for improvement from employees and for implementing or executing those ideas. "Work Out" worked. Why?

A Philosophy of Challenge and Stretch

Welch was always looking for something new to challenge employees. He hated complacency and sitting on one's laurels. He wanted his managers to focus on "stretch" objectives—higher-level goals that forced people to reach higher and higher to achieve them. "Work Out" helped to create this challenge and provide the right incentives for action.

A "Learning Culture"

This, too, was part of Welch's philosophy. He liked to say that "the operative assumption was that someone, somewhere, had a better idea. By sharing knowledge, GE businesses would gain a competitive edge," which would result in better performance.[ix] "Work Out" was premised on this learning culture, based on good ideas and the sharing of important knowledge throughout the company.

The Structure and Process of "Work Out"

Besides the sizable impact of Welch's philosophy, there was the structure and process of "Work Out" itself. Consistent with the present argument, "Work Out" was treated as a case of reciprocal interdependence.

Most "Work Outs" focused on complex problems. To define and solve them, it was necessary to bring together managers and technical people from different functions or operating groups within the Aerospace Division. All these functions or groups were necessary for problem definition and solution. No function or group alone was sufficient to solve the problem. Cooperation and coordination were necessary.

The process of running a "Work Out" demanded that all individuals necessary for problem definition and solution be brought together. "Management by living together" was the norm, as were face-to-face discussions and interactions. Managers couldn't leave or run away when things got hot and disagreements exploded. They had to stay, toe-to-toe and face-to-face, and confront the issues, no matter how stressful or volatile the situation.

"Management by living together" also demanded that no one could leave until an agreement was reached on problem definition and solution. Invariably, an action plan was created, indicating objectives, timelines, and responsibilities for action-plan items. Follow-ups, including additional "Work Out" sessions, ensured that things were accomplished as planned. People were held accountable for defined tasks and simply couldn't shirk their obligations defined by the process.

In essence, "Work Out" was run as an example of decision-making characterized by reciprocal interdependence. The methods of achieving integration or coordination were consistent with this form of interdependence and no doubt contributed to its success. In addition to Welch's philosophy and GE culture, the processes and methods of defining interdependence and coordination needs were important to "Work Out"'s contributions to problem definition and solution and to making strategy work.

An Analytical Process

In sum, an important aspect of integration is the definition and consideration of interdependence. Looking at the issues we've talked about in the last three chapters would suggest the following analytical process:

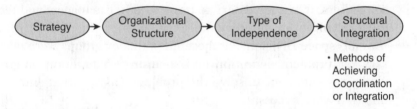

What this shows is that strategy affects structure, which defines interdependence and the units, functions, or people who must work together. Structure and the interdependence defined by it and strategy then determine the methods of coordination or integration necessary to get work done. This figure, in effect, shows what's necessary to execute the strategy shown in the first part of the preceding flow or process diagram.

The same steps and analyses can be undertaken by all managers interested in strategy execution or making strategy work. At the business level, managers first define a clear, focused strategy (see Chapter 3). They then should examine organizational structure, given the demands of strategy (see Chapter 4). Finally, they should define the interdependence created by strategy and structure and develop methods of coordination consistent with the form or type of interdependence noted in this chapter.

Following these prescriptions forces managers to choose appropriate coordination methods. It helps avoid problems of "undercoordination" by matching coordination methods with the task at hand. It also helps avoid problems of "overcoordination," such as setting up committees and other burdensome, time-consuming tasks when they're not needed. Following the preceding prescriptions results in great strides toward making strategy work.

FACILITATING INFORMATION SHARING, KNOWLEDGE TRANSFER, AND COMMUNICATION

The second major topic of this chapter is also an important one. Poor or inadequate information sharing between individuals or business units responsible for strategy execution was rated as one of the largest obstacles to execution by managers responding to surveys in the present research. The data collected from managers involved in execution and my own personal experiences add to these opinions: Information sharing, knowledge transfer, and the communication that supports them are vital to making strategy work.

The obvious next question deals with what facilitates or impedes the information sharing, knowledge transfer, and communication necessary for the effective execution of strategy. What affects the "stickiness" of information flows between or among organizational units? To frame the relevant issues, let's begin with a quick look at two companies, McKinsey and Citibank.

CREATING, USING, AND SHARING KNOWLEDGE

McKinsey and Co.

Everyone knows McKinsey and its reputation in consulting. Perhaps fewer people realize the challenges it faces in the creation, dissemination, and use of knowledge.

It is a large company with offices around the world housing thousands of consultants and staff. Organizational size contributes to the complexity of doing business. It also exacerbates the difficulty of the company's two primary tasks: creating and using knowledge.

As a consulting company, McKinsey must stay on top of things. It must create specialized knowledge that keeps it on the leading edge. As a professional service organization, the knowledge is predominantly in its databases and, more importantly, in the minds of its human resources—its specialists and consultants. Creation of centers of competence and development of "T-shaped" consultants with both broad, general knowledge and deep, industry-specific competence has helped the company develop the expertise and knowledge needed to prosper in an increasingly competitive industry.

But creating knowledge is only half the battle. McKinsey must also focus on using the knowledge across its client base and geographical reach. It must be able to share new information to leverage its learning and avoid costly duplications in knowledge creation. Consultants who deal with client and industry problems in North America need to disseminate their knowledge and insights to colleagues in South America or Europe. "Snowball making" is important, but "snowball throwing," with its emphasis on sharing and using information to service clients and make money, is even more important.

McKinsey uses a number of methods, tools, and processes to integrate and use knowledge. Its "Yellow Pages" lists the firm's experts and areas of knowledge to facilitate personal contacts among its consultants. Common databases of core knowledge are made available through an effective IT system. Practice coordinators are used to facilitate access to information and to coordinate the use of expertise throughout the company. Client service teams focus on the integration of knowledge and its application to clients over the longer term, creating a culture with clients' needs at its core. Efforts are made to facilitate consultants talking to other consultants, specialists talking to generalists, and those with technology-based skills (such as IT) talking with individuals pursuing the "art" or "craft" of getting close to customers.

Before extracting some general principles that can help all organizations share information and knowledge, let's briefly look at the case of Citibank.

Citibank

Like McKinsey, Citibank is a large company with global presence. On the institutional side, for example, it deals with and services large multinational corporations (MNCs) worldwide. It is concerned with "following" MNCs across countries or geographical regions to provide an integrated set of products or services. In so doing, it is deeply concerned with the integration of skills and capabilities worldwide and the sharing of information or knowledge across geographical boundaries.

Of course, the company must simultaneously be aware of regional or local impacts or constraints on its global thrust. Differences in banking regulations, culture, and standard operating procedures by country or region exist, and their impact on banking practices must be recognized. To execute strategy worldwide, both global and local views must be included simultaneously. Following and servicing MNCs effectively requires an understanding of their global needs, but it also requires recognition of local or regional constraints on the methods or services employed to meet those needs.

To achieve the necessary coordination and knowledge sharing and give sufficient attention to local and global needs, Citibank uses a number of methods or approaches. Account manager types are employed to focus on large, important MNCs and take care of their business needs worldwide. These client managers disseminate knowledge about MNCs and coordinate with other managers in different parts of the world. Regional or country managers disseminate information about how to carry on business locally within a country or region. A matrix organization couples managers with global and local perspectives and forces them to confront problems and integrate global business needs with local or regional concerns. Global information systems and databases exist, allowing individuals to tap into a wealth of client or regional information.

These descriptions of McKinsey and Citibank of necessity are brief. Yet they provide insight into how organizations can facilitate information sharing, knowledge transfer, and communication across organizational or subunit boundaries when trying to make strategy work.

METHODS, TOOLS, OR PROCESSES FOR INFORMATION SHARING

The preceding examples suggest a number of formal methods that organizations can use to aid information sharing and knowledge transfer. These formal approaches have received attention in the management literature, so I'll only handle them briefly. There also are informal methods of information sharing. These are also very important, but less attention has been paid to them, so I'll go into more detail on this topic in the next section.

IT Systems/Databases

Creating databases and IT systems to access the data clearly can aid information sharing. The McKinsey databases of core knowledge with broad IT support represent one example. For years, ABB has relied on ABACUS, its information system, to keep top managers apprised of happenings in the businesses or geographical regions. Citibank has its IT systems and databases on its largest multinational customers. IBM deploys its IT expertise to achieve savings through the transformation of business processes and the optimization of manufacturing operations. A host of other companies have done similar things.

Before entering the academic world, I worked for Ford Motor Company in a number of capacities, including as a district field manager. I traveled a region and interacted frequently with dealers. At my disposal was a form, FD 1984 (I loved the symbolism!), which was remarkable. On one page, a wealth of information about a dealer was summarized, including benchmark comparisons to other dealers. Big Brother was clearly watching, and the form made that oversight a manageable task. I'm sure that better dealer summaries or databases exist today. Still, at the time, the FD 1984 was a helpful tool that fostered the sharing of important information and highlighted potential problems for remedial action.

Formal Roles and Jobs

Companies hire and train people to coordinate work and communicate across subunits. Project-management organizations, for example, manage and move projects or products. Project managers may or may not have authority over functional and other personnel who work on their projects. They usually, however, have responsibility to coordinate the contributions of diverse functional groups and manage information flows among contributing personnel. They often act as liaisons, linking diverse groups within the organization. McKinsey, Citibank, Boeing, Microsoft, and other companies routinely use product or project managers to achieve effective coordination. The importance of project management as a tool for managing coordination and knowledge transfer is reflected in the fact that a chapter on the topic has been added to this book (Chapter 13).

Integrating roles are also used to facilitate coordination and information sharing. Insurance companies use customer service personnel to "walk" applications through various functions (underwriting, credit) and keep customers informed about the progress of their applications. The position of "Intelligence Czar" in Washington, D.C. created an integrating role to link and coordinate activities of the many diverse groups currently responsible for intelligence.

In some companies, formal teams or committees are created to facilitate coordination, communication, and information flows. Quality assurance groups, "six sigma" teams, or customer service teams often share this status as integrating units. Customer service teams, for example, usually have members from different functions who bring their points of view and expertise to serving customers. They "own the customer" is a typical beginning to a description of what the team does. Customer service is the higher-level goal, and the team focuses on the process of integrating work across functions or departments to achieve it. The customer service teams at McKinsey are good examples of these formal integrating mechanisms.

Matrix Structures

A host of organizations I've dealt with have some form of matrix structure. In fact, most large companies, especially global players such as Citibank, Boeing, ABB, Booz Allen, and others pursuing coordinated global strategies, rely on this form of structure somewhere for information processing and coordination. In addition to the need for knowledge sharing and integration, use of a matrix is also driven by a scarcity of critical human resources (e. g., few "rocket scientists" whose expertise is needed across sophisticated products like satellites), as well as a need for a dual, simultaneous focus (e. g., global business and country). The simplest way to describe the integrative and information-processing workings of a matrix is to use the "matrix diamond," shown in Figure 5.4.[x] In a global matrix, for example, business managers push products worldwide, while geographical managers make decisions about the best products and use of investment funds within their country or region. Often the two disagree or have different goals or perceptions of how to run a business or a country. Someone must help them reach agreement to allow for the execution of global strategies. This individual must also coordinate valuable information between businesses and regions.

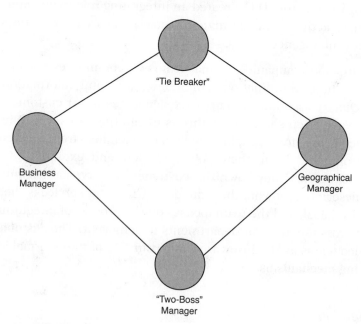

Figure 5.4 The "Matrix Diamond"

Who does this integration and consensus building? The "two-boss" manager is in this dynamic and sometimes stressful position and is absolutely vital to the matrix functioning effectively. This individual must integrate diverse, even conflicting, views. He or she must understand the business manager's problems as well as those within the bailiwick of the country or functional manager. While the job of the two-boss manager was once described to me as "magic worker," a more formal description would simply be integrator and information processor.

If the two-boss manager cannot reduce the conflicts or cannot solve problems to everyone's mutual liking and understanding, the top manager or the "tie breaker" in the matrix diamond steps in, breaks the impasse, and allows work to progress.

The matrix is obviously a complex operating structure. Its goal is lateral communication and coordination, with the co-located two-boss manager integrating business and geographical or business and functional views. It seemingly violates some age-old management principles, such as unity of command, but it does work well, especially when executing strategies in the global arena. More is said about the utility of the matrix organization in a newly added chapter on global strategy (Chapter 11).

INFORMAL FORCES AND INFORMATION SHARING

Everyone knows something about formal methods of fostering communication and coordination such as those just discussed. Yet managers in our surveys still listed poor information sharing as a huge problem when executing strategy. Why?

Because something else must be happening to affect or negate the formal methods. Because knowing what the methods are (for example, a matrix) and knowing how to make them work are two separate issues. Because managers may or may not be motivated to share information and make strategy work.

In my experiences with strategy execution, I have found that managers know the terminology of information sharing and coordination. Everyone has IT systems and formal databases. Everyone knows what an integrator does. Many managers tell me constantly that their companies have been "matricized" in some way.

Yet problems with information processing and knowledge sharing persist. This is so because there also are informal forces at work that affect the outcomes. Let me share with you what some of these forces or issues are.

Poor Informal Contact

The simplest and most common form of information sharing is probably informal contact, regardless of the formal methods employed. People talk to people to seek information and solve problems. A manufacturing manager in New York or Detroit calls or sends a fax to a counterpart in Tokyo, Mexico City, Sao Paulo, or San Francisco. Delivery dates or scheduling problems are discussed and ironed out. A consultant in Germany calls a colleague in Paris to seek help with a client's particularly bothersome problem. A physician doing research in a major pharmaceutical company in Pennsylvania calls an expert in statistics in Germany to help with an important research question. Informal, direct contact between or among managers is arguably the most common form of everyday communication and coordination. Yet even this simple tactic cannot work without same basic underlying prerequisites for success.

Knowing whom to contact, for example, is basic yet critical. Knowing the people, positions, and responsibilities in other locations is necessary for informal contact to work. This seems basic, and yet consider the following comment from a manager in a Wharton executive program:

> *I really wanted to help (a client company) get a nice loan package for his operations in Brazil. But I must admit I didn't know the person who handles this type of loan there, so I mailed the materials I had to the "Loan Manager" in Sao Paulo. I really don't even know if anyone got the papers or helped the customer.*

One remedy is obvious: Publish a directory listing key personnel in different geographical locations, showing their responsibilities and areas of expertise, a la McKinsey.

Go Direct—Not Through Channels

People who can solve problems without getting approvals galore or going through their bosses, their bosses' bosses, and so on, to contact people directly in other offices or parts of the world usually can make informal contact work effectively as a communication and coordination technique. This represents one of the key ideas underlying flat organizations: People can focus directly on a problem without waiting for hierarchical approval. In contrast, the delay of requests as people go through "channels" or undergo numerous checks and approvals often destroys or detracts from the speed and spontaneity of informal, personal contacts.

Create a "Common Language"

As odd as this may sound, people in the same organization may not be on the same page when sharing information or communicating on important issues dealing with strategy execution. They bring different perspectives, technical capabilities, definitions of key terms, or cultural biases that detract from their ability to see and understand divergent points of view. Selective perceptions caused by functional myopia and regional or global differences get in the way of shared ideas and common understanding.

When executing strategy, it is absolutely essential that the strategy be clear, focused, and translated logically into short-term objectives or metrics (see Chapter 3). It is vital, too, that these objectives and measurements be defined consistently to avoid problems of different, competing views of execution outcomes.

Consider a case in which sales performance is measured by revenue, a top-line number, but a function such as manufacturing or an entire division is measured on a bottom-line figure, revenues minus costs. Add to the mix marketing, which is evaluated in part on customer satisfaction. In this case, different metrics almost guarantee different views of strategy execution and reliance on competing performance measures. Sales focuses on volume. It is accused routinely of selling anything and making deals with little concern for costs or the bottom line. Production feels that sales is "giving the shop away." Marketing cares about customers and feels that no one else gives a hoot. Conflicts between or among the functions are common. The division manager sees the conflicts as detracting from divisional performance.

The solution? Focus on common, consistent measures of performance. Define or operationalize the measures carefully. Develop some shared objectives. Place constraints on unilateral, independent measures of performance. Make sales responsible for margins, not just volume. Decide whether costs or customer satisfaction is the driving force behind execution decisions. Determine how and when the functions should cooperate to achieve important results and then hold them accountable. This is not a case where people should be working alone together.

The Power Structure and Culture

Methods of information sharing and coordination are often affected by the power or influence structure of the organization as well as its culture. These factors affect what information is transmitted. They affect who is listened to and who isn't. They affect the relative weight attached to coordination attempts and which transfer of "facts" is believed or discarded.

Power and culture are extremely important to many aspects of execution. Accordingly, they receive additional attention in two later chapters (Chapter 8 and Chapter 9).

ADDITIONAL INFORMAL FACTORS AFFECTING INFORMATION FLOW AND KNOWLEDGE TRANSFER

Let me focus on some additional factors that affect information sharing and knowledge transfer. A Wharton colleague once published an insightful paper about these factors.[xi] I've built upon his work in my own experiences with strategy execution and can share some of my observations here.

Table 5.2 lists factors that affect information sharing and knowledge transfer. These factors reflect aspects of information and organizations, but they also indicate the effects of individuals' motivations on information sharing and knowledge transfer. Some of the factors or issues are new, others touch on things already stated or implied, but all are important, ultimately, to the information sharing and coordination needed to make strategy work.

Table 5.2　Factors Affecting Information Sharing and Knowledge Transfer

---

- Characteristics of the knowledge being transferred:
  - Codified vs. tacit knowledge
  - Proven record of usefulness
- Characteristics of the source of knowledge:
  - Expertise and trustworthiness of source
  - Reliability of source
  - Perceived motivation of source:
- Characteristics of the recipient of knowledge:
  - Lack of motivation (NIH)
  - Lack of absorptive capacity (ability to search for, receive, and evaluate new knowledge depends on the store of existing knowledge)
  - Retentive capacity (ability to use, institutionalize received knowledge):
- Characteristics of the context:
  - Organizational structure
  - Operating structure (existence of coordinative/integrative mechanisms)
  - Incentives
  - Culture

Characteristics of the Knowledge Itself

Codified knowledge can be transferred more easily than tacit knowledge. Writing or following an instruction booklet on "how to assemble a bicycle" is straightforward. "Take part A, insert into part B, and place the entire part into the frame C at location D," and so on. The booklet conveys codified, structured knowledge.

Next, write a set of instructions on "how to ride a bicycle." "First, get on the bike and ride. If you fail, repeat step one."

What else can you say? The knowledge here is "tacit," harder to describe and communicate. It is far less structured than telling people how to put the bike together. Communication in the tacit-knowledge case demands "feel," watching others, practicing, and learning from observing experts. New consultants, for example, learn from experienced consultants. They act as "apprentices" and absorb knowledge over time. They work with their more senior colleagues to learn the "art" of the consulting relationship. Conveyance of tacit knowledge usually requires a hands-on, inter-active approach to information sharing.

Strategy execution and learning are difficult in some organizations because of tacit knowledge. R&D organizations, professional departments or firms (such as legal departments, law firms), con-sulting groups, sales or marketing units, and so on must purpose-ly develop methods or processes to transfer tacit knowledge. This must be taken into account when executing strategy. Teaching consulting skills or how to close a deal often requires observation and hands-on interaction over time. Knowing how to handle group interactions and discussions for new product development usually takes practice and observation of experienced managers at work.

Organizations with large amounts of tacit knowledge to share must be willing to invest in staff and allow the time for interaction, dis-cussion, and emulation that is needed to transfer information effectively. R&D organizations and professional departments cannot be rushed in their attempts to share and use important knowledge.

Characteristics of the Source of Information

Is the source trustworthy, reliable? Have I benefited from using this source previously? What is the motivation of the source? Is there a hidden agenda involved? Am I becoming too dependent on a source, thereby increasing its influence over me?

These are a few questions that often arise when considering the source of information. The answers obviously will affect information sharing and knowledge transfer. Answers to the questions usually reflect previous experiences or encounters with different sources of information. They also could reflect the company's culture.

I once knew a company in which no one trusted anything that marketing had to say. The function was seen as always furthering its own agenda, even at high cost to other functions or organizational subunits. A culture of distrust marked the company, affecting information flow and acceptance.

This distrust led to even more serious execution problems. Marketing bore responsibility for new product development, including significant modifications to existing products. Marketing had to "sell" production on the new products so that production could develop, test, and modify them. But production incurred a large cost to work on new products: Production lines had to be shut down and the flow of work altered. Efficiency was injured because of the discontinuous production, and prototypes had to be produced and tested, disrupting normal operations.

To get production's cooperation, marketing felt it had to "exaggerate" the benefits of the new product. In fact, it often lied about the product's profit potential or the efficiency benefits that ultimately would accrue to production. Marketing promised the world, if only production would help with such an important task.

When the promises proved to be false and production saw the deviousness behind marketing's hype and exaggeration, the distrust and conflict grew even greater. Marketing as a source of information or knowledge was discredited further. Production saw marketing as untrustworthy and unreliable. Most importantly, the execution of product development strategies received almost irreparable damage, representing a major blow to the company's future competitive position.

The perceived motivation, trustworthiness, and reliability of the source are at question here. So, how does an organization affect this situation? By creating and using effective incentives and controls. Setting up the right objectives for cooperation and communication, and then rewarding the appropriate behavior, helps ensure that the sources providing information are doing the right things for knowledge transfer. This example highlights the importance of effective incentives, a topic covered in detail in the next chapter.

The company should also define product development as a case of reciprocal interdependence, as previously discussed. This would force marketing and production to work together, jointly develop the rules and constraints of new product development, and share the rewards and costs of these innovative ventures.

The point is that marketing as a source of knowledge was suspect at best. Something had to be done to avoid permanent damage to the execution of product development strategies and to avoid competitive disaster in the marketplace.

Characteristics of the Recipient

What is the motivation of the recipient? I have seen managers accused of NIH—rejecting information because it's "not invented here." Clearly, the potential recipients don't trust the source, or they feel that their own way of doing things is better. Such rejection, of course, can be costly, leading to duplication and even less fruitful or effective work. What's needed again are incentives to get the groups working together for a common goal. If the recipients and senders of knowledge have something in common or something important at stake, the occurrence of NIH-related problems will diminish.

The "absorptive capacity" of an organization has a major impact on knowledge transfer.[xii] Absorptive capacity (AC) affects the ability of an organization to recognize new information (such as new science, new technologies), assimilate it, and apply it in some way to achieve organizational goals. AC is the result of learning. The ability to recognize and use new knowledge varies as a function of the accumulated base of existing knowledge in an organization. AC, that is, implies a critical mass of knowledge or investment in knowledge-based capabilities (such as R&D, scientists, engineers, IT systems) before new knowledge can be recognized and used to foster and support strategy. Failure to invest in and accumulate AC results in an inability to see, understand, or use new outside knowledge.

Consider a firm without this accumulated base of expertise. Assume next that another firm develops a new technology of some sort. Can the first firm import the new technology, be "second in" with its use, and use it to achieve competitive advantage? Can it import the new ideas and technology for new products or better-performing old products? Can it follow its competitor's lead, imitate the new technology, and remain competitive in the industry?

Without AC, the firm cannot judge the value or potential uses of the new technology. It doesn't have the scientists or engineers who can do an effective technological evaluation. Consequently, it doesn't act. It falls behind other firms with the requisite AC and loses its ability to execute needed new strategies in its industry. Not only can't a firm without AC innovate or be a first mover, it cannot even be an effective follower. It certainly will lose any competitive advantage it once enjoyed.

The solution is clear: A firm must invest in AC if it wants to stay abreast of technological trends or disruptions, adapt successfully, innovate, and continue making strategy work.

Different firms in different industries face different demands on developing AC (for example, high tech vs. low tech), but the basic principle holds for all organizations. Investment in knowledge and accumulation of a critical mass of information are vital to organizational innovation and adaptation. Without this critical mass of accumulated knowledge and capabilities, an organization cannot recognize, understand, or use new, state-of-the-art breakthroughs. It can't easily adapt or change and execute new strategies.

Characteristics of the Context

The context includes organizational structure, whose impact on knowledge transfer has been suggested in Chapter 4 and noted explicitly in this chapter. It simply is important to set up the IT systems and other formal mechanisms for knowledge transfer and information sharing. It's important to use integrators, teams, or matrix structures to achieve effective coordination and communication laterally, across organizational functions and other operating units.

It's also important to know how to make these elements of operating structure work. It's one thing to set up teams or matrix structures for coordination and information sharing. Making them work is often quite another issue. Problems here usually result from one of two sources: (a) technical problems in implementing the operating structure, or (b) problems with incentives, controls, and culture.

As an example of technical problems, consider once more the matrix structure and, specifically, the matrix diamond of Figure 5.4. A common problem with a matrix is not having a "tie breaker," the top role in the matrix. Consequently, conflicts between division and country managers or business and functional managers are not handled or solved immediately. Work comes to a virtual standstill as information moves slowly up two hierarchies. Information sharing suffers immensely. The matrix structure is accused of all sorts of shortcomings. The truth, however, is that it was set up incorrectly. Poor execution guaranteed failure. Technical issues affected performance and knowledge transfer.

The solution? Make sure that a tie-breaker or tie-breaking mechanisms are set up formally when employing the matrix. Addressing this technicality saves the organization a host of operating problems as it attempts to use and share information needed for strategy execution.

The second set of problems—those due to culture or poor incentives and controls—is also important to information sharing and knowledge transfer. Culture, for example, defines a host of things: how a company operates, what it values, how open or "closed" managers are when sharing information, and what's important for individual recognition. Factors such as these clearly can affect the knowledge transfer needed to achieve coordination and execute strategy effectively. A culture of cooperation based on a common, perceived mission will affect execution positively, whereas a culture marked by error avoidance and the need to blame others for poor results clearly will have negative effects on execution outcomes. Again, these aspects of organizational culture or context are discussed in Chapter 8 because of their significance for making strategy work.

Similarly, the incentives and controls employed are important factors affecting information sharing and knowledge transfer. Hoping for cooperation and coordination, but rewarding excessive and inappropriate competition, can only injure information sharing and, ultimately, execution efforts. Again, because of the importance of incentives and controls, Chapter 6 deals with the topic in detail.

This section of the chapter focused on information sharing and knowledge transfer, supporting and reinforcing the previous discussion of interdependence and coordination methods. Communication and information sharing are vital to making strategy work, as managers indicated emphatically by their responses to the Wharton surveys on strategy execution. The various factors discussed in this section affect the "stickiness" of information flows and the usefulness of information to the execution of strategy.

CLARIFYING RESPONSIBILITY AND ACCOUNTABILITY

The third aspect of structural integration, clarifying responsibility and accountability, is also vital to making strategy work.

In the preceding discussions of interdependence, coordination, information sharing, and knowledge transfer, there was a basic but critical assumption that all responsibilities and accountabilities are clear. The presumption was that all individuals know what their roles or jobs are. Managers know with whom they must interact, when, and why, and are fully cognizant of others' tasks or duties.

In reality, this clarity of roles is not always the case. Job-related responsibilities are not always clear, and authority is not always unambiguous. Responsibility and accountability often are blurred when people from different functions or divisions come together, often from different hierarchical levels in the organization. This is especially true in matrix-like structures where both lateral and hierarchical influences can easily cloud the responsibility and accountability picture.

Confusion often results from multiple points of responsibility or when many managers share responsibility. I recall a case at GM when, having learned of some problems with truck transaxels, I asked who was responsible for the quality of the component. I was told, "Around here, we're all responsible for quality. We all worry about it." A further check indeed revealed a number of groups or functions in different organizations and at different hierarchical levels that were responsible for quality, including engineering, quality assurance, plant managers, and production supervisors.

No problem, apparently: Quality appears to be covered adequately. Yet what happens when those responsible for quality are found in different places or have different perceptions or measures of quality? What can happen when things go drastically wrong with quality? What I found was that when everyone is responsible, then no one is responsible. When things went wrong, accountability was also elusive, as managers told me that "someone else really was responsible," not them. Success has many parents; failure is an orphan.

This situation really isn't rare. In fact, it is fairly common, especially in organizations trying to adapt to widespread or rapid change. Roles and responsibilities transform quickly as managers try to cope with change. When many individuals and skills are brought to bear on a problem, the overarching accountability or responsibility often becomes muddled over time. Hence, everyone's responsible; everyone must worry about the problem. Yet the problem is never solved when everyone is responsible and no one is accountable.

Unclear responsibility and accountability in an execution plan or process can hurt efforts directed toward strategy execution or making strategy work. Managers routinely point to this problem as one sorely in need of remediation. This clearly is not a trivial issue. It is worthy of management's attention at all levels of the organization.

RESPONSIBILITY PLOTTING AND ROLE NEGOTIATION

What can be done to confront these problems? One really good technique still is the process of responsibility plotting and role negotiation.[xiii] This process can help identify interdependence and assign responsibility and accountability for tasks or decisions instrumental to strategy execution. This technique has been used successfully by managers at all levels of an organization. Several steps are involved in the process.

1. The first step is to identify a goal or outcome that is related to strategy or strategy execution and is important to the company but that is not being achieved in a satisfactory manner.

   In Figure 5.5, based on an actual case I worked on a few years ago in a medium-size company in Texas, the goal or desired outcome was "new product development." The company's pipeline in this case had dried up, no new products were forthcoming, and the company was losing market share and its competitive advantage. (It had been a market leader for years.) Why new product development had taken such a hit was one topic to be discussed at the company's annual strategy retreat. What to do about rectifying the dismal situation was another, equally important strategic question for the meeting.

Strategic Goal: New Product Development

Major Tasks, Activities, or Decisions to Achieve Goal	Key Positions/People				
	CEO	V.P. Marketing	V.P. Engineering	V.P. Manufacturing	V.P. Finance
1. Do Market Research		"R"			
2. Decision on New Product					
3. Build Prototype					"C"
4. Market Test					
5. Decision on Mass Production					
6. Product Introduction					
7.					
8. Etc.					

R = Responsible for Decison or Action A = Final Say/Accountability for Decision or Action	I = Must be informed after a decision or action C = Must be consulted prior to a decision or action ? = Don't know

Figure 5.5 A Responsibility Matrix

2. The second step in responsibility plotting is to list the major tasks, activities, or decisions that are instrumental to achieving the desired goal or outcome. The people who are important to the goal or outcome and who might be called upon to perform key tasks and activities are also noted.

   Figure 5.5 shows some, but not all, of the key tasks, activities, decisions, and people (functions) involved in new product development in the company being studied, solely in the interest of space. Still, the main idea should be clear: List the key decision-makers and the tasks or activities that must be accomplished to develop new products or extensions of an existing product line.

3. The third step is to define different types or degrees of responsibility. The types must be relevant but simple and few enough to ensure manageability. The codes for types or degrees of responsibility or authority in Figure 5.5 are as follows: R, for those having some responsibility for a task, activity, or decision; A, for the person(s) who is ultimately accountable and who must answer for a decision, activity, or task; C, for those who must be consulted prior to making a decision; I, for those who must be informed after a decision; and ?, when you don't know whether this role is involved or what the extent of its involvement should be.

4. The fourth step is for all managers participating in the process to fill in the matrix by assigning what they feel are the appropriate responsibility codes for the individuals listed, below their function (name, title) and next to the relevant task, activity, or decision. In Figure 5.5, for example, the marketing function or person is seen as having responsibility for the market research necessary for product development. (As it turned out, marketing was also assigned an "A," as having final say over the market research.) Similarly, the VP of finance must be consulted prior to committing funds to building a prototype of any new product.

   The matrix should be filled out individually (privately) at first to avoid excessive groupthink or arguing too early in the process. Also, it is imperative to tap into all participants' opinions to add a richness and diversity of thought to the next steps.

5. The fifth step is to assign participants to a group and combine all participants' responses on just one matrix. In the company case I'm referring to in this example, the responses of individuals in each group were put on one matrix. They were all over the place, indicating strong disagreement about who was responsible for what in the new product development process. This disagreement obviously speaks loads about the underlying problems or obstacles that existed. Differences in perceptions about who is responsible or accountable clearly must have contributed to problems of communications and decision-making in the company's product development process.

6. The sixth step has each group present its single matrix to all participants to highlight disagreements, not only on each group's combined matrix but across the groups as well. Discussion then focuses on why such differences in perception exist and how those differences or conflicts relate to problems with new product development (or whatever the desired goal or outcome listed).

   A word of warning is appropriate here. It is important for the leader or facilitator to control the discussion and the heated debates that often occur during this step. In the company presently being referenced, the CEO had A's for most tasks, activities, or discussions. People (after some hesitation) opened up and hurled criticisms of micromanagement at him. They provided examples of how his interference was screwing up new product development and other important outcomes for the company. Tempers occasionally flared, and breaks were needed to calm things down. But all ended well, as the following steps will show.

7. The seventh step is to have the groups then separate themselves, with each group coming up with one ideal matrix. Based on the discussions, heated arguments, and apparent agreements in step six, each group creates a single matrix, indicating its ideal solution to the assignment of responsibilities and accountabilities for activities related to new product development. Each group, in turn, then presents its matrix to all the participants, and similarities and differences across groups can be addressed and debated.

8. The eighth step is to create one responsibility matrix from the different group presentations. This is done publicly, with the facilitator's goal being one of reaching agreement on the assigned responsibilities and accountabilities for new product development. Successful completion of this step results in one matrix, one unified approach to product development. With this finalized, agreed-upon output, the work of the responsibility and role negotiation process is complete.

9. In the company from which this example was drawn, managers added an additional, ninth, step: publication of a *Guide to New Product Development*. This manual or handbook became a source book, laying out what should be done, by whom, and when for new product development, as well as who was responsible at every step along the way.

Subsequent to the guide's development, actual new product development increased significantly, strengthening the company's competitive position. Its strategy of differentiation once again was being executed with favorable results. "The proof of the pudding is in the eating," and the proof of any process is in its results. Happily, the process in the company worked.

In sum, it is important to clarify roles and responsibilities related to desired strategic outcomes. Without this clarification and an unambiguous assignment of responsibility for critical tasks, decisions, or actions, strategy execution cannot happen. This will cause major problems, as managers told us loudly and clearly.

Unclear responsibility and accountability for execution decisions and actions can kill an otherwise well-thought-out process of execution. Managers interested in making strategy work simply cannot allow this situation to occur. Responsibility for execution decisions and actions must be clearly assigned and understood.

SUMMARY

Three major conclusions or key takeaways were suggested in this chapter. Each is an important aspect of structural integration, and each is critical to making strategy work:

1. It is necessary to define interdependence before choosing or investing in coordination methods. The three types of interdependence—pooled, sequential, and reciprocal—demand different methods or processes of achieving the integration necessary for strategy execution.

   Adding this chapter on integration to the previous chapters on strategy and organizational structure suggests a process that all managers can follow when designing methods for coordination or integration:

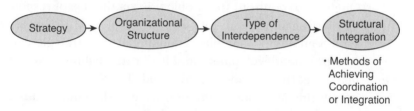

   Strategy affects structure, which determines the type of interdependence involved and the methods needed to achieve effective coordination and information flows. Following this process helps define the coordination methods that are important to making strategy work.

2. Information sharing, knowledge transfer, and effective communication are vital to execution. Poor or inadequate information sharing, in fact, was rated as a major obstacle to strategy execution by managers in the Wharton surveys. This chapter considered many of the formal and informal factors that affect communication and knowledge transfer among those responsible for making strategy work. Managers have an array of formal methods or processes at their disposal, including use of databases, IT processes, formal roles, and matrix structures.

   A focus on the formal, however, is not sufficient. Informal methods or processes can aid or inhibit the functioning of formal methods to achieve information sharing and knowledge transfer. Using informal contacts, direct communication, and a "common language" (clear, agreed-upon metrics and goals) facilitates communication. The characteristics of knowledge senders and users, the type of information transferred, and the context within which information sharing occurs all conspire to facilitate or block the communication needed to make strategy work.

3. Finally, for execution to work, all responsibilities and accountabilities for key decisions and actions must be clear or unambiguous. They must be understood by all managers involved in the execution process. Without clear responsibility and accountability, effective coordination and cooperation simply will not occur. Clarifying responsibility and accountability, then, is vital to execution success.

One way to confront the problem is via the use of responsibility plotting and role-negotiation techniques. This chapter presented an actual example by looking at the strategic need for new product development and how responsibility plotting can help meet the demands of this need. The steps for responsibility plotting and role negotiation were spelled out in this chapter, along with their underlying logic and utility.

Managers who focus on the three major issues presented in this chapter will generate structure and integration methods that are supportive of strategy execution. Another issue, mentioned but not covered in depth in this chapter, is the importance of incentives and controls for operating structure and for making strategy work. Consequently, this is the topic of the next chapter, as we continue to look at ways to execute strategy successfully.

ENDNOTES

i. "Boeing Is Merging Businesses Dealing with Space, Military," *The Wall Street Journal*, July 11, 2002.

ii. Ben Worthen, "H-P Shows Age With Layoffs," *The Wall Street Journal*, May 24, 2012.

iii. Tim Higgins and Jeff Green, "GM Seen Planning Global Reorganization Against Fiefdoms," Bloomberg.com/news/2012.

iv. "At Shell, Strategy and Structure Fueled Troubles," *The Wall Street Journal*, March 12, 2004.

v. Lana Birbrair, "Law Firm Mergers Bounce Back to Prerecession Rate," Report, Law 360, April 2, 2012.

vi. John Hellerman, "Strategic Communications Plans Key to Law Firm Merger Success," *Thomson Reuters News and Insight*, July 24, 2012.

vii. The forms of interdependence defined in this chapter were originally discussed by James D. Thompson in *Organizations in Action*, McGraw-Hill, 1967. They clearly are still useful for a full understanding of interdependence and the need for appropriate coordination mechanisms or processes.

viii. "GE Chief Is Charting His Own Strategy," *The Wall Street Journal*, September 28, 2003.

ix. For a good discussion of "Work Out" and other programs under Jack Welch at GE, see Amir Hartman, *Ruthless Execution*, *Financial Times*/Prentice Hall, 2004, pp. 53–69.

x. For a full discussion of the matrix diamond and matrix structure, see the following: Jay R. Galbraith, *Designing Complex Organizations*, Addison-Wesley, 1972; L. G. Hrebiniak and William Joyce, *Implementing Strategy*, Macmillan, 1984; S. Davis and Paul Lawrence, *Matrix*, Addison-Wesley, 1978.

xi. Gabriel Szulanski, "Exploring Internal Stickiness: Impediments to the Transfer of Best Practice Within the Firm," *Strategic Management Journal*, Vol. 17, 1996.

xii. W. M. Cohen and D. A. Levinthal, "Absorptive Capacity: A New Perspective on Learning and Innovation," *Administrative Science Quarterly*, Vol. 35, 1990.

xiii. Previous work defining and discussing responsibility plotting and the process of role negotiation can be found in the following: L. G. Hrebiniak and W. F. Joyce, *Implementing Strategy*, Macmillan, 1984; Jay Galbraith, *Designing Complex Organizations*, Addison-Wesley, 1973.

6

Incentives and Controls: Supporting and Reinforcing Execution

Introduction

The last element of the execution model presented in Chapter 2 is incentive and controls. Both affect strategy execution. Incentives motivate behavior toward ends or actions consistent with desired execution outcomes. Controls provide feedback about performance, reinforce execution methods, provide a "corrective" mechanism, and allow for organizational learning and adaptation.

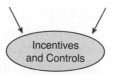

The last point about learning and adaptation is especially important. In industries that are becoming increasingly competitive and, in some cases, extremely volatile, learning quickly from performance and feedback from customers and other stakeholders is becoming central to organizational success. Poor informational feedback can stymie effective change and adaptation and lead to less-than-needed performance results and even competitive disadvantage. This chapter focuses on the main issues or problems related to incentives and controls and how they relate to making strategy work.

ROLE OF INCENTIVES AND CONTROLS

Incentives and controls are last in the logical flow of execution decisions and actions because they must be. Creating sound strategy, structure, integration mechanisms, methods of knowledge transfer, and short-term objectives is necessary for execution. These steps are not sufficient, however. It is also necessary to ensure that people are motivated and committed to making strategy work. Similarly, it is necessary for an organization to be able to change and adapt if feedback reveals problems with execution decisions, actions, or methods.

Execution will fail if no one has skin in the game. Execution will suffer if people are rewarded for doing the wrong things: behavior and actions that are inconsistent with or detrimental to desired execution outcomes. It's that simple: Incentives must support key aspects of the execution process. Increasingly, companies are showing CEOs the door or changing their incentive schemes because key strategic objectives and execution outcomes are not being met.

Controls are also vital to execution success. They allow managers to evaluate execution efforts and make necessary changes. Control systems or methods "round out" the execution process by (a) providing feedback or information about performance against execution objectives, (b) reinforcing execution methods and decisions, (c) providing a corrective mechanism to keep the execution process on track, and (d) allowing for organizational learning to facilitate change and organizational adaptation. These four elements define "controls" in the present approach to making strategy work.

The focus in this chapter is on incentives and controls and how they affect execution. Let's begin with a discussion of incentives.

INCENTIVES AND EXECUTION

Much has been written about incentives and individuals' motivation to perform. Different fields of study, including psychology and management, have saturated us with countless ideas about the links among work, motivation, and effort on the job. Attempts at summarizing this vast literature would be impossible, and this discussion won't attempt it. Instead, it focuses on a few critical incentives-related issues. Let's first introduce a basic point about motivation and incentives that was provided by managers actively involved in the execution process.

A BASIC RULE: DON'T *DEMOTIVATE* PEOPLE

The essential underlying reality in most organizations is that individuals want to perform well. Managers are motivated to seek and attain positive results. They have a high need for achievement, which motivates them to set challenging objectives and work hard toward their attainment.[i] There are exceptions to every rule, of course. Still, virtually all the managers I've known have this drive to succeed, this need for achievement. Organizations usually recruit good people who are motivated to do well.

The basic rule, then, when developing and using incentives is as follows: *Don't demotivate people*. Don't kill, penalize, or handicap the golden goose, the high achiever. Most managers want to perform. Help them do so.

Incentives fuel and guide this basic motivation. They don't cause or create it. Good managers want to achieve. The role of incentives is to support this basic motivation and push it in a direction to facilitate strategy execution.

Execution suffers primarily because of two interrelated problems. First, incentives don't support the right things. The basic, underlying motivation of managers is pushed in the wrong direction, working against successful execution. High achievers respond to incentives; it's vital that the incentives support desired execution-related behaviors and outcomes.

Second, poor incentives demotivate people, even individuals with a high need for achievement. The first problem just mentioned builds upon a strong motivation but deflects it in the wrong direction. The second problem results in an adverse effect on motivation. The wrong incentives turn people off and seriously injure their motivation and drive for excellence.

These problems are basic and important. They should be kept in mind as we discuss incentives and controls and their effects on execution.

GOOD INCENTIVES

Let's build on these basic points and start by stressing that there are many different incentives, but some are better than others.

Generally, good incentives are positive and come in two packages: utilitarian and psychological. The former includes things of extrinsic value (salary, bonus, promotion), while the second is more intrinsic or personal (autonomy, enjoying work, psychological identification with a job or its outcomes). Many rewards, of course, smack of both, as when someone receives a pat on the back or other recognition for work well done, which certainly also bodes well for the prospect of a healthy pay raise or promotion in the future.

Everyone knows about the importance of utilitarian rewards. The view of Nucor's CEO that "motivation is green" needs no interpretation. The statement by Robert Wood Johnson at J&J, "Make your top managers rich, and they will make you richer," is perfectly clear in its meaning. So, too, are the statements of managers in a program at Wharton to the effect that "money is critical, both in its own right and as a way to keep score."

The last point does suggest the psychological side of incentives. "Keeping score" suggests relative position versus peers or colleagues. Pay raises and promotions tell people how they're doing or what their value is to the organization, which clearly implies perceptions of self worth, influence, and achievement.

For our purposes, these managers are suggesting that good incentives are important to strategy execution. What defines "good"? Here are some opinions and ideas reinforced in the surveys or by my own experiences with execution.

Good incentives are tied to strategic objectives or short-term objectives that are derived from strategy. For effective execution, strategic objectives must be reinforced and rewarded, especially at higher organizational levels. At all levels, incentives must support short-term objectives that are related logically to longer-term strategic ends (see Chapter 3).

More and more CEOs, for example, are taking (or being forced to take) incentive deals that focus on company performance and shareholder value. The *Wall Street Journal* reports that CEO pay in 2011 was correlated highly with companies' performance in the stock market. Increases in returns to shareholders resulted in higher CEO pay, whereas decreases in shareholder value had the opposite effect on CEO pay. The relationship between company performance and CEO compensation can be seen at Whirlpool Corp., where nearly 90 percent of CEO Jeffrey Fettig's compensation is tied to the company's financial results. Compensation for John Chambers of Cisco Systems fell 32 percent in the fiscal year that ended July 30, 2012, because of lower company performance.[ii]

When a clear disparity exists between CEO pay and organizational performance, investors today are quick to voice their displeasure. A majority of Citigroup shareholders opposed the bank's pay plan in April 2012, rebelling against the fact that CEO Vikram Pandit received 43 million as the company's shares plummeted 44 percent. Uprisings or outright rebellions have recently occurred in the United Kingdom in protest of top management pay when company performance is down. Shareholders at Barclays PLC voted against the bank's compensation plan. Angry shareholders have turned their sights on pay practices in WPP PLC, whose executives are benefiting from huge paychecks. At the annual meetings of British companies during the first half of 2012, approximately 8.5 percent of shareholders have voted against company pay plans, a significant increase over recent years.[iii] Other examples of the relationship between pay and performance can be seen daily in the business press.

The popularity of programs such as the Balanced Scorecard and other management-by-objectives approaches to goal setting also suggests that efforts are being made to ensure that short-term measures of performance are consistent with desired strategic outcomes. These approaches stress that short-term objectives and incentives are related to the execution of important long-term, strategic objectives. "Strategic thinking" involves the integration of long- and short-term needs, and incentives play an important role in this integration task.

Good objectives are measurable. Managers involved in execution emphasize that they want to know if they've accomplished something of value. This feedback or feeling of worth is consistent with a high need for achievement. Objectives, then, must be measurable. Execution objectives related to strategy that are not measurable convey no sense of accomplishment. They also lead to different interpretations as to what is actually being accomplished. Clear, agreed-upon metrics are critical to reinforcing the right execution-related performance.

Short-term metrics also must be important and relevant to strategic success. I recently was working with a CEO of a small Internet services company. His biggest execution problems, he said, included translating company strategy into short-term, measurable objectives. The strategy focused on differentiation in a competitive, hostile marketplace. Components of differentiation included technical and customer service aspects. His problem? Developing measurable outcomes that both internal staff and customers could agree on and get excited about. Technical people tended to focus on "nerd-like" performance indicators that customers didn't understand. Customers, in contrast, wanted results that clearly tied into real-world outcomes, such as lower costs and programs to help them with their customers.

The two points of view had to be reconciled. First, consistent with the previous section's discussion, strategy had to be translated into short-term metrics. Second, those metrics had to be measurable, relevant, and important to both customers and technical people alike. If what excites and motivates technical people turns off customers, there clearly will be a problem with strategy execution.

After a great deal of work, the problems of relevancy, importance, and measurability were solved and short-term measures supported the company strategy.

Good objectives facilitate accountability. Accountability is really a control issue and will be discussed again later in this chapter, but the last point about measurability demands that it be mentioned here.

Managers in failed or faltering execution programs usually complain that accountability for performance against objectives is weak or nonexistent. Their advice? Make sure that objectives measure something of value and then hold managers accountable for performance against these metrics.

Execution suffers heavily if performance measures aren't used as the basis of managerial responsibility and accountability. Measurability and accountability are vital aspects paving the path to execution success, as the following suggests:

Measurable Objectives → Accountability for Performance Against Objectives → Execution Success

Without accountability, people can never feel that they really have skin in the game. Without clear accountability, the motivational aspects of incentives are basically thwarted or destroyed. Without a focus on accountability and its reinforcement of desired objectives, execution plans suffer because people don't know who's doing what, when, and why, leading to a lack of focus in execution efforts.

Good objectives are never "all or nothing," black or white, or reflective of other such binary distinctions. They refer instead to degree of accomplishment along some continuum of performance.

I worked for Ford Motor Company years ago as a district field manager in marketing. I had clear sales objectives in cars and light and medium trucks. Every ten days, I was judged on whether or not I had made my objectives. The answer was black or white, yes or no. There was no "rounding"—99 percent was a failure, while 100 percent was a success. Even if 99 percent resulted in a trouncing of Chevrolet (one of the important strategic goals), I didn't "make it." I had failed at execution.

The effect of this all-or-nothing approach on motivation is probably obvious. I made sure I always made my objectives. I "lowballed" during planning to ensure having objectives I could easily attain. When the answer to questions about successful performance is yes or no, one tries to ensure success by shooting low, not high. When dire consequences befall those "not making it," the emphasis on lowballing is even stronger, negatively affecting motivation, execution, and the attainment of important strategic and short-term objectives.

Good objectives are not binary, black or white. They reflect degree of performance against some continuous standard. Consider the following simple graphic:

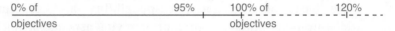

If someone achieves 95 percent of his objectives, is he a failure (black vs. white)? Not necessarily. Other factors must come into play. If I at Ford achieved 95 percent, but my counterpart from Chevrolet in the same region achieved only 75 percent, allowing me to gain market share, should I be forced to bear the title of failure? Granted, I shouldn't receive the same reward as a colleague who achieves 120 percent of important objectives and also beats Chevrolet; she clearly has outperformed me. Still, treating anything less than 100 percent consistently as a failure and not going beyond some simplistic black-white, good-bad judgment will surely lead to game-playing, lowballing, and the massaging and manipulation of data. To use objectives and incentives in such a simplistic way invites reactions inconsistent with execution success.

REWARD THE RIGHT THINGS

Again, the opinions of managers involved in execution and my own experiences weigh heavily here. If strategic plans posit the importance of something, but incentives reward something else, then clearly execution will suffer. It's foolish to hope for one thing while rewarding another. Effective execution demands that this foolishness be corrected. Incentives must support decisions or behaviors consistent with an organization's execution plan.

The stories about cost controls in the early years at Walmart are legion and legendary. Managers sharing hotel rooms to save money. Associates being asked to bring home pens and notepaper from conferences they attend. Walmart buyers calling suppliers collect. Shrinkage incentives directed toward employees, in effect motivating them *not* to steal.

Whether every one of the many stories coming out of Walmart over the years was true is not the issue here. The real issue underlying them, whether fact or folklore, is that people at Walmart believed that frugality is pervasive and good. Cost controls are desirable. The company strategy demands an emphasis on low cost, which is the right thing to incentivize and reinforce. Actions indeed speak louder than words. It is important, then, to recognize and reward the right actions.

It's important to reward performance against agreed-upon objectives. The main point here is to avoid surprises. Objectives related to desired execution outcomes must be developed and clarified up front, and performance appraisal must focus on these agreed-upon measures. The links between rewards and performance then can be forged consistently and unequivocally.

What shouldn't happen is an arbitrary choice of performance measures after the fact. Good leaders do not foster arbitrariness. A sales manager responsible for increased sales volume and market share believes he has performed well, only to be chided for lower margins. A head of engineering focuses on improving the quality of a product, thereby increasing customer satisfaction, but is warned about cost increases in his department and the future dire consequences if costs don't go down.

The relative importance of competing objectives must be established up front in the execution process; measures to evaluate performance cannot be chosen arbitrarily after the fact. If it's important for the sales manager to worry simultaneously about market share *and* margins, then say so up front when execution-related objectives are being negotiated. Lay out the desired relationship between sales volume and margins. If costs provide a necessary constraint on quality improvement or customer satisfaction, clarify this fact for the head of engineering up front, before action plans are executed to achieve departmental objectives.

Managers are telling us something basic here: Avoid surprises and the arbitrary changing of performance criteria after the fact. There is nothing worse than celebrating success against certain metrics, only to be told that performance against other, previously unspecified objectives is sorely lacking.

One last point: Organizations always get what they "pay for." Managers can hope for certain behaviors or outcomes. If the organization actually rewards different behaviors or outcomes, however, what's desired will not materialize. Execution success relies heavily on this straightforward fact of organizational life: Organizations always get what they actually reward, pay for, or reinforce, even if it is occasionally unintentional or unanticipated.

The underlying takeaway in all these examples is simply that organizations must reward the right things. Rewarding the wrong things, even if done unintentionally, will hurt the execution process. Thorndike's age-old law of effect always holds true: Behavior that is reinforced tends to be repeated.[iv] Leaders of execution programs and processes must keep this fact and others discussed in this section squarely in mind.

CONTROLS: FEEDBACK, LEARNING, AND ADAPTATION

The discussion of incentives has repeatedly suggested the importance of controls, which should not be surprising. Incentives and controls are interdependent, flip sides of the same coin. After setting objectives and providing incentives for execution, controls come into play.

THE CONTROL PROCESS

As Figure 6.1 shows, controls provide feedback about performance, reinforce execution methods, provide a "corrective" mechanism, and facilitate organizational learning and adaptation.

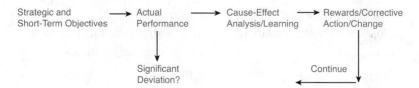

Figure 6.1 The Control Process

Control always begins with a comparison of actual and desired performance, as Figure 6.1 indicates. If there is a significant deviation between the two, it must be analyzed or studied. Cause-effect clarity is the goal; the question is, what caused the deviation? Was it due to an organization's missteps? The unanticipated actions of competitors? The existence of inadequate capabilities or poor incentives? Emphasis clearly is on learning, as managers try to dissect the problem and understand the logical reasons underlying the significant aberration in performance. After learning has occurred, steps then can be taken to provide feedback or correct the situation, leading to change and organizational adaptation.

This picture of the control process is accurate but deceptively simple. The truth is that it contains some significant pitfalls for the execution process. Leadership and sound management are absolutely essential to the avoidance of these pitfalls or problems.

Oticon

Consider the case of Oticon, a Danish manufacturer of hearing aids. In the 1990s, Lars Kolind, president and CEO, decided that he was sick and tired of organizational specialization and his organizational structure. He wanted to get away from excessive hierarchy and a departmental or functional structure that presumably was creating problems. He made a bold move.

What he did was set up a new structure—the "spaghetti organization."[v] The traditional organizational structure was out. A new, fluid structure was in, based on the notion of a fungible pool of human resources or capabilities, people who could choose their own jobs and projects. Job assignment was voluntary. There was little or no formal management control as was the case in the past. A management group reviewed the progress of chosen projects, but it wielded no control over spending and staffing.

Other changes were interesting, to say the least. Additional aspects of the new organization were "one thousand birch trees" and an elimination of all paper. Why birch trees? Only Kolind knew for certain. People moved from project to project, dragging their own trees, desks, and files with them. Projects demanded movement and physical co-location. This movement was seen as beneficial because, among other things, it resulted in informal interaction and chats among people as they moved and encountered each other on stairs (only desks and files used the elevators!).

There was an objective of the new organizational structure and process. It was a 30 percent improvement in competitiveness in three years, giving the name "Project 330" to the execution of the "spaghetti organization" and its related moves. Many people were excited by their new, loose, formless organization.

Results, however, were far from totally happy. Some managers were upset about their loss of position and authority, causing them to resist changes. Some good managers left the company, unhappy with the formless, less hierarchical and controlled organization. Many of the problems noted in Chapter 4 about making flat organizational structures work reared their ugly heads. Severe coordination problems existed, as people could come and go, from project to project, leaving some tasks in midstream and creating performance problems. Hard decisions were sometimes avoided or ignored, as employees felt little responsibility or accountability for any one project in this fluid, nonhierarchical structure. Competition for resources among project teams occurred, with no mechanisms to break ties, set priorities, and move work forward.

There were other problems with the Oticon experiment, but let's focus on its logic, the development of key objectives, and other aspects of control suggested by Figure 6.1. Kolind was sick and tired of specialization and organizational structure, but why? Oticon was experiencing performance problems. Were specialization and a departmental structure part of the problem, negatively affecting performance? This cause-effect relationship and its probable impact on performance were never established, only implied by Kolind's actions.

The key objective—and key input to the control process—was a 30 percent increase in "competitiveness" in three years. But what is competitiveness, and how was it measured? Poor objectives, including those that are ambiguous, not measurable, or subject to varying interpretations, will challenge the control process early when comparing actual and desired performance (see Figure 6.1). In addition, the relevance of the performance objectives can also be questioned without prior explanation of Oticon's past performance problems.

With the constant mass movement of people, the control of projects suffered, and learning couldn't easily occur. Making corrective changes to projects and work flow became difficult. Even simple needs like recording individuals' time on and contribution to different projects or products became challenging.

In essence, the control system of Figure 6.1 broke down. The sound control process so necessary for strategy execution, organizational performance, and adaptation practically ceased functioning effectively.

Oticon did recognize the problems and did, indeed, rebound nicely. Gradually, elements of hierarchy and authority were reinstituted. Coordination methods were reintroduced. Monthly performance reports were brought back as a control tool. Goals were defined clearly, and accountability for performance against them was employed. Many of the elements of the flat "spaghetti" structure were kept but constrained tighter by the added controls. The company also reemphasized strategy, including differentiation via product development and performance, and provided the R&D funding and other resources to support it. Investments in marketing created new customers—for example, young people, overcoming the stigma that hearing devices were only for old people. The emphasis on strategy is a solid reminder that execution begins with a sound strategy and the capabilities needed to make it work.

Looking at the company's 2011 income (EUR 1 billion plus), gross profit (EUR 975 million), and global market share for its diversified product line (original hearing devices, diagnostic instruments, and personal communication) suggests that the original control problems associated with its structural experiment were overcome effectively. Reinstating sound controls undoubtedly contributed to this success.

The Quick-Printing Industry

Some interesting research in the quick-printing or copying industry sheds additional light on the importance of management and controls.[vi] One finding is particularly revealing and significant.

It seems that "mavericks" or entrepreneurs who were part of a quick-printing or copy company, but who left the corporate fold to venture off on their own, performed much more poorly than stores that stayed attached to the corporation. The business or technology hadn't changed, and quick printing is hardly rocket science, so what's going on? What explains these results?

The simple answer is management control. When part of the corporation as franchisees, top management enforced important routines and discipline over them. Management ensured that the company's way of doing business was followed. Objectives were clear, methods of operation were spelled out, and any deviations from acceptable procedures were quickly corrected by top management. These actions ensured product quality and customer satisfaction.

It is management and the controls they impose, then, that make a difference. Top management's ensuring discipline and the following of routines or standard operating procedures positively affected franchisees' performance. Mavericks who went off on their own and rejected the pressure of routines and proven business methods in favor of their own methods and approaches did not fare as well as franchisees who stayed. Even in a simple business like quick-printing, controls can make a difference.

Control Problems in the Securities Industry

Not all control-related stories are happy ones, as attested to by recent examples from the securities industry. Company executives and directors in J.P. Morgan Chase were alerted to risky trading practices in the London office in 2010, two years before the excesses and huge losses became public. The warning flags were hoisted but ignored by top management.[vii] The control system was functioning, but the warnings weren't heeded.

Nomura Holdings, Inc. found in 2012 that its control system had shortcomings that led to leaks of nonpublic information. The information, in turn, allegedly aided and abetted cases of insider trading, as the leaked information was used to gain an advantage in the marketplace.[viii] In this case, the control system apparently failed to alert management quickly enough about shortcomings in the system. The right data simply weren't sufficiently robust, up to the task, and readily available.

Let's now try to extract some general principles of control from the preceding examples and relate them to the process shown in Figure 6.1. Combining these cases with the experiences of practicing managers reported in Chapter 1's research, the goal is to understand control, including "do's" and "don'ts" and what works and what doesn't. Let's look at some guidelines for good controls.

DEVELOP AND USE GOOD OBJECTIVES

Poor objectives can hurt the control process and immediately doom execution efforts. If objectives aren't measurable, the comparison of actual and desired performance that marks the early stages of the control model in Figure 6.1 is problematic and extremely subjective or arbitrary at best. If objectives don't relate logically to strategy or strategic problems that need fixing, the objectives aren't relevant or worth pursuing.

Good strategic and short-term objectives rely on sound planning. The objectives must relate logically to the definition of strategic needs and short-term problems that need attention. Objectives at the operating level in the quick-printing industry were closely tied to strategy and critical needs, but the same cannot be said about Oticon in the early stages of its structural experiment.

Good objectives stress the right things. With poor objectives, the wrong things may be reinforced. Relatedly, with poor objectives, the link between performance metrics and incentives is unforged and unclear. Poor objectives hurt controls. Without clear, relevant, measurable objectives, the control process, which relies on a comparison of actual and desired performance, simply cannot begin to function. Significant deviations from goals cannot be identified. Learning and organizational adaptation are simply not possible.

CONTROLS REQUIRE TIMELY AND VALID INFORMATION

The control process of Figure 6.1 suggests the importance of good information. Planning and objective-setting demand industry and competitor analysis, as well as an assessment of organizational capabilities, and this information must be circulated and be well understood. Deviations between actual and desired performance suggest the collection and dissemination of data. Feedback loops and evaluation of performance rely on sound information.

Good information must be timely and valid. For controls to work, up-to-date information about performance must be valid or correct. Changes in strategy, objectives, or incentives depend on feedback, as do organizational learning and adaptation. The case of Nomura Holdings is one where management didn't receive the timely and valid information necessary to avoid the problems it encountered.

A company entering a totally new market, such as China or Japan, needs good feedback about customer reactions to its products or services. It also needs to know competitors' reactions to the incursion into their market. Are they retaliating? How? Where? Are they attacking elsewhere, such as in Europe, because attention is focused on China or Japan and Europe may be vulnerable? Is the new emphasis on the Far East taking the company's eye off the ball in other markets?

The company's information must also be timely. Old or stale information precludes a timely, effective response to competitors' actions or customer complaints. So, the company entering a new market needs timely, up-to-date information to support strategic actions.

Both timeliness and validity of information, then, are needed. This makes sense for control and the quality of feedback on which to base future strategic decisions. However, there is a catch here, a potential problem, namely the following: *Timeliness and validity of information are negatively correlated.*

Increasing the validity of information by gathering more data from different sources usually consumes more time. A desire for validity and thoroughness, then, can actually hurt timeliness. In contrast, an overly strong emphasis on timeliness runs the risk of generating too hasty and invalid information. Timeliness and validity are not perfectly correlated, but they are negatively related.

Achieving the right balance between timely and valid information is a major challenge facing management, but it's one they must confront. Poor decisions here will affect the quality of information and the feedback that organizations need to ensure successful adaptation to changing or fluid market conditions and to execute strategy effectively. This is an important control-related task needing management's attention.

USE AND ACT ON THE INFORMATION

It's important to act on the information that's collected. It's important to use valid and timely information appropriately to identify and correct problems and move the organization forward. Absent this, learning cannot occur and stagnation or inertia become real, if undesired, outcomes.

Assuming the feedback about performance is good—valid and timely—the next questions are who gets it and can they act on it? Execution relies on good information. Execution also demands, however, that the right people receive the critical information and that they can act on it to make changes, as Figure 6.1 indicates. Without these additional considerations, good information and the control systems that rely on it are virtually useless.

Consider the J.P. Morgan case highlighted previously. The control system worked, providing data about risky investments in the London office. Red warning flags were raised in 2010, but no action was taken for two years. The information was there for the taking, but it wasn't used in a timely, effective manner. What went wrong?

Perhaps the wrong people received the information—people without the authority to act—which represents a flaw in the control process. Perhaps managers seeing the red flags simply didn't believe the information that suggested a serious situation but one never previously encountered. Or, relatedly, perhaps the managers simply didn't know what to do in a new situation. Finally, there might have been a strong reluctance to face the brutal facts, as doing so might have been seen as hurting or causing pain for others.

The point is that valid information existed, but it wasn't acted upon or used to correct a major problem. The control system worked in this case, but management failed, resulting in a black eye for a well-known company.

One more example shows the misuse or lack of use of control or performance data.

I once did some work with the Social Security Administration in Washington, D.C. Administration personnel and I were looking at, among other things, the relative costs of an office-based versus regional-based structure in the Office of Hearings and Appeals. My requests for cost data to test some structural hypotheses were met with a series of responses or reactions:

1. I was told that the requested data probably didn't exist.

2. If the data indeed did exist, I probably couldn't get access to them.

3. If I received access, I would probably find the format of the data not to my liking.

4. If the information was not to my liking, I would have to use it anyway. After all, this is what the administration has.

To make a long story short, I finally got access to the data. Actually, they were very good, helpful data, shedding a great deal of light on costs and how they might relate to organizational structure. I was impressed with the information the organization had routinely collected.

I was also shocked, however. I was the first person to retrieve and use these valuable data in years. No one was using this valuable resource. Control systems rely on feedback, information to fuel organizational change and adaptation. But if no one sees or uses the information, then clearly controls aren't working. Change and adaptation aren't being supported.

This situation may be possible in a government agency that faces no market competition, is supported by tax dollars, and has always been "profitable" by government accounting standards. The same cannot be said about an organization in a highly competitive market, where agility and responsiveness to customer needs and competitors' actions are absolutely essential to survival. Not using solid information in the latter case can only lead to execution nightmares and competitive disadvantage.

FACE THE BRUTAL FACTS HONESTLY

Jim Collins stresses that the "great" companies in his sample always confronted brutal facts openly and honestly.[ix] I couldn't agree more with this aspect of control. The managers in my surveys, like those in Collins', talked openly and convincingly about the need to conduct autopsies when things went wrong. Autopsies are consistent with the analysis of significant deviations and the need for learning and feedback, important aspects of the control model of Figure 6.1. J.P. Morgan didn't face the brutal facts when they first presented themselves, and the company paid for its mistake.

A major strength of GE that I observed time and time again, especially during "Work Out" sessions, was the ability to confront poor performance openly. "Work Outs" were often loud, rambunctious affairs, but the underlying principle driving the discussion was always the same—find out what's causing a problem and eliminate it. Focus on learning and understanding, which can occur only if people confront the brutal facts and dissect a problem.

The sad fact is that many managers really don't want to hear the truth or confront the brutal facts openly, even though this is exactly what will help their companies the most. An industry analyst recently told me that many companies he deals with never accept the brutal reality that they are performing horribly at certain execution tasks, even though these weaknesses may sow the seeds of poor performance, even destruction of the company. These companies want analysts to ignore the bad news, including poor performance vis-à-vis competitors, and report only the good news, even if it means compromising credibility. This may be a special case that combines brutal honesty, ethics, and stock price or market valuation. Still, the avoidance of brutal reality in control systems can only lead to poor execution and performance problems. Conducting autopsies is certainly no fun, but it clearly is an essential ingredient in making strategy work.

Autopsies, of course, won't result in learning and organizational change if people perceive that their main purpose is "finding some idiots to blame for poor performance and please the gods," as one manager aptly expressed it. Execution demands that leaders and followers focus on the issues, confront problems with honesty and a healthy curiosity, and be committed to learning and change. Emphasis must be on embracing error and understanding it, not just on finding, conveniently, someone to blame.

Facing the brutal facts honestly and learning from them are integral aspects of a disciplined, change-oriented culture. This discipline has characterized companies such as Walmart, Southwest Airlines, GE, Crown Holdings, and the firms in the quick-printing or copy industry previously referenced, but not the companies examined by my industry analyst friend. Ignoring the real facts can only hurt strategy execution.

REWARD THE DOERS, THE PERFORMERS

For execution to work, it is absolutely critical that the organization reward the doers, the performers.

Incentives must motivate performance toward desired outcomes. Hoping for one thing but rewarding another is confusing and wrong. So is the neglect of solid performance. The execution process will suffer if the doers aren't recognized and rewarded. It is critical that the organization celebrate success and reward those who helped achieve it.

This simple fact alone can make or break the control process and execution attempts. The model of execution presented in Chapter 2 discusses a number of important decisions or actions that are vital to execution success. Individuals become committed to making strategy work, and incentives ensure that they have skin in the game.

What's absolutely critical next is that the organization celebrates success. Those who perform must be recognized. Their behavior and its results must be reinforced. It is absolutely essential that the doers be rewarded as part of the feedback mechanism noted in Figure 6.1.

Managers have emphasized this point to me time and time again, suggesting that as basic as it is, it is violated often enough to become an execution problem. Their point reinforces the basic argument being made presently: Reward the performers. Give positive feedback to those responsible for execution success and making strategy work.

REWARD COOPERATION

This is becoming an increasingly important issue, one that follows logically from a previous point about the need to reward the doers. The fact is that organizations reward individual performance much more than cooperative achievement, and this can hurt execution.

The world of strategy execution is becoming increasing complex, and it is often the case that task interdependence is high. Individuals' efforts in different functional areas must be combined and coordinated to achieve positive outcomes. Cooperative efforts are needed to achieve integrated results, consistent with the discussion of reciprocal interdependence in Chapter 5. Individual efforts are important, of course, but it is the coordination of those efforts and the cooperation across diverse functions or units that occasionally are vital to execution success.

The problem surfaces when incentives recognize and reward only individual performance and neglect or ignore task interdependence and cooperation.[x]

Incentives and rewards tell people what's important. They motivate certain behaviors but not others. If the controls and feedback of Figure 6.1 foster only individual recognition, the cooperative behavior demanded by increasingly complex and highly task-interdependent execution processes will suffer. As two managers once pointed out when talking to me about the failure of execution programs in their companies that demanded a high level of functional integration and teamwork:

Stars get ahead around here, not constellations.

The execution plan stressed the need for cooperation and coordination. But incentives and performance appraisals recognized only individual performance. The message was very clear about what really counts.

The solution is obvious but rarely simple. The need is to reinforce cooperative behavior. If execution demands highly interdependent activities and the integration of tasks or individuals in diverse functions for success, then group-based incentives may be needed. All individuals on a SWAT team charged with an important task, for example, should be held responsible for the team's output. All should see the same incentives and receive the same performance appraisal upon task completion, an important control element. Not recognizing the need for cooperation and joint effort when interdependence is high can only hurt execution and its outcomes.

CLARIFY RESPONSIBILITY AND ACCOUNTABILITY

The discussion of individual and group-based performance, incentives, and feedback presupposes an important point, namely that responsibility and accountability are clear. This issue was discussed earlier in this chapter and in Chapter 5, but it certainly is important to reinforce when talking about controls.

The control process shown in Figure 6.1 cannot work if responsibility and accountability are muddled or confused. Objectives belong to individuals and, occasionally, teams or units. Without this ownership and accountability for the objectives, feedback cannot be effective, rewards cannot be assigned unequivocally, and a thrust for change cannot work. Assignment of responsibility clearly is much more problematic in a "spaghetti organization" than in a more disciplined organization, which affects performance in significant ways.

It is important, then, to clarify responsibility and accountability for the execution process to work. This is an important element of sound management and control that must be attended to. Accordingly, managers responsible for leading execution are referred to in Chapter 5 and its discussion of role negotiation and the responsibility matrix.

LEADERSHIP, CONTROLS, AND EXECUTION

Control processes and methods routinely test managers' leadership capabilities. Leadership plays a central role in the control process of Figure 6.1. The problem occurs when managers aren't up to the leadership task.

"Do as I Say, Not as I Do."

This is a frequently voiced control-related problem. The charge is that managers ask for one thing but then act as if something else is more important.

One company I worked with wanted increased product development and innovation as part of a new strategy and approach to the market. Innovation, of course, requires experimentation before new ideas or solutions are discovered, tested, and tried successfully. This company's culture, however, was marked by conservatism and risk avoidance, which created an interesting dilemma.

On one hand, managers preached the value of innovation. On the other, their actions worked against the reality of what's needed for innovation. The manufacturing VP, for example, echoed the top management team's stated emphasis on new product development. However, he "discouraged" his subordinates from stopping and reworking production lines to develop and test new product prototypes. Work stoppages are expensive, after all. They hurt scale and scope economies. Needless to say, their leader's actions caused confusion among subordinates about priorities and execution needs.

In another case, a large government agency had developed a program to achieve client satisfaction. The strategy ostensibly placed clients at the core of a social services network, with their needs as the prime generator of other actions and support services.

As a result of increased service to clients, however, professional contact hours and administrative support time increased markedly, causing a significant jump in expense and support activities. Higher authorities in the government bureaucracy soon noted the increased costs with alarm. Feedback on the performance of all the agency's units and programs soon included a heavy emphasis on the need for cost controls.

Client-related efforts, though effective, predictably became secondary to cost reduction. Agency leaders asked for a client focus but acted in a totally different way. The message was clear: Client satisfaction is desirable but only if costs don't increase. It was painfully clear to everyone that: *Actions do indeed speak louder than words.*

Managers, then, must lead by example. What they do is scrutinized by subordinates, regardless of organizational level. What leaders do becomes the benchmark or example for followers to emulate, resulting in controls on behavior or action.

Rework Performance Appraisals

Many traditional performance appraisal methods are terrible. They often destroy teamwork, pit individuals against each other, and promote mediocrity. They destroy risk taking, change, and innovation, often encouraging people to play it safe or maintain the status quo.

These negative outcomes are never intentional, but they often are very real, as I've often been reminded. Companies don't want to cause problems with performance appraisal. Indeed, they try very hard to be objective, even scientific, in their approaches. Still, problems with poor performance appraisals persist, hurting execution.

Performance appraisal and the feedback it gives are critical aspects of the control process of Figure 6.1. As just stated, however, the effects are often negative. The use of forced rankings, for example, is often divisive at best. Forced elimination of "deadwood" creates distrust and injures cooperation. New hires are scrutinized carefully; it's not wise, after all, to hire really good people who increase the probability of your being forced eventually, but most assuredly, into the deadwood category. Risk taking is shunned, as it increases the likelihood of mistakes and poor performance, dangerous outcomes given the nature of the rankings. Innovation suffers if people won't take risks for fear of making mistakes and being forced out of the organization.

An important role of leadership is to mitigate or eliminate these negative effects of poor performance appraisal methods. Even if the company approach, such as forced rankings, is basically problematic, good managers can help overcome the negatives and focus on positive techniques that support execution. What can they do?

1. **They can negotiate objectives for use in performance appraisal.** Insightful leaders don't rely solely on the company's forced ranking or similar systems. They negotiate objectives, the performance against which will determine, in whole or part, the position of the subordinate on the rankings. Use of the agreed-upon objectives tempers or ameliorates the negative impact of the forced-ranking method.

2. **They avoid all-or-nothing objectives at all costs.** The reasons for this were listed previously. Basically, good leaders recognize that nothing good comes from the use of all-or-nothing, black versus white, performance metrics. They know the price to pay includes lowballing or lying, as well as underachievement or constrained performance. They avoid all-or-nothing appraisals.

3. **They demand brutal honesty from subordinates when it comes to analyzing performance and explaining aberrations from the execution plan.** Their main emphasis is on learning, however, not fixing blame or finding scapegoats for poor performance. Brutal honesty facilitates learning and the fine-tuning of execution efforts.

4. **They reward the performers.** They let everyone know what's valued and what counts. They define clearly the parameters of success. They recognize those who contribute to successful execution outcomes. Good managers celebrate success and the people who achieve it.

Managers are important for the success of the control process shown in Figure 6.1. It's important that they lead by example, create a climate of discipline and honesty, and mitigate the negative effects of formal control mechanisms such as performance appraisal methods. This leadership role is vital to execution success.

THE STRATEGY REVIEW: INTEGRATING PLANNING, EXECUTION, AND CONTROL

The consideration of controls completes discussion of the execution model presented in Chapter 2. This provides an excellent opportunity to look back and summarize the main points for execution success considered thus far. The tool or approach we can use for the summary and integration is critical in its own right for successful execution and, consequently, is deserving of attention, namely, the strategy review.

The strategy review is an intensive analysis of strategy, execution, and performance. It allows corporate to test the worth of business plans and execution methods. It's useful for corporate reviews of business strategy and performance. It's also useful within businesses, allowing management to test and evaluate the contribution of functional or product-line strategies to important strategic and short-term outcomes.

The review is not meant to be a mind-numbing "numbers" exercise whose outcome is lots of paperwork and data. It isn't a "gotcha" session in which some people catch others' exaggerations or fabrications and make them look bad. It is intended to be a dynamic, creative, interactive session that focuses on real results and improvement of organizational performance. Its intention is to foster strategic thinking and a better feel for the conditions that lead to competitive advantage and organizational success.

A good strategy review is invaluable. It provides a framework that can be used for integrating planning and execution. It highlights the incentive and control issues discussed in this chapter. It provides an opportunity for communication, the analysis of strategy and execution methods, and testing the reality or feasibility of plans or methods in the real world. It also identifies "holes" or problem areas in an organization's plans or execution methods, allowing for change, adaptation, and corrective actions to improve future plans and execution processes.

Every organization must fashion its own strategy review process. It's not a luxury but a necessity. It's that important. A good review fosters debate and the confrontation of conflict. It facilitates learning. It allows leaders to test their people and develop good managers. It facilitates the integration of strategy across organizational levels. It supports execution.

The strategy review was considered briefly in Chapter 3. Figure 6.2 shows a slightly expanded version of the review and the critical six steps involved. Delineation of the steps isn't meant to suggest some mechanistic, "lock-step" approach or some overly formal view of strategy and execution. It is merely intended to ensure the identification and consideration of important aspects of the strategy review. Organizations certainly should craft their own reviews based on what they feel is most critical and illustrative, given their competitive situations. Let's follow the steps and see how planning and execution decisions come together and make sense.

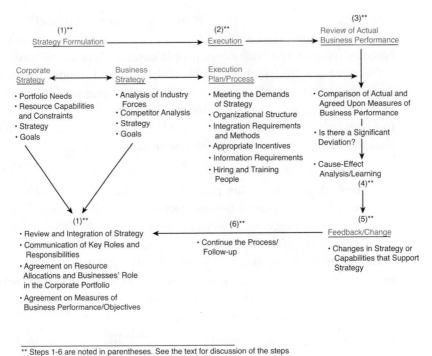

** Steps 1-6 are noted in parentheses. See the text for discussion of the steps

Figure 6.2   The Strategy Review: Planning, Execution, and Controls

STEP 1: STRATEGY FORMULATION

Chapter 3 noted the importance of strategy at both corporate and business levels. Logically, then, the strategy review begins with sound planning (step 1). The review in Figure 6.2 focuses on integrating corporate and business plans. However, the same process as previously noted can be employed at the business level, integrating business strategy with functional or departmental plans.

Corporate Strategy

The corporate level must articulate a strategy as part of the review. In a multibusiness organization, it must create a portfolio model to guide investments and the acquisition or elimination of companies. The description of the portfolio serves as a device to communicate to a business the nature and logic of the portfolio mix and the business' place in it. Corporate needs to develop clear diversification criteria if diversification and portfolio expansion are intended as a corporate strategy.

Corporate planners also need to decide what resources or capabilities are best housed at the corporate level to serve as centralized functions or units to achieve economies of scale and scope or to provide critical support services to the different business units. Investments in technical- or R&D-oriented centers of excellence are part of corporate's consideration of centralization or decentralization of scarce resources or competencies.

Business Strategy

Strategic analysis at the business level must include an in-depth consideration of industry forces.[xi] The focus of industry analysis is on an organization's positioning within the industry and how it tries to differentiate itself from other key players. Analysis is done to determine the power of suppliers and customers and how relative power affects operations and the ease of execution. The business must accurately assess the number of substitutes for its products and services, as there is a positive correlation between numbers of substitutes and competitive rivalry within the industry. The existence of entry barriers must be analyzed, including how to build them to protect competitive advantage and facilitate effective execution. Industry forces affect the intensity of competition in the industry, which, in turn, affects the nature and success of strategy execution programs.

Analysis of competitors and competitive rivalry in the industry is also essential for business strategy formulation and implementation. Who are the main competitors? What are their capabilities or competencies? Which ones are the greatest threats to our domain of strategic activity? What are their current strategies, and how will they compete in the future? Will they retaliate, and how, if we try a new strategic move? These are but a few of the questions that must be answered in a sound competitor analysis.

A business also must conduct an internal review of its resources and capabilities. Whether the company has the requisite capabilities to meet the demands of its strategy is the basic issue being considered. A low-cost strategy, for example, requires capital investments that lead to standardization of production and the achievement of scale economies. It also may require investments in information technology and the development of incentive plans to support the low-cost position. Yet another critical question is, are the right people on board with the requisite training to execute the strategy? Capabilities and human resource needs change over time. Even the "right" people might occasionally have the wrong capabilities or an incomplete set of skills, necessitating remedial action to ensure effective performance.

A sound business strategy can positively affect execution. Creation of entry barriers, gaining market share and power, differentiating one's products and services effectively, developing critical capabilities in support of strategy, and so on, all help to strengthen the business' position and ability to compete, making execution actions and steps a bit easier to implement. It all begins with strategy, as Chapter 3 emphasizes.

Integration of Plans

Corporate and business strategy and the goals they produce are important in their own right. Even more important, however, is the integration of those plans, shown as part of step 1 in the strategy review. This integration was discussed in Chapter 3, and the key elements are listed in Figure 6.2 for consideration.

A first critical step in the integration process is the corporate review of a business' strategy and plans. This is a forum for discussion, communication, and understanding, not merely a dry presentation of numbers and statistics. Businesses aren't on trial here. The purpose is to confront, honestly and openly, the key elements and assumptions of business strategy and how the corporate level can actively support the business' plans. Emphasis is on a qualitative discussion of factors affecting strategy, not on the size and bulk of planning documents.

The review should ideally be an in-depth exercise in creativity, including the discussion of different future scenarios of competitive conditions and company actions. The review is not something to get over with quickly by avoiding key issues or questions. The tough issues or questions, in fact, should be at the heart of the review process, representing the "meat" of business strategy formulation and the relationship between corporate and business plans.

The importance of these points is reinforced by Larry Bossidy and Ram Charan in their book on execution.[xii] Bossidy's experiences at GE under Jack Welch come through loudly and clearly. The strategy review at GE was a positive force for the articulation and communication of strategy, a process also stressed by Bossidy at Allied Signal. My own experiences as a "Work Out" consultant in GE's Aerospace Division also support the importance and usefulness of a results-oriented strategy review. Similar reviews in companies such as Becton-Dickenson, Crown Holdings, and others lend credence to the integrative and informative aspect of a good review rather than its use as a regurgitative or coercive event.

The roles and responsibilities of businesses in the corporate portfolio must be hashed out next between corporate and business planners. Agreement on resource allocations across businesses must also be reached and understood as part of the discussion of roles and responsibilities.

The cash cow at the business level, for example, performs an important function for the execution of corporate strategy. It provides an internal source of funds for corporate distribution. How the funds will be distributed, along with the criteria for distribution, to "stars," new growth companies, or "question marks," must be clearly delineated, understood, and bought into at the business level.

An important outcome of step 1 in Figure 6.2 is agreement on business objectives or the measures of performance that will be used to monitor and gauge business success. Based on the discussion of corporate and business strategies, performance metrics are set up consistent with the role of different businesses in the corporate portfolio. These metrics should vary by role or responsibility, with cash generators being held accountable for different performance measures (low cost, cost reductions) than growth companies or stars (market shares, margins).

STEP 2: THE EXECUTION PLAN

Once business strategy is set and integrated with corporate strategy, the business can focus on its execution plan or process, as shown in step 2 in Figure 6.2.

The execution process pays attention to the execution decisions, actions, or issues discussed to this point in the book. As Figure 6.2 indicates, this would include consideration of the following issues:

- **The "demands" of strategy.** To execute a strategy successfully, the right resources or capabilities are critical. Different strategies demand the development of different capabilities. Without these capabilities, successful performance cannot be attained.

- **Organizational structure.** Strategy affects the choice of structure. Low-cost strategies, for example, usually demand an emphasis on centralization or process specialization in a quest for efficiencies or economies of scale and scope. Complex global strategies often demand the use of matrix or "simultaneous" structures emphasizing two different points of view (such as worldwide business versus country needs).

- **Integration requirements.** Execution cannot be successful without consideration of interdependence across units and the requisite methods needed for coordination, knowledge transfer, and information sharing. A clear delineation of responsibility and accountability is also necessary for successful integration and achievement of unity of effort.

- **Appropriate incentives.** The early part of this chapter focused on good incentives and their role in execution. Execution often suffers because managers don't develop and use incentives that logically support execution decisions and options.

- **Other execution issues.** An organization may focus on yet additional issues necessary for effective execution in its industry or on its competitive landscape. These might include information requirements or IT capabilities; hiring of the right people for certain execution tasks; training and development programs, including top-management executive development programs; and an introduction of a management-by-objectives program to integrate strategic and short-term objectives. Again, the purpose presently is not to be all-inclusive, but simply to provide examples of execution issues that appear in a strategy review.

Whatever the assessment of execution needs may be, the organization must create a *formal execution plan* as part of its business strategy or business plan.

All too often, execution is assumed. Leaders "hand off the ball" to subordinates, and execution and follow-through are taken for granted. This should not be the case.

Step 2 in Figure 6.2 demands that more formal attention be devoted to execution. "Formal" doesn't mean the creation of thick notebooks, scads of words and numbers, and needless bureaucracy. It simply means that execution must be recognized as a valid part of the business plan.

Execution plans must be developed, indicating tasks, time frames, and the people responsible for task completion. "Work Out" worked at GE because the process focused on execution tasks, people, accountability, and ensuring that the important jobs were done in a timely fashion. The same emphasis on execution is needed in every company's strategy review. Attention must be paid to execution issues and obstacles, as the survey data from managers and the model in Chapter 2 argue for emphatically. Nothing less will do if execution is to be successful.

STEP 3: INITIATING THE CONTROL PROCESS

Step 3 in Figure 6.2 begins the process of control. Comparison of actual and agreed-upon measures of business performance is the first step in the control process. These measures could be derived from strategy and the quest for competitive advantage, or they might represent metrics that come from the execution plan. Whatever their origin, actual performance against the objectives initiates the control step.

The main issue is to determine whether there are significant deviations from the desired performance measures. This includes positive as well as negative deviations. If a business is aiming for a 5 percent increase in market share in some part of the world, but achieves no increase or a small, insignificant change, this deviation is very likely significant and in need of attention. However, if the company achieves a 15 percent increase, this also is significant and deserving of additional management scrutiny.

Leaders who only focus on negative aberrations increase the probability of creating a culture of risk aversion or error avoidance, which can seriously impede execution and organizational performance. This aspect of culture is important and is discussed in greater detail in Chapter 8.

STEP 4: CAUSE-EFFECT ANALYSIS AND ORGANIZATIONAL LEARNING

Step 4 is vital to organizational learning and adaptation. It represents a critical aspect of the strategy review.

If significant deviations in performance were identified in step 3, cause-effect analysis is absolutely essential. How can the deviation in business performance be explained? What can the organization learn from the noted aberrations in performance? This is not an easy step. It can backslide into a finger-pointing blame session. It can create defensiveness and closed-mindedness that absolutely destroy curiosity and the ability to learn. Effective leadership is clearly needed to prevent this injurious backslide and keep the review positive, on track, and focused on learning.

Determining cause-effect clarity is difficult, often demanding intensive analysis of data, actions, and the factors that affect or determine performance. A culture or reward structure that supports risk aversion or blaming others won't generate the necessary analysis. Such a climate guarantees an inability to learn and adapt. Individuals simply won't let objective data get in the way of their biased or defensive opinions, which is deadly for learning and change.

Again, leadership is critical. Leaders must confront the brutal facts and explain poor performance. Autopsies are required, but in the spirit of learning and inquisitiveness, not the need to blame or injure others. Creating a climate conducive to learning is essential. Leaders must ask tough questions, and subordinates must respond in kind, with data and opinions that explain performance. Creating such a culture is where managers earn their keep. Again, this issue is revisited in Chapter 8 on managing culture.

STEP 5: FEEDBACK AND CHANGE

If learning has occurred in step 4 and managers understand what caused the significant deviations in performance, then feedback, changes, or corrective actions are possible, as step 5 in Figure 6.2 shows.

Feedback may include rewards or recognition for great performance. It may demand changes in strategy or execution methods based on the brutal analysis of data in the previous step. Business leaders are responsible and accountable for their unit's performance, and feedback is directed toward options and methods to improve it.

Emphasis in step 5 is, of necessity, on preparing for organizational change. The results of the learning process of step 4 must be implemented. Additional capabilities may be required and obtained. Incentives may need modification. Additional coordination or integration methods may need to be introduced and perfected. Business strategy might need to be tweaked to achieve better results for a particular product in a given market or part of the world.

The problem is that managing change, while critical, is also difficult. Because of its centrality and difficulty, the next chapter picks up where step 5 in Figure 6.2 leaves off and considers the enormous task of managing change effectively.

STEP 6: FOLLOW UP AND CONTINUE THE PROCESS

The strategy review does not end with step 5. Indeed, step 5 provides the inputs for a whole new process. Figure 6.2 suggests that continuous attention to key variables is essential for ongoing execution success.

In my "Work Out" experiences with GE, for example, step 6 always defined follow-up activities. If changes were being implemented, additional discussions with key people or additional group meetings were planned routinely. If managers were responsible for new actions or activities, time and attention had to be devoted to determine whether desired changes were actually being executed.

Follow-up is critical to the strategy review and good execution. Left to their own devices, people may leave a strategy review and go back home, hoping that demands will simply go away and life can go back to normal. Inaction is a decision of sorts, the hoped-for result often being an avoidance of change and return to a comfortable status quo.

This cannot happen. The review process of Figure 6.2 requires attention to feedback and change requirements. Learning and change "prime the pump," leading to additional needs, objectives, or fine-tuning of strategy that regenerates and invigorates the review process.

A VP of marketing and planning for a medium-size company recently developed a strategy review process for his company. His remarks to me clearly summarized the value of the exercise:

> The review has helped us immensely. It forced us to develop an execution plan and approach. It emphasized meaningful metrics of performance. It fostered learning and an understanding of what affects performance. Most important of all, it forced people to communicate. Communication between corporate and business staff and across functional areas improved immensely, which really is amazing for this company.

This, then, is the strategy review and how it relates to effective controls, the support of strategy execution efforts, and making strategy work. This chapter also concludes the analysis of components laid out in the basic execution model or overview of Chapter 2.

Our work is far from complete, however. Important contextual factors affecting execution must now be considered in depth, including managing change, culture, and power or influence. The next chapter picks up where the discussion of the strategy review left off, namely with the process of managing change, a vitally important issue for execution.

SUMMARY

There are a number of key conclusions or takeaways suggested in the current chapter. They are as follows:

- Incentives motivate behavior toward ends consistent with desired strategy execution outcomes. Controls provide feedback about performance, reinforce execution methods, provide corrective mechanisms, and facilitate organizational learning and change. Both incentives and controls are important to making strategy work.

- There are some basic aspects of "good" incentives and basic rules for using incentives wisely in the strategy execution process:

  - One such basic rule is that incentives shouldn't demotivate individuals. Most managers are motivated, with a high need for achievement. The last thing incentives should do is injure this need and deflect behavior away from desired execution outcomes.

  - A related fact is that incentives fuel and guide motivation. They don't create it. The role of incentives is to support motivation and guide behavior in the right direction.

  - Good incentives are tied to strategic objectives or short-term objectives that are derived from strategy. Incentives, then, foster strategy execution at all levels of an organization.

- Good incentives reward the right things. It's foolish to hope for certain execution outcomes and then reward other outcomes or behaviors.

- A final point to keep in mind about incentives is that "organizations always get what they pay for." Individuals respond to incentives and give the organization exactly what it is rewarding, even if the results are inconsistent with strategy execution. Rewarding the wrong things, even if done unintentionally, always hurts the execution process.

- Controls provide feedback about performance, reinforce execution methods, provide a corrective mechanism for an organization, and facilitate learning and change, as Figure 6.1 clearly indicates. For controls to work effectively and support execution, rules or guidelines must be followed.

- For execution to work, it is absolutely essential that organizations reward the doers, the performers. Only then will appropriate execution-related behaviors be reinforced and guaranteed.

- It is absolutely necessary that the control process face the brutal facts openly and honestly when execution-related performance is poor. It is imperative to conduct autopsies for organizational learning to occur. Without the analysis of facts and the learning it leads to, organizational change or adaptation is jeopardized.

- The control process cannot work if responsibility and accountability for execution-related tasks are unclear. It is necessary, then, to clarify responsibility and accountability for controls to work and strategy execution to be successful.

- Controls need timely and valid information to work effectively. A balance between timeliness and validity of information must be achieved, a major problem confronting managers given that these two aspects of good information are inversely correlated.

- The role of leadership in the control process is central and pervasive. Problems occur when leaders aren't up to the leadership tasks vital to controls and execution.

  - Setting an example for subordinates that is consistent with execution-related objectives and behaviors is an absolute must. "Do as I say, not as I do" is a policy that will destroy the control process and hurt execution results. Actions, indeed, do speak louder than words.

  - Good leaders also know how to use performance appraisals effectively. Leaders, for example, must avoid the use of all-or-nothing objectives. They must demand brutal honesty from subordinates. And they must recognize and reward the performers, the doers who contribute to execution success.

- Finally, this chapter stressed the necessity of conducting a strategy review. Such a review process is critical to supporting the planning and control process and making strategy work. The strategy review is not a luxury or an option; every organization must fashion its own strategy review to execute strategy effectively. A good review fosters discussion, clarifies corporate and business strategy, helps set execution-related objectives, allows leaders to test and understand their people, and facilitates learning and organizational change. It is important to the success of strategy execution efforts.

Discussion of the strategy review ends where the next chapter begins, namely with the important task of managing change. Attention can now turn to this critical aspect of making strategy work.

ENDNOTES

i. Discussion of the need for achievement first began with David McClelland, who also talked about the need for power and the need for affiliation. See *The Achievement Motive*, Appleton-Century-Crofts, 1953; also see his *The Achieving Society*, Van Nostrand Reinhold, 1961.

ii. Scott Thurm, "CEO Pay Moves With Corporate Results," *The Wall Street Journal*, May 21, 2010.

iii. See "CEO Pay," Ibid; see also Dana Cimilluca, David Enrich, and Cassell Bryan-Low, "In U.K., Spats on Pay Escalate," *The Wall Street Journal*, May 16, 2012.

iv. Edward Thorndike, *The Elements of Psychology*, A. G. Seiler, 1905.

v. The changes at Oticon drew worldwide attention. Googling Oticon "organizational structure," "spaghetti organization," and so on revealed hundreds of references to the Oticon experiment. These included academic articles, popular press coverage, and case studies done by the Harvard Business School and other leading universities. The "looseness" of the new organization simply conflicted with the need for focus, direction, discipline, and control demanded by strategy execution and superordinate goals. Autonomy and discretion are wonderful; too much autonomy and discretion, however, can lead to confusion, anarchy, and a lack of strategic and operating focus.

vi. A. M. Knott, "The Dynamic Value of Hierarchy," *Management Science*, 47(3), 2001.

vii. Dan Fitzpatrick, Gregory Zuckerman, and Joan S. Lublin, "J.P. Morgan Knew of the Risks," *The Wall Street Journal*, June 12, 2012.

viii. Atsuko Fukase, "Nomura Finds Weakness in Controls," *The Wall Street Journal*, June 12, 2012.

ix. Jim Collins, *Good to Great*, Harper Business, 2001. The need to conduct autopsies was also emphasized by Larry Bossidy and Ram Charan in their informative work, *Execution*, Crown Business, 2002.

x. See L. G. Hrebiniak's *The We-Force in Management*, Lexington Books, 1994. This book focuses on interdependence and the other conditions that affect coordination and cooperation in organizations.

xi. Michael Porter's *Competitive Strategy*, Macmillan, 1980, provides a well-known and complete discussion of industry forces and their relation to competitive advantage and profitability.

xii. Larry Bossidy and Ram Charan, *Execution*, Crown Business, 2002.

7

Managing Change

Introduction

Successful execution requires the effective management of change. Indeed, execution is often synonymous with change, as key actions and steps are taken or modified to make strategy work.

Analysis to this point has often referenced or implied the importance of change for strategy execution. It is now time to talk explicitly about the critical importance of managing change. The inability to manage change effectively can destroy or seriously hamper otherwise valid and complete execution plans.

MANAGING CHANGE: A CONTINUING CHALLENGE

The topic of managing change has received a huge amount of attention. The literature in psychology, sociology, and management has contributed volumes on the subject. The popular press has added its share of articles on the issue. Metaphorical treatments of change combining fact and fiction have grown in number and captured readers' imagination, such as Spencer Johnson's wildly popular work on coping with change.[i]

Despite all this attention, managing change is still an ongoing execution issue. The inability to manage change is mentioned consistently as an ongoing execution problem.

The Wharton-Gartner and Executive Education surveys list the inability to manage change as a critical strategy-execution problem. The data collected in the discussions after the original research further support the findings about the centrality and importance of change management for the execution of strategy. Moreover, the issue of managing change is virtually always in the news. Consider, for example, just a few recent change-related cases and issues:

- When Hiroaki Nakanishi became Hitachi's president in 2010, the company was in very bad shape, losing money hand over fist, over $12.5 billion in the four preceding years. In 2013, Hitachi is in the midst of an amazing turnaround, thanks to Nakanishi's aggressive change program.[ii] Under his guidance, Hitachi has changed from a slow-moving, inert company to an active one. Old, unprofitable businesses were spun off— mobile phones, computer parts, flat-panel TVs—and intense strategic attention was paid to more profitable, big-ticket items, like power plants, rail lines, and water treatment facilities. This represents a major change that even its early critics now recognize as a bold and profitable move. Early resistance to change folded as the logic of Nakanishi's change strategy became clear and the company's performance improved.

- Sony, in contrast, facing the same or similar industry-related problems as Hitachi, hasn't changed as significantly. It's locked into business as usual in many respects, and the inability to change and move into new strategic directions is hurting its bottom line. Sony, for example, has lost money selling TVs for years on end, but it remains wedded to the industry segment, refusing to pursue an exit strategy, a la Hitachi. The result? In May 2012, Sony announced its fourth straight year of losses, with a record net loss of approximately $5.8 billion.[iii]

Two companies—Hitachi and Sony—same industry, but one changed aggressively and the other appears mired in the status quo. One company seemingly embraces change, while the other doesn't, raising interesting questions about strategy and its execution.

- In March 2012, United Continental Holdings, the world's largest airline, "flipped the switch" in a massive attempt to merge elements of the two partners, causing all sorts of change-related problems.[iv] It merged United and Continental reservations systems, websites, and frequent-flier programs in one quick move, but the results were far from effective or pretty. Problems mounted fast, leaving a host of grumbling customers, confused company personnel, and head-scratching industry analysts. CEO Jeff Smisek apologized for the massive problems related to the change, admitting that the company added stress and complexity to its operating systems by trying to implement or execute so many changes simultaneously. A perceived need to "bite the bullet" and execute complex change quickly had good intentions behind it, but the actual results left much to be desired and many problems needing repair.

Businesses often grow more complex as they change over time. Product and market diversification through organic growth or acquisition add new elements to manage and new problems to confront, which can challenge strategy execution. The problems are exacerbated when the change is rapid, with many things being changed simultaneously.

- The example of Lego was cited previously. The company expanded feverishly into all sorts of businesses: theme parks, television programs, watches, clothes, and so on. The outcome of this diversification was dismal. Rapid change and poor strategic choices added complexity that challenged planning and execution. Too many competitive problems and worries due to the changes provided obstacles that couldn't easily be overcome. Only when the company again embraced its simpler

roots did a state of normalcy—and profitability—return.[v]
Large, complex change proved to be a mistake at Lego, a situation that, thankfully for the company, was rectified by focusing again on its simpler roots and capabilities.

- Avon Products has been undergoing a change process that is challenging the well-known "Avon Lady Calling" company.[vi] Long-time CEO, Andrea Jung, the "face woman" for Avon and other companies like GE and Apple on whose boards she sat, took the venerable company through a series of subtle changes that led to her being replaced by Avon's board. Jung tried to create a retail brand and strategic thrust to enable the company to grow and compete with the likes of L'Oreal or P&G. Slowly, the company turned away from its tried-and-true direct sales model. The company's attention was diverted away from emerging markets like China and Brazil due to this strategic change or refocusing. Other problems added to the mix—for example, an investigation of bribery in China, and SEC investigation into alleged information leaks—the results of which included lagging sales and a stock that lost half its value in 2011.

  Sherilyn McCoy was appointed CEO in the spring of 2012, and her change task is enormous. Her challenge is to return Avon to its door-to-door direct sales roots and customer-centric processes and capabilities. Negative changes that mounted slowly but inexorably will have to be rebuffed in another change process that will indeed prove to be challenging and difficult.

- The revolving door is again working at Yahoo.[vii] Marissa Mayer became the sixth CEO in the last five years, counting interim chief executive Ross Levinsohn. She clearly is qualified, bringing insights about consumer websites and advertising from Google. She's a good PR person as well, which will help her with managers and win outsiders over to her plans for Yahoo.

The downside, however, is the revolving door and the endless stream of changes the company has been enduring. Frequent changes breed a lack of steadiness and unstable leadership, and these facts will add to Mayer's problems. Her immediate predecessor, Ross Levinsohn, had developed a strategy for Yahoo, presumably with execution requirements, and Mayer's rejection or modification of his plans may add to the turmoil facing the company. Change, indeed, especially repeated change, can prove bothersome and challenging.

There are, of course, many other examples. But the recent ones provided, coupled with the continued prevalence of change-related issues in the popular press, raise interesting questions. If the topic of change management has been researched and discussed so often and extensively, why is it still such a big problem? Why is managing change always a potentially disruptive issue, despite the learning and insights that apparently have accumulated over time?

There are, I believe, two general answers to these questions, at least when the issue is strategy execution and its associated changes. First, managing strategic change is terribly complex and difficult. The number of interdependent factors and obstacles that affect execution clearly increases the complexity facing leaders of change efforts. Second, the emphasis in strategy-execution programs or processes has not focused enough on certain aspects of change management that directly affect execution results. Let's pursue these points further.

STEPS IN MANAGING CHANGE

There are six basic or generic steps, issues, or decisions in the management of change, most of which were implicitly at work in the preceding examples:

1. **Size and content of change.** The first step is to decide on the focus of change efforts. What is it that needs changing? How big is the problem or threat facing the organization, and how should the organization respond?

2. **Time available for change.** How much time does management have to execute the change? Does the organization enjoy the luxury of time, or must it act quickly? Why do some leaders see that it's time to change, while others see the same problems and decide that the time isn't ripe for change?

3. **Tactics in the change/execution process.** How should the change be executed? Should it proceed in "bits and pieces" or all at once? Should it be implemented slowly and methodically or quickly, to get it done in one fell swoop? Are there problems with rapid, complex change?

4. **Clear responsibility or accountability.** Who is responsible or accountable for elements or aspects of the change process? Are responsibility and accountability clear to all involved in change?

5. **Overcoming resistance to change.** It is vital to overcome resistance to change or new execution efforts. Overt and especially covert resistance can kill or injure change efforts and execution in a big way.

6. **Monitoring the change.** Are the changes working? How tightly or loosely should the change process be monitored? What methods for tracking change should be employed? Monitoring results and progress and tweaking or modifying the change process are important to achievement of desired execution results.

All six issues are important and central to sound change management. Overcoming resistance to change is vital and is discussed in Chapter 8. Clarifying responsibility and accountability is also extremely important. This issue has already been discussed in Chapter 5 in the discussion of coordination and integration, and in Chapter 6 where the requirements for effective controls and the steps in an effective strategy review were spelled out. The need to monitor and track changes was also an important part of the discussion of controls and the strategy review in Chapter 6.

The present position is that more attention must be paid to the first three issues. The size of a strategic threat or opportunity and the time available for change interact in ways that heavily impact the third issue, how the change process is managed. How the process is managed, in turn, presents both potential costs and benefits to an organization. Put another way, the present argument is that:

> The relationship between (a) the size of a change and (b) the time available for change determines how the change is executed, the costs and benefits of change, and the prognosis for success.

These aspects of change and strategy execution are important and in need of attention. Knowing how the size and "speed" of change affect the execution of change and the costs and benefits of different approaches to change is absolutely essential to change management and sound execution.

A MODEL OF CHANGE AND EXECUTION

Building on the previous points, let's construct a model of change and execution that is useful to managers concerned with making strategy work.

COMPONENTS OF THE MODEL

Size of the Change

The content of change efforts must be chosen carefully. Priorities must be set. Strategic change initiatives must be important and few. There is a real danger in doing too many things at once, a point emphasized in an example noted previously and, again, later in the chapter.

The content of change must obviously reflect and react to the size of a strategic threat or opportunity facing an organization. Size matters when it describes problems that top management must cope with when managing change. The size of a problem or opportunity is instrumental in marshalling resources and developing commitment to the change process. The bigger the problem, the more complex the content needed to confront it, and the harder it is to manage change effectively.

An important question here is why some organizations see the need for change while others react slowly or not at all to strategic and operating threats. Some top managers see a large problem and react, while others stall or maintain the status quo, despite performance and other problems that seem to cry for action.

Managers and their organizations fail to respond to demands for change and define an attack against large problems for four potential reasons:

1. **They don't believe the problems are real or significant.** "This too will pass" is the chosen mantra as managers wait for things to change on their own.

2. **This situation is fueled and supported by inertia and its focus on the status quo.** Relatedly, they are shocked by the negative data they're seeing and don't want to make a mistake by responding quickly to perceived threats that they feel are outside the realm of possibility. Some caution is praiseworthy, of course, but not perpetual paralysis due to disbelief of data suggesting that major problems exist.

3. **The capabilities to understand and react to change don't exist.** To understand and apply lessons learned from competitors' technological innovations, for example, a company must have the engineers, scientists, and technical skills and capabilities to analyze and understand the change-related issues that are unfolding. Without the necessary expertise, reaction to technological changes, even large, significant ones, is problematical.

4. **Managers feel that definition and reaction to large changes are not their problem or responsibility.** Their answer to needed change is "not me," or "someone" will handle it; it's not part of my job title or requirements. This is avoidance, often supported by poor incentives, inability to confront risks or uncertainty, or even a desire to avoid attention or attract criticism.

Time Available for Change

Assuming that managers perceive the need for change, the next major decision is how long they believe they have to execute the change. The time element must be considered carefully. The effects of shorter time horizons include increasing the number of changes or change components that must be considered simultaneously. Generally, the shorter the time horizon, the greater the complexity of the change process, as more and more critical factors must be taken into account at once.

Velocity of Change

When many change issues must be considered in a short period of time, the "velocity of change" is high. Generally, the higher the velocity, the greater the costs or problems associated with the change process. High velocity, though occasionally necessary and often exciting, is usually associated with low success in managing change, as is emphasized below.

RELATING CHANGE TO EXECUTION PROBLEMS

The combination of these components creates a rough but useful model of the change process (see Figure 7.1).[viii] The model, in turn, helps define execution-related problems that emanate from the process of change.

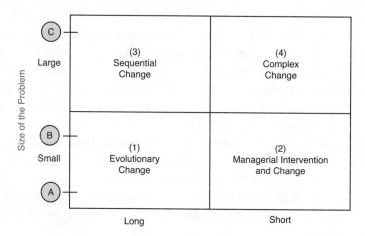

Figure 7.1 A Model of Change and Execution

The x-axis in Figure 7.1 exhibits a time dimension or the Time Available for Execution. Again, this is an important issue for leaders of change, as time defines the velocity of change and the potential problems that result from "speed." The time variable is separated into "long" and "short" time frames to simplify the discussion.

The y-axis in Figure 7.1 focuses on the size of the threats or opportunities confronting an organization. For present purposes, discussion focuses on threats or problems. The y-axis, then, is simply labeled as Size of the Problem. As previously mentioned, larger problems demand more resources and managerial attention (change "content") than smaller problems. Large problems can complicate the process of change and affect change efforts and their outcomes. Similar to the time dimension, the size of the problem is also expressed in binary terms as "large" or "small."[ix]

Situation A: Many Small Changes

Let's focus first on a common, everyday situation in organizations—a myriad of small problems in need of managerial attention or change. This is situation A in Figure 7.1.

This situation is known to all managers. Rules and standard operating procedures (SOPs) exist in every organization. They usually tell people how to handle small problems or changes that crop up routinely. The quick-printing industry example referenced in the previous chapter provided insights into the importance of management controls (hierarchy) and SOPs for the handling of routine problems or changes.[x] Management earns its keep by responding to problems and developing or changing routines and SOPs that effectively cope with and solve the emerging problems. This information is then passed on to all offices or businesses within the organization to ensure that the same effective SOPs are used routinely throughout the company. However, sometimes even the rules and SOPs don't exactly cover a problem, and managers must exercise discretion to handle it. This, of course, is why we have managers.

Managers throughout the organization, then, are handling problems, many of which are similar or identical. As a district field manager at Ford, I followed the SOPs. I routinely handled dealers' requests, sometimes "bending the rules" or doing dealers favors to expedite sales or solve problems. These usually weren't major issues, so I just handled things the best way I could.

There always was a potential problem brewing, however. Other managers handled things their own way. Others responded to the same problems in their zones or regions in different ways. Suboptimization surely existed, as multiple approaches to problem solving were being employed, not the best approach. Because the problems were small, the costs of this suboptimization were low and went unnoticed by higher-ups in the company.

Occasionally, however, a problem got larger. It grew a bit in severity, demanding hierarchical attention (situation B in Figure 7.1). The problem still was not huge or strategic, but it loomed larger and demanded additional attention.

A dealer in one region, for example, might feel that the company's decisions or solutions to problems routinely favored another dealership in some way. Or a large dealership with facilities in multiple regions might believe that the inconsistency of company methods or actions across regions (for example, when "bulking" cars, handling credit issues, or deciding on new car allocations) was creating financial problems or uneven treatment of dealers.

The bottom line was that occasionally someone complained. A dealer would go over the field manager's head and complain to someone at the district or regional office. A person higher up in the organization was now involved in a growing problem, clearly with the intention of not letting the problem get larger or out of hand.

This individual would routinely call all field managers and other relevant personnel together. He would define the problem and then ask all of the gathered personnel, "How have you been handling this problem or issue?" The various managers would reply, and something extremely interesting often occurred. When the managers heard the different approaches to handling the problem, there often were comments such as:

"I've been doing xxxxx this way for years. When did we start doing it *that* way?"

"When did this happen? When did we begin handling this problem like that? Did the company change its policy?"

These comments are striking because they reveal that the organization had changed over time. Ways of doing things had evolved in different directions. Evolutionary change had occurred (box 1 in Figure 7.1). The evolutionary changes weren't purposeful or planned by the organization. Different people handled the same problems differently. Suboptimization was occurring but was insignificant. No one even noticed until small, routine problems became slightly larger and more salient issues in need of attention.

Evolutionary change happens in all organizations. It is routine and rarely noticed until small, minute problems become larger and loom as significant issues if action isn't taken. The time frame for evolutionary change is long because different decisions can be made or different actions taken ad infinitum, as long as no one calls attention to the problem or demands a unified, consistent approach to problem solving. If and when the latter does occur, the time frame to confront the problem is substantially reduced and action is taken. What types of action?

Typically, when a problem gets larger and moves from A to B in Figure 7.1, the approach to problem solving changes. The movement is to box 2. A regional manager sets up a committee or task force of field managers, tells them that multiple ways of solving the problem are no longer tolerable, and asks them for their recommendations as to the best approach for all managers to follow in the future.

This is an example of a managerial intervention and change, as Figure 7.1 indicates. Someone defines the problem, shortens the time available for change or execution, and demands a solution to the problem.

Responsibility for the change is usually that of an individual or group charged with finding a solution to the problem. When the job is done, life goes back to normal, with managers routinely responding differently to many small problems and issues. There is an equilibrium of sorts until a new, bigger problem arises, demanding a new managerial intervention in a shortened time horizon. Most organizations face this type of situation routinely, as problems "spring up" and need quick resolution.

Situation C: A Large Strategic Problem

This situation in Figure 7.1 is much more serious. A major strategic problem looms, demanding significant change.

A competitor's strategy creates a new business model, potentially rendering ours obsolete and demanding a significant change in strategy. Hitachi's spin-off of unprofitable products like TVs and moving into new product areas present challenges to Sony. Will the company respond to Hitachi's new strategic thrust? A significant change in strategy is indeed a large problem, and Sony must carefully weigh its options.

Or a competitor's new product threatens a blockbuster product, demanding action on our part. The direct challenge to Sanofi's prescription drug, Plavix, and the potential loss of exclusivity and profits on the drug were major problems for Sanofi to cope with, even as the company prepared for a takeover of Aventis, another large strategic problem.

Recent threats to the McNeil unit of J&J resulting from poor product quality certainly represent a major problem for both the division and corporate parent that cannot be taken lightly. Causes of the problem could include many factors, including J&J's strong emphasis on decentralization and strategic business unit autonomy. This suggests that solutions to the problems may indeed be complex, challenging both organizational structure and process.

Given the existence of large strategic problems that must be confronted, Figure 7.1 suggests that the handling of these problems is a function of top management's perception or assessment of the time available for strategy execution. The execution horizon is the driving force behind the choice of change methods.

SEQUENTIAL CHANGE

If managers believe that the time available for execution is long, Figure 7.1 indicates that sequential change is employed. What's a long versus short time frame depends, in part, on economic factors, industry forces, and competitive conditions. To DuPont, Boeing, or Ford Motor Company, a long time horizon may be five-plus years because of capital and investment requirements. In contrast, I once reviewed a business plan for a designer and manufacturer of women's clothing in New York. In the plan, as I recall, long term was six to nine months, or two-plus "seasons" in the clothing market. As one manager put it at the time, "If we miss two or more seasons, we're really in deep trouble. The fashion business doesn't allow many major mistakes." Clearly, industry and competitive conditions come into play when considering the time dimension.

However it's done, top management decides on the time horizon for execution. If the decision is that there is ample time to execute a strategy, a sequential process can be followed. A sequential intervention means that the organization reduces a large change into smaller, more manageable pieces or proportions. It handles each piece or aspect of the change process before moving on to the next.

Under sequential change, what we see is a chain of activities or steps, with movement to the next step determined by analysis or outputs at a prior step in the process, as shown in this simple graphic:

$$A \nearrow \begin{array}{c} B \\ \searrow \\ B^1 \end{array} \nearrow C \longrightarrow D \longrightarrow E \longrightarrow Etc.$$

To solve a strategic problem and initiate the change process, market research, industry analysis, or interviews with customers determine that a particular type of product or service or competitive strategy could work in a defined market segment (A). Two prototypes (B and B1) of a product or service are developed and field tested in a sample market, and product performance and customer reactions are observed. Modifications are made, resulting in a new product or service , which is tested further. A decision is made, and the product is placed in mass production , with the company ultimately expanding distribution to yet additional market segments.

Or, employing the model of execution of Chapter 2, a change in corporate strategy may necessitate a change in structure or even a change in business strategy for a unit in the corporate portfolio. A revised business strategy could precipitate possible changes in business structure or the coordination mechanisms employed to achieve effective integration and unity of effort. Incentives, then, would at minimum have to be examined to see if they adequately support the new strategic and short-term objectives of the company. These are examples of a sequential logic and approach to change. Large problems are reduced to smaller, more manageable proportions, and the analysis focuses on one element of the process before moving on to the next.

"One element" in the change process could include a small number of items or issues being considered simultaneously. In a previous example, two product or service prototypes were considered (B and B1) at the same time. The two together make up a single step in the sequential change process. Each element in the sequential change process may contain a small number of issues that are considered concurrently, the emphasis being on "small," as is explained later in the chapter.

Another way of looking at sequential change is to see it as a series of smaller "managerial interventions" (see Figure 7.1). Large changes, that is, are reduced to smaller changes that individuals or groups focus on and solve as part of the sequential chain of activities or steps just noted. Box 3 in Figure 7.1 in many cases is simply a series of smaller changes derived from box 2, with the accumulated steps taking place over a longer time period.

Bank of America (BOA) followed a slow, sequential change process after completing its acquisition of FleetBoston.[xi] Although many changes clearly were in store, including some sizeable job cuts, BOA didn't execute large, major changes quickly. Rather, it studied big problems carefully and focused on handling them in a sequential change process to avoid making big mistakes. In contrast, United Continental Holdings "flipped the switch" in March 2012 and eschewed a sequential change process, opting instead to change many things at once, which resulted in major problems. These examples suggest that there may be some benefits attributable to a slower, more deliberate sequential change process.

Benefits of Sequential Change

This process of change has some obvious benefits. It is methodical and paced. It represents a type of planned or rational change, as each step is engaged only after the prior step is satisfactorily completed.

The step-by-step process allows managers to celebrate success and reduce resistance to change. Naysayers and doubters can be shown the results of market research and the initial positive reactions of customers to a new product. The success of the first stages in the change process can be used to win over doubters who were originally against the entire change initiative. The initial success allows an approach that says to the doubter or resistor, "You felt that the proposed new product would never work or sell. Yet initial reactions are positive and successful. Will you come on board and support the new product initiative, now that you've seen the early results?"

The celebration of success also supports the strategy-execution process. Positive results affect buy-in and ownership in a positive way. A "pat on the back" can be given to those achieving positive interim results, which reinforces their motivation and commitment to the planned change.

Sequential interventions allow for clear cause-effect analysis. The effects of an incremental change in the serial process can be more readily observed than the effects of many simultaneous changes. Coordination and learning are thus easier to achieve in this more controlled version of change management.

A sequential process also allows for incremental investments of time and money. Everything need not be invested and put at risk all at once. Small portions of an investment can be done with minimal risk, lowering the overall risk profile and uncertainty for the organization. There is no need to "bet the entire house" on a new venture. Under a sequential change process, management is betting on smaller pieces and only after achieving some measure of prior success.

Of course, it must be recognized that there is a potential downside to sequential change. The benefits just mentioned are hardly guaranteed. Potential costs must be considered by the leaders of strategic change.

Problems with Sequential Change

Sequential Interventions Take Time

The elements of the change process are spread out over months, even years. One danger is that people lose sight of the ultimate goals of the change process. The desired execution outcomes lose their salience or significance because short-term issues dominate managerial work. Leaders of change must constantly reinforce execution efforts, remind individuals of the ultimate outcome being pursued, and keep people focused on the change process. The long execution horizon presents an additional problem for leaders of sequential change. Simply, other factors come into play. Exogenous forces change. Competitors' actions or plans change, consumers become more price conscious, or government antitrust decisions hold implications for a company's own strategic scenarios. The sequential change process must always be adapting to these external shocks.

There are, of course, both positive and negative exogenous stocks; even positive events can tax the change process. The sudden and amazing growth of hydraulic fracking and potential increase in natural gas supplies, for example, are presenting challenges to some companies. UGI Utilities is one company being forced to make alterations to its strategic plan because of these positive external developments. Safety and infrastructure improvements (e.g, new pipelines) must be made. Managers must carefully weigh investment options, talent requirements, training programs, and other execution needs as the company undergoes change to meet the sudden growth of a new market segment. A previous process of sequential change is being interrupted by external events and demands that must be met. Top management is well aware of the new challenges facing the company and is actively involved in planning and executing the requisite changes.

An organization's internal capabilities may also change over time. Critical human resources may leave the organization. Developments in R&D or in IT systems may necessitate alteration of a sequential execution plan to account for the new developments. As with exogenous changes, managers must be attuned to internal changes and account for their impact on a sequential intervention with a long execution horizon.

Transitions Must Be Managed

In a sequential change process, the passing of the baton must be managed carefully. The sequential picture, A→B→C, seems simple and inherently logical. Work done in marketing on customer needs is passed routinely to engineering for product design. The transition from one group to another is obviously necessary and attended to by key players in both functional groups. The process, however, is not always seamless.

An insurance company I worked with closely provides a good example of transition management. Customers calling the company seeking information about the status of their application increasingly become dissatisfied with the explanation that "it's somewhere in the system," in some functional area (e.g., underwriting, credit) with no clear date of emergence. The solution? Create a transition manager position. New applications were assigned a manager who would walk the application through all processes of evaluation. Calls from customers went directly to the appropriate manager who informed them as to the location and status of their applications. The transition manager aided coordination and provided a valuable information link for customers.

A word of caution is in order, however. Chapter 5 noted significant problems with knowledge transfer and information sharing in organizations. People in engineering may not trust marketing's research methodologies. An NIH ("not invented here") syndrome may lead to the rejection or modification of transmitted information. Cooperation may be affected by a climate or culture of distrust based on previous bad experiences between functions needing to work together.

In brief, the logical and obvious transitions between groups, functions, or organizations under sequential change processes must occasionally be managed actively and carefully. Transition managers may be required to carry information and the explanations of data development from unit to unit. An engineering person may act as a liaison to marketing, perhaps even be part of marketing's deliberations. The goal of this two-function participant is to facilitate information flow and acceptance of data by the two groups.

Other mechanisms to facilitate transitions under sequential interventions may be needed. Transfer pricing under conditions of vertical integration is one such obvious mechanism. Formal project- or product-management systems are yet another, as noted previously. The point is that the required transitions cannot be left to chance. They need the active attention of managers as they cope with sequential strategic change.

Sequential Interventions May Be Boring

This is a point that has arisen more than a few times in my change-related work. Managers may see sequential change processes as less than exciting. They see the logic of serial changes that feed one into another. They espouse the benefits of planned or rational change. Still, the logical, sequential process is seen at times as mundane, an exercise in project management more than an exciting challenge in managing strategic change.

The leader's job here is obvious but not always easy. Use of intermittent feedback or rewards, the celebration of interim successes, partial strategy reviews of goals and performance, and other such activities are necessary to keep key personnel's eyes on the ball. Important industry or competitive changes could go unnoticed because of this boredom or malaise, and leaders of sequential interventions must work to ensure that appropriate attention is continuously paid to important execution outcomes.

The costs and benefits of managing large, strategic changes in a sequential fashion are noted in Table 7.1.

Table 7.1 Costs and Benefits of Sequential and Complex Changes

	Sequential Change	Complex Change
Benefits	Planned, rational change. Methodical and paced.	High "speed"; large problems are confronted quickly.
	Opportunity to celebrate success and reduce resistance to change.	Complex change is exciting, seldom boring.
	Clear cause-effect analysis, allowing for organizational control and learning.	Creation of esprit de corps.
	Incremental investments can be made.	
Costs/Problems	Sequential interventions take time.	Coordination and control are difficult.
	Exogenous forces and organizational capabilities change.	Cause-effect clarity is low.
	Transitions must be managed.	Learning suffers.
	The change process may be "boring."	Certain performance criteria must be relaxed, and managers cannot be held accountable for them.

COMPLEX CHANGE

If the leaders of large-scale, strategic changes feel that the time available for execution is short, complex change is the result (box 4 in Figure 7.1).

With complex change, the strategic problem facing the organization is large. Many aspects or elements of change are needed to respond to and cope with the problem. And given the short time for execution, they all must be handled or done simultaneously. This, then, is a defining characteristic of complex change: Everything important is going on at once during the intervention. The short time frame demands the simultaneous consideration of key change variables to beat the time constraint.

There arguably are some benefits of employing a complex change. Large problems are confronted faster. This approach increases the speed of response to change, which may be touted as an advantage. Things are attacked and attended to quickly rather than being drawn out.

Complex changes can also be exciting. They certainly seldom are boring. Managers at all levels of the company roll up their sleeves and pitch in, all at once, to confront and solve a major strategic problem. This pervasive, overriding approach often breeds a camaraderie of sorts, an esprit de corps, as C-level managers "toil in the soil" with middle managers, get their collective hands dirty, and solve the organization's vulnerability before a large strategic threat.

Speed and camaraderie are seemingly both attained when confronting change. This sounds wonderful, a positive testament to the virtues of complex interventions involving big problems and many individuals or functional units simultaneously.

If this sounds too good to be true, it's because it usually is too good to be true. The seemingly positive aspects of complex change notwithstanding, this change process teems with problems. It flirts with disaster. It creates a number of issues that virtually guarantee the failure of change and poor execution outcomes. Indeed, let's make the following assertion:

> *Complex change should be avoided, if possible. Unless it's absolutely inevitable, a complex intervention should rarely be used purposely and willingly. Complex change courts disaster and, more often than not, guarantees the poor execution of strategic change.*

To managers who say they enjoy complex change, these indeed are fighting words. Obviously, this strong statement needs justification. How can I or anyone raise such emphatic storm warnings about complex change? To answer the question, let's consider some of the problems routinely encountered with this approach. Examples can then be used to highlight the problems in actual change situations.

Problems with Complex Change

At least four major problems characterize complex change. The overall difficulty of this change process is exacerbated by the fact that all four problems are always present. These, then, are not separate, intermittent problems; they are constant elements of the change that, together, increase the difficulty of change management and jeopardize execution outcomes:

1. **Coordination and control are difficult.** Under complex change, it is difficult to set up effective coordination mechanisms and controls. Too much is going on at once. Different individuals or units are responding to change-related problems in real time, at once, and this simultaneous treatment of multiple problems in multiple areas or geographical settings defies easy coordination.

   A ranking manager in the National Hurricane Center in Miami once attended a Wharton executive program. He suggested that his organization routinely faced huge problems of coordination and control during major hurricanes (a big problem!). When a huge storm hits, people are working everywhere to save lives (first) and property (second). Different organizations and resources are marshaled into action (the Red Cross, National Guard, State Police, Army Reserve, emergency medical personnel, local hospitals, and so on). They all respond to the problem, handling things as they occur and change, usually according to their organization's own rules and standard operating procedures.

   So much activity in so many different organizations, all with their own methods and hierarchical arrangements, provides a nightmare for coordination and control. A command center is set up. However, the many decentralized activities that are occurring in the teeth of a vicious storm that rarely acts in a predictable manner make establishment of centralized controls extremely difficult at best. That organizations such as the National Hurricane Center can perform at all under such adverse conditions is remarkable.

United Continental Holdings created major turbulence for itself and its customers by moving too fast and changing too many business elements or processes simultaneously— reservations systems, websites, frequent flier programs. Coordinating and controlling problems when too many programs or projects are being worked on at once creates a herculean task not easily addressed.

The large global law firm is beset with many problems as it grows. In addition to complex legal issues that vary by country or region, there also are financial matters, currency problems, marketing issues, budgeting needs, political changes, regime instability, different time zones, and so on that together add to the problems of lawyer-managers. If the lawyers try to handle all of these problems or challenges at once or deal with rapid, large changes simultaneously, coordination and control become difficult, if not impossible. Law-related issues are difficult enough; the management issues only increase the intensity of the situation.

Too much is going on to handle all things at once. Complex change clearly threatens the ability to control global growth of the large law firm. The organizational structure and decision-making process of the large global firm are different in 2013 than they were just a decade or so ago, challenging coordination and control mechanisms.[xii] Handling this complexity is a prime task, and a new management structure must be added to the normal lawyer-based operations, a new but challenging job-related need, a point returned to in the chapter on service organizations.

In 2012, Knight Capital Group was hurt by a computer-trading malfunction. The problem highlighted a risk that now is gaining increasing attention: ever-faster stock trading in increasingly complex markets. Increased velocity of trading is taxing companies' abilities to keep up with the market. According to one perceptive analysis, traders and others are asking "if speed kills."[xiii] The present view is that speed can kill or, at minimum, it can present major problems as companies try to accomplish too much too fast.

The same problems of coordination and control exist in any organization facing a major strategic problem and the need to tackle it on many fronts simultaneously. A major competitive threat or external discontinuity (for example, a major innovation or technological "revolution") may demand a change in strategy, pricing, distribution, incentives, marketing plans, and manufacturing schedules. If all must be done simultaneously, within a short execution horizon, one can easily see the problems of control and coordination that can arise in such a situation.

2. **Cause-effect analysis is difficult, if not impossible.** Assume a company is in the throes of a complex change. By definition, time is of the essence, and many things are going on at once. If one were to "package" and depict the change process, it might look like the following:

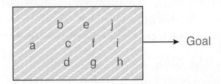

What we see is an organizational "black box" of sorts with many activities, tasks, or change programs (a–j) going on at the same time, the intention being to solve a problem or achieve some goals as quickly as possible.

Assume next that the change process fails miserably. The goal isn't attained, and the organization suffers major, but hopefully not irreparable, damage. Clearly, an autopsy is in order, and the reasons underlying the failed change must be identified and understood.

The problem is that a clear cause-effect model cannot be drawn. It is nearly impossible to explain with great certainty exactly what happened. It is difficult to explain what went wrong.

Did single elements in the "black box" of tasks, activities, and programs affect goal attainment independently of the others, as the following suggests?

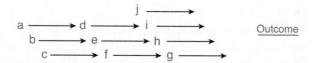

Did a through j, that is, have separate, independent effects on the outcome, as the preceding picture shows? Or were there interactive effects? Did a subset or various subsets of the ten tasks, activities, or programs interact with each other to negatively affect the outcome, as the following suggests?

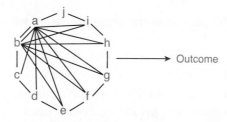

Considering that there are a huge number of possible binary combinations of a through j and a host of other combinations or permutations of three or more variables in interaction, explaining what caused the failure is virtually impossible. What explains the outcome when so many things are going on simultaneously? Nothing does, at least not easily and transparently. Cause and effect remain uncertain and unclear.

3. **Learning suffers.** The result of an unclear model of cause and effect leads logically and inexorably to yet another problem: Learning cannot occur.

   A failed major change is serious. Many resources were dedicated to the complex change, including a great deal of management's time, efforts, and commitment. At minimum, the organization wants to learn from its mistakes and prevent the reoccurrence of such a huge change-related failure in the future.

   The problem is that it can't learn. The unclear cause-effect relationship when many tasks or activities are being attended to simultaneously prevents learning. Given the difficulty of determining the independent and interactive effects of a through j on change outcomes in the previous example, what would the organization do differently in the future? What corrections in the set of tasks and activities that were handled concurrently in the complex change would be made? Which tasks or activities would be eliminated or reinforced?

There are no simple answers to these questions. Learning is not an easy option when failure results under complex change. Top management surely will try to make some educated guesses as to what needs fixing, but this represents an exercise in judgment at best.

4. **Relax the performance criteria against which people are held accountable.** The only way to make a complex change work is to reduce its complexity. The need is to focus on a small subset of simultaneous tasks, activities, or programs and not hold individuals accountable for performance in other areas. In other words, set priorities, focus on key performance outcomes, and let other performance measures slide.

Why is this cure listed as a problem of complex change? Because organizations usually aren't willing to relax or eliminate the performance criteria against which people are held accountable. They insist that managers continue to do it all. They won't let managers focus on some aspects of change and let others slip or go to Hades. They'll usually ask the overworked and embattled managers involved with complex change to:

"Do the best you can."

Being asked to "do the best you can" is usually the kiss of death. Without relaxing the number of measures that managers are responsible and accountable for, the complex change won't work. The change will be seen as a failure, and the managers involved will often be tainted by it and be seen as failures by the organization.

Asking subordinates to do everything well is basically inconsistent with sound performance management. Amir Hartman's study of successful business leaders and "ruthless" execution found, simply, that these individuals do the following:[xiv]

- Focus on a few select performance measures when managing, including when managing change. They take great care not to dilute the need for focus with too many competing measures that can detract attention from critical goals and change needs.

- Believe that a broad set of measures slows down execution and severely complicates the management of change.

Consistent with this assertion, Hartman is arguing, in effect, that setting and using too many targets, forcing managers to focus on all of them simultaneously, and refusing to back off and relax the performance criteria against which managers are evaluated and held accountable can only lead to a nightmare for the organization trying to cope with complex change. Clearly, a focus is needed on a smaller number of critical change objectives.

Let's consider a few actual examples to bring the preceding points to life and show the negative consequences of complex change.

The National Hurricane Center

This organization succeeds because it sets priorities and relaxes less important performance criteria.

Faced with a hurricane and the complex coordination problems previously mentioned, the center focuses on its primary goal: saving lives. Saving property is a distant secondary goal, and little else matters.

Imagine if other performance criteria weren't relaxed. Picture a situation in which managers were held accountable for "sandbag utilization per life saved" or some other such hypothetical measure. Imagine the anxiety or angst of managers and workers toiling during a major storm if they knew they would be held accountable for the efficient use of sand and sandbags!

Is this an unrealistic example? Perhaps not, if one considers other real-world examples depicting similar issues.

General Motors: A Case of Quality Improvement

I once observed a case of needed quality improvement involving transaxles at GM. Quality problems had surfaced, and the company wanted to do something about them.

The first major problem was that early analysis uncovered a host of individuals or units responsible for quality of the affected component. Ultimate accountability, however, was unclear. This was a case of "when everyone is responsible, then no one is responsible." The situation was eventually cleared up, and individuals were assigned the responsibility of tackling the quality problem.

One individual (whose identity is not in my notes but whose plan was given to me by James Powers of Corporate Strategic Planning) had a novel approach to the problem. He and his unit would focus solely on certain, clearly defined quality parameters and solve the problem. The company would have to agree to relax or eliminate other, less important performance indicators against which he or his unit was usually evaluated. One example is overtime expense. Whereas overtime expense is usually a measure that plant managers or department heads would be held accountable for, the plan in question would have had upper managers disregard overtime expense and similar metrics while the main focus was on quality improvement.

Higher-ups in GM in their infinite wisdom rejected the proposed plan. They realized the difficulty, of course, of focusing on a complex issue such as quality improvement while also being held accountable for a host of other performance measures. Still, their advice was, "Do it all; do the best you can," under the trying circumstances.

The manager and his people, however, remained adamant: They refused to do it all. They would solve the quality problem but only according to their plan of action, which required the relaxation or elimination of many normal or routine measures of performance. This stubbornness was clearly risky, as it presented an ultimatum to higher management. Still, the manager persisted, arguing that his approach was the best way to tackle and solve the complex problem at hand. To try and "do the best you can" and meet a large number of performance objectives simultaneously would surely culminate in failure or unhappy results.

The company finally relented. They accepted the plan with its focus on the key quality issue and relaxation of secondary measures of performance. The plan worked, and the quality improvements were achieved in a relatively short period of time, much to the credit of those in charge of execution.

GE: The "Stars" Versus the Second Team

Another example comes from my experiences as a "Work Out" consultant in GE Aerospace.

I often worked closely with an extremely capable and committed manager. At one point in time, in addition to his tasks as part of a "Work-Out," this manager was involved with another, very difficult project. The situation clearly was a complex change. The problem being solved was huge, and the time frame was short. The manager (I'll call him Bob) and his charges, a cross-functional team, had reacted cautiously and somewhat reluctantly when first asked to tackle the problem. They knew the low probabilities attached to the successful outcome of the complex situation that was presented to them. Still, being good "company men," they agreed to the task. They agreed to do the best they could with a tough assignment.

Progress on the complex change was haltingly slow. A focus on one area was met with new problems or unanticipated shocks in another. Despite the hard work, hours spent, and total commitment of the change team, positive results were scarce and short lived.

One day, after an especially frustrating and unsuccessful attempt at making a dent in an important technical component of the overall change, Bob asked if I'd meet him for a drink after work. He'd like, he said, to talk over a few things pertaining to the project. I suspected, ominously, that something was up, and was I ever right.

Bob announced, after a drink and the exchange of general pleasantries, that he was leaving the company. This shocked me, as he clearly was seen as a star with a bright future. He was accepting a great new job in a higher position with better pay, so the move was a positive step in his career. Yet he did add something that was, at the time, very disconcerting.

Bob mentioned that the complex project he was laboring on was getting him down. Hard work was getting him and his team nowhere. Too much was going on at once to allow a good handle on the problem, and the prognosis for success really looked bleak.

He also said that he worried immensely about the prospect of failure in a company such as GE that really focused on getting results. In fact, he envisioned a scenario he didn't like. He and other top-notch people ("stars," the "first team") had been assigned a huge problem to solve. The task was difficult and complex, but again, they were encouraged to do their best. Now it began to look like they could not succeed with the task. Bob then explained what he really feared would happen.

He feared failure, of course, as he was definitely a high achiever. He also feared that the "first team" would be tarnished in the eyes of many. He said he saw it happen before. The first team, the stars, falters and fails. Everyone will say it was an impossible task to begin with, so failure or at least major problems were not unexpected. The first team's efforts are acknowledged, but the bulk of the original problem still exists.

The company then redefines the problem. It reduces its difficulty and even breaks it down into smaller chunks. A "second team" is assigned the new task, and they usually fare much better than the first team could with a much more difficult and complex task. The second team succeeds where the first team couldn't.

Bob's fear, based on his perception of the situation, was that his status within the company could be tainted. As silly as it sounds, he said, he felt that what is perceived becomes what is real. If he and his first-team colleagues were perceived as failures, this indeed could become part of the company folklore or insidious reality over time. This, he offered, could affect his career advancement in some way.

Was Bob paranoid or just wrong? Perhaps both, but this case is not totally far fetched. Companies do hurl individuals into the fray of complex changes, and performance suffers for all the reasons just noted. Does the performance mishap—or possibly multiple mishaps—affect the perception of an individual's value to the organization? It certainly is possible, and probably likely, in a competitive climate that stresses results and consistent performance. In a company where results count greatly, failure to produce them, even when constrained by the difficulties of a complex change, could easily be seen over time as managerial failure.

The intention here is to emphasize that examples abound to show that complex change is difficult and problematic. It often fails because of the following four reasons (listed in Table 7.1):

- Coordination and control are extremely difficult to achieve when many changes are happening simultaneously.
- The cause-effect analysis that is vital to explaining significant deviations in performance is virtually impossible.
- The organization cannot easily learn from its mistakes.
- Organizations are unwilling or reluctant to reduce the number of performance criteria against which individuals are held accountable, which can guarantee poor performance.

The last requirement—that organizations focus on as few critical performance or execution outcomes as possible—is absolutely vital to making complex change work. The more tasks, activities, or change programs that must be attended to simultaneously, the greater the velocity of change, the pressure on individuals, and the probability of failure or major change-related problems.

Faced with large strategic problems, an organization should rely on sequential change, despite its unexciting nature. If complex change is inevitable, then the warnings and issues presented on the vagaries and difficulties of complex change must be acknowledged and addressed by management in as effective a way as possible. At minimum, top management must reduce the number of performance criteria against which individuals are held accountable to give the change a chance and increase the probability of success.

OTHER FACTORS AFFECTING CHANGE

There are, of course, other factors that affect the success of change attempts that are needed to make strategy work. This chapter focused on how the nature of a change— defined by its size and the time available for execution—affects how the change is managed and the prognosis for success. These issues, it was argued, are usually not discussed well in the massive literature on change and, thus, are in need of attention.

Again, however, our task is not yet complete. Managing change and execution successfully demands that attention be paid to two additional issues: (a) managing culture and cultural change, and (b) understanding power or influence in organizations. Both affect execution success and whether strategy works. Both affect the process of change, as an organization copes with competitive conditions and challenges over time.

The next chapter picks up where this one leaves off. Chapter 8 deals with managing culture and cultural change, including how to overcome resistance to change. Chapter 9 then considers the role and impact of power and influence on the strategy-execution process and its outcomes.

SUMMARY

There are a number of key points about managing change that are important to the success of execution. They are as follows:

- Managing change is important for strategy execution. Execution often implies change in key factors such as strategy, structure, coordination mechanisms, short-term measures of performance, incentives, and controls. How change is implemented often means success or failure of strategy-execution efforts.

- Managing change is still a major execution problem, as the data reported in the present research strongly suggest. In fact, the Wharton-Gartner, Wharton Executive Education surveys, and follow-up research and discussions with managers noted the inability to manage change as the single biggest obstacle to effective strategy execution. The problem is due in large part to the complexity of the steps required to manage change effectively. These include the following:

- Assessing accurately the size and content of a strategic change
- Determining the time available for the execution of change
- Determining the steps or tactics to be employed in managing the change
- Clarifying responsibility and accountability in the change process
- The need to overcome resistance to change
- Setting up controls to monitor the results of change management

■ This chapter focused on the first three issues, as these have not been systematically considered in the literature on change management. Specifically, the impact of the relationship between (a) the size of a change problem and (b) the time available for execution on how a change is executed is explored. Four approaches to change—evolutionary, managerial, sequential, and complex—are analyzed in depth, along with their costs and benefits for an organization.

■ A major conclusion of this analysis is that complex change is difficult and sometimes dangerous, often resulting in poor change management and failed execution. Complex change occurs when the strategic problem facing an organization is large and the time frame for execution is short, resulting in many change-related tasks or activities being attended to simultaneously. This simultaneous treatment of many difficult change issues is characterized by four major problems:

1. Coordination and control are difficult to achieve when many tasks, activities, and change-related programs are being attended to simultaneously.

2. Cause-effect analysis explaining significant deviations in performance is virtually impossible.

3. Organizational learning is jeopardized because of the lack of cause and effect clarity.

4. Organizations are not willing to reduce the performance requirements for which managers are accountable, which virtually guarantees poor outcomes under complex change.

■ When the strategic problems facing an organization loom large, sequential change is preferred. It is logical to break the large change into smaller, more manageable pieces or elements and manage change sequentially, focusing on each element only when the previous one is completed satisfactorily. There is a downside to sequential change—it takes time, unanticipated factors can impinge on the process over time, and it is unexciting—but it is an effective way to handle large changes rationally and methodically.

■ Other factors affect the success of change management, including culture and overcoming resistance to change. These are considered in Chapter 8, the next chapter that deals with effective execution and management of change.

ENDNOTES

i.   Spencer Johnson, *Who Moved My Cheese?*, Putnam, 2001.

ii. Daisuke Wakabayashi, "Hitachi President Prods Turnaround," *The Wall Street Journal*, May 11, 2012.

iii. Ibid.

iv. Susan Carey, "United Merger Turbulence Hits Elite Frequent Fliers," *The Wall Street Journal*, May 24, 2012. See, too, Susan Carey, "United's CEO Apologizes for Service Woes," *The Wall Street Journal*, July 27, 2012.

v.   See Schumpeter, "Simplify and Repeat," *The Economist*, April 28, 2012.

vi. "Changes Needed at Avon Are More Than Cosmetic," Knowledge@Wharton, April 25, 2012.

vii. "As Mayer Brings the Pizzazz, Yahoo Waits for the Magic," Knowledge@wharton, July 17, 2012.

viii. An early, "barebones" version of this model and its components without an in-depth discussion of execution-related issues and problems can be found in L. G. Hrebiniak and William Joyce's *Implementing Strategy*, Macmillan, 1984.

ix. Use of binary variables for continuous variables such as time and size of change may not represent an ideal way to operationalize these factors. Still, for the purposes of this discussion, use of binary distinctions such as "long" and "short" time frames is useful and valid for describing the effects of variables such as size and speed of change on execution outcomes.

x. A. M. Knott, "The Dynamic View of Hierarchy," *Management Science*, Vol. 47, No. 3, 2001.

xi. "Shareholders OK Merger for Creating No. 3 Bank," *Philadelphia Inquirer*, March 18, 2004; "Bank of America Vows Slow Post-Merger Change," *Philadelphia Inquirer*, April 2, 2004.

xii. See Jennifer Smith and Ashby Jones, "Practicing Business," *The Wall Street Journal*, May 7, 2012. The management issues in these large global law firms are treated later in Chapter 12. The present discussion is intended only to raise the issues surrounding the difficulties of coordination and control under conditions of complex change.

xiii. Tom Lauricella and Scott Patterson, "With Knight Wounded, Traders Ask if Speed Kills," *The Wall Street Journal*, August 3, 2012.

xiv. Amur Hartman, *Ruthless Execution*, Prentice-Hall/Pearson Education, 2004.

8

Managing Culture and Culture Change

Introduction

Managing culture is important to strategy execution. A solid alignment of culture and execution methods fosters execution success, while a misalignment can create horrendous problems.

James Burke, a past CEO of Johnson & Johnson, was emphatic and succinct years ago when he explained his company's outstanding performance and ability to handle crises by stating that, "Our culture is really it." Even at the time of his death in 2012, J&J still focused on its "Credo" as a statement of culture and how to compete and treat customers and employees. Culture is alive, openly discussed, and important at J&J. We can add a simple fact to Burke's statement: Culture can make a big difference in execution.

In contrast, a "corporate culture of concealment" was blamed by Mitsubishi Fuso Truck and Bus president Wilfried Porth when explaining his company's cover-up of defects in its products.[i] Similarly, a House subcommittee was told that Enron's culture was "arrogant" and "intimidating," discouraging employees from blowing the whistle on shady deals going on within the trading company.[ii] Culture clearly affects behavior.

Recent research supports assertions about the effects of culture. One in-depth research project found that a company culture geared to high standards and a strong emphasis on results produced outstanding performance at both Campbell's Soup and Home Depot.[iii] Another well-known study found that a culture of discipline was instrumental in producing positive execution results at Circuit City, Nucor, Walgreens, and other companies.[iv] Cultures that support risk taking have been associated with such outcomes as innovation, cooperation, and product development in yet other analyses of the impact of culture.[v]

Culture is pervasive and important. It affects and reflects methods of strategy execution. Yet, despite its importance, some caution is in order. As is emphasized in this chapter, culture is affected by other factors or conditions. Culture shapes behavior but is also affected by behavior and the factors that shape behavior. A practical question, then, is what is the relative importance of culture versus the factors or conditions that shape or affect it?

A related issue or problem is that managers often don't know how to change culture effectively. They understand fully that culture affects execution, but their attempts at culture change fall short. The purpose of this chapter is to explain culture and show how to change culture, when necessary, to achieve execution success.

WHAT IS CULTURE?

There are many aspects of culture, which makes it a complex phenomenon. At the societal level, it refers to the development of intellectual and moral faculties via education and learning, the enlightenment and excellence of taste acquired by aesthetic and intellectual training, the tastes and behavior of a group or class of people, and a stage of advancement of a civilization, among other things.[vi] These aspects of culture, while interesting, are not extremely helpful to leaders of organizational change and strategy execution.

What is more interesting and to the point is organizational culture. This normally includes the norms and values of an organization, including the vision shared by organizational members. Culture usually has a behavioral component, defining the "way an organization does things," including decision-making, how it competes, how much risk it tolerates, the emphasis it places on ethics or fairness in its transactions, and how people treat or evaluate one another's actions and contributions to the organization. Culture also refers sometimes to the outcomes of these behaviors, including organizational creativity or innovation.

For our purposes, let's use the following simple model of culture and behavior:

Culture ⟶	Behavior
• Shared Values and Norms • A Common Vision/Credo • Common Goals, Incentives	• "The Way We Do Things" • How We Compete • How We Treat Each Other • Risk Taking, Innovation

Culture refers to the shared values, vision, or "credo" that creates a propensity for individuals in an organization to act in certain ways. Goals and incentives reflect and reinforce this propensity to act, and the result of this cultural bias is reflected in actual behavior. While admittedly simple, this model suggests some important characteristics of culture and behavior in organizations that affect execution.

CULTURE IS IMPORTANT FOR EXECUTION

It is necessary to talk only briefly to someone from J&J about the importance and contribution of its "credo" over the years to understand this assertion about the importance of culture. Critical decisions and their consequences are constantly held up against the "credo" by J&J's management to help them assess the relative worth of strategic decisions and execution methods. The "credo" is a live and pervasive aspect of J&J's culture that affects behavior.

In my experience, culture is so important in some companies—for example, Nucor, Google, and GE—that new hires must virtually pass muster on an informal "cultural due diligence" before they are hired. Someone who once interviewed at Google told me that people he spoke to cared little about his academic background and professional accomplishments. They were concerned much more with his ability to meld with the team he might be joining.

More and more companies are conducting formal cultural due diligence before entering mergers or executing acquisitions. Southwest Airlines spent two full months analyzing the cultural compatibility of Morris Air before acquiring it. In contrast, insufficient early cultural due diligence probably added to the woes of DaimlerChrysler as it tried and failed to work out the kinks in its merger. An emphasis on cultural due diligence is becoming increasingly prevalent and important because of culture's impact on execution.

CULTURE IS NOT HOMOGENEOUS

While some aspects of organizational culture may be pervasive and homogeneous throughout an organization, other aspects are more heterogeneous.

Organizations, as with a country or a society, have subcultures. Manufacturing personnel have different goals, values, perceptions, or time frames for decision-making than the scientists in R&D. Marketing people see the competitive world differently than individuals in operations or engineering. While culture refers to values, incentives, or behavioral guidelines that people share, subcultures sometimes define differences in these same characteristics within the organization. To simplify the present discussion, reference will be made primarily to organizational culture unless an explicit example of subcultural differences on execution is introduced.

CULTURE AFFECTS PERFORMANCE

For our purposes, this is a critical aspect of organizational culture. Culture affects performance. The simple model just introduced can be changed to look like the following:

Culture ⟶ Behavior ⟶ Organizational Performance

Culture elicits and reinforces certain behaviors within organizations. These behaviors, in turn, affect organizational performance in vital ways. If this weren't true, culture would hold little interest for managers involved in execution efforts. Because it is true, it is necessary to pursue this point further to ensure a better understanding of the role of culture in making strategy work. Consider just a few examples of the effects of culture on performance:

■ A recent article addresses changes during a "lost decade" at Microsoft that, by 2012, had created a culture at the company clearly antagonistic to innovation and change. The culture moved from innovation and market leadership to a bureaucratic and "cannibalistic culture" that hurt performance, according to the article.[vii] For example, a performance appraisal system, "stack ranking," is a forced-ranking appraisal system that drove employees to compete with each other, leading to a climate hostile to cooperation. A "Windows-based bias" worked against new products that didn't work with Windows—for example, the e-reader—negatively affecting innovation. Prior success, interestingly, led to a culture based on old or traditional products and management processes that stifled change and, over time, led to internal problems and poor organizational performance. Success, indeed, can breed a culture of inertia, leading to negative results, according to this article.

■ Sony seems to be bound to a traditional Japanese culture that makes it difficult to shed businesses, people, or products in any attempt to update strategy and affect performance. It still makes and sells products like TVs even though the company's performance in this product area has been dismal for a better part of the last decade. A tradition-bound company culture makes strategic change difficult, which clearly is affecting performance. In contrast, Hitachi's major moves in 2012 exiting poorly-performing businesses suggests a company culture that is less constrained and more risk-accepting than that at Sony.

- Corporate culture clashes are a leading cause of merger-related problems. A ten-year study of 340 major acquisitions by Mercer Management Consulting, Inc., suggests the negative impact of culture clashes on performance outcomes and the execution of diversification strategies.[viii]

- Josef Ackermann's streamlining of management structures at Deutsche Bank and the introduction of Anglo-Saxon methods of doing business while eliminating old German ways were done to improve performance. He and others felt that the bank's shedding of some aspects of its German past and cultural constraints was absolutely essential to its achieving global growth.

- An effect of culture of a different sort is interesting and worthy of attention. When Advanced Micro Devices Inc. (AMD) held a meeting for an important chip announcement, some big PC companies were noticeable by their absence. AMD's chief executive, Hector Ruiz, said at the time that the companies didn't attend because Intel "intimidated" them, and fearing retribution, they opted out of the meeting. According to Ruiz, they didn't want "to risk angering Intel by becoming 'too visible' in supporting AMD," a rival chip maker.[ix] Intel's culture, he felt, is prone to retaliation, which can affect the behavior of other companies. Whether true or not, the case defines an interesting perception of company culture and how it can affect the actions of others.

- A major structural move by GM in 2012 is squarely aimed at the elimination of "fiefdoms" that, the company argues, have created a culture antagonistic to company performance.[x] Fiefdoms, it is argued, result in splintering of effort, a loss of nimbleness and efficiency, and a culture of slow-moving consensus. How the current regional managers react to increased centralization, a loss of power and influence, and a new culture based less on regional autonomy and more on corporate control is an interesting issue that needs to be tracked and amplified. Changing culture long nurtured by decentralization and an emphasis on regional control and performance won't be an easy task.

- Finally, the storied culture at Southwest Airlines that emphasizes a "family" atmosphere, core values built on doing things well, and advancement via performance, not only motivates workers, it also has contributed to the company's success as one of the most profitable U.S. airlines. Culture has affected Southwest's performance. It will be interesting to see if recent problems, including increased competition and labor unrest, affect this enviable performance record.

Many other examples can be noted, but it is clear that culture affects performance. Culture and culture clashes certainly affect the execution of strategy.

ORGANIZATIONAL PERFORMANCE AFFECTS CULTURE

This is a significant point that is not always obvious in discussions of culture. Much more attention has been paid to the effects of culture on performance than the obverse, the effects of performance on culture.

The logic underlying the assertion that performance affects culture is straightforward and compelling, and it is based on previous discussions of feedback and controls in Chapter 6 and managing change in Chapter 7. If organizational performance is poor, cause-effect analysis is undertaken to explain the negative deviation. This analysis usually results in decisions about what must be changed to improve performance. But changes in critical variables aimed at improving performance—such as changes in incentives, people, capabilities, or organizational structure—can affect culture. These changes and the modifications in behavior they produce can shape the "ways an organization does things." They can affect core values and norms in which organizational attributes are seen as important or significant.

The reverse impact of behavior on culture is suggested by the similar actions of two different CEOs—Edward Zander and Sanjay Jha—who tried to change the culture at Motorola to improve reaction to the marketplace. Both bemoaned the lack of "urgency" in the company. Both argued that a technological culture was driving product-related decisions—that is, an "inside-out" approach to market strategy that focuses on technology and stresses "build it and they, the customers, will come." Both argued, instead for an "outside-in" approach where the company reacts to and serves customers' needs and wants. But how does a CEO change an entrenched technological-based culture to a market- or customer-based one? He does it by changing people, capabilities, and incentives—actions that change behavior and priorities and, in turn, can effect a change in culture. Hiring aggressive new people and rewarding them for servicing customers can result in new ways of competing and, eventually, culture change.

Motorola's split in 2011 into two companies—Motorola Mobility and Motorola Solutions—also had culture-change overtones. The new structure allowed greater focus on two different markets and increased the autonomy and ability of top managers to deal with customers who were different and in need of tailored strategic and operating responses. Structural change can lead to behavioral change that can affect or change how a company competes and operates, which can affect culture. Notwithstanding the sale of Motorola Mobility to Google in May 2012 and the introduction of new top management teams and new cultural issues due to the need for integration of the two companies, the actions noted prior to the sale—hiring new aggressive people, adding new capabilities, changing incentives, and modifying organizational structure—were aimed at changing behavior, which, over time, can have a profound effect on culture.

In effect, the simple model previously shown is again being modified slightly to add a feedback loop:

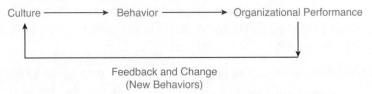

The point suggested by this model is simple but important: Culture both affects organizational performance and is affected by organizational performance. Culture is not a one-way street. Culture is both an independent, causal factor and a dependent variable that indeed can change, however slowly or reluctantly.

Let's now take the argument one step further to explain culture change. Let's try to integrate the effects of culture and what affects culture and culture change into one useful model. The effects of culture on strategy execution and the effects of execution on culture can then be seen more clearly, allowing leaders of culture change to deal more effectively with execution-related issues.

A MODEL OF CULTURE AND CULTURAL CHANGE

Figure 8.1 depicts a model of culture and culture change. The top part of the model (steps 1–4) shows the effects of culture. More importantly, the bottom part (steps 5–8) shows how to change culture, which is the main point of interest at the present time.

THE TOP LINE: THE EFFECTS OF CULTURE

The top line in Figure 8.1—steps 1 through 4—shows the effects of culture on behavior and organizational performance.

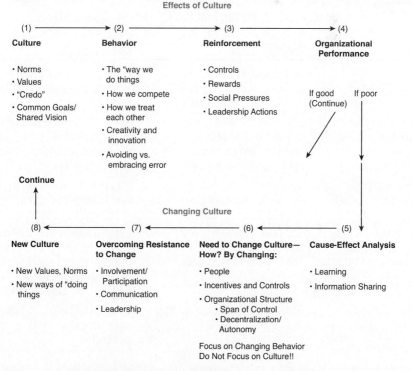

Figure 8.1 Managing Culture Change

Step 1: Culture

Again, culture comprises the main values, norms, "credos," or belief systems of an organization. It defines and creates a propensity to act in certain ways. This step assumes that an organizational culture is in place.

Step 2: Behavior

Culture affects individual and organizational behavior, the "way we do things." Behaviors include how companies compete, how people treat each other, the extent of risk taking, and desired outcomes such as creativity and innovation. For example, culture can affect the degree to which organizations avoid or embrace error, the effects of which can impact heavily how an organization operates and executes plans on a daily basis. Table 8.1 lists some examples of different behaviors, performance outcomes, and managerial "mindsets" in organizations that avoid and embrace error.[xi]

Table 8.1   Effects of Avoiding Versus Embracing Error in Organizations

	Avoiding Error	Embracing Error
Controls	Top-down, repressive, or constraining; emphasis on "being right" at all times.	Emphasis on self-control; emphasis on getting the facts.
When a mistake or problem is alleged	Deny the problem or play it down; if cannot deny problem, emphasis on blaming someone else.	Admit the error; determine and analyze the causes so as to prevent recurrence; conduct "autopsies."
Individual needs being met	Survival; defensibility of actions against threats or accusations of others is critical.	Higher-level need satisfaction due to growth, learning, and acceptance of challenge.
Setting of objectives and performance standards	Top-down, unilateral; little participation or negotiations; "all-or-nothing standards."	Participative process; effective discussion and confrontation of conflict; goals and performance standards are not "all-or-nothing" or "black and white."
Attitude toward change	Resistance to change is high.	Embraces change as unavoidable, necessary, and beneficial.

	Avoiding Error	Embracing Error
Interpersonal orientation	Guarded; low trust; alienation.	Open; high levels of trust; emphasis on cooperation and joint efforts.
Innovation and creativity	Low.	High.

The point of Table 8.1 is to show that culture affects behavior in big ways, some of which may occasionally be negative. In extreme cases of risk avoidance, culture creates an emphasis on blame, survival, and low trust. It hurts organizational learning and fosters high resistance to change. Error avoidance is disastrous for creativity, innovation, and successful organizational adaptation.

In contrast, organizational cultures that embrace errors treat mistakes as necessary components of risk taking. Top managers I've known have argued that a company focused on innovation and new approaches to competition inevitably makes mistakes. Some have said openly that, if people aren't committing errors or making mistakes, they aren't trying to innovate. It's that simple. When the unavoidable mistakes are made, these managers focus on conducting "autopsies" and facing the brutal facts. They also embrace change as unavoidable and beneficial for the achievement of organizational goals, including those related to execution. Clearly, culture can exert positive and negative effects on behavior in organizations, potentially affecting execution outcomes.

Step 3: Reinforcement of Behavior

As Chapter 6 stressed, incentives and controls guide and reinforce behavior. The reward structure tells individuals what's important. It reinforces behavior that is consistent with organizational goals and culture. Leadership actions likewise signal what behaviors and outcomes are valued by the organization. The sum total of activities in step 3 in Figure 8.1 is to reinforce desired behavior and aspects of culture, creating a form of peer pressure and hierarchical influence on doing the right things.

Step 4: Organizational Performance

Culture affects performance. If performance is good, there usually is a positive alignment of culture, goals, behavior, and reinforcement methods. All is in sync. Good performance lends credibility to the top line in Figure 8.1. The effects of culture are positive, and all is right with the world. Poor performance, however, poses a problem. Poor performance indicates that something isn't working. It is necessary to discern what the underlying problems are, which takes us to step 5 in Figure 8.1.

Step 5: Cause-Effect Analysis

Step 5 provides an important transition between the top line in Figure 8.1 (Effects of Culture) and the bottom line (Changing Culture), so it is mentioned in the discussion of both topics. Consistent again with the discussion of controls in Chapter 6 and change in Chapter 7, significant deviations in performance, positive or negative, must be explained. This example focuses for discussion purposes on poor performance only, meaning significant negative deviations from desired goals or outcomes. What is needed is a complete cause-effect analysis to explain the negative performance. This is a necessary prerequisite for organizational change. Without cause-effect clarity, learning and organizational change are simply not possible.

Assume for a moment that cause-effect analysis indicates that major changes are needed. New competitive or industry forces exist, technological innovations have rendered current methods virtually obsolete, and new strategies and ways of doing business are necessary. Assume, too, that top management decides that cultural change is needed to facilitate and support the massive changes in strategy and operations that are required. The question, then, is how does one change organizational culture to support execution of the new strategy?

THE BOTTOM LINE: CHANGING CULTURE

The bottom line in Figure 8.1 deals with culture change. The process of change begins in step 5, with the cause-effect analysis just discussed. The results of this analysis, including the underlying problems negatively affecting performance and the logic behind the contemplated changes, must be fully understood and communicated adequately. Cause-effect analysis tells us what went wrong and why. But this knowledge or learning is useless unless it gets to the right people, individuals who can act on the information. This information, then, must be transferred and communicated effectively.

The first step in changing culture, then, is communication and information sharing. The reasons and logic underlying the need for change must be complete, unambiguous, and compelling. The data supporting and justifying change must reach the right people.

Refer momentarily to the discussion of complex change in Chapter 7. When the causes of poor performance cannot be determined because of the many forces or factors under complex change that are going on simultaneously, learning cannot occur. Cause-effect analysis sheds little or no light on the causes of poor performance.

It follows logically that under these conditions, communication and information sharing about the need for change cannot occur. The reasons and logic for change are not complete, unambiguous, or compelling. Cause-effect analysis yields no clear results. The first step in changing culture, then, cannot be achieved. Effective communication and information sharing cannot occur.

This is why step 5—cause-effect analysis—is so important for culture change. Without it and the communication of findings that result from this analysis, culture change is on a shaky footing. It is doomed from the outset.

For purposes of discussion, assume that the cause-effect analysis is complete, clear, and compelling. Assume, too, that the results of this analysis and the need for change have been communicated clearly and completely to the right people. The culture change process can then move on to step 6 in Figure 8.1.

Step 6: Changing Culture

This is a critical step. It suggests that, to change culture, it is not wise or effective to focus directly on culture. To change culture, that is, don't focus on culture itself or the underlying defining aspects of culture: values, norms, and "credos." Don't try to change attitudes, hoping for a change in behavior. Focus instead on behavior.

The logic here is twofold. First, it is virtually impossible to appeal to people to change their beliefs, values, or attitudes. Requests of managers for more open-mindedness in decision-making or more tolerance of subordinates' mistakes or risk taking sounds nice, but they usually have no impact whatsoever on managers' underlying beliefs, values, and attitudes, or execution-related behavior. Managers will say that they'll try to do things differently, but such a promise usually bears little fruit. Behavior doesn't change easily in the face of requests to do so.

Second, it is important to recall that culture both affects behavior and performance and is affected and reinforced by behavior and performance. Culture and its effects are not a one-way street. Culture affects behavior, but behaviors also affect and reinforce culture. It is possible, then, to posit the following relationship:

Behavior ⟶ Culture

Changing behavior, that is, can challenge cultural norms and, ultimately, change them. Culture is a dependent variable, affected by behavior, as well as a causal variable, affecting behavior.

In light of these points, how does one change behavior and, ultimately, culture? The answer is by changing people, incentives, controls, and organizational structure, as Figure 8.1 suggests.

Hiring new people often results in bringing fresh ideas, capabilities, and new ways of doing things into an organization. New skills and capabilities create a need or drive for action and for ways to exercise and use the new capabilities. Bringing in people with rare or desired technical capabilities virtually creates a situation in which individuals yearn to use their skills and create new and exciting programs, processes, and results. New capabilities can indeed drive new behaviors.

Transferring incumbents of jobs to other positions and replacing them with fresh blood can do much to effect changes in culture and the norms supporting it. The fastest and most effective way to eliminate complacency is to bring in people with a sense of urgency. Trying to appeal to complacent people to change alone won't work. Bringing in fresh blood from inside and outside the organization can change things faster.

The CIA has been under fire in the past because of its intelligence shortcomings. Critics of the intelligence community have pointed to an increasingly ineffective, bureaucratic approach to execution of the agency's work.[xii]

An intelligence organization must perform two tasks. It must (a) collect data on information and then (b) analyze that information, looking for coherent patterns or emerging facts. According to the critics, the collection of intelligence data is being done well; it's the shortage of qualified analysts that's causing the problem. There's an insufficient number of experts who can analyze multiple data sources, detect underlying patterns, and effectively "connect the dots," according to those critical of agency performance. Bureaucrats have been replacing qualified analysts, and execution of the analytical side of intelligence work has suffered. The remedy? Bring in new blood. Bring in analysts who know how to discern patterns in information or intelligence data. Search for and hire people with the right capabilities. Doing so will transform the CIA's culture back into the analytical juggernaut it used to be.

Collins's argument about getting "the right people on the bus" also suggests the impact of people on behavior, execution, and culture change.[xiii] Hiring the right people, individuals with certain desired characteristics—skills, aggressiveness, achievement-orientation, dogged determination, and so on—can affect execution and culture.

Changing incentives and controls likewise can bring about culture change. Rewarding people for performance or competitive success goes a long way in changing a culture in which rewards had been based on seniority or official titles only. Incentives guide behavior in new directions and add value to the pursuit of new ways of doing things. Likewise, controls reward the new, desired behaviors and outcomes, reinforcing their importance and creating new norms and values about the appropriate ways to act and compete.

The right incentives and controls can even effect change in the "wrong" people. Managers may exhibit complacency in execution simply because that's what the organization rewards and reinforces, even if unknowingly. Changing incentives and controls may bring out the right behaviors in at least some portion of a group of "wrong" or complacent managers. Combining new people with new incentives and controls is clearly an aggressive way to change behavior, execution methods, and culture.

Changes in organizational structure also can affect behavior and lead to cultural change. Flattening organizations, for example, usually leads to larger spans of control, by definition. Larger spans, in turn, mean that individuals must exercise autonomy and discretionary decision-making in a more decentralized structure. Relying on a superior is possible when spans of control are small. When spans are large, reliance on hierarchy to solve problems virtually disappears as an option. Individuals must take the bull by the horns and make decisions, as they are unable to easily pass on their problems and concerns to a higher hierarchical position.

One can easily argue that exercising autonomy in a flatter, decentralized structure surely affects culture. The need for autonomy becomes a core cultural value. The exercise of discretion and autonomous decision-making becomes valued, and individuals come to resent any incursions on or detractions from their managerial freedom and self-control. Structural change indeed can bring about cultural change.

> When changing culture, it is far wiser and more effective to focus on changing people, incentives, controls, and organizational structure. These changes affect behavior that, in turn, brings about changes in culture.

Popular but Ineffective Approaches to Culture Change

This book began with an early example of changes in a division of AT&T. The CEO at the time knew he would have to instill a new culture and spirit into the organization. He would have to change some core values and norms. To accomplish something new and totally foreign—successful performance in a new, highly competitive landscape—culture change was absolutely essential. It wasn't something nice to do or a luxury; cultural change was vital and necessary.

The first attempts at culture change mirrored those of many other companies. The focus was on appeals to change, telling key managers that their mindsets would have to be different to compete successfully. Appeals were made to think differently (think "strategically") and form a new cultural thrust that centered on competition and new, value-added measures of performance.

Emphasis early on was also placed on teamwork and building a cohesive top-management team to handle the challenging new competitive thrusts. Again, this is consistent with the actions of many companies as they hold retreats, raft white water, climb rocks, have paint-gun battles, and so on, all in the name of team building.

The simple fact is that these early attempts at cultural change are often useless and ineffective. Appeals for teamwork and cultural change sound great. Teambuilding activities are fun, and they might have some positive effects in the short term. The problem is that when all is said and done, when the teambuilding exercises are over, managers return to the same organization, the same structure, the old incentives and controls, and processes that characterize the same old decision-making and power structure. In a brief period of time, everything is back to "normal," with the familiar, same-old ways of doing things. The old culture is intact. Nothing has changed.

It may indeed be that some things actually deteriorate. I remember vividly the comments of one manager who, upon getting "back to normal" after a period of off-site teambuilding in a company undergoing change, remarked on the value of his experiences:

> *I always felt that my boss was closed-minded and intolerant. After spending a week with him and others becoming sensitized to critical areas of teamwork and cultural change, I now am positively sure of it. He'll never change, and this is frustrating.*

If appeals to teamwork and admonitions about culture change go unheeded, what does one do to affect culture? Again, the answer is seen in Figure 8.1.

Effective Leaders Change Incentives and Controls

If a new competitive industry is looming, managers can change incentives to reward competitive success. Put more pay at risk. Tie rewards to performance. Stop rewarding people solely for "getting older."

Forging a link between performance and rewards will change behavior. It will also increase the value of the new behaviors because they are instrumental in achieving positive feedback and desired rewards. The reinforcement of competitive behavior will lead to a new culture, a new set of values or beliefs about performance and the right ways to conduct business.

Some recent articles have looked at CEO performance and incentive compensation in the 2011-2012 period and found that, more and more, shareholders are demanding that CEO pay be consistent with and reflect corporate performance.[xiv] The impact of these demands, however, goes beyond the CEO suite. They raise the more general issues of (a) the importance of compensation schemes at every organizational level and (b) the ultimate impact of the incentive-performance link on organizational climate or culture. Top managers as role models reinforce the need for a culture or context in which "free-riding" is eliminated and people are rewarded for results. Leaders can affect culture in this way; what's appropriate for the C-level group certainly should be reflected throughout the organization.

Other articles and studies support this link between leader behavior and company culture.[xv] Leaders can bring about culture change, directly and indirectly, via their behavior and definition of what is worthy of attention, including what factors affect incentive compensation.

Effective Leaders Change and Develop People

Some people simply won't like a change in incentives, controls, or structure. They'll resist wholeheartedly, desiring a return to the old comfortable incentive methods and ways of doing business. Faced with this situation, managers may opt out. They leave the organization or take jobs elsewhere in the same company where incentives and controls are not tied to actual performance.

But happily and more importantly, in these situations new people come in. Individuals attracted by jobs with clear linkages between performance and rewards enter the organization or change jobs within it. Typically, they are managers with a high need for achievement lured by the prospect of accomplishment, positive feedback, and control over the conditions that affect their rewards.

The importance of organizational development or training processes cannot be overstated here. Managers with new skills and capabilities need not come from without; they can be developed internally. The need is for organizational leadership to commit resources to this task. A commitment to existing people via company development programs is a powerful signal that can affect company culture in a positive way. These programs signal a strong commitment to existing human resources and the development of new, useful skills among current employees, which can positively affect performance, commitment to the organization, and company culture.

People with positive mindsets about the links between performance and rewards provide grist for the cultural mill. They help create a new culture. Bringing in or developing managers with the requisite skills and motivation to compete brings about a needed cultural change.

In brief, savvy managers I've known have changed culture, not by appealing to managers' beliefs, attitudes, and values but by fostering changes in behavior. Behavioral change in response to new incentives and controls can affect culture change. Bringing in or developing people with fresh ideas and new capabilities lays the foundation for culture change.

Structural Change and Culture Change

Changing structure, too, can bring about culture change. I recall a situation at Sears in which top management was concerned about undue corporate influence on decisions made at the store level. Corporate staff and regional managers were seen as having too much say over local decisions about product lines, merchandising methods, and competitive strategy at its many, geographically dispersed stores. The immediate issue was how to minimize centralized interference in operations that had to become increasingly decentralized due to competitive conditions. The longer-term, strategic issue was how to create a culture of autonomy, action, and a desire for local control at the store level to foster quicker local reactions to competitive trends and consumer tastes.

To create the desired store culture, Sears could have appealed to corporate and regional managers to butt out of store operations, keep a low profile, and let store managers control the bulk of local decisions. An appeal could have been made simultaneously to store managers to exercise autonomy and take charge of their operations. But management at the time was smart enough to know that such admonitions simply wouldn't work. Old habits die hard. A culture based for years on the values of centralized control wouldn't easily succumb to simple requests to do things differently.

What Sears did made sense. They eliminated or consolidated many of the regional management positions. They, in effect, increased the span of control of the remaining regional managers, thereby making it difficult for them to interfere in or tightly control local decisions. The store managers, in turn, were forced to exercise their discretion and autonomy and make decisions for their stores. A culture in which centralized controls were the way they did things for years was directly challenged by behaviors that clearly would lead to different methods of management.

The attempt to change operations and, ultimately, to infuse a new culture based on locally dominated decision-making worked well in some stores, but not in others. The new structure and methods alone weren't sufficient to cope with the many changes and strategic challenges that eventually confronted Sears and the retail industry. Still, the example has merit in that it shows how changes in structure can affect culture more directly and effectively than simply appealing to people to change their values and accepted ways of doing business.

Similar structural changes can be found at Walmart. The company has certainly relied on centralized controls, for example, when opening new stores. Standardization rules here. New stores all have the same departments and product lines as existing stores; centralization and standardization mark the model of expansion and definition of what new stores look like and how they serve the public.

Yet, early centralization usually gives way to increased decentralization as stores must cope with local competitors and local customer preferences and demands. Centralized control has its place, but local autonomy is increasingly critical to Walmart's success. The need is to create a culture that focuses on decentralization and the ability to respond quickly and effectively to local industry forces and customer tastes, while also preserving some of the benefits of the centralized model.

To execute this plan to foster a culture of local control, autonomy, and decentralization, the company pushes many decisions down to the store level. Stores become profit centers. Large departments are treated as "stores within stores," and they also are profit centers under the control of local management. Managers are granted large amounts of autonomy, but are held responsible for performance. Incentives are tied to performance objectives, and rewards are based on results against those objectives.

For present purposes, the point of the preceding examples is to show, consistent with the model of Figure 8.1, that when changing organizational culture:

■ It is not wise or beneficial to focus directly on culture. Appeals to individuals to change deeply embedded values, norms, or accepted ways of doing things hardly ever work, despite the admonitions to do so.

■ Attempts at cultural change that emphasize teamwork and challenging "games" (whitewater rafting, rock climbing, and so on) are fun, but they'll never bring about culture change if other critical organizational variables or characteristics do not also change.

- To achieve cultural change, it is necessary to focus on critical individual and organizational variables or characteristics, namely people, incentives, controls, and structure. The goal is to alter behavior and perceptions of what's important and rewarded, knowing that these alterations can result in changes in organizational culture.

- This approach to culture change can work because culture both affects behavior and is affected by behavior. Culture exerts its effects (it's an "independent" variable), but it is also affected by people, incentives, controls, and structure (it's also a "dependent" variable). Culture can change in response to other changes.

Step 7: Overcoming Resistance to Change

Even if steps 1 through 6 in Figure 8.1 are executed flawlessly, there still may be a problem. A few key managers may resist the culture change or the new execution methods—modifications in incentives, people, controls, and structure—that are directed toward culture change. It may be necessary, then, to reduce resistance to change, which is step 7 in Figure 8.1.

Much has been written about resistance to change. The underlying logic in most of these treatments seems to be that, when managing change and trying to overcome resistance to it, it is essential to focus on the positive and avoid the negative aspects of change.

The active involvement or participation of key players in the planning and execution of change, for example, can reduce resistance. Most individuals resist changes or new execution programs that are foisted upon them. They resist new methods that are "surprises" or that they had no hand in developing. Some participation, discussion, and involvement in changes that affect culture usually have a positive effect.

It also is important to define the benefits of an intended execution plan and the proposed changes, cultural or otherwise. The benefits of change must be advertised, along with the new values and drivers of excellence. If culture change is expected to add new and exciting elements of work, this fact must be clear. New incentives tied to performance, increased autonomy in a new, decentralized structure, and opportunities to learn, grow, and advance are examples of positive aspects of new execution methods and culture change that can be emphasized to reduce resistance to change.

A related point is that it is important to advertise the preservation of the best aspects of the old culture when managing change. These include such elements or characteristics as an entrepreneurial climate, informality among colleagues, and a client orientation. Preserving what's good and familiar during times of change can reduce resistance to the new methods or situation being proposed.

Changes in culture or execution methods may have some negative effects. Even here, the "negatives" can be turned into "positives" of sorts. Certain jobs may be eliminated or altered (a "negative"), but ensuring that displaced employees will have the first crack at training for the new jobs is a "positive." Or outplacement services for displaced managers within the company can be set up to help them find new jobs in the same division or at other divisions or locations (a "positive"). Or, while there may be a reduction in the number of administrative jobs (a "negative"), the reductions will be accomplished by natural attrition and projected retirements (a "positive").

Culture change may create uncertainty and perhaps even fear about job security issues, new responsibilities, and different ways of doing things. Accentuating the positives of the change is important to reducing resistance to it.

DaimlerChrysler tried to focus on the positives when, in the earliest stages of its merger, it announced that, in a merger of equals, layoffs would not occur. Growth would actually create new opportunities, it argued, which represented an exciting and positive aspect of the merger. The fact that the merged company couldn't deliver on its promises only hastened the downfall of the venture. Add to this the huge differences in culture between the German and American company, and the negative fate of the venture was sealed.

Sound communication and information sharing are important to reducing resistance to culture change. The advertising of positive aspects of change and the reduction of uncertainty require effective communication.

I recall an attempt at new execution methods and culture change in a medium-size company in which the prime requisite for success was actually considered by the CEO to be "communication, communication, and communication." Without effective communication about the need for change, top management felt that a negative climate would ensue. Their stated preference was to communicate openly to prevent the development and dissemination of misinformation that could increase resistance and hurt the change process. This emphasis on communication and information proved to be most beneficial and useful.

If people don't have information, they'll make it up to fill the void. Nature abhors an informational vacuum. Rumors thrive in this fertile soil, and most hold negative implications for change. It is far better to be proactive and forthright and focus on communication of the positives of change and the actions required to ameliorate the negatives.

Uncertainty is a terrible thing during episodes of change. The rumor creation and manufacturing of stories or scenarios to reduce it, however, actually increase uncertainty and exacerbate the negative consequences of change. Lying or playing games with the "facts" is also taboo. People ultimately see through these diversions or prevarications, and the result again is resistance to change and a real threat to execution success.

Successful culture change and strategy execution demand a communication plan that stresses positive aspects of the change and informs people honestly about their options and opportunities. A communication plan indicates the individuals who must receive information about changes in execution methods. Individuals directly affected by new execution methods should be communicated with on a face-to-face basis, individually or in small groups. A change in structure, for example, should be communicated to and discussed openly with those directly affected by new reporting relationships or new assignments and responsibilities. Individuals indirectly affected, such as staff personnel who work with or support line managers directly affected by the structural change, can be informed in more efficient ways such as e-mails, mass meetings, company newspapers, and videoconferencing.

Massive and purposeful communication is critical to reducing resistance to change. It cannot be left to chance. Without a purposeful plan aimed specifically at those directly affected by new execution methods or by changes in incentives, controls, people, and organizational structure, an organization is courting disaster. Rumors and informal conversations will consume valuable time and detract from ongoing, everyday performance. Misinformation will increase uncertainty and anxiety, further affecting performance negatively.

Finally, leadership is central to the process of reducing resistance to culture change. In fact, the impact of leadership is noticeable along the entire bottom line of Figure 8.1.

Effective leaders play a major role in culture change. They are important to the cause-effect analysis that identifies areas of needed change. They clearly are instrumental in changing and managing key people, incentives, and organizational structure. Leaders play a significant role in controls, as they provide feedback to subordinates and help evaluate individual and organizational performance. Leadership is critical to the task of conducting autopsies and facing the brutal facts when change processes related to execution aren't working.

Perhaps most important of all is the leader's role in reducing resistance to culture change or changes in execution methods supporting the new culture. Managers must lead by example. "Do as I say, not as I do," tolls a death knell for the new behaviors required to effect culture change. Leader behavior is action oriented and instrumental, but it also is intensely symbolic. It tells people what's important. It adds credibility to, or detracts heavily from, the perceived worth and impact of credos, values, espoused ethical standards, and an organization's public persona. Whether or not central leadership figures are seen to be supportive of new execution methods, communication plans, incentives, and different ways of doing business will determine the success of culture change and the reduction of resistance to it.

Step 8: The Impact of Change

The effective treatment of steps 5 through 7 in Figure 8.1 will result in culture change. It usually will not occur overnight, however. Culture change will definitely happen if the need for change is well documented and communicated, and an execution focus on incentives, people, controls, and organizational structure is directed toward behavior change and new ways of doing business.

Excessive "speed" or moving very fast when it comes to culture change sometimes sounds desirable but is dangerous. Occasionally, speed kills. A new culture cannot easily be legislated, coerced into being, or ordered on demand. People must see and believe in the need for change and the logic of the new execution methods to support it. New values, norms, ways of doing things, and propensities to act can be developed, but these results usually take some time.

Assume, however, that a company feels it is in dire need of speed when it comes to culture change. Assume that top management wants quick results. What elements of steps 5 through 7 on the bottom line of Figure 8.1 can be eliminated in the name of speed?

The short answer is that none of them can be eliminated. Cause-effect analysis and the need for change still must be clearly documented and communicated. A focus on behavioral change via new people, incentives, controls, and structure is still necessary. However, there are risks associated with speed, and they must be kept squarely in mind.

Hiring a bunch of new people—for example, an entirely new top-management team—can facilitate new values, norms, and ways of doing things. However, it also can create apprehension and increase resistance to change. Sudden and massive leadership changes create uncertainty. They can cause a retrenching of sorts as individuals in middle-management positions play a game of wait-and-see to determine which way fair and foul winds might blow. While new people can speed up culture change, the reactions of others may actually slow down the change process.

A related problem was mentioned in Chapter 7. If many changes are made very quickly and simultaneously in people, incentives, controls, and organizational structure, the result is a complex change. If the change fails—people resist, a new culture is rejected—then what? Cause-effect analysis explaining the failure is difficult, if not impossible. What caused the failure? Was it the new incentives? The new controls? The new people? The new structure? Was it a combination of factors in interaction? Which ones? In brief, excessive speed can inhibit learning and increase resistance to change. Moving fast may obscure the underlying forces at work, making it difficult to explain failures and learn from mistakes.

There will be times when management feels that speed is essential. There will be instances when "quick" culture change is needed. Even here, the steps in the bottom line of Figure 8.1 cannot be ignored. They must be attended to effectively, and care must be taken to manage the complex change carefully. Doing many things at once can challenge coordination, control, and learning, as Chapter 7 showed. Focusing on the key aspects of culture change, while relaxing other performance criteria against which people are usually held accountable, is absolutely essential for success.

SUMMARY

Changing culture is difficult, but it can be accomplished. Here are the "rules" or steps for managing culture change that can be derived from Figure 8.1 and the preceding discussion.

RULE 1: THE REASONS FOR CHANGE MUST BE CLEAR, COMPELLING, AND AGREED UPON BY KEY PLAYERS

Cause-effect analysis and learning are vital to successful change. Explaining poor prior performance is a *sine qua non*, an essential ingredient, before changes in execution methods or the logic of culture change is accepted as legitimate and necessary.

RULE 2: FOCUS ON CHANGING BEHAVIOR—NOT DIRECTLY ON CHANGING CULTURE

Appeals to individuals to change rarely work. Requests to change beliefs, values, or ways of doing things rarely achieve the desired results. It is better instead to focus on changing behavior, which can lead to culture change. New people, incentives, controls, and organizational structures can motivate behavioral change and lead to changes in organizational culture.

RULE 3: EFFECTIVE COMMUNICATION IS VITAL TO CULTURE CHANGE

A communication plan must be developed. People directly affected by changes must be communicated with directly, face-to-face or in groups. Information sharing is important to controlling or squelching rumors and other sources of misinformation that can inhibit change. There can never be too much communication when managing culture change.

RULE 4: ADEQUATE EFFORT MUST BE EXPANDED TO REDUCE RESISTANCE TO CHANGE

Effective communication of the positive aspects of change helps to reduce resistance. Communications dealing with potential "negatives" of change can reduce their impact. Methods aimed at improving participation and involvement in defining or defusing change and its consequences can also help, such as "Work Out" sessions at GE and other companies that identify key issues and collectively and openly reduce the resistance to new execution methods or culture change. The instrumental and symbolic roles of leadership are also important to the reduction of resistance to change.

RULE 5: BEWARE OF EXCESSIVE SPEED

Speed in managing culture change may be desirable or necessary. It is, however, fraught with problems. Changing too many things simultaneously and immediately can confuse the change process and make coordination and communication difficult. Excessive speed can breed uncertainty and increase resistance to change. Moving too fast can hurt the learning process and cloud the need for change, with dire consequences. If excessive speed is absolutely essential, the approach to managing complex change developed in Chapter 7 must be adhered to closely.

Managing and changing culture are difficult tasks. They are part and parcel of the overall process of managing change. It is recalled once again that the ability to manage change effectively was listed by managers surveyed for this research as the most critical requirement for the successful execution of strategy. Managing culture and culture change clearly share this criticality and importance in the execution of strategy.

Only one more major topic must be handled before trying to summarize the content of this approach to making strategy work: the role of power and influence in the execution process. The impact and importance of this role already have been suggested, but it is time now to consider this topic in greater detail. This is the goal of the next chapter on power, influence, and execution.

ENDNOTES

    i.   "More Problems for Mitsubishi as Six Are Arrested," *Philadelphia Inquirer*, June 11, 2004.

   ii.   "Enron's Watkins Describes 'Arrogant' Culture," *The Wall Street Journal*, February 15, 2002.

  iii.   William Joyce, Nitin Nohria, and Bruce Roberson, *What (Really) Works*, Harper Business, 2003.

  iv.   Jim Collins, *Good to Great*, Harper Business, 2001.

   v.   L. G. Hrebiniak, *The We-Force in Management: How to Build and Sustain Cooperation*, Lexington Books, 1994.

  vi.   See *Webster's New World Dictionary* or *Webster's New Collegiate Dictionary* for these and additional definitions of culture.

 vii.   Kurt Eichenwald, "Microsoft's Lost Decade," *Vanity Fair*, VF Daily, July 3, 2012.

viii. "When Disparate Firms Merge, Cultures Often Collide," *The Wall Street Journal*, February 14, 1997; "The Case Against Mergers," *Business Week*, October 30, 1995.

ix. "AMD Says Intel Intimidates Clients," *The Wall Street Journal*, September 24, 2003.

x. Tim Higgins and Jeff Green, "GM, Seen Planning Global Reorganization Against Fiefdoms," Bloomberg.com, August 17, 2012.

xi. An excellent early and still relevant discussion of avoiding and embracing error can be found in Donald Michael's *On Learning to Plan and Planning to Learn*, Jossey-Bass, 1973; see also L. G. Hrebiniak's *The We-Force in Management*, op. cit.

xii. Many of the arguments against the effectiveness of CIA operations have been summarized in L. G. Hrebiniak, *The Mismanagement of America, Inc.*, iUniverse, 2008. A good early, but still relevant, discussion can be found in Herbert Meyer's "Intelligence Tenets," *The Wall Street Journal*, June 14, 2002.

xiii. Jim Collins, *Good to Great*, op. cit.

xiv. See, for example, Scott Thurm, "CEO Pay Moves with Corporate Results," *The Wall Street Journal*, May 21, 2012; Joann Lublin and Dana Mattioli, "A Few Disconnects in CEO Pay," *The Wall Street Journal*, May 21, 2012.

xv. See, for example, Steve Denning, "How Do You Change an Organizational Culture?" *Forbes*, July 23, 2011; Peter Bregman, "A Good Way to Change a Corporate Culture," Harvard Business Review Blog Network, June 25, 2009.

9

Power, Influence, and Execution

Introduction

Successful strategy execution indicates an ability to gain support for a particular course of action or execution plan. Making strategy work often entails getting others to perform in certain ways or change their behavior. Leading execution and culture change presupposes an ability to influence others.

Power is social influence in action.[i] Power always implies a relationship. It normally involves some likelihood that one actor in the relationship can influence another actor. In similar terms, power defines the probability that one person or organizational unit can carry out its own agenda, despite resistance from another person or unit.

Strategy execution and managing change imply the importance and use of social influence or the exercise of power. The influence structure of an organization can seriously affect the success of execution efforts.

Opinions of managers actively involved in execution lend credence to these assertions. Respondents in the current research noted the impact of power or social influence. Their message was that attempts to execute a strategy that "conflicts with the existing power structure" face a dim prognosis for success. Attempts at execution and organizational change that go against the fabric of influence face a steep, uphill battle.

Power and influence clearly are important for execution and organizational change. It is far easier to execute a strategy that has the support of powerful people than one that breeds and fuels the ire of influential players. This seems patently obvious. Yet, as important and obvious as the ability to influence others is, interviews with managers still uncovered important questions in need of clarification:

1. What is power, and where does it come from? What creates differences in power or influence in organizations, especially among "equals," people of the same rank or at the same hierarchical level?

2. How can knowledge of the power structure be used to improve the success of execution efforts?

The first questions are important, as managers sometimes cannot adequately explain power beyond the obvious aspects of hierarchy or personality. "I'm the VP, and he reports to me; that's all you need to know," was one manager's statement to me about power in his functional area.

There's much more to power beyond hierarchy, however. Mid-level managers often have influence far greater than their position in the organization would suggest. People at exactly the same hierarchical level on the organization chart often enjoy different levels of influence. Though formally they are "equals," some of the people are "more equal" than their peers. Years ago, David Mechanic wrote about the power of lower-level participants on execution outcomes in organizations, and his findings about power still hold sway today.[ii] It is simply vital to understand the sources of power to foster and succeed in execution attempts.

The second question follows logically from the first and is especially important for all managers below C-level positions, meaning virtually everyone else in the organization. The issue here, especially for upper or middle managers charged with making strategy execution work, is how to use power effectively, even if one doesn't possess it personally. The issue basically is how to tap into others' influence and use it as your own to facilitate execution.

The purpose of this chapter is to shed light on the origins and use of power in making strategy work. The goal is to understand power beyond the obvious explanations of hierarchy or personality and show its relation to execution and important outcomes.

A VIEW OF POWER AND INFLUENCE

Hierarchical position certainly affects power or influence. There's no denying the impact of position. The CEO outranks his or her direct reports, and the same is true of VPs and their subordinates. Yet we all have seen or met "weak" CEOs and VPs. They have the position, but they have little influence over others. They are figureheads with limited power.

Personality also comes into play. "Natural" or charismatic leaders exist, and they certainly wield a ton of influence over their followers, sometimes well beyond the bounds of their formal authority. For years, the influence of Jack Welch, Lee Iacocca, or Percy Barnevik was much more than even their lofty formal position would indicate.

There's much more to power, however. All power differences simply cannot be explained by hierarchical position and personality. Other factors are at work. The present view is that:

> *Power or social influence both affects, and is affected by, strategy formulation and execution in organizations. Planning and execution rely on and are affected by power, but they also create power differences, thereby affecting power.*

Let's analyze this statement further. Let's determine what power is, where it comes from, and how it relates to strategy execution.

Figure 9.1 provides an overview or model of power and influence in organizations. For discussion purposes, let's begin with strategy formulation.

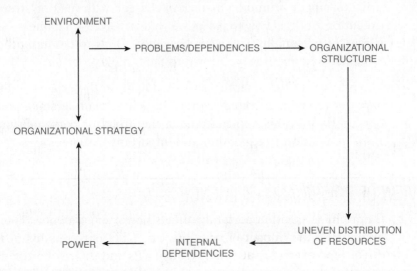

Figure 9.1 Power in Organizations

STRATEGY AND ENVIRONMENT

Organizations confront environments of varying complexity and uncertainty. They must deal with or co-opt them to survive. Strategy, in effect, defines how an organization positions itself to allow it to deal with its environment effectively.

At the business level, for example, organizations analyze industry forces, competitors, and their own capabilities to determine how best to position themselves and compete. The resultant strategy defines how the organization plans to cope with its environment. The double-pointed arrow in Figure 9.1 suggests that some organizations have enough market strength within their industries to affect their environment (for example, a monopoly or a large firm in an oligopolistic industry), while others are virtually helpless before environmental forces (for example, a firm in a perfectly competitive market). In effect, some firms have high strategic choice because of their ability to influence critical external forces or conditions, whereas other firms face deterministic environments within which the firm is effectively controlled by external forces.[iii]

PROBLEMS OR DEPENDENCIES

For all organizations, the formulation of strategy defines problems or dependencies that must be solved or handled for the strategy to work. In General Motors (GM) or Ford Motor, for example, the introduction of robotics was part of a strategy to lower costs while improving product quality. The relationship between the use of robots and outcomes such as cost reduction and product improvement was well documented. Cause-effect relations were clear and compelling: Using robots had predictable positive effects.

But the road to robotic heaven was strewn with potholes. There were critical problems or dependencies that had to be dealt with. Unions, for example, at first resisted the introduction of robots because, in addition to increasing efficiency, they also led to layoffs or the displacement of workers. The unions, of course, represented a critical dependency for GM and Ford. The companies depended on the unions for its labor supply, a key factor of production. A strike called by the UAW in objection to the robots could curtail or cease production. Labor represented a critical dependency or problem that had to be resolved for the low-cost strategy to work.

A consideration of the pharmaceutical industry reveals similar problems or dependencies related to strategy. In this industry, innovation and product development are critical concerns. The potential of a company's "pipeline" is a driving force in its economic or market valuation. A strategy of differentiation in the marketplace based on product development depends mightily on innovation. A critical dependency on R&D and new-product development clearly is central to making strategy work.

Companies have experimented with new ways of finding drugs because of this huge dependency and the problems that ensue if new drugs aren't found. For example, pharma companies have spent billions of dollars on machines to create thousands of chemical compounds and then test them with robots. The goal in doing this is to generate a flood of new products and profits to the pharma industry. Most critics have called this machine- or technology-based incursion into R&D an expensive failure. Machines have turned out compound after compound with no useful results. Replacing a dependency on real scientists with machines simply hasn't worked.

The example does show emphatically, however, that pharma companies realize that a critical problem or dependency exists. Innovation must occur if their strategy is to succeed. The formulation of strategy creates demands for the development of critical capabilities (see Chapter 3), as well as problems or dependencies that must be solved or confronted if the strategy is to work.

ORGANIZATIONAL STRUCTURE

How does an organization respond to the critical dependencies or problems defined by strategy? A typical way is to create or adapt an organizational structure to respond to the demands of strategy, as Figure 9.1 notes. This is a logical extension of the argument made in Chapter 4 that strategy affects the choice of structure. Structure now is responding specifically to the problems or dependencies created by the strategic plan.

In the GM or Ford cases, a unit responsible for industrial relations or collective bargaining handled the union "problem" when introducing robotics into the manufacturing process. Without the dependency on labor, such a unit would never exist. Structure clearly is a response to the existence of a union and the dependencies on it that developed over time.

In the pharmaceutical case, R&D units respond to the need for innovation and product development. Reliance on the research prowess of scientists in multiple R&D units around the globe has been the typical response to the strategic need for new drugs. The structure of the organization—multiple R&D units—reflects the demands of strategy and the needs created by it.

The result is a dependency on scientists to solve the innovation-related problems necessary for survival. Indeed, the typical large pharma company has multiple R&D facilities as part of its structure. J&J, for example, has approximately 240 SBUs or operating companies, some of which are designated as "prime companies," sources of innovation and new product development. The redundancies and extra costs associated with multiple R&D units in this form of structure obviously must be seen as worth it, given the need to make an innovation strategy succeed.

Other pharma companies are taking another path to confronting critical dependencies and creating a fuller product pipeline: namely, mergers and acquisitions that almost instantly provide new products and treatments that have already been approved and are in the marketplace. Valeant Pharmaceuticals International, for example, made 13 takeover bids in 2011 alone, succeeding in 11, to beef up the company's product line.[iv] The company is avoiding the substantial risks associated with R&D, while simultaneously confronting the problems or dependencies required to make its strategy work. Its approach, in effect, is adding new structural units to the organization via the M&A route, consistent with the present argument that structure is important to the handling of critical problems or dependencies facing the organization.

Other examples abound, but the point is clear: Structure serves an important function, given the problems or dependencies created by strategy. Its creation and adaptation over time reflects and responds to the problems or critical strategic dependencies needed to gain competitive advantage.

UNEVEN RESOURCE ALLOCATIONS

Not all structural units are equal, however. Over time, some elements or units of organizational structure are seen as solving bigger problems than other units. Some are seen as responding to critical dependencies, whereas others are seen as responding to less critical issues. Some units simply provide more value-added results to the organization than other structural units.

The result is inevitable: an uneven distribution or allocation of scarce resources, as Figure 9.1 indicates. Units seen as confronting critical dependencies facing the organization benefit from this uneven allocation of resources. Important units simply get more: bigger budgets, more people, greater access to top management, participation in key strategic-planning sessions, a heavy impact on policy decisions, and more IT support. These units, in effect, get more control over scarce resources and their deployment.

Where does all of this lead? What results from this uneven distribution of scarce resources favoring structural units that confront and solve the critical dependencies or problems facing the organization?

INTERNAL DEPENDENCIES AND POWER

The answer to these questions, as shown in Figure 9.1, is that these favored structural units create internal dependencies. Others depend on the units for a host of things—information, new products, sales forecasts, profits, prestige or brand enhancement, engineering solutions—depending on the function's or unit's task and expertise.

R&D units, for example, create internal dependencies. The rest of the organization relies on them for new products and continued competitive advantage, points emphasized in the pharmaceutical example. Recall, too, the centrality and importance of Bell Labs in its heyday at AT&T. Bell Labs was special. It made scientific discoveries at the leading edge of technology, gave AT&T new products, and enhanced the reputation of the company. Other units needed and depended heavily on Bell Labs. The research unit enjoyed an abundance of resources and used them well. The virtual destruction of a powerful and productive Bell Labs within AT&T over time indeed was painful to observe.

When I was a manager at Ford Motor, marketing was king of the hill. In an extremely competitive environment in which a market share point translated positively and heavily to the bottom line, the company depended on marketing for sales and share. Marketing received virtually all the resources it asked for because of its centrality and importance to sales and profits. Ford Division was basically a marketing-oriented organization.

Because of its favored position, other units depended heavily on marketing. This function's performance supported other functions' budgets and reason for being and controlled the work done elsewhere in Ford Division. Marketing, for example, made up or influenced the production schedule for cars and often changed the product-line mix of units to be built, usually to the chagrin of manufacturing. There were complaints but usually to no avail, as marketing was relied on for its valuable contributions and, consequently, had the upper hand. Marketing had created powerful dependencies on itself within Ford Division.

Definition of Power

It is now possible to define power, or at least the potential for power, in a useful way. Consistent with this discussion, especially the notion of dependency created by strategy, structure, and the resource-allocation process, the following definition of power is feasible and realistic:

> *Power is the opposite of dependency. If B is totally dependent on A, A has power and influence over B.*

Let's clarify this notion of dependency and power and then provide some examples. Assume the existence of two individuals or structural units in an organization, A and B. The preceding definition suggests two conditions that give rise to power differences between A and B:

1. **A has power over B in direct proportion to A's having something B needs.**

   If an individual or structural unit owns or controls something that another individual, unit, department, or function needs to perform a job or achieve its goals, then the potential for power exists. If A has or controls something B requires—information, technological knowledge, human resources, money, or other capabilities or competencies—then A has the potential for power and can exert influence over B. The phrase "potential for power" is used because this first condition, while necessary, is not sufficient. Another condition exists that affects power.

2. **A's power is also related to its ability to monopolize what B needs.**

If an individual or structural unit, A, has or controls something that another individual, unit, or function (B) sorely needs, and B cannot get it elsewhere, then B is totally dependent on A. A has power over B. A's ability to exercise influence over B is extremely strong and compelling because of the dependency *and* monopoly relationship.

Power, then, is the opposite of dependency. Dependency can be observed when one unit or individual copes with uncertainty or provides scarce resources to other individuals or units. If the degree of substitutability is low, meaning the valued resources or knowledge cannot be easily obtained elsewhere from another individual or unit, then dependency is strong, and the power of one individual or unit over the other is consequently also very strong and unilateral.

USING POWER AND INFLUENCE

Individuals or units with power certainly can wield it. Other individual factors may come into play, however, affecting how those with a potential for power actually exercise it.

The recent celebration of the fortieth-plus anniversary of the Mustang and Ford's revamping of the continued hot seller takes me back to an interesting anecdote about power and influence.

The great success of the Mustang in the 1960s really could be attributed to two individuals: Lee Iacocca and Donald Frey. Iacocca was in marketing and Frey was in engineering, and both collaborated heavily on the design and introduction of the car. Actually, Frey probably contributed a great deal more than Iacocca. He and his team created the car in only 18 months, with Frey leading the design and development process. He clearly played a huge role. Yet, when one thinks of Ford and the Mustang, Frey's name never comes to the fore. It is Lee Iacocca whom people usually associate with the car's success. His flamboyant and dominant personality enjoyed the exercise of influence and being in the spotlight.

In contrast, while Frey certainly shared a high potential for power or influence, he eschewed the limelight, preferring to work behind the scenes. He exercised his influence in technical circles—he received the National Medal of Technology and was influential in improving automobile safety and performance—but he never achieved the name recognition, standing, and breadth of influence of Iacocca. Frey seemingly had a low need for power and attention, and that affected how he chose to use or not use his power position. At the time of his death in 2010 at the age of 86, only auto enthusiasts and insiders were fully aware of Frey's massive contributions and his rejection of the power spotlight.

Top managers such as Iacocca, Jack Welch, and Percy Barnevik certainly used their influence to affect strategy and the direction of a company, as Figure 9.1 shows. What happens, of course, is that the chosen strategy often reflects and perpetuates the organizational power structure. Those in power create strategies that support or feed off their bases of power.

For years, top people in Ford came from marketing, a logical occurrence because of that function's power within Ford Division, a marketing-oriented organization. In contrast, the track or path to top management at GM was traditionally through the finance organization. Clearly, strategy formulation within the companies reflected and supported the prevailing power bases. Those in power developed strategies that would build on their power position and perpetuate their influence over the strategy-making process. Power begets and perpetuates power; those who have it strive to keep it.

Another CEO, Kenneth Olsen, the inimitable leader of DEC for over 30 years, passed away in February 2011. He, like Donald Frey, received the National Medal of Technology and was well known, but my remembrance of him perhaps is a bit different than others' recollections of this brilliant technical genius.

In the heydays of DEC, Olsen once told me that his company was basically "an engineering company." Olsen's top people were engineers, whom he trusted for the right answers to DEC's strategic problems. This reliance on engineering worked well for years. However, the inability to develop a sound marketing group because of engineering's power did come back to haunt the company. The marketing of the company's first major PC—the "Rainbow"—was disastrous. Marketing simply couldn't get things done, especially when engineering disagreed with aspects of the product development and marketing plan. DEC wasn't a marketing organization, and the lack of this function's influence was readily apparent to outside observers.

Motorola, too, for years was an engineering-dominated company. Interviews I conducted with key managers prior to one of the Vice Presidents' Institutes—a key executive development and leadership program—stressed what people saw as a growing negative aspect of the company's traditional engineering strengths and influence on strategy.

New product development, a critical aspect of strategy, was driven too much by engineering, these managers argued. Product development was too much of an "inside-out" process. New "toys," technologies, or a new "box" would be driven into production, often without someone ascertaining adequately whether customers wanted the new product. An "outside-in" approach would have ascertained that customers wanted certain problems solved. They wanted an integrative approach, using existing technologies, to solve problems and make their companies more effective. They didn't desire new, standalone technologies that didn't get to the core of their problems. Some managers in Motorola felt that it was time for customers to exert more influence on strategy formulation rather than having engineering dominate the product-development process.

Changes at Motorola since these observations by managers have been somewhat promising, as the strategy has seemed to focus more on customer needs. The company had a big hit with its Razr flip-phone, for example, which suggests a closeness to the market and a greater response to customers. However, by the time Google bought Motorola Mobility in 2011, the company had slipped and lost some market influence. Strategic changes and power shifts are occurring, as Google-Motorola tries to challenge Apple and others and carve out a niche for its products. Whether the revamped company can compete effectively and restore its luster is still a question in need of additional validation.

COMING FULL CIRCLE: CONCLUSIONS ABOUT POWER

Discussion of the impact of power on strategy and the perpetuation of power by those involved in strategy formulation brings us full circle in Figure 9.1, where we began with a consideration of the effects of strategy. The major conclusions of the analysis thus far are as follows:

1. Power is the opposite of dependency. Differences in dependency denote differences in power.
2. Power both affects, and is affected by, the processes of strategy formulation and execution in organizations.

Power is social influence that arises from differences in dependencies. It's affected by choices of strategy and structure, and the resource allocation decisions that follow logically from these choices. Power, in turn, drives the choice of strategy and consequent execution needs. Individuals in power usually want to retain or perpetuate it, so choices of strategy clearly reflect the power of individuals creating it. Power, then, both affects and is affected by strategic processes in organizations.

Although this is interesting, we must take the analysis one step further. It's important that managers involved in execution understand power. It's absolutely vital, however, that managers also know how to use the power structure to further the ends of strategy execution. Let's consider next what Figure 9.1 and the preceding discussion are telling us about the relationship between power and execution.

POWER AND EXECUTION

Managers must note and profit from the following three important takeaways about the relationship between power and execution:

1. The need to define power bases and relationships in their organizations.
2. The importance of forming coalitions or joint ventures with those in power to foster execution success.
3. The need to focus on value-added, measurable results to gain influence and achieve successful execution outcomes.

DEFINE POWER BASES AND RELATIONSHIPS

This is a necessary first step in an attempt to use power effectively. Using a model or approach similar to that in Figure 9.1, the first step for managers at any level of the organization is to "map" out the key dependency relationships affecting power or social influence.

Who are the main players affecting what I do in my job? What departments, functions, or other structural units does my department, function, or unit interact with and depend on? Which units depend on my unit's provision of knowledge, technical support, or physical outputs? What are the points of dependency or needed cooperation? Are there other sources of the needed knowledge, technical support, or physical materials besides the unit(s) providing these important inputs?

These and similar questions are intended to ascertain the key factors affecting power or influence in organizations. Consistent with this discussion, these key factors are as follows:

1. **Dependency relationships.** Who is dependent on whom and for what? Is the dependency mutual or reciprocal, or is it unilateral? Unilateral dependencies denote strong power relationships. Those who totally depend on others for vital knowledge or other resources are in a vulnerable position, with low bargaining power and little influence.

2. **Degree of substitutability.** Are there many sources of the needed information or resources, or does a particular unit or individual have a monopoly over the information or resources? Recall that the ability to monopolize the vital resources that others need is an important contributor to power and influence.

3. **Centrality of an individual or unit.** The degree to which an individual or unit is linked to others in the flow of communications or resources is often linked to power. Organizational units that routinely interact with many other units are highly pervasive. Units that can cause an organization to literally shut down by not performing their tasks or functions are highly

essential. An accounting department is typically pervasive; all units need and rely on accounting information. However, it may not be as essential as a technical service department that has the skills and knowledge needed to repair an important computer-based technology or manufacturing process that keeps the organization functioning. Being essential is usually more strongly related to power and influence than being well connected.

4. **Coping with uncertainty.** Many organizations routinely face high levels of uncertainty. Individuals or units that cope with and reduce uncertainty for other individuals or units usually increase the dependency of others on them, thus increasing their power. This "uncertainty absorption" allows for the definition of "facts" or information that others need to do their job. It also reduces tensions or problems related to ambiguity, thereby providing a kind of psychological benefit, again increasing dependency and power.

The marketing function within companies may derive some of its power from uncertainty absorption. It provides sales forecasts to production and other units, which reduces uncertainty and provides the facts needed for those units to operate. The marketing group could also influence other functions' tasks or operations—for example, production of products or services—despite the other functions' resistance to marketing's demands, which again suggests the latter's influence in the organization.

A CEO of a company or president of a country has valuable advisors and "insiders" who provide important information and intelligence. These advisors reduce uncertainty and provide data that the CEO or president can use to make critical strategic decisions. The top person's reliance or dependency on the key people increases their standing and power in the organization.

These four conditions or behaviors, in effect, are valuable assets in an organization. Reducing uncertainty, having low substitutability, and enjoying high centrality lead to dependencies and, consequently, differences in power.

Individuals and units in an organization benefiting from these dependencies affect execution. They can get others to buy into their agenda and execution plans. Other individuals and units need the powerful individuals and units to execute their own plans, actually intensifying the power relationship but simultaneously achieving desired execution outcomes for the company.

FORM COALITIONS OR DEVELOP JOINT VENTURES WITH THOSE IN POWER

The previous discussion suggests that forming coalitions or joint ventures with those in power is an effective way to gain support for an execution plan or methods. Cooperation around a common execution goal can foster positive results. Getting powerful people on your side or in your corner can help to overcome resistance to new execution methods or processes.

The most basic coalition is formed between a manager and his or her boss. Selling a superior on the merits of a new strategy or methods of executing that strategy is necessary for success. Convincing the boss of the merits of execution gains hierarchical support, a base of power and influence. Convincing the boss to intercede with his or her boss to support the execution plan locks three different hierarchical levels into the execution process. Gaining the backing of three levels lends credibility to execution and its intended results, and it advertises to others the viability of actions directed toward making strategy work.

Other coalitions and joint ventures also support power. An attempt by nurses at a large Philadelphia hospital to make sweeping changes in procedures was doomed to failure until they were successful in gaining the support of a large block of physicians. Demands made by the combined nurse-physician coalition were met within a reasonable period of time with only a few modifications to the original nurse-only generated demands. The joint venture simply created a larger power base that couldn't be ignored.

Changes in product specifications proposed by sales stand a greater degree of success if engineering supports the modifications. Manufacturing may resist if sales alone is pushing for the changes. Shutting down production to experiment with new products or to develop prototypes of new models clearly reduces efficiency and takes away from the volume, standardization, and repetition needed to achieve low-cost production. The added urging of a respected or powerful engineering unit may convince manufacturing sooner about the logic and feasibility of sales' requests.

Powerful coalitions can affect the execution process and organizational change immensely. Joining forces creates power bases by combining the potential for power of individuals and units, allowing for more effective execution than the individuals or units could achieve acting alone.

FOCUS ON VALUE-ADDED, MEASURABLE RESULTS

The driving force implicit in the model of power in Figure 9.1 and the discussion of key power-related factors or conditions is basic yet extremely important:

> *Individuals or units that create value obtain power. Results clearly count. An execution plan must show the benefits that will accrue to the organization from effective execution for it to be taken seriously.*

To gain power and facilitate execution, execution plans or methods must focus on value-added, measurable results. There must be a positive cost-benefit outcome. Individuals in power won't support execution if they don't see recognizable benefits for the organization. Coalition formation won't occur if parties to a potential joint agreement don't see a "win-win" situation, a sharing of positive results. It is easier to marshal support for execution when higher-ups and others in the company believe that measurable benefits are forthcoming.

A key word here is "measurable." Execution plans that promise "soft" outcomes—greater support, more management commitment, cooperation, a friendlier culture—are usually doomed to poor support and failure if the soft outcomes are not translated into hard metrics. This is not to say that soft measures aren't good or desirable. It simply means that measurable outcomes that people value and can touch, see, and feel usually generate greater backing than poorly defined or less certain execution outcomes. Let me use an example taken from a Wharton Executive program to support the point.

The Case of the Frustrated VP

In my Wharton executive program on execution, managers bring real problems to attack and solve. Emphasis in the program is on practical and common execution problems, their actual solution, and on making strategy work. One such participant I've labeled as the "frustrated VP."

This woman was the first female to achieve the rank of VP or higher in her company. She described the company as having a "tough, male-dominated, cigar-chomping, scotch-drinking culture." After a few good-natured ribs from male program participants about the company "sounding like a great place to work," she presented her problems, one of which I'll try to summarize as succinctly as possible.

At a meeting with the company's executive committee, she and a few of her male colleagues presented their strategic functional plans—including plans for execution—for the committee's approval. According to her:

> The sales/marketing guy presents his plan, real fast, "boopity-boop," over and done. The reaction of the committee? Real positive. Notification of full funding and commitment soon followed.

> Next, the manufacturing VP presented his plan, with basically the same result. A fairly quick presentation, bang-bang, with quick consensus about the value of the functional plan and the proposed execution process.

> Then it was my turn. As the new VP of HR, I presented a few interesting and important strategic thrusts and talked about implementation. I was really prepared. I was new to the officer group, and I wanted to impress my peers with my knowledge, careful preparation, and sound planning.

So, what happened? There was little visible enthusiasm during my presentation. There were quite a few probing questions and even a couple of snide remarks that generated a few chuckles at my expense. The executive committee said it would consider my plan and let me know its recommendation ASAP. The bottom line is that I didn't get close to what I was asking. They didn't like my plan, and it's frustrating.

This represents the gist of her story. Her plan had a rocky journey through the approval process and was "clearly underfunded." The "old-boy" network took care of its own, in her opinion, but she suffered indignity and frustration at what she saw as a major setback.

As is typical, the other participants in the Wharton program and I had questions. We probed, wanting to know the details of her and the other managers' plans. The questions and ensuing discussion were blunt, factual, and to the point, as a more complete picture of her company's plan-approval process came into focus. For present purposes, I'll take one small portion of the discussion and summarize the main issues.

The first questions dealt with the quick approvals of the plans of the manufacturing and marketing VPs. After a lot of probing, it was clear that their presentations weren't shallow, "boopity-boop," incomplete plans at all. The manufacturing VP discussed introduction of a new technology, closing an outdated plant, and the need to work with the union on execution. Basically, his presentation, pieced together from the probing questions and answers, went something like this:

My main recommendation is introduction of (new technology) in four of our five plants, with a gradual cessation of operations in the fifth. Here are the important facts. The purchase cost of the technology amortized over X years is $_____. The benefits include a reduction in variable cost per unit produced over that time period of $_____, reducing overall yearly cost of operations by Y percent. If we look at the net present value (NPV) of expenditures vs. cost savings over the life of the new machines, the NPV is positive and actually winds up returning a hefty positive Z percent ROI over the period. In addition, besides the cost reductions, we can expect a significant improvement in product quality, which will improve drastically our position with customers, especially in the mid-market where we've had tough times with (a named competitor) over the last few years.

The presentation (as did that of the marketing VP) focused clearly on facts and measurable results. Discussions focused on costs and benefits, including increased margins. The NPV model was analyzed, including determination of the appropriate discount rate. Measures of quality were discussed, including the determination of quality improvement at the production levels envisioned. The real costs of closing the fifth plant were clarified, the result being a slight reduction in the NPV figure, which was still positive. The additional costs of an elaborate plant-closing process were juxtaposed against the benefits of goodwill with the union (an intangible) and the costs of avoiding a strike or work slowdowns (a real, tangible number).

Though there were additional questions, the essence of the presentation hopefully is clear. The Wharton program participants' probing revealed that there was real "meat" in the VP of manufacturing's remarks. It focused on costs, quality, and NPV, outcome measures that the executive committee could see clearly and understand fully. Now let's consider our beleaguered VP of human resources' presentation and draw some parallels or distinctions. I'll take only one portion of her plan for illustration purposes.

Part of her proposed plan dealt (appropriately!) with executive education. She wanted to increase spending dramatically because of the obvious benefits of training and investing in management talent. "People are our most important asset," she argued, and expenditures on increased executive education will only strengthen the value of this asset. She proposed, too, that training be expanded to include more mid-level manager programs to increase the managerial pool for the future. The cost of the expanded training was significant but well worth it, she insisted, because of the benefits, including a better-trained, happier, and more loyal workforce.

Can we identify a problem here? The basic gist of her argument is that executive education is good, a worthwhile expenditure, and that benefits include happier, more loyal employees. But, she is saying, these benefits come at a significant, high cost. The measures of the beneficial outcomes are subjective, at best, with no real metrics provided. The executive committee could see and measure the costs in her presentation very easily, but they had to grapple a bit with the supposed benefits.

The bottom line is that they saw an increase in expense with no verification of the increase in benefits. They primarily saw costs and a budget increase. Period. Their reaction was to say that her plan was too expensive and that full funding was quite impossible. She needed to revise her budget requests accordingly.

So, what was the advice to her? What did we suggest she do to change her plan and approach to the executive committee while simultaneously reducing her anxiety and frustration level? Rather than reiterate all the advice and discussion that ensued, let me tell you what our VP of human resources actually did to follow our advice.

First, she defined a real problem that all members of the executive committee—indeed, all significant stakeholders—could agree with. She focused part of the new plan on turnover. She pointed out correctly that turnover in the company was exceedingly high. In fact, she provided data to show that turnover was the second highest in the entire region.

Second, she provided data on the cost of turnover. Some of these data were real and hard and some were estimates, but even they nonetheless could be translated into real, hard numbers. For example, replacing a top-level manager who left for a position elsewhere usually meant hiring the services of a job placement or "headhunter" firm. The service such a firm provides is not cheap: a fee of up to 100 percent of the found executive's annual salary. This fee clearly is a cost of turnover. Similarly, it takes a while for the new manager to get up to snuff in the new job. Clearly, the manager's salary and fringe benefits during the learning period can be treated as a cost of turnover. The suggestion to her was to consider six months of salary and fringe benefits as a real cost of turnover. (Six months is an estimate, of course. The logic is real, however, and it's now up to the executive committee to prove she is wrong, a task not easily done.) Other costs were similarly defined as costs attributed to turnover.

Third, she did some extensive research and found that articles in professional journals and popular magazines alike had discovered links between turnover and managerial education and training programs. Devoting time, money, and attention to managers actually increases their commitment to a company, sometimes contractually (for example, an agreement not to leave the company for X years after completing a company-paid-for executive MBA program), sometimes psychologically (committing to the company because of a perceived inducements-contributions "contract"). This link between turnover and managerial education programs was critical, as it allowed her to take her plan to a new level.

Fourth, she rewrote her original HR plan and budget with a different thrust and tone. A goal of the new plan was to reduce managerial turnover. Why? Because reduction of turnover would reduce the real costs of turnover. More specifically, the new plan contained a specific objective to:

> *Reduce the cost of turnover by X dollars by reducing the actual turnover among middle- and upper-level managers by Y percent over a period of three years.*

One of the action plan items or methods of reducing turnover and its costs was to increase the number of middle- and upper-level managers participating in management training or executive development programs, in-house and out-of-house. In essence, she defined the following causal link:

Executive Education ⟶ Reduces Turnover ⟶ Lowers Costs

Her terms were well defined, including the costs of turnover. The link between management education and turnover was spelled out and supported substantially. The NPV of the future cash flows from training and cost reduction was shown to be positive. She showed that education and training were not expenses to be eschewed at all costs, but rather were investments in cost reduction and the building of core capabilities in management for the years ahead.

The new budget and HR plan were approved unanimously by the executive committee. (She kept me abreast of things well after the Wharton program was completed.) Committee members remarked about the plan's logic and the compelling relationship between training or education and cost reduction. Her new plan clearly had a different impact than the prior one.

The point of the example, first, is to show that any plan, strategic or operating, must have an execution focus on measurable results and clear value-added outcomes. Approvers of the plan must be able to see and measure real costs and benefits for the execution plan to be accepted.

Second, power in organizations depends on these real value-added contributions. Individuals and units that add value increase their influence. High-performance individuals and units create dependencies on themselves while also increasing their centrality and importance, leading to enhanced power and influence. Power depends on one's perceived contributions to an organization's bottom line or competitive position in an industry.

Finally, a history of successful execution and positive results not only increases power or influence, it also helps future plans and future requests for funding get approved more easily. Power positively affects future planning and execution. People and units with solid track records find that their influence within the organization facilitates the development and execution of future strategic and operating plans. Power can positively affect execution in many ways, including generating the needed support for future plans.

Table 9.1 summarizes the main lessons learned from the case of the frustrated VP. Comparing the original, rejected plan to the accepted one reveals some basic points about performance, power, and execution success. Basically, the example stresses the importance of (a) agreed-upon, measurable factors (turnover and its cost), (b) clear cause and effect (how actions reduce turnover), a strong cost-benefit analysis (positive NPV), and the importance of solid metrics (measurable outcomes).

Table 9.1　The Frustrated VP: Lessons Learned

The Rejected Plan	The Accepted Plan
Seen as an "expense," raising costs.	Focuses on a real, costly problem—turnover.
No clear cause-effect relationship between plan and outcomes.	Cause and effect are clear; execution of proposed plan affects turnover.
No value-added outcomes or benefits.	Cost-benefit analysis is shown with positive net present value.
Lack of metrics, no measurable objectives or outcomes.	Use of solid metrics, agreed-upon measurable outcomes, or measures of value added.
The result of the accepted plan?	Delivery of positive, measurable outcomes increases power or influence and positively affects present and future execution success.

Execution plans fail when these basic elements are lacking. Increased power or social influence usually accrues to individuals whose execution plans are marked by the elements on the right side of Table 9.1. Performance affects influence. Plans that deliver positive, measurable outcomes benefit both the organization and the individuals responsible for them.

A FINAL NOTE ON POWER: THE DOWNSIDE

Power is important for execution. It can facilitate the accomplishment of an execution plan. Power differences are inevitable, given the assumptions and discussion of Figure 9.1, and these differences reflect the results of positive contributions to an organization's ability to compete effectively and prosper. Power, then, has an upside that cannot be denied or denigrated.

There also is a potential downside to power, however. The first and most obvious problem is that power perpetuates itself, a point stressed previously. People in power tend to want to stay there. They formulate and execute strategies that support their skills, power bases, and contributions to the organization. Obviously, this is not a problem if those in power are doing the right things.

If the strategy is wrong, however, if the power elite doesn't respond adequately to environmental changes calling for a different competitive strategy, then major problems can occur. If the individuals in charge persist in doing what they've always done primarily to maintain their position, this may lead to competitive disadvantage.

A recent article, mentioned previously, raises questions about Microsoft's "lost decade," in which poor management decisions allegedly hurt the company.[v] Destructive policies like "stack ranking"—a forced ranking of managers—created ill will, forced good managers to leave the company, and created terrible internal competition. A focus on and excessive loyalty to Windows allegedly blinded managers to the merits of non-Windows related products. What created and drove these problems in a lost decade marked by waning company performance? In part, the power structure that became more bureaucratic, rigid, and unchanging over time. The view of the key top people created an inertia toward progress and internal problems, according to this 2012 article, with the power structure at the core of the restrictive climate. Microsoft is releasing new products at the time of this writing—Windows 8 and its Surface Tablet—and it remains to be seen if they help loosen the strictures of a controlling power structure.

Ron Johnson became CEO of J. C. Penney in 2011 with a mandate to reinvent 1,100 retail stores and gain traction in a highly competitive industry with players like Macy's, Kohl's, Walmart, Sears, and Target. His actions thus far have proved less than effective. The reasons offered for Penney's problems are many and varied, as many industry pundits are heaping criticisms on the company, its strategy, and Johnson's decisions.[vi] An underlying implication in these criticisms is that Penney's power structure and culture are totally at odds with Johnson's planned makeovers. The company, pre Johnson, exhibited a slowness to adapt, a kind of mass-production, one-size-fits-all model that reflects a slow, bureaucratic power structure not attuned to new, volatile, and challenging competitive conditions. The feeling one has after reviewing critics' comments is that adherence to the "old ways" of competing, coupled with a stifling power structure, has maintained a strategy that has outlived its effectiveness in a new retail industry. Johnson may yet succeed, but his attempt to add new life to a worn company faces many challenges. (Note: In early April, 2013, Johnson was fired and "Mike" Ullman, who preceded Mr. Johnson, was rehired as Penney's CEO to turn around a still-ailing company).

The case of DEC is worth another mention. The dominant group in DEC for years was engineering. It ruled the strategic roost. The dependencies on engineering were strong, and that ultimately proved to be a problem. When the need for marketing and customer service grew more acute in an increasingly competitive PC market, DEC couldn't respond effectively. Engineering still ruled, and some individuals in this function actually believed that other "soft" functions such as marketing were not very important or useful.

The company had built an effective and powerful top coalition around engineering. This worked well when the main strategic problems were technical and dependency on engineering paid huge dividends. When the market changed, demanding more of the soft skills such as marketing, the same power structure proved burdensome. Marketing didn't have the resources or enjoy the political clout that would have enabled the company to respond to competitive pressures from increasingly sophisticated and demanding customers. Many of DEC's problems could be attributed to its power structure:

> *Power is usually slow to change. Those in power normally wish to maintain it. Power can support execution, which is a positive aspect of it. Power, however, can also create inertia, negatively affecting change and organizational adaptation.*

The Critical Role of CEO Leadership

Changing the power structure when it is wrong and dysfunctional depends very much on top-management leadership, especially that of the CEO and board of directors. The CEO and the top-management team can change strategy, people, structure, responsibilities, and the allocation of scarce resources, decisions, or actions that affect the power structure. Indeed, some of these high-impact decisions can only be made by a CEO, executive committee, or company board. Only such a high-level person or team can affect the dependencies among major operating units, thereby determining who has influence over whom. This obviously is not an easy task. It often is an unpopular one. Still, it must be done.

In this situation, the CEO must rely on sound cause-effect analysis to explain performance problems and the need for change (see Chapter 7). The reasons for change must be clear and compelling. Communication of the changes, especially those involving resource reallocations, must be complete and pervasive, cutting off dysfunctional rumors and covert manipulations of information and the "facts." Careful, occasional use of external analysts and consultants may help the CEO or management team prepare and present a case for the changes that will alter the power structure. Similarly, obtaining the support of the board of directors or large shareholders can result in a powerful coalition to push for the necessary changes.

In the absence of strong leadership at the top when organizational performance is poor and strategic change is necessary, other groups will definitely step in, take control, and alter the power structure, sometimes usurping the power of top management. Both shareholders and boards of directors are increasing their influence of late, partly in reaction to company performance and partly due to a perceived need for changes in strategy and the power structure. Consider just a few examples:

- In 2012, the directors of Chesapeake Energy Corp forced CEO Aubrey McClendon to step down as chairman, bowing to pressure from shareholders over his personal dealings, influence, and the company stock's poor performance.[vii] The year before, a shareholder rebellion over McClendon's compensation had the board introduce performance-based incentives, a muscle flexing by shareholders and the board alike. The CEO's ability to influence loans to favored companies was also curtailed.

- Barrick Gold Corp., the world's largest gold miner, ousted CEO Aaron Regent because of poor company performance.[viii] The ouster, coming in the wake of the 2011 takeover of Barrick by Equinox Minerals, also suggests that there could have been some power struggles about the new direction of the acquired company and the increased exposure to political and economic risk as Barrick altered its product and geographical focus at the insistence of the acquiring company. Reading between the lines often suggests power-related factors in addition to economic or strategic issues.

■ In 2012, Samsung Electronics appointed a new CEO, Kwon Oh-hyun, who led the company's chip business for the preceding four years. Simultaneously, the company announced that the power of the new CEO would be diminished.[ix] Samsung wanted more separation between its consumer and component businesses and a better way to handle the conflicts that arose between them. The decision was made that the consumer product divisions wouldn't report to and be under the control of the new CEO. Rather, the consumer group would report instead directly to the company chairman who would play the decisive role when the consumer and component businesses conflict. The power of the new CEO was clearly limited by the company, and the result was a dramatic shift in the power and importance of the component businesses.

■ CEOs simply aren't the bosses they used to be, according to an interesting article about CEO power and control.[x] The article points out that, increasingly, under pressure from investors, more companies than ever are splitting the roles of CEO and chairman and reducing the power of the CEO. The numbers are significant: More than 20 percent of the companies in the S&P 500 have appointed an independent outsider to the role of chairman, a significant increase over the last six years (12 percent in 2007). The result is basically a "second seat of power," according to the article. CEOs who also held chairmanship positions could influence boards' agendas, decisions, and actions; they held power and ran the boards accordingly. The separation of CEO and chairman roles, with chairmen being separate and not appointed by the CEO, allows the board to become a more effective counterweight to the CEO's power and influence. Again, CEOs aren't the strong bosses they used to be in many companies.

■ A previous discussion of incentives and controls in Chapter 6 noted how shareholders and company boards are increasingly linking CEO pay to company performance. This link between compensation and company outcomes clearly is intended to control CEOs and ensure that their decisions and actions are weighed more carefully against the common good of investors. CEOs who don't perform have been shown the exit door in many companies in this exercise of owner power, and new examples of this phenomenon can be seen virtually every week in the business headlines.

The point of these examples is to show that boards and shareholders will take action if CEOs and their top executives won't change dysfunctional power structures that affect performance. The advice to these high-level, high-profile managers—indeed, to all managers with responsibility for strategy formulation or execution—is simple and straightforward.

Understand the Power Structure

This is an obvious yet basic need. Analysis of the decisions and forces at work in Figure 9.1, including the effects of structure, resource allocations, and dependencies, is a vital first step. Understanding power is an essential requisite for changing power. Knowing what have traditionally been the bases of power is absolutely essential to altering the influence structure and overcoming resistance to change by those who fear the loss of power.

Be Bold and Make the Necessary Moves

Changing the power structure is very much like changing culture. Appeals to those in power to change and relinquish their influence, thereby eliminating some aspects of a dysfunctional power structure, typically fall on deaf or unsympathetic ears. The only way to change power, similar to changing culture, is to focus on the conditions that bestow power.

To change power, it may be necessary to change strategy, as different strategies make different demands on organizational skills or capabilities (see Chapter 3). Whether or not one changes strategy, it may be necessary to alter structure and integration methods in response to the demands of strategy (see Chapter 4 and Chapter 5). If structure changes, this could lead to different resource allocations and dependencies on different individuals and groups within the organization. The dependencies, in turn, could lead to different levels of centrality and importance of these individuals or units, thereby affecting the power structure.

Not all changes in power demand such big, bold moves. Within departments or functions, managers need not concern themselves with strategy and structure, but can focus on resource allocations and changes in people or decision-making responsibilities and authority. Still, even within divisions, departments, or functions, managers must be aware of the fact that power is the opposite or obverse of dependency. Power cannot be changed until dependencies are changed. Changing dependencies, even at lower organizational levels, is a bold and difficult move. People with power are reluctant to lose it, no matter where they happen to be in the organization.

Overcome Resistance to Change

The manager effecting changes in power must be able to overcome resistance to change. Again, the process and requisite steps are similar to overcoming resistance to cultural change (see Chapter 8). The cause-effect analyses, effective communication, and leadership capabilities documented in the previous chapter come into play once again when considering changes in the power and influence structure. Nothing less than a full commitment to change and a full understanding of the key factors and conditions affecting power will work when contemplating and executing a needed change in power.

If a power structure proves to be dysfunctional and an organization is losing competitive advantage, profitability, and market share, it must be changed. Reluctance by top management to do so will inevitably lead to continued performance problems and steps by shareholders or directors to right the situation. Biting the bullet and instituting change is tough, but it's still better than being the target of outsiders' forced changes.

SUMMARY

A number of important conclusions can be drawn from the present chapter's consideration of power influence and execution. They are the following:

- Power affects strategy execution. The data collected from participants for Chapter 1's survey research indicate that attempts to execute strategy that violates or goes against the power structure of the organization always face difficulties and are often doomed to failure.

- Power is the opposite of dependency. An individual or unit, A, has power over another individual or unit, B, if two vital conditions are met. A has power over B if (a) A has something (information, resources) B needs and (b) B cannot get it elsewhere. If A has something B needs and is able to monopolize what B needs, then B is totally dependent on A, and A has power over B.

- In organizations, the demands generated by strategy affect structure. The structural units solving the critical problems of the organization are rewarded in an uneven distribution of scarce resources. The uneven distribution of resources leads to the differences in dependencies that create power differences.

- Having power facilitates the formulation and execution of strategy. In the absence of power and social influence, an individual or unit (department, function) can form coalitions with those having influence to foster and support execution methods and plans. The logic is that of the joint venture: Joining forces and creating power bases by combining the potential for power of individuals and units allows for more effective execution than an individual or unit could achieve acting separately.

■ To receive support, execution methods and plans must produce clear, measurable, and positive value-added results. Hierarchical superiors or potential joint venture or coalition partners will not support execution if they cannot see and measure its results and value-added contributions to the organization. Individuals and units with a history of producing positive results gain credibility and additional influence over time in the organization.

■ The desired perpetuation of power by those who have it creates a potential downside for the organization. People in power may persist in doing what's necessary to perpetuate their powerful positions, even if their actions are inappropriate under different or changing competitive conditions. If this happens, the role of the CEO and his or her executive team is essential to changing the power structure. Emphasis must be on changing strategy, structure, or resource allocations, which in turn can affect dependencies and the definition of new power relationships. Power differences are inevitable. The trick is to ensure that power or social influence furthers the achievement of organizational goals and the execution of strategy.

ENDNOTES

i.   The notion of power as a relational social influence and an ability to act, despite resistance, can be traced back to Max Weber's *The Theory of Social and Economic Organization*, Free Press, 1947. See also Robert Dahl's *Modern Political Analysis*, Prentice-Hall, 1963.

ii. David Mechanic, "Sources of Power of Lower Participants in Complex Organizations," *Administrative Science Quarterly*, Volume 7, 1962.

iii. Lawrence G. Hrebiniak and William F. Joyce, "Organizational Adaptation Strategic Choice and Environmental Determinism," *Administrative Science Quarterly*, September 1985.

iv. Ben Dummett, "For Drug Maker, M&A Does the Work of R&D," *The Wall Street Journal*, April 18, 2012.

v. Kurt Eichenwald, "Microsoft's Lost Decade," *Vanity Fair*, July 3, 2012.

vi. See, for example, Margaret Bogenrief, "Ron Johnson Really Is Destroying J. C. Penney," *Business Insider*, October 15, 2012; Jae Jun, "Why J. C. Penney Is Not Worth Buying," *Seeking Alpha*, October 23, 2012.

vii. Russell Gold, "Chesapeake Board Crimps CEO's Power," *The Wall Street Journal*, June 9, 2012.

viii. Alistair MacDonald and Edward Welsch, "Barrick Gold Ousts Its CEO," *The Wall Street Journal*, June 7, 2012.

ix. Evan Ramstad and Jung-Ah Lee, "New Samsung CEO to Have Less Clout," *The Wall Street Journal*, June 8, 2012.

x. Joann Lublin, "More CEOs Sharing Control at the Top," *The Wall Street Journal*, June 7, 2012.

II

Applications

Chapters 1-9 presented the key factors and decisions necessary for successful strategy implementation or execution. The chapters were guided by a model of execution and, taken together, provide a roadmap for the process of making strategy work. Those chapters presented the essence and *raison d'être* of the execution task.

The present version of *Making Strategy Work* takes an additional, important step. The following chapters present applications of the basic execution approach to real-world, challenging situations and show how strategy can be implemented effectively in these situations. The emphasis is on a useful application of the present model to problems and opportunities managers face routinely in today's highly competitive world. Part II, "Applications," in large part reflects a response to the requests of managers who felt that application of the present approach would be helpful and informative in their ongoing work on strategy execution.

Chapter 10, "Making Mergers and Acquisitions Work," focuses on making merger and acquisition strategies work. This chapter appeared in the original edition of this book, and it has been brought up to date to ensure its continued utility and relevance.

Chapter 11, "Making Global Strategy Work," is a new chapter. The previous edition of this book devoted insufficient attention to global strategy, and this chapter corrects this oversight. The emphasis, again, is on applying the present model and approach to global implementation issues, a timely and important topic in today's fiercely competitive world.

Chapter 12, "Executing Strategy in Service Organizations," is also a new chapter that responds to the requests of many managers for additional coverage of the service and not-for-profit sectors. Does strategy implementation or execution in service organizations follow the same rules and principles as their product-based counterparts? This and other questions are tackled and answered in this new, informative chapter.

Chapter 13, "Project Management and Strategy Execution," is a new, but slightly different, application-oriented chapter. It shows how project management can be applied to, or used along with, the approach to implementation presented in this book. In response to requests from previous readers of *Making Strategy Work*, it presents project management as a possible aid or complementary facilitator of some aspects of the process of making strategy work. It shows how project management can be useful and supportive of strategy execution. It also emphasizes, however, potential pitfalls that must be avoided when employing project management in the implementation process.

Part II of this book is meant to be helpful in providing insights into making strategy work in important settings or situations. Accomplishing this purpose would clearly represent a positive outcome for both the practicing manager and interested academics or students of the strategy execution process in complex organizations.

10

Making Mergers and Acquisitions Work

Introduction

This book shows how a logical, integrative approach can address execution obstacles and opportunities and lead to execution success. It provides a valuable guide for future execution decisions and actions. This chapter takes one more step to show the usefulness of the present approach to strategy execution.

The purpose of this chapter is to apply the book's concepts to a real execution problem. It shows how the present model and insights can actually be used to foster positive execution outcomes for a complex strategy. It shows how to make mergers and acquisitions work. It details M&A decisions against the present model and takes a step-by-step approach to M&A execution.[i]

MAKING MERGER AND ACQUISITION STRATEGIES WORK

WHY FOCUS ON MERGERS AND ACQUISITIONS?

M&A activities are common, important, and consume huge amounts of resources, including management's time. They are always in the news. They are exciting. These attempts at growth and diversification fuel the imagination as they purport to drive future profitability and shareholder value.

The logic underlying M&A activities sounds virtually unassailable.[ii] The motives behind M&A include, but are not limited to, new sources of growth, when organic growth is stifled or hampered by industry or competitive forces; attempts at diversification to attain new product or service lines; a search for complementary countries or regions in a quest for global expansion; and simply a desire to expand within an industry to gain market power, control industry forces, and reduce operating costs. Some recent examples of M&As that build upon these points of logic include the following:

- Pfizer announced in 2012 that it intends to buy NextWave Pharmaceuticals to add an attention deficit hyperactivity drug to its line of products. Similarly, in the same year Bayer acquired Shiff Nutrition, Inc., to add vitamins and other products and increase its position and presence in the lucrative over-the-counter market in the U.S.[iii]

- Chinese companies have been flexing their economic muscle of late by actively acquiring companies to diversify their product lines and geographical footprint. Food Group of China, for example, agreed to acquire a majority stake in U.K.-based Weetabix in an attempt to extend its product line and influence worldwide. Chinese companies have eagerly taken advantage of Europe's economic woes, for example, as companies like State Grid and China Three Gorges are raiding Spain's assets in a buying spree.[iv] This recent activity is expected to continue as China expands its global reach.

- The announced blockbuster merger of U.S. Airways and American Airlines in 2013 is intended to achieve most of the

M&A benefits noted above. The outcome of a successful merger will be the largest airline in the world, by traffic, which will hopefully lead to lower costs and scale economies; increased market power, leading to greater control of "suppliers," pilots' and attendants' unions; new global routes, thereby increasing product or service lines; and simply greater growth and profitability than could be achieved by organic expansion.

- Japanese companies are also getting into the M&A act. In fact, in 2012, Japanese companies were second only to the United States in foreign acquisitions, logging more than 700 deals in that year alone. The goal: Increase earnings while enlarging companies' global footprint. For example, Softbank's acquisition of Sprint/Nextel allows entry into the large U.S. market and creates one of the largest telecommunications companies in the world (90 million subscribers) to better compete in a highly concentrated industry. A desire for geographical reach, size, and competitive clout clearly seems to underlie Softbank's move.[v]

- Hitachi, another Japanese company, announced plans in October 2012 to buy British nuclear venture, Horizon, for $1.12 billion. The purpose of the acquisition is to help double Hitachi's revenue from its nuclear power business while simultaneously reducing exposure to low-margin consumer electronic products.[vi] Hitachi outdid rival Westinghouse Electric, a unit of Toshiba, thereby expanding a key business while also limiting a major competitor's growth options, another purpose or goal of M&A activity.

- The example of Valeant Pharmaceuticals International was mentioned in a previous chapter but is worth another mention here. In 2011, the company made 13 takeover bids and won 11. Why such aggressive activity? To replace the work of slower-moving, more expensive, and risky R&D activities in an effort to expand the companies' pipeline of products and treatments more quickly and effectively. In effect, M&A activity is seen as an alternative to R&D for new product attainment and growth.[vii]

- Smaller companies also are getting into the M&A act. In the New York metro area alone, there were more than 80 mergers or acquisitions involving CPA firms in the years 2008 through 2011. The goals are identical to those of larger companies—that is, create size, obtain market power, achieve economies of scale, and combine complementary capabilities or service.[viii]

These are but a few recent examples of M&A activity to show their intended logic or goals. There are countless other recent examples of M&A or contemplated M&A activities involving a host of companies, including some big names—Ryanair - Aer Lingus and LAN Airlines – TAMSA—in the airline industry in addition to American-U.S. Airways. The point is already clear, however: M&A is big business and the stated goals of this activity are consistent across companies and industries. M&A activities are indeed common and important, driven by the reasons noted previously.

The sad truth is, however, that most mergers and acquisitions, despite their popularity, fail or founder. They don't deliver on their goals and management's promises. A number of articles and special reports show convincingly that there is a strong case against M&A.

A ten-year study of 340 major acquisitions by Mercer Management Consulting is significant because it validates the fact that most business marriages do not work. The study found that a full 57 percent of the merged companies lagged behind industry performance averages three years after the transactions had been completed. Many of these mergers destroyed shareholder wealth. They failed to deliver. They wasted valuable resources and presented real and opportunity costs to investors.[ix] Similarly, a study by the Boston Consulting Group showed that, of the 277 deals it analyzed, 64 percent actually resulted in a drop in shareholder value.[x] This certainly isn't solid performance or a recommendation for M&A activity.

Yet one more recent analysis affirms the bleak results of these previous studies. This study, whose results were published in March 2011, reviewed hundreds of M&As from around the globe and 70 technical papers on M&A over a 30-year period, and its findings are shocking and supportive of the earlier facts about M&A success, or lack thereof.[xi] The study found that approximately 70 percent of M&As fail to achieve the expectations forecasted for them; that more than 50 percent actually destroyed value; and less than 30 percent could be labeled as successful.

Some well-known examples of past problematic marriages include Quaker Oats and Snapple, AOL and Time Warner, Morgan Stanley and Dean Witter, Citicorp and Travelers, and Daimler-Benz and Chrysler. And M&A problems certainly aren't going away, as evidenced by some recent attempts at combination that have exhibited, are currently exhibiting, or are anticipating signs of stress and poor performance even before the M&A process is complete:

- In the Softbank-Sprint Nextel deal just mentioned, critics are already arguing that the typical sources of cost savings are lacking, suggesting that one important justification of M&As of this type holds little validity.[xii] Sprint's shareholders are scratching their heads, wondering about the logic of the deal and whether the combination can deliver on Softbank's goal of fixing a troubled mobile carrier and gaining traction in a competitive industry.

- Kraft's hostile takeover of Cadbury for $19-plus billion in 2010 has faced rough going. Senior Cadbury management (120 out of 170) left the company in protest. Integration costs were sky high ($1.3 billion), with projected savings only one-half as much. Profits fell due to the high integration costs. Critics have argued that there was poor due diligence on Kraft's part, too-hasty attempts at integration, and insufficient attention paid to the vast cultural differences between the companies, leading to major problems.[xiii]

- Renault's partnership with British racing car company, Caterham Cars, is a strategic alliance, not an outright merger or acquisition, but the goals of such a combination are similar to those of M&As. (Indeed, such alliances are often precursors to more formal M&A arrangements.) The real challenge to making the alliance work is similar to that often heard in many mergers or acquisitions: overcoming vast cultural differences between the companies involved.[xiv] A popular expression is that "opposites attract," but this isn't the usual case in M&As where opposite cultures can spell disaster for attempts at company integration and concerted joint effort. Time will tell if the entrepreneurial culture of Caterham meshes smoothly with the more staid, established culture of a larger Renault.

■ The U.S. Airways-American Airlines merger faces rocky times ahead before the newly created airline flies without turbulence. Integration of the two airlines will be challenging, at best, as new routes, operating procedures, computer systems, labor contracts, frequent flier programs, and perhaps even culture clashes come into play. The huge problems that plagued and are still tormenting the United-Continental merger suggest strongly that the future integration of the airlines will not be easy.

■ In July 2012, Delta Airlines shocked the business world when it decided to buy the Trainer, Pennsylvania, oil refinery from Conoco Philips. This is a gutsy move at vertical integration to guarantee a steady supply of low-cost jet fuel, and such an acquisition can wind up looking really good or really dismal. This clearly is a diversification into a totally different industry, and the success of the venture depends on a number of factors, including the demand for and price of fuel and Delta's ability to manage a business outside its core capabilities. Management skills certainly come into play in making an acquisition strategy of unrelated diversification work. Questions about the move linger and, again, time will tell whether this was a sound move, and whether vertical integration can offer Delta some advantage in a competitive commodity market.[xv]

■ Finally, consider the well-publicized potential merger between European Aeronautic Defence and Space and BAE Systems, a merger that never got off the ground due to politics and national concerns with the merger. Despite the strategic and commercial benefits of creating a worthy opponent for Boeing, the merger failed to gain lift and take off.[xvi]

Strong protectionist and political objections have, in effect, killed the prospects of what appears to be a logical economic combination. The French, British, and German politicians needed to compromise, but fears of job loss and erosion of power scuttled the deal before it could materialize. Politics indeed makes for strange bedfellows; politics also can prevent the sharing of beds by complementary and not-so-strange bedfellows.

The problems with M&A will not go away; they will be around for a long time. Not only have there been failures or problems in the past, there certainly will be many more mergers and acquisitions that will founder in the future. The real question—and the critical one that needs explication—is why M&As founder or fail. Why is there such a devastatingly poor record for these expensive but popular activities? A few recent examples of challenged M&A activities were just presented. What do they and the many other examples available teach us about why M&As often founder or fail?'

WHY DO SO MANY MERGERS AND ACQUISITIONS FAIL OR FOUNDER?

The answer to this question is straightforward: They fail because of poor planning and poor execution. The following list shows some aspects of poor planning and poor execution that explain poor M&A results.

Poor Planning	+	Poor Execution	=	Poor M&A Results
• No Compelling Strategic Rationale		• No Clear, Logical Approach to Execution		• Poor Financial Performance
• Inadequate Due Diligence		• Conflicting Cultures		• Erosion of Shareholders Value
• Overstatement of Expected Synergies		• Poor Integration		• Decreases in Customer Satisfaction
• Too High a Price Paid		• Poor Leadership		
		• Excessive Speed		
		• Poor Management of Change		

Let's summarize briefly some of the main issues and problems that characterize poor planning and poor execution. Time then can be devoted to a discussion of how the present approach to execution can address the problems and help make M&A strategies work.

Poor Planning

Bad planning generates execution problems. It may also doom a merger or acquisition from the outset.

No compelling strategic logic. M&As represent major strategic decisions. They also are expensive, both in terms of real and opportunity cost. Accordingly, the logic behind such major decisions must be developed carefully. The motivation for acquisition or merger activity must be clear in terms of desired results— growth, global expansion, diversification—and a detailed and logical plan must be developed to support the expenditure.

This logical, planned approach, sadly, isn't always the case. High market capitalizations and excess cash on hand can burn a hole in CEOs' pockets. M&A activities often reflect feelings of "wealth" and a penchant to spend rather than sound strategic analysis of what sustains long-term value.

Related to the previous point is top management hubris or greed. "Bigger and better" is a driving force that CEOs occasionally succumb to, leading to M&A activities for the wrong reasons. Excessive pride ("I can handle this huge merger easily") and personal benefit also come into play. Once, after asking a CEO why he was pursuing global diversification and after hearing some of his stock answers about growth and shareholder value, he added, "Besides, a CEO of a large, diversified company makes much more money and wields much more influence than a CEO of a smaller, nondiversified company."

This was a great rationale for him, obviously, but not necessarily a sound strategic footing for diversification and an enhancement of shareholder value.

A compelling and logical strategic rationale is needed to justify an M&A strategy. If the rationale isn't clear and compelling, critical stakeholders won't jump on the bandwagon, and execution will be more difficult and problematic.

Inadequate due diligence. This is a critical aspect of planning for M&A. Due diligence, including cultural due diligence, is vital to M&A success. An acquiring company must carefully analyze a target industry and potential candidates. "Hard" data—industry forces, resources and capabilities, industry attractiveness, market power, competitors, and the foundations of expected synergies and costs savings—must be studied carefully. So must the "soft" issues revolving around culture and the similarities and differences between potential merger partners. People, culture, values, and attitudes rarely mesh easily. It is often easier to integrate distribution channels than divergent cultures.

Sound planning and due diligence must prepare the merger for the need to handle and integrate hard and soft measures if the M&A strategy is to work. Poor due diligence usually results in poor execution outcomes.

Too high a price paid. Paying a premium for an acquisition in M&A is the rule, not the exception. Paying a high premium means that the probability of earning back the cost of capital is virtually nil. Paying a 50 percent premium, for example, would mean that a company realizing synergies in the second year after purchase would have to increase the return on equity of the acquisition by 12 percentage points and maintain it for nine more years, just to break even.[xvii] On average, this isn't going to happen.

Good planning is necessary to keep the price in line, given the synergies and other benefits that realistically can be expected from an acquisition. Poor planning increases the costs to everyone, especially the shareholders who entrust their money to managers who, they hope, will look out for their best interests.

Poor Execution

Not having a logical approach to execution. Having a logical approach to execution is necessary for the success of M&A strategies. The importance of this for all strategies was emphasized by managers in the current research, and it is especially true for M&A strategies. Executing diversifications without a well-thought-out execution plan and process is simply asking for trouble. This book has developed execution guidelines and a model that will be applied to the case of making M&A work later in this chapter.

Poor integration. This is often the big deal killer. Structural integration must be done well if a merger is to achieve any success.

The melding of organizational functions or divisions and clarification of responsibilities and authority in the merged organizations are important to effective and efficient postmerger performance.

Even more important for M&A success in some cases is cultural integration. Due diligence on the planning side can prepare an acquiring company for culture conflicts and related problems. Even with good planning, however, cultural integration can be a formidable challenge that, if done poorly, can hurt the execution of M&A strategies. Attempts at making diversification strategies work that ignore the management of culture and culture change are usually doomed to failure.

Costs of execution. Often overlooked are the costs of execution beyond the obvious expenses incurred by acquisition strategies. Structural and cultural integration demand management's time and involvement. Unclear execution responsibilities can increase decision time and create frustrations. Managers may leave the company or "drop out psychologically" because of the frustrations and unclear direction of change. Consider, again, the mass exodus of managers from Cadbury when the company was swallowed by Kraft in a hostile takeover. This indeed represents a significant cost.

Execution activities also create opportunity costs, as time spent on M&A execution means that less time is available for other managerial tasks. Time spent on execution may detract attention from other critical industry forces and competitive conditions, thereby injuring organizational performance. Real and opportunity costs, including management taking its eye off the ball to handle execution bottlenecks, clearly represent a potential problem when trying to make M&A strategies work.

"Speed kills." Moving quickly in M&A transactions and integration is often touted as a good thing. But excessive speed can be dangerous. As heretical as this sounds, speed in integration and culture change can have a serious downside.

A high "velocity of change" and the need to handle many conflicting factors at once when integrating an acquisition can create a highly complex change and lead to disastrous outcomes. Excessive speed can hurt integration and execution success.

Poor change management. Execution of M&A strategies usually involves change, and the ineffective handling of change will thwart or seriously injure execution. Key questions or issues include whether to make changes quickly or manage them over longer periods of time. Obviously, decisions must take the speed or velocity of change into account, including benefits and costs of alternative change approaches to making M&A work. Leadership is also critical here, as managers at all levels of an organization must deal with change and overcome resistance to it.

The issue of trust. One more issue needs to be mentioned—trust. Trust between the parties involved in an acquisition can affect both planning and execution. A lack of trust can affect the sharing of information and the validity of due diligence data. Trust clearly can positively affect cultural integration, the setting of performance objectives, and the structural integration of a new business into the corporate fold. Managers on both sides of an M&A strategy must be open and honest with each other to facilitate execution.

This, then, is a brief summary of planning and execution problems related to the performance of M&A strategies. The literature on M&A, opinions of managers in the present research, and my experiences suggest that these problems can seriously affect execution results.

The critical question is where do we go from here? How can we improve the odds of success for the execution of M&A strategies? Given that so many mergers fail, any change in success will save countless dollars and frustrations. But how does one address the huge problems just noted and improve the chances for success?

One answer to these questions is to apply the ideas and concepts developed in this book. The following sections apply the present model and concepts to the critical issue of making acquisitions and consolidation work. They go through the steps, decisions, and actions necessary to confront the execution problems and issues just noted and make M&A strategies successful. Upon completion of this task, you can judge for yourself how useful and practical the present approach to execution really is.

USING THE PRESENT MODEL AND APPROACH TO EXECUTION

CORPORATE STRATEGY

The present approach to execution begins with corporate strategy (see Chapter 2). As was just stressed, planning affects execution outcomes. Poor corporate strategic plans usually beget poor execution results.

Corporate strategy is typically concerned with portfolio analysis, financial issues, acquisitions, and diversification or divestiture strategies, as Chapter 3 stressed. It is concerned with the mix of businesses in the corporation and resource allocations across businesses to maximize shareholder value. When considering M&A strategies, the corporate task or responsibility looks like the following:

Corporate planning involves due diligence in the analysis of possible target industries and candidates for M&A activity. Industry forces and conditions must be analyzed, including industry concentration, the power of suppliers and customers, the strength of competitors, and the barriers to effective entry.

In the case of related diversification, when the candidate company for acquisition is in the same industry as the acquirer, much is already known about industry forces, structure, and competition. Emphasis now is less on learning about the industry and more on analyzing how the acquisition will alter market or competitive forces in that industry. The acquisition, for example, may increase market power over suppliers due to the buying power of a larger post-acquisition organization. Larger size may also lead to a low-cost position in the industry. Candidate attractiveness thus is more important than industry attractiveness in the case of stick-to-the-knitting, related diversification. If an industry or strategic niche within an industry is attractive, a list of suitable acquisition candidates can be drawn up and carefully analyzed. Due diligence requires a thorough examination of the candidate's finances, resources and capabilities, current strategy, potential for growth, and appropriateness as an addition to the corporate portfolio.

The Hewlett-Packard-Autonomy debacle raises many planning related questions and emphasizes the critical importance of solid due diligence. HP bought Autonomy in 2011 for $10 billion and only one year later recorded an $8.8 billion write-down. HP claimed that accounting and other irregularities at Autonomy overstated its revenues and worth. Autonomy's management countered, saying HP's reasoning is flawed and makes no sense. The bottom line, however, seems to point to inadequate due diligence on HP's part. Previous top people at HP—for example, former CEO, Mike Hurd—had argued that Autonomy was overpriced at half the amount HP wound up paying. Coupled with other HP acquisitions that went sour—for example, a $14 billion acquisition of EDS and huge write-down of it in 2012—the issue of poor due diligence at HP certainly has gained traction in many circles and shown how poor planning can hurt acquisition success.

Due diligence also demands cultural due diligence of the acquisition candidate (see Chapter 8). What are the driving cultural values? What is the company's credo or vision? What is its approach to compensation and how it makes important decisions? Is the candidate vastly different in terms of style, culture, structure, and how it does things? What is the power structure (see Chapter 9), and will it clash or meld easily with the existing corporate power structure?

The importance of due diligence cannot be exaggerated. Due diligence in M&A on the "hard" issues—market position, financial resources, technological assets and capabilities, distribution networks—is important for success. But due diligence on the "soft" issues is also important. Ignoring them is like walking into a minefield of potential culture clashes. Moreover, "hard" issues often breed "soft" issues; focusing on the former while ignoring the latter can spell disaster.

In the BP-Amoco merger, for example, the two companies had different "hard" strengths: One focused upstream on exploration and R&D, the other more on downstream capabilities such as marketing and retail distribution. But the obvious differences also suggested harder-to-detect issues. The people, skills, attitudes, and culture generated in an R&D-type "upstream" organization in any industry are quite different from those in an organization dominated by sales, marketing, and a "downstream" market mentality. These differences can affect execution success.

In the Renault-Caterham alliance announced in 2012, due diligence was apparently done on cultural matters. The long negotiations between the two companies was made difficult due to the cultural differences between the two companies. The fact that the companies recognized the vast cultural differences, however, is a positive sign. Ignoring the "soft" cultural issues and focusing only on the "hard" issues—car design, cost, product development, distribution—would likely detract from the viability of the strategic alliances going forward.

Daimler-Benz certainly knew the "hard" issues of the automotive industry when it went after Chrysler. It might have erred a bit in its analysis of Chrysler's cost structure, but for the most part, due diligence on the "hard" issues was fine.

Where Daimler-Benz faltered was in its due diligence on the "soft" issues. The cultural differences between the German and American companies were huge. The vast differences between compensation schedules caused major cultural and perceived equity problems. A job of due diligence on the "hard" issues was offset by poor cultural due diligence, a fact that affected the execution of the "merger of equals." Due diligence on the "softer" issues is a must for M&A success.

Kraft likely paid too little attention to cultural issues in its acquisition of Cadbury. The company focused on product line, geographical growth into India, and the cost of the acquisition, but it apparently paid less attention to the cultural differences between itself and Cadbury. The fact that so many senior Cadbury managers fled from the company post acquisition was indeed telling. These senior people clearly saw an incursion or outright raid on company values and operating autonomy, a fact that Kraft officials obviously hadn't built into their acquisition approach.

Sound corporate planning and due diligence represent a critical first step in the M&A process. Deciding on a viable acquisition candidate and negotiating a fair price, coupled with due diligence, allows the transaction to go forward on a positive note.

CORPORATE STRUCTURE

The next major step in executing the corporate M&A strategy is the choice or modification of organizational structure, given the new acquisition. Strategy affects the choice of structure, as was emphasized in Chapter 4 dealing with structure and execution, and Chapter 5 on managing integration and information sharing, and this choice is affected by M&A transactions.

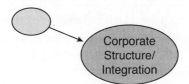

Choice of structure depends on the type of acquisition strategy being executed. The typical related diversification usually involves the melding of two organizations in the same industry that are alike in many ways. Their similarity usually means an execution emphasis on the reduction of duplications and costs and an attempt to attain synergies by consolidating the companies.

Related diversifications in terms of markets and technologies usually call for greater centralization of structure, as like units are combined to service the merged organization. Core central functions provide the scale and scope economies that drive down operating costs. Centralization also allows for the development of centers of excellence to serve the entire organization. Related diversifications, then, typically call for some centralization of structure and the expertise and scale and scope economies it implies.

The case of unrelated or mixed diversification is a bit trickier. An acquired company, though in a different industry, may share similar technologies, manufacturing operations, marketing capabilities, or distribution channels. On the other hand, some or all of these same characteristics may be quite different. The rule developed in Chapter 4 emphasizes that common, similar elements become centralization candidates, while differences usually drive the choice of decentralized structures.

If technologies are similar across the companies, for example, a corporate R&D group or a centralized engineering function may be in order. The postmerger organization simultaneously may be characterized by separate divisions or SBUs to reflect differences in customers, markets, or distribution channels. Centralization and decentralization exist side by side because of the mix of technological and market similarities and differences.

Another example is provided by looking at vertical integration backward or forward, a typical unrelated diversification. This diversification also raises the question of structural choice: Should the newly purchased unit stand alone, as a separate division or profit center, or should it be melded into an existing corporate function as a cost center?

The answer in most vertical integration attempts is often straightforward. The newly acquired vertically integrated unit is typically in a different, if adjacent, industry. It usually is more logical to maintain the separate identity and functioning of the unit or company. Delta Airlines, for example, is wise to leave its oil refinery acquired from Conoco-Philips as a separate, standalone unit run by managers and engineers with refining experience. It makes little sense to bring control of the new unit into an airlines company, under the supervision of individuals who know nothing about refinery operations.

The case of a newly acquired company that has been a successful profit center and profit generator can present a slightly more difficult problem when the company is in the same or similar business as the acquirer.

Assume, for instance, that a company in the chip-making business acquires another chip maker, but one with different, more technically sophisticated and innovative products. Retaining the new company as a separate profit center generates cash and usually maintains focus on R&D, technological change, and product development, as the company continues to compete effectively in the industry. The fruits of its labor, however, are shared by all, including competitors that buy the acquired company's products and technological advances. The autonomous company, in effect, is funding innovation for the industry, including competitors.

Conversely, bringing the new unit into a cost center reporting to an existing function such as manufacturing increases the acquiring chip-maker's control, but this option may forego market share and the R&D capability of a separate profit center. The cost-center move also risks a dramatic drop in production, adversely affecting economies of scale. Another issue deals with autonomy. Top-flight scientists and engineers may leave the acquired company, rebelling against the loss of autonomy and being put under the authority of a cost center director. Maintenance of the profit center model allows the key scientists, engineers, and managers to maintain their autonomy, status, and influence in a standalone company rather than be relegated to a new, confining bureaucratic structure. The key personnel had previously enjoyed a culture wherein their knowledge and capabilities contributed to a professional, expertise-based culture of autonomy and self-control, and threats to this situation will likely be rejected.

Structural choice also affects the degree of structural integration required by the acquisition strategy. Under related diversification, the acquisition must be melded into the organization structurally. With unrelated diversification, interdependence is lower and integration requirements are also consequently lower. Structural integration simply isn't as urgent when the acquired company is to remain as a separate, standalone profit center.

The structural integration of two companies is no easy task. The many acquisitions in the banking industry worldwide in the past couple of decades usually had efficiency or cost-cutting goals. The inability to deliver on cost-cutting promises could be attributed in part to poor structural integration. Melding of similar organizational units to reduce redundancies and create synergies sounds straightforward, almost easy. The many problems that exist with related diversification in the banking industry suggest that the consolidation process is not at all easy, but exacting and difficult.

Effective integration makes serious demands on an organization. The time and resources required are often underestimated. The integration process takes time. The individuals or team responsible must have the experience to deal with conflict and generate agreement between factions or management teams with different views of what the merged company should look like and how it should operate. The integration process deals with many variables or factors—people, structure, incentives, responsibilities, culture, and so on—adding to its complexity. The process also needs to focus on strategic issues and the ultimate goals of the merger or acquisition as a guide to integration activities and processes. Integration is, at once, a strategic task, as well as one focusing on the micro, "devil-in-the-details" issues.

Structural integration also holds important implications for organizational power and influence. At the formation of Citigroup, much time was spent figuring out whether the group from Travelers or the managers from Citibank would dominate the critical positions in the combined structure. Recalling from Chapter 9 that structure is related to strategic problem solving, the distribution of scarce resources, and the formation of dependency relationships that lead to differences in power and influence, it is no wonder that structural choice and integration consumed so much attention within Citigroup when executing its M&A strategy.

Structural issues were treated in depth in Chapters 4 and 5. This summary is merely trying to emphasize that, to make M&A strategies work, the corporate level must choose an appropriate structure to realize the benefits of its acquisition strategy. The appropriate mix of centralization and decentralization is needed to maximize the performance, most notably, the efficiency, and effectiveness of the new, combined organization. Structural integration is needed to realize the benefits of cost cutting and avoidance of expensive duplications in the combined organization.

In addition to structural choice and integration, cultural integration of the merger partners is also vital to the execution of diversification strategies, as suggested by previous examples. This is another important task confronting corporate decision-makers trying to make M&A work, and it deserves a bit more attention.

CULTURAL INTEGRATION IN M&A

Cultural integration is important for M&A success. Except for pure conglomerate-type mergers in which acquired units are totally independent, standalone entities ("pooled" interdependence; see Chapter 5), cultural integration comes into play.

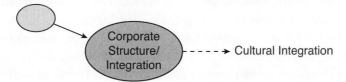

As important as cultural integration is for success, it is often neglected or woefully mismanaged. It often creates problems with making acquisition strategies work.

The poor performance of many companies in the studies of acquisitions (cited previously) can be attributed in part to corporate culture clashes. The consultants and other M&A specialists involved in the studies point to the fact that culture clashes have become a significant causes of many M&A failures.

Sony and Matsushita's hardware-software dreams may have been grandiose and crazy from the start, almost guaranteeing that they would turn into horrific nightmares. However, the Japanese managers were worlds apart from the "Hollywood smoothies" they chose to run the combined companies.[xviii] The culture clash turned out to be one of the big deal killers.

Daimler-Benz and Chrysler again can be mentioned. The vast differences between German and U.S. cultures have already been noted, but other important cultural differences also came into play. Premerger Chrysler was more informal, often taking a "buccaneering" approach to problem solving and new product development, with cross-functional teams working together and interacting heavily in a reciprocally interdependent setting (Chapter 5). In contrast, Daimler-Benz had a more traditional silo or "chimney" structure in which engineering ruled and marketing or design people mixed infrequently with engineers and played much more of a secondary role. These differences in style and process make cultural integration difficult, challenging the viability of an acquisition strategy.

The Sprint-Nextel merger of "equals" never fulfilled its promises. There were huge technical problems as both companies' technologies were vastly different, allowing for no easy integration. Cultural factors also came into play, with a lack of cultural integration only adding to the technological problems. The decision to shut down the Nextel network by the middle of 2013 surprised few in the industry. Poor planning and poor integration had doomed the merger of equals. It will be interesting to see what transpires after Softbank's acquisition of Sprint-Nextel in terms of cultural integration.

How, then, does one achieve effective cultural integration? Table 10.1 summarizes a few practical steps toward this end.

Table 10.1 Achieving Cultural Integration in Mergers and Acquisitions

---

1. Create individual or "SWAT" team responsibility for integration:
   - Responsibility for integration
   - Integration objectives defined
   - "Riding herd" and pushing the integration agenda
2. Take immediate steps to help clarify personnel orientations and reduce uncertainty:
   - New IDs, business cards, as needed
   - Information regarding the new merged company: phone numbers, e-mail addresses, benefit programs, health plans, stock options, reporting relationships, and communication links
3. Define the new desired culture:
   - Key values and drivers of excellence
   - Results or outcomes desired, as well as strategic rationale
   - Advertise the new, exciting elements of work (growth opportunities, increased responsibility, new promotion possibilities) and other positive aspects of the merger

4. Maintain and reinforce the best characteristics of the old culture:
   - Entrepreneurial climate, informality, client or customer orientation
   - Holding on to familiar "anchors," performance strengths
5. Institute communication programs to reduce uncertainty and facilitate the culture change process:
   - Provide forums for communication and open confrontation of problems
   - Q&A sessions
   - "Work Out" programs
   - Advertise training for new responsibilities
6. Develop and reinforce incentives and controls that support the new culture:
   - Supporting new behaviors and acquisition objectives
7. Manage change effectively:
   - Tactics and methods of managing change, including culture change
   - Overcoming resistance to change

Assign Responsibility for Integration

The first step is to assign responsibility for the integration task. Assigning an individual or preferably a "SWAT" team with the job of "riding herd" or pushing the integration agenda and ensuring that critical tasks get done is a good initial step. If someone isn't directly responsible for cultural integration and paid to worry about integration success, this important task will not receive sufficient attention.

When choosing members of the "SWAT" team, one must consider the operational strengths and weaknesses, cultural similarities and differences, and the power structures of the two merging organizations. Agreement must be reached on the team's composition. Usually, both organizations are equally represented, but top-management agreement may be reached about greater inclusion of one side or the other based on strategic or operating needs.

This initial step of assigning responsibility, while basic, is critical. Choosing an integration team signals a great deal to members of both companies about the merged company's commitment to making the acquisition strategy work. Assigning accountability for integration emphasizes its importance and its central role in making a merger successful.

Orient Personnel Immediately

There are simple yet critical early steps that the organization or "SWAT" team can take immediately to aid cultural integration. Orientation sessions or messages ("town-hall" meetings, in-house TV broadcasts, e-mails, and printed flyers) can focus on issues that may seem trivial at first but are important for ease of integration. Clarifying simple things such as "how to answer the phone" in the merged company reduces stress. So does immediately providing new identities and position descriptions via new IDs and business cards. Information regarding the new company—such as phone numbers, e-mail addresses, health plans, benefit programs, reporting relationships, and so on—can reduce uncertainty, define employees' new space in the company, and go a long way toward eliminating small, nitty-gritty annoyances that collectively can stall or injure the process of cultural integration.

Define the New Culture

It is important to be proactive and define the new, desired culture of the merging company, as Table 10.1 indicates. Setting expectations is critical to integration success. Key values, beliefs, and drivers of excellence should be clearly communicated and reinforced. Results or value-added outcomes expected as a result of the merger should be explained, as well as the strategic rationale behind the consolidation. Any new and exciting elements of work or new opportunities created by the merger should be advertised, such as growth opportunities, promotion possibilities, and new positions.

It is vitally important to publicize what the merger means for everyone and not just focus on the aspects of it that are critical only to top management or institutional investors. Doing everything possible to emphasize the widespread positive impact of the merged company can begin to firm up understanding and commitment throughout the organization, smoothing the transition and aiding development of a new climate or company culture.

Save the Best of the Old Culture

Cultural integration doesn't mean automatic rejection of all old values and previous ways of doing things. Positive aspects of the previous company culture should be retained and their retention clearly advertised to all. An entrepreneurial climate, informality, or customer orientation that has always served the organization well should not be automatically discarded. These aspects of the old culture should be advertised and played up strongly.

"It is important to have something familiar to hold on to" is the way quite a few managers have expressed their feelings to me about the importance of cultural or organizational "anchors" in M&A transitions. Even people who can handle change and ambiguity well have emphasized the importance of the security, safety, and familiarity that accompany these "anchors" or points of stability when going through the throes of a merger.

Institute Communication Programs

Good communication is absolutely essential to cultural integration and reducing resistance to change. Rumors develop and fly as a result of M&A activities. Uncertainties abound, especially around job-security issues. These sparks of discontent can easily fuel a blaze of resistance to cultural integration and cause the merged company countless problems.

Providing communication forums is critical to integration success under M&A. Q&A sessions, "work-out" type programs, and open-house discussions allow for fact finding, venting of emotions, and avoidance of misinformation. Training or educational programs do much to advertise new, exciting opportunities created by the merger. They also provide a forum for communication and dissemination of information useful for cultural integration.

It is important to handle negative information openly and directly. If redundancies are likely to result in consolidation and a displacement of personnel, the company should communicate clearly what will be done to mitigate personnel reductions. "No layoff" policies, retraining programs, and processes to help move people into new jobs should be advertised to reduce security concerns.

Establish Appropriate Incentives and Controls

It is important that incentives and controls support the new culture in a merged organization, as Chapter 6 suggests. Incentives must be consistent with and support new behaviors and the achievement of acquisition objectives. They must motivate cooperation and integration in the new organization, not excessive competition or other dysfunctional behaviors.

The uneven compensation schedules in Daimler and Chrysler created problems for the postmerger integration process. Grossly different pay for similar positions in a merger of equals motivated competition and some ill feelings among managers whose work and contributions were undervalued. DaimlerChrysler executives knew that these disparities had to be confronted and annoying differences eliminated if the merger was to get on a solid, cooperative footing. Sadly, the disparities weren't handled effectively.

In mergers such as Morgan Stanley-Smith Barney (now, in 2013, simply Morgan Stanley), or Citicorp-Travelers, important goals deal with cross-selling of products and services across supposedly related or interdependent businesses. Yet much of this ballyhooed cross-selling and integration never materialized in these cases. One reason is that incentives didn't clearly support or encourage the desired behaviors. Managers and marketing people feel no great urge to work laterally and push other divisions' products and services if incentives don't support such behaviors. Relatedly, if incentives and benefits of one-stop shopping aren't clearly communicated to customers, they will independently continue to seek and choose a variety of financial services on their own from an array of different companies.

If incentives don't motivate and support the new desired outcomes and behaviors in a merged company, cultural integration will suffer. Chapter 6 emphasized the importance of rewarding the "right things," and this advice is particularly salient when trying to meld two organizations.

Effective controls and strategy reviews are also important to structural and cultural integration. Because these reviews in M&A situations involve business-level objectives and performance in a corporate review, these issues are discussed later in this chapter when considering controls at the business level and reviews of business performance.

Manage Change and Transitions Effectively

This is also a critical step in achieving cultural integration, as Table 10.1 and previous discussions have indicated. Because managing change is so important for many aspects of M&A success beyond just cultural integration, more detailed attention is paid to it in separate sections and discussions later in this chapter where managing change and managing cultural change are the topics of discussion.

The tasks of structural and cultural integration are vital to achieving effective execution of an M&A strategy. Careful planning and dutiful attention to structure and integration are important responsibilities of the top-management team committed to M&A success. Let's now turn to the next steps in making acquisition strategies work.

BUSINESS STRATEGY AND SHORT-TERM OBJECTIVES

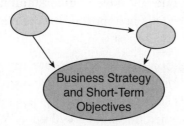

The newly acquired business in the corporate portfolio must formulate or clarify its strategy. Effective integration of corporate and business strategy is impossible if the latter isn't clear and its role or position in the corporate portfolio isn't accepted and well understood.

Business strategy involves analysis of industry forces, competitors, and resources and capabilities, as each business unit attempts to position itself to compete in its industry and attain competitive advantage (see Chapter 3). This summary simply adds that, to make M&A work, the strategy of the acquired unit must support and be consistent with corporate strategy.

The goals of the corporate M&A strategy should already have been laid out as part of the company's compelling strategic rationale for pursuing an acquisition. These goals presumably are clear, drivers of the prior search for and choice of an acquisition candidate. The new organization's role in the corporate portfolio should have been carefully considered by corporate strategists prior to the acquisition.

Much more is needed for execution success, however. Corporate expectations are important, but they must be communicated to the newly acquired business. The role of the new business in the corporate portfolio must be understood and embraced by the acquired company and the parent organization alike.

If corporate expects the acquisition to function as a cash generator, its performance is central to the success of the corporate portfolio strategy. The new company's generation of cash may be critical to resource allocations to other businesses, especially those in emerging or growth industries where cash requirements are high. The poor performance of the acquired organization in this regard can seriously injure the attainment of corporate strategic goals. Consequently, a clear understanding of and commitment to a business strategy is important to the success of the corporate M&A strategy.

The communication between corporate and business executives is also important for the execution of the acquired business's strategy. Expectations surrounding resource allocations to the new business must be hashed out and agreed upon. What the business gets or gets to keep from its own earnings surely has an impact on business-level performance. The goals or performance standards that the new business will be held accountable for also will affect business performance, and these too must be negotiated fully and openly between corporate and business management. Conflicting expectations must be confronted.

There clearly is an interactive, symbiotic relationship between corporate and business strategy and objectives that affects execution outcomes at both levels of the organization. This relationship is shown in Figure 10.1.

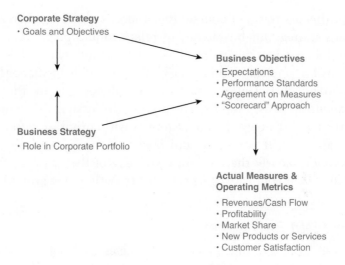

Figure 10.1   Relationship Between Corporate and Business Planning and Execution

Figure 10.1 shows, first, that corporate and business strategies must be integrated and consistent with each other. Good planning and the integration of plans are important to the success of M&A strategies (see Chapter 3).

The figure shows, second, that objectives and performance metrics must be determined for the newly acquired business. Performance standards and measures must be agreed to by both corporate and business management. These objectives are related to a business' role in the corporate portfolio. They also will be used in an evaluation of business performance at a later point in time.

A "scorecard" or management-by-objectives approach is needed to integrate corporate and business plans and objectives (see Chapter 3).[xix] Corporate and business strategies must be translated into performance metrics at the business level, as Figure 10.1 shows. Emphasis is on the data or information that will appear on "dashboards" showing the health and performance of the combined postmerger companies. Corporate and business planning results, then, in a set of business-level objectives and performance metrics that can be used to track execution success. The failure to institute these tracking metrics can negatively affect the execution of the M&A strategy.

All this assumes, of course, that there is a clear, coherent corporate strategy for businesses to relate to and help execute. Major problems occur when corporate strategy and its portfolio assumptions are unclear or don't exist to guide and help shape the development of business strategy and objectives. In these cases, execution clearly suffers. The present discussion also assumes that business strategy is consistent with corporate strategy (see Chapter 3). If corporate and business strategies clash or are in conflict, clearly the corporate strategy of the acquirer must prevail. The dog must wag its tail, not the other way around.

Strategic and Short-Term Objectives

After corporate and business strategies and objectives are fully developed, communicated, and integrated, it is time to focus on executing business strategy—in this case, that of the acquired company.

A scorecard or management-by-objectives approach again comes into play. The need now is to translate strategic objectives into short-term operating metrics at the business level (see Figure 10.1). The strategic objectives of the acquired business have been hashed out and committed to, as the previous discussion stressed. What must happen next is a cascading or translation of strategic objectives into short-term, measurable, operating objectives within the acquired business.

As suggested in Chapter 3, formal approaches such as MBO or the Balanced Scorecard can help with this process of translation. If M&A objectives at the business level include cash generation or increased customer satisfaction, for example, these strategic needs must generate operating measures down through the organization that are consistent with the M&A objectives. Higher-level goals must be translated into lower-level goals if execution is to be successful.

This aspect of execution—integrating strategic and short-term objectives within a business or operating unit—is central and important in all attempts to make business strategy work. The role of the business leader is to ensure internal consistency of objectives and efforts in the quest to fulfill the new business's intended role in the corporate portfolio.

BUSINESS STRUCTURE/INTEGRATION

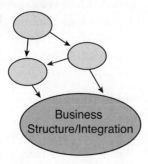

The present approach to execution (see Chapter 2) emphasizes next that strategy and short-term objectives again drive structure, now at the business level. The job of the business management team is to create and manage an organizational structure consistent with business strategy (see Chapter 4). Integration and information sharing also must be attended to within the new business, consistent with the points about interdependence and coordination emphasized in Chapter 5. The preceding discussion argued that corporate strategy affects the choice of structure; the present point is that business strategy also affects the choice of structure and integration methods.

An additional aspect of integration that is important is the possible structural integration required between corporate and business levels. The existence of corporate functions or centers of excellence defines the centralized expertise or capabilities that the acquired business unit may have to tap into and employ to execute its business strategy. Information sharing between a corporate R&D function and the newly acquired business's engineering or product-development units, for example, may be critical to the acquisition's ability to develop and deliver new products or technologies.

Steps or methods to facilitate this integration and information sharing include the use of informal and formal methods (see Chapter 5). Rotation of technical people, joint meetings or scientific symposia, or teams comprising members of both groups can facilitate integration. So can "dual" or "matrix" reporting relationships, in which business-level R&D people report to a business leader while simultaneously reporting, solid-line or dotted line, to a centralized R&D group. Effective post-acquisition integration is the need being met by methods such as these.

PROJECT MANAGEMENT

A brief mention should presently be made for the use of project management in achieving integration and facilitating the required translation of strategic to short-term objectives. Chapter 13 goes into more detail about the project-management tool, but it deserves some attention at the present time.

Project management provides a path to desired results. It helps develop a plan of action to attain the objectives or performance measures vital to execution success, including aspects of the plan vital to successful integration or coordination. The path usually shows a timeline that also lays out the key responsibilities of the people involved in goal attainment and the steps needed to coordinate their actions and decisions.

Project management can also aid the development of sound communication methods. Moving projects along, evaluating interim performance against goals, and making revisions to the plan of action all demand communication and discussion and the confrontation of problems and opportunities so vital to making strategy work. The results of this project assessment and progress provide the needed information and feedback so critical for control, the integration of operating procedures, and the refinement of execution tactics.

An analysis of project management is undertaken in Chapter 13, a new chapter at the end of this book. The emphasis is on showing how project management can facilitate or aid strategy execution and contribute to its success.

INCENTIVES AND CONTROLS

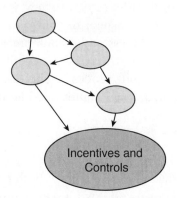

The role of incentives (see Chapter 6) again comes into play. If corporate R&D and engineering at the business level must work together to achieve important product development objectives, the incentive to do so must exist and be positive. Incentives must support important M&A strategies and goals. Perceptions of inequality in incentives certainly can affect the performance of integration teams comprising members from both parties to the merger.

Incentives must also support and reinforce important short-term objectives within the newly acquired business. The translation of business strategy into short-term operating objectives must be reinforced, and incentives are important to this reinforcement. They are vital to execution and achievement of the short-term objectives that the management-by-objectives process or Balanced Scorecard approach identified in a prior execution step.

Controls are also important, especially in the early post-acquisition stages of M&A activities. The strategic objectives and role of the newly acquired organization in the corporate portfolio have been set. Structural and cultural integration have begun and are in process as the new business commences performance in its new role. It is important next that corporate reviews the performance of the new unit to ensure consistency with corporate needs and to provide feedback to the acquisition as to how it's performing its agreed-upon role in the corporate portfolio.

The Strategy Review

The importance of the strategy review was noted in Chapters 3 and 6 as an important aspect of control and performance assessment. This review process and its outcomes are also important for the execution of M&A strategies, especially in early stages of the postmerger integration process. The essence of the strategy review, it is recalled, looks something like this:

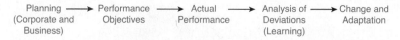

Planning ⟶ Performance ⟶ Actual ⟶ Analysis of ⟶ Change and
(Corporate and   Objectives   Performance   Deviations   Adaptation
Business)   (Learning)

The planning stage in M&A involves both pre-acquisition planning at the corporate level and postmerger planning between corporate and its business acquisition. The importance of the planning stage has already been noted when discussing the integration of corporate and business strategies in the M&A process.

The critical phase of the strategy review process occurs when actual performance of the new unit is assessed and analyzed. The analysis of an acquired business's performance against agreed-upon objectives is important for making the acquisition strategy work. Assume for a moment that the performance of the acquired company is not up to expectations, meaning that there is a significant deviation between desired outcomes or objectives and actual performance.

One goal of the strategy review as a control device is to analyze and explain what went wrong. Learning is the desired end here. Confronting the brutal facts is essential. Was the strategic plan sufficiently focused? Were competitors' capabilities underestimated? Did the acquired firm have the necessary people, products, distribution, and other capabilities to achieve its goals? Did industry forces change to present unforeseen challenges and increase the intensity of competition in the industry, thereby negatively affecting profits? Was the corporate or business plan too robust, resulting in unrealistic expectations of the new firm in the corporate portfolio?

The purpose of the strategy review, then, is to explain and explicate past performance. This is important, but not sufficient, however. The strategy review has two more functions or purposes. The first function characterizes all such reviews; the second is applicable primarily to a newly acquired company and, thus, is important for M&A success.

The first purpose or function of the strategy review, beyond explaining past performance, is to look ahead and try to understand and shape future performance.

While the term "review" clearly denotes a view of the past, it also must include learning, a look ahead, and potential modification of future strategy and execution efforts. The past must be considered, but future scenarios and strategic thinking must also be the rule. Some typical issues or questions in a review geared to the future include the following:

- How did competitors and customers respond to our products and services in the past? How will they respond in the future? What data support the predictions?

- Are competitors making changes in response to our strategic move that will affect us in the future? Building large, new plants could signal competitors' future emphasis on volume, cost reduction, or a new low-cost strategy with aggressive price competition. Hiring key top management could also signal a change in strategy.

- Will competitors add new capabilities to compensate for prior shortcomings or to meet our strengths? Adding new salespeople or distribution channels could signal competition on new fronts or in new market segments.

- Are customers' needs or demands changing? Increased competition, especially price competition, could give customers more power to make demands, including for expensive product changes or extensions that challenge a company's cost structure.

- Are new CEOs coming aboard in the industry, promising an industry shake-up and new forms of competition in response to industry consolidation?

- Is anyone in the industry close to a technological breakthrough that can make existing technologies or manufacturing methods obsolete?

These and similar questions force participants in the strategy review to look ahead and anticipate future needs, opportunities, and problems. This is true and valuable in any organization. The review cannot be confined only to an analysis of the past and regurgitation of data that may not be meaningful in future competitive scenarios.

The strategy review involving a newly acquired company has an additional important function. Its purpose is the continued integration of the acquisition and development of a better strategic fit between the new company and its corporate parent.

Planning for the acquisition focused on both hard and soft data. Industry and competitive forces were studied, and the role of the acquisition in the corporate portfolio was carefully weighed. Performance criteria were set, and resource allocations were made. There were also considerations of issues such as cultural integration, the development of managers for their new roles in the merged company, and the leadership and communication skills needed to make the M&A strategy work. The latter issues, too, must be reviewed, discussed, and possibly changed to aid the integration of the new company.

The strategy review provides an opportunity to see where additional new processes or methods could be developed to facilitate communication, uncertainty reduction, and assimilation of new employees. Most, if not all, of these integration issues have already been addressed in a portfolio of older, established companies. Shortly after an acquisition, however, there always are integration issues that weren't considered in the acquisition planning stage. The strategy review allows participants to see which issues are still causing problems and need attention, increasing the review's utility in making M&A strategies work.

As always, the need is to focus on clear, measurable performance metrics. I've been part of post-acquisition reviews in which managers complained about poor morale, uncertainty, conflicts, commitment in the acquired company, and how these issues were affecting postmerger integration and performance. My response has always included, among other things, a demand for greater specificity:

- What are the measures or indicators of poor morale? Has turnover increased? Have exit interviews revealed problems?

- What performance measures are down, indicating problems? What other factors could be affecting performance besides postmerger integration problems? How can one tell if coordination is poor, negatively affecting decision-making and results such as customer satisfaction?

- How does one know that conflicts are real and debilitating? How can their effects be identified, measured, and corrected?

- What are the indicators of poor or insufficient communication that supposedly are hampering postmerger integration? What communication methods or processes should be added and why?

These and similar questions are intended to add value to the post-acquisition strategy review. Reviews should not resemble or degenerate into gripe sessions. They can serve a useful function in the postmerger integration process, provided that they focus on important measures of performance and the factors that impact them.

Analysis of data in the strategy review results in learning. It also identifies areas of change that are needed to fine-tune the execution process and facilitate the achievement of M&A goals.

MANAGING CHANGE

Executing an acquisition strategy always involves change, and managing change well clearly is important for M&A success. Chapter 7 dealt with the tactics and steps that a company can take to execute change over various time intervals. Chapter 8 looked at the softer issues involved in managing culture and cultural change. Both chapters contain important advice for making mergers and acquisitions work. Let's first consider the issues raised in Chapter 7.

Executing change under M&A strategies is a huge task. The first critical decision is to determine how much time the acquiring company has to execute its acquisition strategy. The time available—the implementation horizon—determines how the large change is managed and controlled and what kinds of problems will likely arise. Questions here include the following:

- How much time for change is available? Is it important to move quickly to reap the benefits of consolidation? Why?

- Do we have the luxury of time? Can major post-acquisition changes be instituted logically over, say, a one- to three-year period?

- Is it possible to attack the easy changes first, the "low-hanging fruit," and then attack the more difficult changes in a more piecemeal, planned fashion?

Decisions about the time available for change determine whether a sequential change approach is possible when integrating the new acquisition and managing the M&A process, or whether a faster, complex intervention is necessary. The former is more logical and slower, breaking down large changes into smaller, more manageable pieces and executing changes sequentially, with more attention to detail and achieving successes along the way. In contrast, the latter does everything at once, simultaneously changing many things under the short perceived time constraints defining the complex intervention.

Chapter 7 stressed that there are strengths and weaknesses of both sequential and complex change approaches. Sequential change allows for incremental investments, learning, and the celebration of success along the change-management path. It takes longer, however, allowing competing issues to crop up and challenge the change process.

Complex change, in which many things are changed simultaneously, is fast, but coordination is troublesome, learning is difficult, if not impossible, and the prognosis for success is usually poor. If complex change is absolutely essential, the only way to make it work, Chapter 7 stressed, is to relax or eliminate many of the concurrent performance criteria against which people involved in change are normally held accountable. Complex change taxes organizational resources and should not be taken lightly.

Some changes under M&A strategies can usually be done quickly. These often are the smaller changes, the "low-hanging fruit," that can easily be picked in the early stages of post-acquisition integration. Elimination of obvious functional redundancies or sharing established capabilities or competencies right away are examples of issues that management in the merged company can agree with and act on quickly.

Larger changes brought about by the acquisition take more time, planning, and care in execution. Melding entire sales forces or distribution channels and changing invoicing procedures overnight may affect customers negatively, thereby demanding more time and forethought. Elimination of R&D units holds important implications for innovation, and scientific or technical capabilities shouldn't be scrapped without careful analysis. Introducing an entirely new IT system to eliminate disparate legacy systems and achieve communality of information and information processing is a huge task that, if done quickly and poorly, can severely hurt operations, decision-making, and customer satisfaction.

When the shareholders of Bank of America and Fleet Boston approved their companies' merger, Bank of America management spent the next day "reassuring employees and customers that change would be slow and for the better."[xx] The bank announced some quick changes, but it also emphasized that other changes that could negatively affect internal operations or customer service would be executed gradually. For example, integration of the banks' complex computer systems was handled carefully and not rushed. Deep cuts in branches and personnel also were handled gingerly. Management stressed that the bank would take its time to avoid the problems seen in recent mergers of other institutions. The bank, then, was talking about slow, deliberate change in major areas.

Beware of excessive speed. A popular mantra among M&A analysts is that "speed in integration is good." Yet data reported earlier regarding the vast number of mergers and acquisitions that founder or fail suggest that something is definitely going wrong. One culprit might be that excessive speed, resulting in complex change, does major harm.

The problems with complex change have already been noted in Chapter 7, including the difficulties with coordination and learning and the poor prognosis for the success of change. By stressing speed in the postmerger integration process, proponents of quick integration are actually arguing for complex change and its attendant difficulties. This obviously can affect integration and the execution of M&A strategies.

Excessive speed in the execution of complex M&A strategies may do more harm than good. Speed increases the complexity and velocity of change, which can definitely work against M&A success.

When Kraft acquired Cadbury, it forced one-time integration costs of $1.3 billion and moved quickly to integrate the two organizations. Profits fell, senior Cadbury managers deserted the ship, and cultural clashes ruled the day. Excessive integration size and speed created major problems for most of the new organization. I say "most" because one critical unit or region for Cadbury was not part of the speedy integration—India. India was basically left alone to deal with changes due to the acquisition at its own pace. Integration wasn't fast and complex, and the velocity of change was slow. The result? Cadbury/India fared quite well, with close to 30 percent revenue growth in 2010. A decentralized, slower approach seemed to work well in direct contrast to the typical speedy integration and controlling efforts by Kraft in the remainder of the merged company.

The speed of integration and the quick implementation of many changes clearly plagued the United-Continental merger. Operating problems resulting from one-time, quick changes in reservations systems, revenue-accounting processes, and even the frequent-flier program wreaked havoc on the merged company. Speed definitely increased complexity and change velocity, adding to the problems of the joined companies' M&A activity.

Reliance on speed in the execution of complex strategies such as M&A may cause yet other problems. The intense focus of managerial time and attention devoted to making strategy work may distract management from other tasks, including tracking and reacting to competitors' actions and changing competitive conditions.

Boeing's performance suffered greatly when it was distracted by the execution of its merger with McDonnell Douglas. Similarly, the Morgan Stanley-Smith Barney merger, with its huge implementation problems, could have deflected attention away from the marketplace and hurt the development of programs to foster cross-selling and the satisfaction of complex consumer needs.

A focus on fast integration in M&A may cover up an inability to plan change carefully and think things through. Worse yet, if speed is associated with decisiveness and "macho" action, while slower planned change somehow is seen as a weakness, then the execution of M&A strategies surely is in jeopardy. Speed doesn't necessarily imply being tough or being able to "bite the bullet" and get things done. Tackling complex change doesn't suggest a positive management style any more than using a slower, sequential change process suggests an overly cautious, timid style.

The effects of speed and complex change must be weighed carefully when executing M&A strategies. The costs and benefits of complex change must be compared to those of a slower, sequential change process. The bottom line is that speed is good for "low-hanging fruit" and other relatively easy, visible execution problems, whereas less speed and more thoroughness are better for larger, more impactful, and more difficult execution-related changes.

MANAGING CULTURE AND CULTURE CHANGE

Executing M&A strategies also demands an ability to manage culture and culture change effectively (see Chapter 8). Southwest Airlines spent months exploring cultural compatibility with Morris Air before acquiring it. It tried hard to determine whether Morris's employees and style would fit with its can-do attitude and *esprit de corps*, and the effort paid off handsomely. In contrast, the Price-Costco marriage lasted only ten months due to an inability to create a single unified culture, suggesting a poor attempt at cultural due diligence, change management, and integration in this merger.

The intended BAE Systems and European Aeronautic Defence and Space merger never got off the ground in 2012 due to vast cultural differences, not between the companies, but among the countries that had a stake in the companies and a concern with merger results. Protectionist attitudes, concern with jobs, and control of the possible new venture created problems. Cultural and political barriers added to a climate that wasn't conducive to deals across countries in Europe. These factors, in toto, added to a climate in Europe that wasn't a "happy hunting ground" for M&A deals.[xxi] This climate of concern effectively killed a merger that looked promising from an economic point of view.

Cultural differences abound when executing mergers and acquisitions. These differences are seen in many areas, including the following:

- Style of management
- Centralized versus decentralized decision-making
- Upstream versus downstream emphasis on the value chain
- Incentive and compensation packages
- Control systems (risk-averse or risk-accepting companies, different performance appraisal methods)
- Functional competition versus cooperation
- Entrepreneurial versus a top-down, command-and-control decision-making climate
- Professional versus bureaucratic orientation (reliance on rules, standard procedures)
- Internal (production) versus external (customer) orientation

Managing culture effectively requires that these differences be noted and critical ones targeted for change. Inability to resolve cultural differences will certainly come back to vex or harm the execution of an M&A strategy.

A critical point emphasized in Chapter 8 is that, when changing culture, it is not advisable to focus directly on changing culture itself. Changing culture by appealing to managers to think and act differently is a losing proposition. Examples were provided to show that changing culture is more successful if the focus is on changing people, organizational structure, incentives, or controls.

To change the "decision style" of corporate management after a new acquisition, one can appeal to them to change. For example, an appeal can be made to corporate personnel to assume a more entrepreneurial or decentralized style of decision-making to allow the acquisition to cope with its own industry problems. Will such an appeal for change work, given that a centralized or top-down structure has been the norm for years? Not likely. Such appeals sound good, but they alone rarely produce results.

To change corporate "decision style" as an element of desired culture in managing the new acquisition, Chapter 8 emphasized that changing people, structure, incentives, and controls has a higher probability of success. Increasing spans of control, for example, forces behavioral change because it is more difficult to exercise top-down control when spans are large. Large spans foster a "hands-off" management style. Even if a manager still desires to micromanage, it simply is more difficult to do so, given the larger number of organizational units or subordinates. Changes in behavior would likely occur, defining a new management style. Changing corporate structure or redefining corporate managers' responsibilities can help eliminate close control of an acquired business's activities.

Bringing in new people likewise can effect behavioral change, leading to culture change. New people bring in fresh ideas, motivations, and new capabilities, which can affect decision style and the way things get done. Moving managers internally after an acquisition has been made also can result in cultural change. New people may respond strongly and positively to different incentives developed to foster integration and motivate new behavior consistent with M&A goals. Placing Kraft people in charge of General Foods (GF) operations and GF people in charge of Kraft operations early in their merger did much to signal the importance of integration and the impact new people can have on culture change.

Changing the power structure may also be a necessary ingredient in successfully managing culture and culture change in the post-acquisition organization. Differences in power in the premerger organizations must be addressed after an acquisition. The roots of power and the dependencies that support them (see Chapter 9) must first be understood. If changes in power are necessary, the CEO or top-management "SWAT" team can alter structure and resource allocations, resulting in changes in dependencies and power in the new, post-acquisition organization. The changes in power and influence can be instrumental in changing culture and making the M&A strategy work.

This suggests another problem with mergers. So much time and attention can be devoted to the two companies as partners in a "merger of equals" that real power differences in the acquirer-acquiree relationship are overlooked or ignored. It's rare that two companies contribute the same value or have the same power in a combination of companies. The influence and contributions of each must be confronted and discussed to integrate the two organizations effectively. Ignoring the power structure is not wise in M&A activities.

The debacle that emerged in the $26 billion Duke Energy-Progress Energy merger in 2012 also suggests a power play that may affect integration and perhaps the success of the merger.[xxii] Bill Johnson was fired as CEO of Duke just hours after completion of the merger. This sparked all sorts of negative reaction from shareholders and the North Carolina Utilities Commission about power struggles and strategic and operating issues that were never brought to light while the merger was being evaluated. The director of Duke Energy's board incurred the wrath of the utilities commission when it was explained that Johnson withheld information from the board prior to the merger causing the commission to wonder what other secrets or power plays were hidden during the due diligence phase of the proposed merger.

The sudden change in the CEO position acted as a lightning rod to highlight a host of concerns, causing some to worry that Duke's execution of the merger would be negatively affected by the utilities commission's and shareholders' distrust of information being disseminated by the company. Execution plans, for example, including rate hikes to fund changes and integration requirements, could be jeopardized by a dubious utilities commission, causing major headaches for the merged company. The announced departure of the new CEO who took Johnson's place—Jim Rogers—only adds to the merger fiasco that has been playing out, surely signaling a rocky execution road ahead for the company.

It is absolutely imperative to reduce resistance to the changes that result from M&A activity and the new company and culture involved. The preceding advice on cultural integration is certainly applicable to the task of reducing resistance to change. The emphasis on personnel orientation, definition of culture, advertisement of the huge opportunities provided by a larger, merged company, and massive doses of communication clearly can help in this regard. Additional discussions of culture change and power relationships in Chapters 8 and 9, respectively, provide yet additional suggestions to help reduce resistance to changes brought about by M&A activities.

THE CRITICAL ROLE OF LEADERSHIP

The importance of sound leadership is vital to all the steps or actions necessary to make M&A strategies work. The critical activities just noted can work only if managers assume an execution-biased role. Aspects of this active and demanding role in M&A include the following:

- An ability to analyze, understand, and "sell" execution needs and decisions
- A need to "ride herd" on the integration of an acquired company to ensure that the steps needed for structural and cultural integration take place
- An ability to develop and use positive incentives for change
- An ability to temper a strong penchant for "numbers" and past performance with strategic thinking and a view toward learning and future performance
- An understanding of power, culture, and resistance to change and how to overcome obstacles in these areas

- A knowledge of managing change effectively, including when to use "speed" or complex interventions and when to proceed incrementally, in a sequential, paced intervention
- Open-mindedness and a high tolerance for ambiguity and uncertainty

Poor leadership can kill or seriously injure execution efforts. Good leadership demands both analytical skills and insights and an ability to handle issues that arise during postmerger or post-acquisition activities. A balance of sorts is needed with an ability to meld the "hard" and "soft" issues critical to execution success. These admittedly are demanding leadership prerequisites, but they're necessary when trying to make M&A strategies work.

SUMMARY

Making M&A strategies work is difficult. Much is at stake, and success depends very much on managing a complex set of activities or actions. This chapter applied aspects of this book's approach to the successful execution of M&A strategies, emphasizing the key steps, actions, or decisions it espouses.

The highlights of this approach are shown in Figure 10.2. The execution process begins with sound planning and corporate strategy and then takes a logical, integrated journey through organizational structure, structural and cultural integration, business strategy and its integration with corporate planning, business structure, agreement on performance metrics, strategy reviews, and the inescapable need to manage change and culture effectively. The basic premise is that a practical, unified approach to executing M&A strategies is needed, along with the necessary leadership capabilities to make it successful, and this chapter provided such an approach.

Figure 10.2 Highlights of Process Aimed at Making M&A Strategies Work

Results of M&A activity for the last few decades have been poor. Few mergers have delivered on their promises to achieve synergies and enhance shareholder value. Few have justified their premium prices. Few have been able to integrate disparate or culturally divergent firms to produce positive results. Cultural collisions with negative outcomes have been the rule rather than the exception.

This chapter shows what can be done to make M&A strategies work. Although focusing on the M&A challenge, this chapter also suggests the utility of this material for leading effective execution and management of change across all industries, organizations, strategies, and execution challenges. You can choose and use aspects of this approach to help make strategy work in your own organization.

ENDNOTES

i.   Pure "mergers of equals" are relatively rare in the M&A arena. The bulk of transactions are acquisitions by cash, stock, or both. Even pure mergers must go through the steps laid out in this chapter to achieve success—integration, cultural due diligence, managing change, and so on—so no further differentiation between mergers and acquisitions need be made in this discussion.

ii.   See, for example, Daniel Fermon, *Mergers and Acquisitions: Recovery in 2011-2012*, Insight/Economic, January 9, 2010.

iii. "Pfizer Will Buy Small ADHD Drug Maker for $700M," *The Philadelphia Inquirer Briefcase*, October 23, 2012; Fredrick Geiger, "Bayer Acquires Vitamins Maker Schiff for $1.2 Billion," *The Wall Street Journal*, October 3, 2012.

iv.   Laurie Burkitt, "Chinese Food Company Eats English Breakfast," *The Wall Street Journal*, May 4, 2012; Pablo Dominquez and Prudence Ho, "China Buys Up Spain's Assets," *The Wall Street Journal*, May 30, 2012.

v.   "Why Softbank's Sprint Deal Is a High-Wire Act," Knowledge At Wharton Today, October 16, 2012.

vi.   Kana Inagaki and Konstantin Rozhnov, "Hitachi to Acquire Horizon Nuclear Venture," *The Wall Street Journal*, October 31, 2012.

vii. Ben Dummett, "For Drug Maker M&A Does the Work of R&D," *The Wall Street Journal*, April 18, 2012.

viii. *Analysis of M&A Activity in New York Metro Area for CPA Firms*, RF Resources LLC, January 2012.

ix.   See the results of the study and related discussion in "The Case Against Mergers," *Business Week*, October 30, 1995; see also "When Disparate Firms Merge, Cultures Often Collide," *The Wall Street Journal*, February 14, 1997.

x.   "Investment Banks Arranged $1.2 Trillion in Mergers in '03," *The Philadelphia Inquirer*, December 30, 2003.

xi.   Steve Coote, "M&A Success and Failure," *VSC Growth*, March 2011.

xii. Daisuke Wakabayashi, Anton Troianovski, and Spencer Ante, "Bravado Behind Softbank's Sprint Deal," *The Wall Street Journal*, October 16, 2012.

xiii.   Scott Moeller, "Case Study: Kraft's Takeover of Cadbury," *Financial Times*, January 9, 2012; Alex Webb and Amy Wilson, "Was Cadbury a Sweet Deal for Kraft Investors?" *The Telegraph*, April 24, 2011; Guy Beaudin, "Kraft-Cadbury: Making Acquisitions Work," *Bloomberg Business Week*, February 9, 2010.

xiv.   David Pearson, "Renault's New Partnership," *The Wall Street Journal*, November 6, 2012.

xv.   Linda Loyd, "Questions Linger in Delta's Purchase of Trainer Refinery," *The Philadelphia Inquirer*, July 16, 2012.

xvi.   Andrew Peaple, "Europe Raises Merger-and-Acquisition Defenses," *The Wall Street Journal*, November 6, 2012.

xvii.   The data on gains, profitability, and time to break even on an acquisition investment are from a study by Mark Sirower, as reported in "The Case Against Mergers," *Business Week*, October 30, 1995.

xviii.   "How to Merge," *The Economist*, January 9, 1999.

xix.   Robert Kaplan and David Norton, *The Balanced Scorecard*, Harvard Business School Press, 1996.

xx.   "Bank of America Vows Slow Post-Merger Change," *The Philadelphia Inquirer*, April 2, 2004.

xxi.   Andrew Peaple, "Europe Raises Merger-and-Acquisition Defenses," *The Wall Street Journal*, November 6, 2012.

xxii.   Rebecca Smith and Valerie Bauerlein, "Duke Director Pressed on Ouster of CEO After Deal," *The Wall Street Journal*, July 21-22, 2012; Rebecca Smith, "Duke Pins CEO Swap on Closed Plant," *The Wall Street Journal*, July 19, 2012; and Valerie Bauerlein and Rebecca Smith, "Ousted CEO Says Duke Wanted to End Deal," *The Wall Street Journal*, July 20, 2012.

11

Making Global Strategy Work

Introduction

This is another chapter on application of the present model and concepts to real-world execution issues. It follows logically from the previous chapter on diversification via M&A and represents a topic of interest to many organizations in an increasingly global economy.

Global strategy represents a form of diversification. It adds organic growth to a company's methods of expansion, short of full-scale merger and acquisition, while not eliminating M&A as a source of global diversification. A global strategy usually represents some degree of unrelated diversification, given the focus on different markets, customers, cultures, and modified products or services in different regions of the world. It certainly also can contain related elements as companies attempt to employ core capabilities, technologies, and products across a wider geographical reach.

Much of what was covered in the previous chapter on M&A applies to making global strategy work, so repetition of the main points presently would be redundant and unnecessary. The need for sound planning, due diligence, a viable entry strategy, informed structural choice, effective coordination, clear responsibility and accountability, appropriate incentives and controls, and the other requirements covered under making M&A work certainly are relevant, and a quick review of Chapter 11 will clearly show its application to the execution of global strategy as a type of diversification.

Making global strategy work, however, does present additional implementation challenges or problems that the global manager must handle. The expansion beyond national boundaries, while increasingly commonplace, does present the need for additional decisions and actions to make global strategy work.

Consider for a moment just one promising, yet challenging, aspect of the global market: the developing world. Developed markets—for example, Western Europe—currently offer few exciting global investment options, but developing markets—for example, China, Singapore, South Korea, and Brazil—present new opportunities. In 2000, developing countries accounted for 20 percent of global GDP, but in 2012, this figure rose to 38 percent, a 90 percent increase. Companies like 3M, Caterpillar, and P&G have done well in these emerging markets, but they have also been buffeted by volatility and sudden nasty surprises in the marketplace.[i] For example, 3M watched as chip sales in China, which had been strong, suddenly just collapsed in a recent sales quarter for the company. This was a shock, but surprises are becoming more common in the global arena outside the developed countries.

What we have in developing markets, then, is increasing opportunity, but also increased risk and volatility. Companies must adapt to these conditions. Sound planning, partnering, feedback mechanisms, and talent management are needed to make global strategy work. In all global markets, even developed ones, companies must handle political, currency, and economic risks. These facts of life represent a "given" for all organizations in the global marketplace.

Yet, not all companies face the exact same problems in their global venturing. Not every global player invests heavily in developing countries with their risks and problems. Global goals and strategies vary, and plans of execution must reflect these variations or differences. The remainder of this chapter focuses on different, "generic" types or forms of global competition and the decisions and actions needed to make the different types of global strategy work.

TYPES OF GLOBAL GROWTH AND EXECUTION DECISIONS

It is useful to attack the issue of making global strategy work by first recognizing that different stages or types of global expansion exist and each has its own set of issues or challenges that must be addressed. These stages or types include early or basic international presence, full-scale multidomestic operations, and the coordinated global strategy that represents more than a basic multidomestic presence and operations. Companies don't need to progress through the various types or stages of growth, but it is entirely possible that some companies grow in this manner. For present purposes, emphasis is on the different types and their challenges. The chapter makes no assumptions about movement through the various types as stages of development.

EARLY OR BASIC INTERNATIONAL PRESENCE

This type represents the basic entry into global strategy. A company may "dip its toe" into international waters via an international division, usually a marketing arm of the company. It typically exports products or services. It might pursue simple joint ventures or strategic alliances to gain access to local markets, manufacturing, and distribution channels, as well as service-related capabilities. More complex joint ventures or alliances may come later, and these are treated later in a separate section of this chapter.

This early stage of global growth is still marked by a heavy domestic influence. A highly centralized structure is still the norm, with most global decisions made at corporate headquarters. Key investment and operating decisions, including marketing, are usually made in the home office, not in the decentralized settings of country or region. Implementation of this strategy depends significantly on centralized decision-making and control.

Making this type of strategy work typically involves cultural due diligence and an understanding of how the international arm of the company must work with foreign interests. Contracts between the home and local companies, for example, regarding the availability and distribution of products, are usually fairly simple and straightforward and rarely cause major cultural or domain-related problems. Still, it is not wise to dismiss culture-related issues, even in this simple form of global operation, as cultural differences can come into play to challenge the success of offshore operations. Cultural due diligence is always a good idea when executing even this basic form of foreign participation.

Most large companies today either skip or pass through this basic, centrally-controlled form of global expansion in favor of more sophisticated and demanding types. The global world is flat and competitive, and "dipping one's toe" in the international arena is usually bypassed for more elaborate global arrangements, especially in large firms. These more elaborate forms of global strategy demand additional, more sophisticated, often more complex methods of execution to make strategy work.

THE MULTIDOMESTIC GLOBAL ORGANIZATION

The multidomestic company competes in international arenas, but with a greater investment and more elaborate organizational structures. This is the typical form of global presence as companies have presence in many global regions, with this presence marked by significant investment decisions.

The stakes and costs of international competition increase dramatically under this form of global expansion. Direct foreign investment is low or nonexistent in the previous stage. In contrast, direct investment increases dramatically at this point. The company is forced to replicate itself on foreign soil, building plants, creating local service and distribution networks, and hiring more local managers. The pressing need is to get closer to foreign markets and make decisions locally, so as to better serve markets that are becoming increasingly heterogeneous and in need of special or differentiated handling. These requirements have major implications for organizational structure, incentives to achieve the requisite market differentiation, and human resource policies.

Consider the following companies and their recent decisions in the global arena: Procter & Gamble, GE, Halliburton, and Rolls-Royce. P&G is relocating the headquarters of its global skin, cosmetics, and personal-care division to Singapore, leaving Cincinnati behind.[ii] This is a clear movement away from its traditional centralized structure, representing the obvious importance of Asia's fast-growing market. The company has been making similar moves in other divisions, clearly reflecting a desire to get closer to important customers and markets. These aren't simply cosmetic moves; they represent major structural changes as implementation steps in response to global competitive forces. Other consideration may also play a part—for example, tax advantages—but the overriding factor seems to be a desire to decentralize and get close to important global markets.

The other companies mentioned have made similar moves. GE moved its X-ray business from Wisconsin to Beijing; Halliburton headquarters was moved from the Netherlands to Singapore; and Rolls-Royce moved its Global Marine headquarters from London to Singapore. The moves and expanded geographical footprints include most of the functions or capabilities needed to make the companies' global strategy work. These represent structural moves toward decentralization, reinforcing the importance of structure as a variable important to the execution of global strategy.

Though a common form of global expansion, multidomestic presence is a challenging, often difficult type of global strategy to execute for at least three reasons: increased costs, control problems, and a major change from a centralized to a more decentralized form of organization. To understand this, consider a common form of organizational structure under this type of global presence—the worldwide product division (see Figure 11.1).

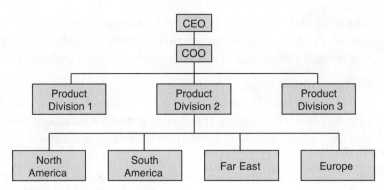

Figure 11.1 Worldwide Product Divisions

Under this structure, each product division is responsible for its line of goods and services abroad. Each division organizes geographically, by region or country, as Figure 11.1 shows. Each division is relatively self-contained and autonomous, acting as a global profit center responsible only for its products worldwide. Interdependence laterally is often low, as division heads find little need to coordinate activities extensively with their counterparts in other divisions.

Incentives are based wholly, or in large part, on SBU or divisional performance, reinforcing the independence and separate nature of the businesses. Incentives usually motivate concerns with divisional or local performance, not corporate performance. Care must be taken to ensure that these motivations do not create excessive competition across divisions for scarce resources that ultimately results in suboptimization and negative corporate performance. Maintaining corporate strategy and effectively controlling the independent pieces of the overall portfolio can present a formidable challenge. Similarly, creating a corporate identity for managers in addition to their divisional or country allegiance can be difficult. The relationship between corporate and business strategy, highlighted in Chapter 3, is important here: Each affects the execution of the other's strategy, and this is true in global as well as domestic competition.

Creating a structure based on worldwide divisions can be expensive. Key functions like manufacturing in many cases must be replicated in all divisions. The company, in effect, must reproduce itself many times over. This raises costs dramatically. If the benefits of the increased investments and related costs in multidomestic operations aren't seen quickly enough, shareholders and others might balk at the higher costs and pressure management into bad cost-reduction steps and measures that hurt strategy execution.

Multidomestic companies obviously still can contain productive centralized elements or functions that service all divisions (e.g., a common legal staff). It's rare that complete decentralization is the rule. The discussion presently is simply intended to show that the general trend toward decentralization can increase real costs due to duplication. This trend, however, can potentially create additional problems, some of which may now be noted.

Another aspect of the structure noted in Figure 11.1 can affect the execution of a multidomestic global strategy. As mentioned previously, the worldwide divisional structure indicates a move from a centralized to a more decentralized organization. The early stage of global venturing was marked by centralized control and home-office rule. The multidomestic form of global expansion demands that many functions like manufacturing, sales, distribution, even R&D, be decentralized, controlled at the divisional or local level within a region or country. The increasing number of companies— for example, Microsoft, GE, and P&G—that have decentralized functions like R&D after years of more centralized controls reinforces the notion of decentralization as an important execution element in this form of global competition.

This decentralization often demands major changes in the globally expanding company, something that can cause resistance by corporate personnel. Centralized corporate staff perceive loss of power and influence and oppose it. New human resource policies favoring local hiring and regional talent may conflict with previous centralized hiring and selection procedures. The increased costs of replication of functions may be used as ammunition against the movement to a more decentralized, autonomous organization, challenging the successful execution of the multidomestic strategy. Centralized units or functions always exist to serve all businesses; the probability of conflicts over decision-making and authority, however, usually increases with a move to increased decentralization in the expanding organization.

The human resource issue can be mentioned as an example of this potential conflict or tension. Are skills and capabilities developed locally to run and control the decentralized businesses, or do centralized corporate centers of excellence or HR functions exert their influence on local decisions and operations? Where should critical capabilities be developed and nurtured to best serve the execution of strategy? People are at the core of organizational performance; the issue is where these critical resources are located, developed, and used in the pursuit of strategic goals.

Finally, culture again comes into play. Care must be taken to avoid culture clashes between the company's previous way of operating and the local, decentralized methods of management. Important, too, might be differences in values and local mores or habits that can challenge the successful execution of the multidomestic strategy. Companies like Walmart learned the hard way that imposing a business model and culture on operations in foreign nations simply doesn't work and that culture-related factors can inhibit or destroy attempts at global diversification.

Table 11.1 summarizes the issues involved in making the multidomestic strategy work. Answers to the questions raised must be addressed to ensure the successful execution of global moves.

Table 11.1 Strategy Execution Issues in the Multidomestic Organization

Issues	Comments/Questions
Strategy	■ Has adequate due diligence been performed?
	■ Is there stakeholder buy-in to the level of required investment?
Structure	■ The location of scarce resources is an issue.
	■ Centralization vs. decentralization must be addressed: Each has benefits and costs.
	■ The locus of decision-making—who has the final say—must be decided and clear responsibility defined.
	■ Conflict resolution processes need to be addressed.

Autonomy & Controls	■ Local autonomy vs. corporate center control is an issue that flows from the discussion of structure.
	■ Need to monitor performance to avoid suboptimization due to autonomous divisions performing at the expense of overall, collective performance.
Incentives	■ Support for local/regional performance is necessary.
	■ Reinforcement of corporate objectives is necessary.
	■ Need to develop incentives and performance appraisal methods to support international presence and development.
Talent	■ Commitment to the development and mix of local skills and talent.
	■ Using company and local talent to ensure effective performance of foreign units.
Culture	■ As always, the need for cultural due diligence is paramount.
	■ Melding company and country cultures effectively is a need, so as to…
	■ …Avoid harmful culture clashes.
Managing Change	■ Overcome resistance to change when centralized responsibility and control move to more decentralized operations.
	■ Obtain buy-in for new ways of implementing strategy and the costs associated with increased global presence.

THE COORDINATED GLOBAL STRATEGY

The last type of international expansion is the coordinated global strategy. The key word here is "coordinated." Competitive advantage under this global strategy is derived, in large part, from the sharing and leveraging of skills or capabilities across country boundaries. Countries or regions may enjoy comparative advantages, for example, in labor costs or other factor prices. The trick is to leverage the low-cost position into competitive advantage elsewhere. Or, a company may enjoy a technological capability that represents a core competence. Again, the need is to share and integrate its core competence across product lines and country boundaries.

A product under this form of global competition may move from country to country with value-added investments of some kind along the way until the product reaches its final market. An electronics business in country A lends its technical capabilities before the product benefits from additional technological advances at a company in country B, or the power train expertise of a company in country C, before the final product (e.g., a locomotive or power plant component) reaches the ultimate consumer.

In cases such as this, methods of coordinating, sharing, and integrating are extremely important for successful implementation of the global strategy. Sharing and leveraging denote the need for coordination, which further implies a need for effective communication and control across divisional and country boundaries. The "seamless" or "boundaryless" organization becomes a working metaphor and operating reality, as the need for sharing laterally, across countries or products, challenges traditional notions of authority and "turf."

Incentives, controls, and structures must be created or modified to support this "lateral" emphasis on sharing and cooperative behavior. The autonomy and independence of worldwide divisions or product lines must be tempered to motivate concern with the increased interdependence suggested by the coordinated global strategy. Confronting increased interdependence effectively is critical to making this type of coordinated global strategy work (see Chapter 5 for a definition of types of interdependence and their effects).

How do companies create the sharing, communication, and controls needed for successful execution of this form of global strategy? I believe there are three ways to achieve the needed coordination, control, and perceptions of interdependence and cooperation. All three raise additional execution issues—for example, those related to effective incentives, structure, and human resource policies. They are as follows:

- Creating effective global managers
- Employing lateral or matrix-type structures
- Forming strategic alliances

Creating and using global managers. The coordinated global strategy relies very much on the capabilities or skills of effective managers. An effective cadre of global managers, though a small group, can be critical to the success of this form of global strategy.

Effective global managers are, first and foremost, integrators. They work across country or division boundaries to ensure the dissemination of knowledge and the application of a company's core competence in a pursuit of global competitive advantage. They create personal relationships to increase the speed and effectiveness of programs being implemented. They understand and mediate conflicts between divisions with a worldwide product focus and country operations with a decidedly more local focus. Their travels and contacts make them useful for the collection and dissemination of information vital to the establishment of effective feedback and control systems.

Performing as a global integrator isn't an easy role. Percy Barnevik of ABB once said that global managers are made, not born. This group of vital human assets is created via rotating assignments, experience in various countries, and the opportunity to interact with people of different nationalities and cultural heritages. In this case, familiarity breeds understanding, as well as an ability to see superordinate goals and issues that transcend purely divisional or country concerns. The effective global manager represents a unique breed. The success of the coordinated global strategy often depends in no small part on this cadre of effective managers.

Lateral forms of organization. Despite their problems, matrix or lateral forms of organization are still useful, even vital, to the implementation of coordinated global strategies. They attempt, in effect, to combine global perspective and worldwide operations with local markets and conditions. Figure 11.2 exhibits a simplified matrix structure with an area marketing manager in the dual-reporting role with two bosses. Figure 11.2, in effect, suggests the matrix diamond discussed in Chapter 5, with product line and geography as the two areas in need of integration by the two-boss manager. In this case, the COO is the tie-breaker when conflicts occur and must be resolved.

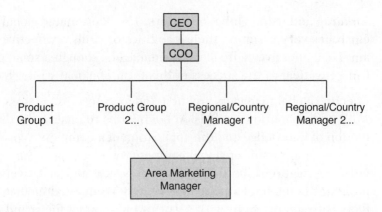

Figure 11.2 A Simple Matrix Structure

Figure 11.2 can be redrawn in even a more simple, straightforward way, building on the notion of the matrix diamond:

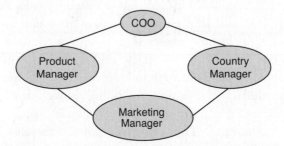

The two-boss manager is the integrator, the important link between the product group and country managers. If he or she reports to a regional manager, the integration would include cross-country communication and coordination within the region. Making the matrix form of organization work, however, is not always as simple and straightforward as the previous statements might suggest. The underlying logic is premised on the desire to serve both product and country needs *simultaneously* in critical strategic and operating decisions. The dual focus, however, can also generate conflict, as the needs, goals, and plans for businesses and countries are not always in perfect harmony.

There is also the issue of duality of control faced by co-located personnel; that is, managers with more than one boss, like the area marketing manager shown in Figure 11.2. This dual-reporting relationship is necessary to facilitate communication and coordination across businesses and regions by making the co-located manager's role into an integrating force. Duality of control, however, violates the rule of unity of command or control, and exacerbates problems of decision-making and performance appraisal. The "dual hierarchy" suggested by the binary focus can also result in slow decision-making and the overloading of different hierarchies with conflicting information.

Despite these difficulties, this lateral form of organization can help make the coordinated global strategy work. Effort is required, however, to ensure successful coordination and effective performance. To make this structure work, it is necessary to ensure that:

- The logic of the matrix form is well understood by the managers serving the various roles. The integrators or co-located managers especially must understand their role and how conflicts, while virtually unavoidable, can be handled in an expeditious manner.

- The individual in the dual-reporting role in the matrix must be well trained and fit for the job. Managers with low tolerance for uncertainty or conflict will have a difficult time adapting to a demanding, integrative role.

- Top management support for incentives, job-rotation policies, and performance appraisals that reward and reinforce such duality of perspective are clearly vital to effective implementation of this structural form. Accordingly, care must be taken to heed the advice in Chapter 6 about the central role of incentives and controls in making strategy work.

- The role of tie-breaker must be well defined and functional. Conflicts at the lower portion of the matrix that are not easily adjudicated cannot be left to fester and remain problematical. The tie-breaker must be defined and the process of resolution clearly laid out to avoid endless, counterproductive conflicts.

Lateral coordination mechanisms are clearly central to the success of the coordinated global strategy. These structures are difficult to pull off, and dedication of managers to the task is essential for success.

STRATEGIC ALLIANCES

In global competition, joint ventures or strategic alliances often play a key role in making strategy work. It is abundantly clear that such alliances can help companies accelerate learning, take advantage of technological diffusion and change, and avoid unnecessary duplication of capabilities already created by others. They are important to the argument here because they can also facilitate the communication and information exchange needed for the execution of all global strategies, including the coordinated global strategy being considered presently.

Traditional forms of organization have limits. Vertical integration and the direct investment it signifies can actually hinder innovation and technological change. Direct foreign investment increases holdings, but it also increases the size and complexity of operations. Different structural units across the world can lead to "silos" of sorts, across which communication and sharing of variable knowledge can be severely inhibited, negatively affecting the execution of global strategy.

Consider again, the recent move by GM to centralize certain critical functions to increase corporate control and reduce the impact of silos that had developed in the company's international arena.[iii] The argument, laid out by GM, is that fiefdoms or silos had developed over time, inhibiting the flow of valuable knowledge or information needed to execute the company's global strategy. The assumption behind GM's move is that coordination and knowledge sharing can occur more easily when key functional areas share centralized space and are more closely aligned than they are in a more decentralized form of organizational structure. Whether centralization is the answer here, only time will tell (see Chapter 5), but the intent of the structural move is certainly clear.

Generally, internal expansion and the inevitable creation of hierarchy can negatively affect flexibility, speed of response to markets, and the free flow of information so desperately needed to implement global strategies that demand ongoing coordination and knowledge sharing. Strategic alliances can help to facilitate this knowledge exchange. Certainly, alliances don't always represent a panacea, but they can help to execute global strategy. They are based upon the "trading" of up-to-date knowledge or skills. They generate speed and flexibility in responding to market needs; agreements are usually built more quickly and efficiently than things constructed with bricks and mortar. They overcome many of the size, complexity, and inertia properties of large global organizations, including the restrictions placed on communication and interaction by large, independent, structural "silos." The bottom line is that there is a complementarity of benefits or assets; each member of the alliance gives something and receives something in return.

In essence, strategic alliances, employed wisely, can facilitate the implementation of global strategies. They overcome many of the limits or negative consequences of traditional forms of organization and can facilitate quick response and adaptation to changing international threats and opportunities.

Table 11.2 summarizes some of the issues that must be addressed to execute the coordinated global strategy. Not every organization faces every issue or problem simultaneously, but there is a high probability that the global manager, over time, will need to confront and solve many of the issues or problems noted in Table 11.2.

Table 11.2   Execution Issues with the Coordinated Global Strategy

Issues	Comments/Questions
Strategy	■ Melding corporate and business/regional strategies is crucial.
	■ Regional/business managers must be aware of their contribution to overall corporate strategy.
	■ Sharing core competence globally is an important corporate task.
	■ Deciding on locus of decision-making and responsibility (corporate, region, or business) is part of the strategy discussion.

Structure	■ Location of scarce resources is a critical issue.
	■ Balancing centralization (corporate) and decentralization (region, business) of decision-making is important for success.
	■ Achieving coordination or integration across interdependent units or regions is necessary for the strategy to work.
	■ Using matrix-type structures is often necessary, and the logic of this structure must be understood.
	■ Establishing tie-breakers (in matrix, between corporate and regions, across interdependent units) is necessary for effective decision-making and coordination.
	■ Developing and using strategic alliances to accelerate learning, gain access to local distribution, share technology, and generate speed in responding to local, divergent markets can help execute this global strategy.
Autonomy & Controls	■ Clarify local autonomy vs. corporate controls.
	■ Establish conflict resolution processes.
	■ Create information and knowledge-sharing processes to provide feedback about performance and integration needs across interdependent regions or businesses.
Incentives	■ Create incentives to motivate the sharing of knowledge across units or areas in need of integration.
	■ Clarify incentives for "two-boss" managers in matrix structures.
	■ Develop incentives to support cooperation and avoid suboptimization of businesses and regional units working at cross purposes.
	■ Establish performance appraisal systems to develop and reward global managers.
Talent	■ Develop a cadre of global managers as necessary.
	■ Rotate key managers through different regions/businesses to facilitate knowledge sharing and problem solving and develop a global perspective.
	■ Provide education and training based on feedback about global performance.
	■ It may be important to emphasize a "core" language to facilitate communication and create a core staff to ensure control and consistent performance.

Culture	■ Commitment to cultural due diligence is vital to strategic success.
	■ Effort must be made to align country and company cultures and avoid disastrous cultural mistakes.
Managing Change	■ Confronting and resolving conflicts between or across regions and businesses and changing responsibilities is important to a fluid global organization.
	■ Overcoming resistance to change when centralized responsibility and control is moved to decentralized regions or businesses or to manager-integrators is important for organizational functioning globally.
	■ Obtaining buy-in to ongoing changes in a fluid structure in need of integration is necessary for the successful execution of the coordinated global strategy.

The decisions or steps involved in the execution of all global strategies are presented in Figure 11.3. The type of global strategy drives or affects decisions about structure, requisite talent, coordination, incentives, controls, and change management, as the previous discussion has shown. The figure highlights the importance of culture and cultural due diligence, as these issues are particularly salient in global organizations.

Figure 11.3 also shows clearly that the factors involved in the implementation or execution of global strategies virtually mirror, and are totally consistent with, the general model developed in Chapter 2 and applied throughout this book. Global strategy admittedly raises some questions or issues that go beyond the general model—for example, cultural differences by country or region, geographical distance or dispersion of organizational units, regional risks and uncertainties, and some talent issues related to effective global managers—but, in the main, the same factors apply to global execution as are relevant for the implementation of all strategies. An entirely new model isn't required to foster successful global execution; rather, modification or tweaking of the general model presented in this book is sufficient to understand and achieve the effective implementation of global strategies.

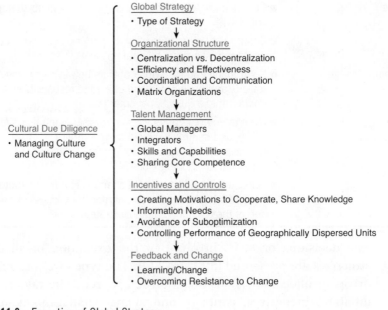

Cultural Due Diligence
• Managing Culture and Culture Change

Global Strategy
• Type of Strategy
↓
Organizational Structure
• Centralization vs. Decentralization
• Efficiency and Effectiveness
• Coordination and Communication
• Matrix Organizations
↓
Talent Management
• Global Managers
• Integrators
• Skills and Capabilities
• Sharing Core Competence
↓
Incentives and Controls
• Creating Motivations to Cooperate, Share Knowledge
• Information Needs
• Avoidance of Suboptimization
• Controlling Performance of Geographically Dispersed Units
↓
Feedback and Change
• Learning/Change
• Overcoming Resistance to Change

Figure 11.3 Execution of Global Strategy

SUMMARY

This chapter has discussed the execution of global strategies. Global strategy represents a form of diversification, as an organization seeks to add new markets, customers, products, or services to its portfolio growth and profitability. Some risks are involved as companies plan to expand globally—for example, greater risks in developing countries—but global strategy still represents a form of diversification to achieve growth.

It is useful to attack the issue of making global strategy work by recognizing first that there are different types of global expansion and that each has a few of its own challenges or needs. The types of global strategy include early or basic international presence, the multidomestic global organization, and the coordinated global strategy. These types are marked by increased complexity in making strategy work, with the coordinated global strategy representing the most complex situation in which to achieve successful execution. The discussion in this chapter looked at each type of strategy and analyzed the problems or issues endemic to each in a quest for successful execution.

Despite these endemic peculiarities, this chapter also emphasized that no new drastically different models are needed to understand and achieve the successful execution of global strategies. The same general model developed and employed throughout this book suffices in this regard. Making global strategy work requires decisions about organizational structure, coordination, requisite talent, incentives, controls, and change management, which is similar generically to the process of executing all strategies. Some modification or tweaking of the general model may be required to allow for the greater impact of factors like culture, geographical dispersion and control issues, and the need for a special breed of global manager, but the basic model is still workable; there is no need to introduce an entirely new model of making global strategy work. For example, coordination or integration of organizational units is important to the execution of all strategies. Integration in the Coordinated Global Strategy certainly demands additional attention and methods, but these demands represent an extension or refinement of the basic execution model, not the need for an entirely new model or approach.

In sum, the execution of global strategies varies with the type of strategy being pursued, but the variables or factors involved in execution are basically the same across all types of strategy. Some factors or variables may deserve heightened analysis in the global arena—for example, structure, talent, coordination, and culture—but these same factors or variables come into play when making all strategies work. The differences are those of degree, not of kind.

ENDNOTES

i. Justin Lahart, "Emerging Risk for Multinationals," *The Wall Street Journal*, Heard on the Street, November 15, 2012.

ii. Emily Glazer, "P&G Unit Bids Goodbye to Cincinnati, Hello to Asia," *The Wall Street Journal*, May 11, 2012.

iii. Tim Higgins and Jeff Green, "GM Seen Planning Global Reorganization Against Fiefdoms," Bloomberg.com/news/2012.

12

Executing Strategy in Service Organizations

Introduction

The United States has become a service economy. Approximately 77 percent of U.S. GDP in 2011 was accounted for by service businesses, compared to 22 percent for manufacturing and 1 percent for agriculture. The projected percentages look to remain the same for 2012. There's no denying the obvious: Service businesses are predominant and important in the United States and, indeed, the world economy.

The impact of services is even greater than the previous numbers suggest. There is a large and growing segment of services in product-based companies. Functions or corporate center groups in companies—for example, IT, HR, finance, executive development, and company "universities"—are like service organizations in many respects as they complement and facilitate the operations of product creation and delivery. Service capabilities are important, even in product-based companies, and they must be employed so as to aid the execution of corporate and business-level strategies.

Relatedly, the growth of government services over the years provides another example of service businesses. Agencies or units like the Social Security Administration, Veterans Administration, Internal Revenue Service, and so on, all are examples of service-oriented businesses that function to serve customers or clients. These service businesses are not-for-profit entities, a fact that further emphasizes the importance of goals related to customer or client satisfaction. Service-type agencies, units, or businesses abound in the government, adding to the centrality and importance of services for organizational performance.

For present purposes, the pervasiveness and importance of services raise an obvious question: Is strategy execution in service businesses or functions similar to or different from execution or implementation in product-based businesses? Alternatively, the issue is whether managers need additional weapons in their execution arsenal to make service-based strategies work.

Some managers in the Wharton surveys and discussions insisted strongly that "service businesses are different" or that "execution is easier in manufacturing or product businesses than in service businesses." Managers in the not-for-profit service arena were most vociferous in arguing for these differences. Is there any validity to these assertions? Are service businesses "different" in important ways? This is what the present chapter is about: answering these and related questions about execution in service businesses.

The short answer to these questions is that:

> *Service businesses are just like their product-based counterparts in most respects when executing strategy. They must worry about and confront the same or similar issues. One class of service businesses, however, does present some additional challenges, a point explicated below.*

Let's begin the analysis of execution in service businesses by looking first at some obvious similarities with product-based, manufacturing organizations.

SIMILARITIES: EXECUTING STRATEGY IN SERVICE BUSINESSES

There are some obvious similarities between service and product businesses. In fact, some service companies sell products. McDonald's sells food products that, for sure, are perishable, but products nonetheless. Insurance companies sell products like term insurance with neatly packaged folders and policy declarations that one can hold, read, and store with one's important legal papers. Walmart sells products, millions of them, around the world. These companies advertise, try to differentiate their products or offerings, develop programs to get close to customers, seek market share and power, and so on—execution activities similar to those in product-based companies worldwide.

Beyond these basic comparisons, many other similarities exist between service and product businesses. Consider briefly the key variables related to successful execution that have been considered in previous chapters, and the similarities are clear and compelling.

STRATEGY

Strategy, for example, is still central and critical in service companies. Most service businesses formulate and execute strategy much like their product-based counterparts. They analyze their industries and make note of industry structure and forces. They need to do competitor analysis and decide how to position themselves in an industry or strategic group so as to gain competitive advantage. They must decide on a strategy and pursue the skills and capabilities needed to execute their chosen strategy, and then hope that the decisions and capabilities create entry barriers to potential imitators seeking to emulate their successful positioning. The creation of entry barriers around capabilities, size, and economies of scale help insulate the service company and facilitate execution, similar to the results in product-based companies.

Walmart relied early on a first-mover strategy. It entered small markets that competitors felt were much too small to support large retail stores. It differentiated itself early as the cost leader and moved quickly to open new stores, thereby moving close to customers seeking what Walmart was offering. With size and growth, Walmart became the cost leader, generating additional profits and growth.

The low-cost strategy of Walmart resulted in a huge market share that generated a focus on standardization, repetition (opening new stores with a set pattern and set of operating procedures), and the holy grail of high volume. Investment in IT and creation of relations with suppliers were critical aspects of the company's execution plan, and they further cemented the company's power and centrality in the industry. Economies of scale and scope were huge.

Execution of a strategy based on size, economies, power over suppliers, and getting close to customers and markets created entry barriers, power over customers, and few substitutes (stores and product breadth) for many years. These capabilities and actions related to strategy allowed for effective execution growth and an enviable market position. It's simply easier to execute strategy when entry barriers, power over suppliers and customers, and other favorable industry forces provide a protective shield against easy imitation and competitive challenges. Walmart simply took advantage of this situation.

Walmart admittedly did have trouble executing its global strategy. It tried to foist its business model and methods on customers in France, Germany, and Indonesia, for example, but the attempts performed poorly or failed. The problems here reflect those considered previously in Chapter 11 on making global strategy work, especially culture-related problems. The basic premise still holds, however; Walmart's focus on strategy execution mirrors that in most product-based companies.

JetBlue, Southwest, and other no-frills airlines rely on a low-cost strategy. They make decisions not to do things other more expensive airlines do (strategy defines decisions about what a company won't do, as well as what it will do). Capabilities are developed and people are trained to support the strategy. Investments support the execution of the low-cost approach; reliance on one aircraft at Southwest (the Boeing 737), for example, reduces pilot training and parts inventory costs. A focus on secondary as well as primary airports represents a "distribution" aspect of execution to get close to customers while lowering landing and take-off costs/fees.

Hospitals like the Children's Hospital of Philadelphia (CHOP) focus on pediatric care and invest heavily in technology and physicians' capabilities that support the execution of its focus/differentiation strategy. CHOP also relies on marketing and advertising as part of an implementation plan of outreach and education to physicians and potential client families worldwide.

Publicis executes its differentiation strategy by developing technological resources (e.g., Internet-based services) and consulting capabilities to aid the performance of its advertising-purchasing customers. Increasingly, it is hiring talent capable of working closely with customers as consultants, which generates skills and capabilities that clients desire and leads to more effective strategy execution. Its size as the second largest advertising firm in the world creates entry barriers, reduces the threat of easy imitation, and results in scale economies, all of which enable execution of its differentiation approach.

Many of these same strategy-driven activities and concerns can be found in not-for-profit service organizations. Granted, the absence of profit goal typical in competitive settings sets these organizations apart somewhat. However, they still must define goals and their strategy to achieve desired ends. They face competition of sorts from other not-for-profits for scarce resources or limited budgets—for example, in government agencies or organizations. They must support their strategies with needed talent and skills, and they certainly must differentiate and justify themselves in terms of value-added actions or services.

Even profit is a concern of sorts in not-for-profit organizations. A wise manager once remarked to me that "the only thing nonprofits generate is additional nonprofits." His argument was that, even in not-for-profits, a healthy concern with the "bottom line" is critical, along with a concern for the value-added aspects of performance or, as he put it, the "bang for the buck" the organization generates. Non-for-profit organizations are "profit-oriented," he argued, even if profits are disguised and not labeled as such. These organizations need to create strategies or plans to control costs, nonprofits, and performance, just like other organizations.

In service organizations, strategy is critical, the first step in the execution process. Programs of planning, competitor analysis, and industry analysis result in a choice of strategy. Strategy then, makes demands on organizational resources and capabilities to support the execution of the chosen strategy. This is identical to the process of planning and execution that marks product-based companies. Service companies are remarkably similar to their product-producing cousins in this regard.

ORGANIZATIONAL STRUCTURE

Structure also comes into play in the execution of service strategies, in most respects similar to its role and contribution in product-based situations. Consider the large firms in banking, consulting, or accounting—for example, Citibank, McKinsey, and Booz-Allen—and their global organization structures. Decentralized operations and units exist to service local needs and respond to customer demands that vary by country or region. Simultaneously, centralized units or corporate centers exist to provide consistent worldwide service in key functional areas or areas of knowledge or expertise.

Occasionally, more sophisticated structural combinations emerge to integrate and share knowledge across units or industry groups in the global area. Booz-Allen, for example, for years operated by layering decentralized operations over centralized resources to form a kind of global matrix. Industry-focused groups were served by functions and areas of expertise that were vital to the performance of the industry groups. A simple version of this overlay and matrix, and one adaptable to many companies, might look like the following:

Functions/Disciplines	Industry Groups		
	Financial Services	Technology	Manufacturing
Strategy	──────→ X ──────→	X ──────→	X
Operations	──────→ X ──────→	X ──────→	X
IT	──────→ X ──────→	X ──────→	X
Marketing	──────→ X ──────→	X ──────→	X

For industry-oriented consulting or accounting projects, experts from various functions or areas of expertise are available as resources to aid performance in companies in different industry groups. Functional experts may even move across industry groups, sharing knowledge and experience across a broad spectrum of organizations. This lateral sharing and communication facilitates the execution of strategy.

Similar matrix structural forms can be seen in many companies where emphasis is simultaneously on country/region, on one hand, and business, on the other. Managers in dual roles report, at once, to regional or country managers and home office business managers responsible for global operations. This structure fosters knowledge sharing in a coordinated matrix structure, again aiding the execution of strategy. Chapter 11 discusses the use of matrix or lateral organizational structures in support of global strategies focusing on geography and product or service lines.

Structure can provide market or customer focus in service organizations similar to that in product-based companies. NewsCorp is contemplating splitting itself in two, separating the entertainment businesses from the newspapers. The structural split would allow for enhanced strategic attention and market focus for the different businesses. The logic and use of structure is exactly like that in product-based companies such as GE, P&G, Kraft, PepsiCo, and others. Even universities organize by colleges, structural units that allow a focus on customers and competitors in the same academic fields.

The point is clear: Service organizations are much like their product-based counterparts in the use and centrality of organizational structure in the strategy execution process. Much like the operations of P&G, GE, Halliburton, Rolls-Royce, and others, service companies like banks and consulting companies focus on mixes of centralization and decentralization to build on core expertise while serving and getting close to diverse regions, customers, or markets.

TALENT, CAPABILITIES, AND NEED FOR TRAINING/SKILL DEVELOPMENT PROGRAMS

A focus on talent and capabilities is also seen in service companies to support and implement chosen strategies, the same focus observed in product-based organizations. Hospitals dedicated to cures or treatment in complex clinical areas seek the best physicians, support staff, and technologies to back their efforts. Insurance companies endeavor to find the best people in risk assessment and actuarial skills. Universities search for highly qualified research professors to differentiate themselves in a competitive academic environment. Consulting firms seek the brightest and the best when they recruit at well-known MBA programs around the globe. Execution of consulting services demands up-to-date, critical knowledge to support client-based strategies.

Decisions about talent and capabilities are important for strategy execution, but they might even have additional effects on operating and execution decisions. One recent significant study shows, for example, that from January 1995 to June 2011, corporate investments in technology and equipment in the United States increased significantly.[i] The study data also show an increase in GDP over the same period, as well as an increase in company profitability.

Given these investment decisions—themselves reflective of strategy execution choices—and given the growth of GDP and profitability, one would expect other execution decisions to follow logically. One such decision deals with hiring and employment. The data here are indeed significant, but not what one might expect: Employment actually declined significantly over the time period studied. Despite positive investments, GDP growth, and company profitability, employment of human resources actually decreased. What happened here, and is it significant?

As companies invest increasingly in technology—read "computers or robots" and the requisite software—these machines do more and more in terms of decision-making, communication, and integration of work, themselves aspects of strategy execution. But the reliance on robots and computers also reduces the reliance on some kinds of human capital while, simultaneously, increasing the importance of other human skills and capabilities. Certain jobs are lost in greater volume than the new jobs needed, resulting in the decline of overall employment. Moreover, if people can't easily be found to staff the new and demanding positions, outsourcing and perhaps internal training will occur.

What we see, then, is a logical trend of sorts. Investments in technology like computers reflect execution decisions to support strategy. These decisions, in turn, further affect execution by changing the mix of skills or capabilities needed by the advanced technologies. Some jobs are eliminated, while other new jobs are created. This results in outsourcing to support strategy if the needed skills aren't readily available in-house.

Hopefully, this technological trend will also result in retraining programs to allow some people to reinvent themselves as productive employees. Given the trend in jobs lost and gained as a result of technology, a trend that is certain to continue with increased reliance on technology, it is obvious that strategy execution decisions must include training or retraining programs to develop and keep important human capital. Companies clearly must retrain and retain employees so as not to succumb to excessive outsourcing, a trend that can increase coordination and control problems significantly. Companies must also commit to and keep valuable employees, which clearly can affect organizational culture and "buy-in" in a positive way.

Investments in talents and capabilities, then, are themselves critical for effective strategy execution. But these decisions and investments further affect job creation and elimination, hiring practices, training programs, and activities like outsourcing—that is, additional execution decisions. Investments in capabilities actually produce a chain-type or serial effect on additional execution decisions, resulting in both intended and unintended consequences.

These results can be observed in both service and product-based organizations. Clearly, service organizations support execution of their strategies with the acquisition of critical resources and capabilities, including the best technologies and people available, which is no different than what is done in product-based companies. Where the requisite skills aren't available, service companies should invest in training programs, just like their product-based counterparts.

INCENTIVES AND CONTROLS

Incentives are vital to strategy execution, regardless of type of organization, service or otherwise. The type of incentive predominant in service and product companies certainly may vary, but the bottom line is that incentives support and reinforce strategy and related long- and short-term objectives in all organizations interested in the successful execution of their plans. The investment banking industry may focus almost exclusively on money as an incentive or reward, while the university health-care system focuses on title, tenure, and centrality in decision-making in addition to money, but the underlying issue is the same: Incentives must support the execution of strategy and the attainment of related objectives.

A common mantra in service organizations is "we don't have incentives" like those in product-based companies. This statement is misleading, if not totally incorrect. Some service companies indeed have bonuses and large monetary rewards as incentives. Even in "poorer" service organizations or government agencies there are rewards and incentives. Individuals who assume and remain in their jobs over time— teachers, nurses, professors, government bureaucrats, physicians, and so on—clearly are motivated by something valuable to them—for example, serving the common good, free time, control over choice of jobs or projects, prestige, even money, even if not in the "big bucks" category. Individuals who work and commit to an organization and its goals certainly must see clear incentives to do so.

Controls, too, come into play in service organizations. Feedback on performance against objectives is vital to organizational learning and adaptation, in both service and product-based companies. Sound controls are needed to avoid calamitous problems by catching them as soon as possible and taking corrective action.

This last aspect of control obviously wasn't heeded at J. P. Morgan when billions in losses were uncovered due to risky practices by London-based traders. While the losses made headlines in 2012, the first indications of the losses actually appeared two years earlier, but the company apparently ignored the warning signals.[ii] The control system in place seemingly created sufficient concern that discussions were held about confronting the London traders as early as 2010, but clearly something went wrong. The miscues and poor investments were allowed to continue, culminating in serious damages and a black eye for J. P. Morgan. Controls and their feedback provided needed data for change to occur, but this clearly didn't lead to a desired outcome. The overall process and results suggest "a serious breakdown in internal controls and risk systems" at the company.[iii]

Weaknesses in internal controls led to serious leaks of information in Nomura Holdings, Japan's biggest brokerage, while weak controls at MF Global resulted in the company's CEO, Jon Corzine, engaging in practices that eventually led to the company's demise.[iv] Again, warning signs were present, but weaknesses in controls resulted in aberrant behavior at great cost to both companies.

Incentives support or guide desired execution-related behavior, while controls signal aberrations from desired courses of action and allow for corrections and organizational adaptation. This is true in both service and product-based organizations.

THE LOGICAL CONCLUSION?

It is obvious, even from the few examples provided, that service businesses in banking, education, accounting, health-care, and so on focus on the same factors in the execution of their strategies as product-based organizations. Common concerns and issues in the implementation or execution process exist, regardless of type of organization.

The similarities notwithstanding, there are those who still argue that service organizations are different from their product-based counterparts in some critical areas. Accordingly, let's consider some of the more commonly noted differences and evaluate their merits and possible impact on strategy execution and organizational performance.

SERVICE BUSINESSES: POSSIBLE DIFFERENCES AFFECTING STRATEGY EXECUTION

PRODUCTION AND CONSUMPTION OF SERVICES

In many service businesses, there is a simultaneous production and consumption of services. This suggests that companies cannot inventory services the way product-based companies can. The empty airline seat is lost once the airplane takes off; the seat space cannot be inventoried. A legal conference with discussion between lawyers and clients is over and done at the completion of the conference and the imparting of knowledge or advice. Socratic dialogue and classroom interaction underlie educational processes, but the teaching and learning moment is short-lived, representing a simultaneous production and consumption of knowledge.

Strategy execution in cases such as these may demand repetitive sessions of interaction to share or impact knowledge. Execution depends in large part on knowledgeable personnel who can get close to clients or customers and sell the value of their advice or insights. Marketing activities may need to be strengthened to generate demand and sell that airline seat before its value is lost, at least until the next flight.

These activities, while important, are not always so different from activities in product-based companies. Capable talent is needed to provide customers with knowledge and insight about the merits of a given product. A lost sale to a customer is lost forever if the customer rejects a product in favor of a substitute. A service component is often critical to the sale of a product and to customers' perceptions of "quality" of sales and service, which may be a short-term, even fleeting result of company-customer interaction.

Products can be inventoried while services cannot, representing a real difference. This may lead to strenuous marketing activities and real-time emphasis on publicizing performance issues or cost reductions to lure customers before the service is lost forever. Airlines, for example, work closely with companies like Orbitz and Travelocity to change and post prices in real time, hoping to attract last-minute travelers to their inventory of seats on given flights.

In many service organizations, then, the "product" is fleeting, not prone to inventorying. Strategy execution activities must focus on marketing, incentives, and customer-oriented programs to effect a sale before the service is lost forever. These activities are especially critical with differentiation strategies, as the organization must prove its services' worthiness and benefits before the opportunity to sell the service disappears.

ARE SERVICES PERSONAL?

Some argue that services are intensely personal compared to the more impersonal situation of buying a product, say, on the Internet. Yet, even here care must be exercised. Using an ATM at a bank can hardly be considered personal service. Automated carwashes are anything but personal; people appear only when something goes dreadfully wrong with the automated process.

Even movie theaters rank high on impersonality of service. Long ticket lines persuade customers to use the computer kiosk with its impersonal approach to ticket selection. Regardless of how many screens show movies, there usually is one centrally located popcorn machine serving long lines of customers. A large machine focuses on economies of scale and large-scale production, not personal service beyond the "do you want butter?" question. Using a few poorly trained high school kids for the popcorn/candy counter does help to execute a low-cost strategy, but the result is hardly intensely personal.

The experience on many airlines is rarely personal and pleasant. In the past, airline travel was billed as an exciting way to seek personal freedom, far-off places, and simply a nice and quick way to get from point A to point B. Things have changed quite a bit, typically for the worse. Long lines, e-tickets, fewer services, incremental charges for everything, small and uncomfortable regional aircraft, fewer nonstops, airport hurdles, and so on all conspire to make air travel anything but personal. Even first class on some carriers is anything but first-class, personal service. The growing emphasis on cost containment has created a production-type mentality that works against any notion of a personal service experience. The basic low-cost strategy is more often correlated with impersonality, not personal treatment.

These examples are hardly mind-boggling or uncommon, but they show that common assumptions of services as intensely personal experience don't necessarily hold. Many services are intensely impersonal as a matter of fact, casting doubt on this popular notion of service organizations.

THE MEASUREMENT ISSUE

Another common argument is that, in services, one "can't measure what we do." Services businesses, the argument goes, often defy the easier measurement of performance associated with the manufacture and sale of goods. I've worked with lawyers, HR people, IT specialists, and others who routinely use this argument as proving a difference between service and product-based functions or businesses. One group of lawyers I worked with in Washington, D.C., for example, consistently argued against a zero-based budgeting process in their government agency by using the "can't measure what we do" assertion or, relatedly, "only lawyers can judge lawyers' performance." Measurement by others, they argued, isn't possible or desirable. A version of this theme is fairly common among many service providers.

Again, the argument in most cases has little merit; measures or performance metrics can always be developed. IT specialists or HR functional people can approach their internal "customers" and ask questions like those raised in a previous chapter discussing the translation of strategy into measurable objectives:

How do you, as a customer, evaluate the IT/HR services we provide for you? What criteria do you use to evaluate our performance or our department's contribution to your performance in the organization?

Given two hypothetical IT or HR departments, assume that one is highly effective and one highly ineffective or even incompetent. How would you tell the two apart? What criteria would you use to differentiate between the high-and-low-performing service units?

Questions like these, at minimum, can begin to provide feedback to service groups or functions about how others measure and value their services. Without measurement of performance, there can be no useful assessment of the contribution of a unit, department, or job to the execution of a strategy. Even the lawyers in the aforementioned government agency, faced with a loss of standing, people, and money due to continued resistance to the zero-based budgeting process, eventually made all sorts of comparisons of their services to the costs and quality of outsourcing the same services. They eventually came up with ways to measure what they did for the agency. A bit of pressure resulted in decent measurement metrics developed by the lawyers themselves, increasing organizational and professional acceptance of them.

Granted, measurement isn't always easy. The U.S. Department of Interior is responsible for all national parks. Some personnel there have expressed concern to me about measuring performance. What are the salient metrics? Usage or number of people who visit is one criterion. Customer satisfaction is another, although it's difficult to collect sound data on this dimension across so many diverse park locations. Costs always come into play, but it's difficult to relate expenditures to specific value-based outcomes.

Nonetheless, despite the difficulties inherent in the task, department personnel are actively engaged in defining measures of performance. Budget allocations before a cost-conscious Congress (at least in some areas!) demand that they do so. Areas or agencies seen as "soft" desperately need to create measures showing what they do and why it's important if they want to avoid the budget axe. Measurement in the Department of Interior is difficult, but necessary to prove to others that the dollars spent on department services and activities are worthwhile expenditures.

Without measurement, there can be no controls and feedback needed for effective organizational adaptation over time. Without measurement, controls, and evaluation, performance metrics become "subjectives," not objectives, in the execution process, and this can lead to trouble as perceptions of subjective performance clash. Simply put, measurement is vital to strategy execution in service and product-based companies alike.

The obvious conclusion thus far is that service and product-based organizations are alike in many respects. They both worry and attend to many of the same execution requirements or factors. I mentioned previously, however, that strategy execution is different and more challenging in certain kinds of service organizations. Let's add to what we've discussed already by looking at a way to envision or categorize service companies, units, or agencies so as to be able to draw distinctions among them and show how certain service organizations can pose challenges to the process of strategy execution.

CATEGORIES OR TYPES OF SERVICE ORGANIZATIONS

Table 12.1 shows different types of service organizations displayed against three variables: machine/equipment-based companies, people-based organizations, and degree of personal/impersonal service. I came across these distinctions in an article years ago, and it has proved useful to me in practice.[v]

Consider the far-left position in Table 12.1. The organizations here are good examples of the impersonal service organization. ATM-machine banking, car washes, and Internet services hardly qualify as personal with close-to-the-customer interaction. Emphasis is on fast machine transactions with some scale and scope economies. Movie theaters provide some personal interaction, but not much; centralized kiosks push large-scale production and scale economies, as emphasized previously.

Table 12.1 Categorizing Service Organizations

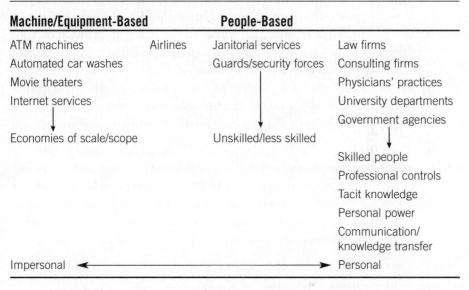

Machine/Equipment-Based		People-Based	
ATM machines	Airlines	Janitorial services	Law firms
Automated car washes		Guards/security forces	Consulting firms
Movie theaters			Physicians' practices
Internet services			University departments
↓			Government agencies
Economies of scale/scope		Unskilled/less skilled	↓
			Skilled people
			Professional controls
			Tacit knowledge
			Personal power
			Communication/ knowledge transfer
Impersonal ◄──────────────────────► Personal			

Airlines are clearly machine- or equipment-based. Decisions about buy versus lease arrangements, fuel efficiency, discounts for volume purchases, and widespread use of e-tickets suggest impersonality and reliance on computers. Some service is offered by ticket agents or flight attendants, but the overall experience on most carriers is less than personal, as suggested previously. Granted, some airlines score better than others on the personal dimension; airlines, then, in Table 12.1 are shown to be not as impersonal as the other services listed.

The point is that machine-based service companies, especially the large ones like the airlines, are impersonal, and they invest in capabilities that support and help execute basic low-cost strategies. Even "good" airlines that differentiate themselves somewhat with personal touches (e.g., Singapore Air, Cathy Pacific) worry about operating costs and scale economies in a low-cost approach to operations. These large service companies are very much like their product-based cousins in their emphasis on technology, scale, repetition, standardization, and cost containment, and their execution decisions and actions reflect this basic fact.

It's on the people-based side of Table 12.1 that we observe some significant characteristics that affect strategy execution. People-based organizations on the far right of Table 12.1 score higher on the Personal dimension than those on the left. Dealing with certain organizations—janitorial services, guards or security personnel—is rarely a problem. It's the characteristics or qualities of organizations on the far right in the table—again, the most personal—that separate them a bit from their product-based counterparts and present the greatest challenges to strategy execution.

The far-right of Table 12.1 basically lists service organizations in which strategy execution can be problematical. Included here are law firms, physicians' practices or physician groups in hospitals or other health-care organizations, consulting firms, university colleges and departments, and even some government agencies where professional services rule.

These people-based organizations are usually staffed and run by professionals. They are not always solely professional organizations—for example, law firms or physicians' practices with many clerical, administrative, or managerial staff who are not physicians or lawyers and who follow different administrative rules or practices—but they have a large number of professionals who often must work with the administrative or managerial personnel. Consulting firms, hospitals, and many government agencies meet this description of professionals working within administrative boundaries and dealing with bureaucratic rules and procedures. This emphasis on professional staff or professionals in administrative settings can affect the development and execution of strategy. Let's consider this point in more detail.

DEFINITION OF GOALS AND STRATEGIES

One issue is often differences in the definition of key goals and the strategies to achieve them. In the Social Security Administration, for example, professionals focus on client service and satisfaction as key goals while administrators focus on costs and next year's budget cycle. Physicians and administrators in large hospitals often differ in defining what precisely are medical versus management matters and who should make key decisions. Each group has goals and ideas about how to execute to achieve them and, more than occasionally, the varying perceptions of how to proceed result in conflict.

The mention of goals raises another issue in these professional organizations—the measurement problem. What metrics should be used to measure performance in government agencies? In the legal department or group that exists in a service provider? In the Department of Education? Definitions of performance may vary substantially in the university where professors' metrics (research, publication, professional standing) may occasionally clash with administrators' emphasis on costs, activity (percentage of time spent on research and teaching), and output (number of publications per salary expenditure).

It was argued previously that measurement is often difficult, but always possible. The present point is that different groups or factions in service organizations—professionals versus administrators—may go through the process of measurement, difficult as it is, only to find that the definition of goals or performance metrics of one group or faction is different from and conflicts with the goals or metrics of the other. The lack of common ground exacerbates the measurement problem and creates conflicts between groups that can injure efforts to find agreed-upon execution methods and performance metrics.

Groups of professionals, as mentioned previously, also may profess that "you can't measure what we do." Often, this argument is used to hide behind a wall of "nonmeasurability" and avoid evaluation of performance against goals by "outsiders." Processes and questions such as those outlined earlier to discern the criteria or metrics customers and others use to define effective performance are ignored or avoided, if they are developed by outsiders, not by the professionals themselves. The situation is only worsened when disagreement exists as to what really are the critical goals to pursue and what specifically can be used as metrics to measure and evaluate performance.

In some cases, goals are unclear, and the strategies to attain them are nonexistent or poorly defined. In a company where profitability is a goal, support by a strategy of differentiation that shows value to the client is often the case. The strategy of the large government agency usually is not as clear and well defined, however. How specifically does one "compete" against other government agencies for budget and standing? How does an agency increase or enhance client satisfaction? In most organizations, strategy is developed with an eye to increased performance and the attainment of competitive advantage. Where performance is not easily measured and competitive advantage is not a critical focus, the role and impact of strategy are problematical, as are any attempts at concerted execution efforts.

If strategy and related outcomes or goals are unclear and in conflict, the execution of strategy clearly is compromised. If professional groups resist and avoid measurement metrics related to performance, execution is problematical and open to conflicting views of results. When ambiguity about goals and strategy reigns, successful execution is not a fruitful or likely proposition.

PROFESSIONAL VERSUS ADMINISTRATIVE CONTROLS

Another critical issue, and one obviously closely related to the previous discussion, is that of authority and control over key decisions and actions about strategy formulation and execution.

Professionals demand self-control and definition and use of authority based on expertise or a body of professional knowledge. Administrative, hierarchical, or "bureaucratic" authority cannot be allowed to stifle, confront, or negate professional authority. Physicians, professors, and consultants have knowledge derived from education and practice, and key decisions, it is felt, should be based on this body of knowledge, not on bureaucrats' authority or hierarchical standing in an organization.

There is clearly an impact on planning and strategy execution under this professionally based view. Conflicts occur as viewpoints clash as to what are professional and administrative issues and who should resolve them. Professionals, in effect, believe that their model of professionalization and self-control trumps any model of administrative control over key outcomes and how to attain them.

The large consulting firms occasionally face the problem of priorities and controls. Professionals in special interest groups or functional or practice areas of excellence sometimes begin to look like academics in departments of a university. Professionals value knowledge creation as a critical goal or *raison d'être*; managers and administrators see knowledge use to generate business and profits as the main goals of these functional areas of expertise. Creating and using knowledge are complementary, of course, but strenuous emphasis on one or the other can occasionally cause a difference in opinion between professional and managerial staff as to who should control strategic and operating decisions. Who is more valuable and logically in control—knowledge creators or knowledge users? This is the underlying issue that can spark problems or conflicts in a number of areas, including performance appraisal, and raise the issue of professional versus administrative control.

A similar problem can often be seen in clashes between R&D organizations or units and the businesses or functions they serve. Centralized or independent R&D functions often delight in the "R" of R&D, focusing on science or research that is interesting on its own. Managers in businesses or functions who need help with real problems in a competitive market focus more on the "D" of R&D, developmental work that is practical and useful for problem solution.

The difference in goals and control of the strategies to achieve and apply them can cause clashes between R&D professionals and their internal customers. The researchers—for example, PhD scientists, physicians, or engineers with advanced degrees—often want professional standing and self-control over the definition and development of sound research. They resist controls imposed by nonprofessionals or outsiders, including the managers who seek R&D services. This may be seen by business practitioners as elitist and contrary to organizational goals. A clash between professional and administrative controls often ensues, hurting a coherent approach to strategy execution based on the work of R&D units.

KNOWLEDGE AND POWER

In all of the previous examples, professional knowledge and professionals' desire to control its development and use were often at the core of the execution issues discussed. Controlling professionals is a bit like "herding cats," a difficult if not impossible task. Professionals' desire to control knowledge, as well as strategy, goals, and performance evaluation, almost guarantees additional problems in an organization's attempts at planning and execution.

The nature of knowledge itself can add to the problems already identified. Codified knowledge is different than tacit knowledge, and it is easier to transmit and control. The "bicycle" example of Chapter 5 highlights the differences: Writing instructions on how to assemble a bicycle is easier and clearer than instructions on how to ride a bike (Step 1: Get on bike and ride; Step 2: If you fall, refer back to Step 1). Tacit knowledge is more difficult to describe and communicate. It is unstructured and "soft," compared to codified knowledge.

In people-based, professional service organizations, it is the professional who wants to control, interpret, and use tacit knowledge. Depending on professionals performing these tasks increases their power, as Chapter 9 suggests. Power is the obverse or reverse of dependency: A has power over B if (a) A has something B needs, and (b) A can monopolize and control whatever it is that B needs. If A controls something valuable, B depends on A completely and A has power over B.

In the professional, people-based, personal organizations in Table 12.1, professionals work hard to control tacit knowledge. Only they can interpret, understand, and use tacit knowledge for their own and organizational ends. Lawyers interpret fuzzy legal precedents; physicians alone focus on illness and disease, and they want also to control administrative matters that affect diagnoses and patient care decisions; consultants often fight to control tacit knowledge in dealing with clients, arguing that they alone, through experience, have the "feel" for important but delicate client services.

Professionals enjoy the power or influence that accompanies control of tacit knowledge, and they often are reluctant to share it.

Consultants have told me personally that they are reluctant to share knowledge; the more widespread the understanding and control of tacit knowledge, the less the organization depends on them, damaging their base of power. Power or social influence has its rewards, and professionals want to keep and use it in the organization.

This control of information and the power derived from it obviously can affect both strategy formulation and, especially, execution. How things get done, who decides what, how coordination occurs, and who is responsible for what objectives and even organizational change, all can be affected by professional control. Action plans created by outsiders or nonprofessionals are rejected or, at minimum, viewed with skepticism. Professionals rule in professional, people-based organizations, service units, or government agencies, in both for-profit and not-for-profit settings, and strategy execution activities or decisions related to the use of critical knowledge are often controlled jealously by them.

CONCLUSION: A DIFFICULT SETTING FOR STRATEGY EXECUTION

The present analysis has suggested that strategy formulation and execution in many service organizations mirrors the same processes found in product-based companies. Banks, insurance companies, airlines, and many others focus on strategy, positioning, goals, and the execution-related decisions regarding talent, technological capabilities, organizational structure, incentives, and controls that are critical to effective performance. These organizations also focus on organizational change, as they adapt to evolving competitive conditions over time.

If there is a difficult setting for strategy execution, it is in the people-based, professional service organization on the far right in Table 12.1. Included here would be for-profit and not-for-profit organizations staffed by a significant number of professional employees or experts. The nonprofit group represents a particularly difficult arena for action because of the lack of a profit goal and the dedicated, focused activity such a goal provides. The difficulties in these people-based, professional organizations include the following:

- Unclear or competing visions of strategy and goals
- Competing views of professional and administrative staff regarding goal definition and managerial processes related to goal attainment
- Professionals' need for self-control and emphasis on expertise or knowledge as the basis of authority, rather than an emphasis on hierarchical or positional authority
- Poor measurement metrics in areas of service, including measures of value-added activities, performance metrics, and customer satisfaction
- The existence and use of power or influence that underlies strategy execution decisions and actions

These and other issues provide challenges to the performance of people-based, professional service organizations, especially those in the not-for-profit category. The critical next question, then, is how can strategy execution be managed in these difficult settings? What steps or actions can managers take to facilitate planning and execution in these organizations, government agencies, or service-oriented functions? This is the task to which we now can focus our discussion.

STRATEGY EXECUTION IN PEOPLE-BASED PROFESSIONAL SERVICE ORGANIZATIONS

A number of key decision or action areas are central to making strategy work in these organizations. The first deals with the general setting within which the majority of implementation steps or execution actions take place.

THE SETTING FOR ACTION: A CASE OF RECIPROCAL INTERDEPENDENCE

Chapter 5 pointed out that the case of reciprocal interdependence is the most complex form of interdependence and the hardest to manage and coordinate. Realistically, it defines the situation in which most strategy formulation and execution decisions and actions are made in professional service organizations.

Figure 12.1 depicts a view of reciprocal interdependence, building on the discussion in Chapter 5.

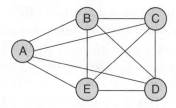

Figure 12.1   Reciprocal Interdependence

The defining characteristics of this form are as follows:

- All players deal routinely with each other and all have a vested stake in some outcome. This is a network group structure, not a hierarchical one.

- All participants, A through E, are *necessary* for decision-making. All necessary skills, functions, or areas of expertise are needed to make decisions. Think, for example, of physicians, nurses, and administrators who must decide on a major program in a hospital. Or consider administrative decisions in the Social Security Administration where the inputs from physicians and the legal staff are vital to support those decisions. All bring necessary skills or capabilities to the table.

- Individual players, or subsets of players, while necessary, are *not sufficient* for decision-making. Physicians and nurses making decisions without the presence or inputs of administrators run the real risk of conflict. Similarly, administrators making decisions without the inputs from physicians and nurses face the problem of members of the latter group vetoing that which they weren't part of or privy to in the decision process. In this situation, reliance on power or even forcing behavior comes into play, usually with disastrous results.

■ Decision-making under these conditions of high interdependence demands effective communication, face-to-face interaction, and clarification of responsibility and accountability, with each player, group, or faction understanding its own role and that of others in the network.

This form of interdependence and its defining characteristics are often critical for decision-making in professional service organizations. Key players, equals in the decision process, must interact, communicate, and reach agreement on decisions, including those related to strategy formulation and execution. Professionals, key functional people, administrators, and other stakeholders, for example, customers or clients, are jointly responsible for decisions or actions. Nonparticipation by an important group or faction usually spells failure for decisions made in the absence of, or without the consent of, an important group.

Let's take the analysis one step further and consider (a) critical strategy execution decisions and actions, and (b) how they must be made in a professional service organization or government agency marked by high levels of interdependence.

DECIDING ON STRATEGY AND GOALS

Decisions about strategy and strategic goals must precede strategy execution decisions. In some professional service organizations, this isn't a major problem. Consulting firms have customer service and profitability as major goals and strategies stressing differentiation or cost leadership support and generate performance consistent with the goals. In these firms, an executive group comprising professionals (knowledge creators, scientists, engineers), functional areas of expertise (IT, HR), program directors, even client or industry representatives work together to formulate plans and lay out execution requirements. The same type of all-inclusive group would be used to consider major changes in strategy, type of client served, or execution investments. The decision-making process isn't always smooth, but the clear goals and need to perform in a competitive situation usually results in agreement among key decision-makers, even after heated discussions.

In the university or teaching hospital, the process isn't always as straightforward. Goals of physicians (stellar patient care) and professors (outstanding research, a sound learning environment) are easily expressed, but the strategies to achieve them aren't always stipulated clearly. Strategy can be inferred often from investments in classroom or health-care technology, but inferences aren't always correct or ascribed to by everyone.

To clarify goals and strategy, meetings of key professional and administrative personnel are required; the high interdependence of professional knowledge, technology, and functional expertise demands face-to-face interaction and discussion. Communication is central to reaching agreement on goals and the methods of achieving them. Without this intense interaction and communication, ambiguous goals and strategies will remain and increase the difficulty of choosing the right execution tactics or steps. Without this clarity, conflicts and other problems are certain to emerge in people-based, professional organizations.

A really good example of poor strategy and execution was recently provided by two hospitals in the Philadelphia area. On Wednesday, July 18, 2012, Abington Health System and Holy Redeemer Health System called off a merger the two organizations had announced only three weeks prior. The primary impetus for the stunning reversal was extreme pressure from outsiders and hospital insiders who opposed a ban on abortions and other procedures at Abington Hospital that was part of the merger agreement. Why did this problem and quick turnaround occur?

The merger strategy was originally announced with fanfare and with some of the usual goals attributed to typical mergers or acquisitions. A larger organization, it was felt, could achieve scale economies or efficiencies that would be beneficial. The merged organization could also deal better with competition and be better equipped to handle the anticipated overhaul of the U.S. health-care system.

What went dreadfully wrong was the hospitals' violation of the tenets of decision-making required for success under the conditions of reciprocal or shared interdependence. Key players were ignored, causing problems. Essential stakeholders screamed when the merger and its conditions regarding abortion were announced. Members of the community felt disenfranchised because they had no say in the matter regarding "their" hospital in Abington. Pro-choice groups attacked the merger. Even pro-life groups were upset that bans on undesirable hospital procedures didn't go far enough. Physicians threatened to boycott or leave the merged institution, extremely upset and disappointed that Abington and Redeemer didn't even consult them before signing a letter of intent for the merger.[vi]

Individuals and groups that should have been involved in the merger strategy and the definition of key execution related goals and procedures were ignored and left out of the decision process. The face-to-face interaction and discussion of key issues never materialized, and a handful of essential decision-makers were never involved in the communication and decision network that exists under conditions of high interdependence.

Key strategic and operating decisions in people-based professional service organizations must take account of the essential players or decision-makers and ensure their participation in the communication network shown in Figure 12.1. The tenets or rules of decision-making under conditions of high, reciprocal interdependence must be met. Critical decisions will otherwise fail and create additional dysfunctional consequences, such as lack of trust and probable conflict in future strategic and operating matters.

In effect, in people-based, professional service organizations, inclusion in decision-making is the first requirement for success. Face-to-face interaction and active discussion are needed. Responsibility and accountability must be clarified, with the roles of key players clearly identified. Processes for the resolution of conflict—which often is inevitable—cannot be avoided; rather procedures or processes for the confrontation of conflict must be developed and employed to solve major execution-related problems.

DEFINING MEASUREMENT METRICS AND CAUSE-EFFECT CLARITY

As noted previously, some professional service organizations have problems with the development of performance metrics or outcomes. Related to this point is the often-unfulfilled need for clear cause-effect models that show the relationship between organization or agency actions and the resultant metrics. Cause-effect clarity is low, detracting from the proof that execution methods are indeed working.

Consider the case of General Motors and Facebook. In May 2012, GM announced it would cease advertising on Facebook because it felt that the ads had little or no impact on consumers' automobile purchases.[vii] Marketing experts or professionals in Facebook argued otherwise, but GM sought more proof—clearer cause and effect relationships—that advertising on Facebook has a direct impact on sales. Professional service organizations often face this problem of links between action and results, with unclear links detracting from the perceived efficacy of execution actions or steps.

The case of Publicis is another example of the same phenomenon. Customers of Publicis began arguing a few years ago that all advertising companies were alike in their services and that there was no direct causal link between their services and desired customer-related outcomes like sales. This is a case where the outcome metrics are defined, but the causal links between execution actions and outcomes are unspecified or unclear.

Publicis created a decision structure like that illustrated in Figure 12.1. Sessions were held that included customers, functional experts from IT and marketing, and managerial personnel discussing the issue. Joint agreements were reached. Publicis, for example, vowed to prove the existence of links between its advertising and customer sales. Publicis even suggested payment plans that paid Publicis less at first, but more later if the link between its advertising and outcomes like sales could be unequivocally demonstrated. This is a significant attempt at proving a cause-effect connection, and advertising efficacy and results are eagerly being evaluated currently.

People-based, professional service organizations, such as government agencies, face the difficult task of defining clear outcome metrics and the cause-effect models linking actions to results. This is a common issue in the Social Security Administration,

Department of Interior, and other government bodies. These organizations or agencies can use the same decision processes as those noted in the discussion of Figure 12.1 to define agreed-upon measurement metrics and the causal path to their attainment, as these organizations indeed are trying to do at the present time.

Other agencies or government bodies aren't faring as well; they're not forcing the issue to measure results and define their plans or strategies to achieve them. The approach under conditions shown in Figure 12.1 certainly needs radical, progressive thinking and action, which clearly is more demanding and difficult than simply doing the same-old things and complaining about how difficult management is. Admittedly, it isn't always easy or politically feasible to attack the lack of metrics and show how to achieve them, but it is necessary if organizations desire to increase their management and execution capabilities.

All organizations must worry about and prove cause-effect clarity between execution activities and desired outcomes or performance metrics. People-based, professional service organizations, especially not-for-profit types, definitely must work harder to show such causal links, but this is a necessary, if challenging, task to prove the worth of execution decisions and actions. Reliance on all-network groups, following the model depicted in Figure 12.1, can assemble critical decision-makers and foster the interaction and communication needed to get the desired results.

STRUCTURE AND COORDINATION PROCESSES

Focusing on organizational structure and related processes, such as those dealing with coordination and integration, can help the development of effective execution in people-based, professional organizations. Again, the task may be challenging, but it is important for effective implementation of strategy and operating plans.

Consider for a moment the increasing complexity facing law firms as they grow from small businesses to huge multimillion dollar firms with geographically dispersed practices. Issues of planning, budgeting, outsourcing, strategic alliances, complex tax codes, especially in the global arena, and similar industry changes demand new skills and management processes when planning and executing strategy. Some of these complexities can be addressed by lawyers, but many go beyond legal training and demand new management skills and capabilities. The solution: a different-looking management structure with new processes of coordinating and executing work.

Law firms are changing to handle the increased complexity and management demands.[viii] The model of the law firm is changing in terms of organizational structure and process. The C-level suite in large law firms is looking increasingly like that in the business firm, with positions filled by professional managers to handle many of the nonlegal matters noted previously. Lawyers are free to do legal work, while managerial positions are created to do important nonlegal tasks that affect the bottom line. These new managers often bring fresh ideas, talent, technologies, and operating procedures to the firm, helping to reduce costs, tackle new opportunities, and generally support the firm's strategy and goals. Granted, state rules and ABA requirements must be met. In some states, for example, there are prohibitions against total ownership of law firms by non lawyers. Still, changes in management structure and process are characterizing and changing the law firm of old.

Concepts related to structure and requirements for effective coordination are also appearing with greater frequency. In the law firm, meetings reflecting the interactive processes noted above under conditions of reciprocal interdependence are becoming more common for purposes of integration and coordination of legal and business matters. These represent important steps for strategy execution.

Large hospitals are providing similar changes in structure and process to improve management and profitability. Recent data reported by the Pennsylvania Health Care Cost Containment Council showed that profit margins were up slightly in hospitals in the Philadelphia region.[ix] The most profitable situations seem to be in hospitals achieving cost efficiencies, increases in volume, technology investments, integrated patient care, acquisitions, and alliances or partnerships with other hospitals.

The last three items—integrated care, acquisitions, and alliances—suggest an emphasis on structure and processes of coordination around agreed-upon goals. Mergers and acquisitions demand structural integration of hospitals, often resulting in scale and scope economies. Effective coordination across clinical areas with patients at the focal point represents a sound approach to management in these professional organizations.

Effective coordination also demands clarification of responsibility and accountability across functional or clinical areas, again representing the use of structure and process as management tools in the execution arsenal. Chapter 5 noted how the use of a responsibility matrix can facilitate the clarification of responsibility and accountability. The present view is that tools like this can be employed effectively in people-based, professional service organizations. The prime condition for success, again, is that the professionals, administrators, and other key personnel get together, discuss goals and issues face to face, and foster the problem-solving capabilities of groups like those shown in Figure 12.1 to clarify responsibility and accountability and solve other execution-related problems. This is an example of high interdependence and "managing by living together" that can help solve complex problems.

EFFECTIVE INCENTIVES

Without effective incentives, execution flounders badly. Incentives must support agreed-upon goals and fuel the motivation of all personnel, including professionals, toward desired outcomes. As mentioned previously, the sad lament often heard is that incentives don't exist in many people-based service organizations, especially the not-for-profit sector. These organizations, the argument is offered, are not like their for-profit cousins, so execution automatically suffers, and effective implementation is only a dream, not a reality.

I participated recently in an executive development program for top managers in the IRS in India, and among the most common laments about the ineffectiveness of execution was this notion of a lack of incentives and the impact of this deplorable situation. I've heard similar arguments from countless managers in a host of not-for-profits, including large government service organizations and health-care nonprofits.

In all of these cases, I challenged employees to list the reasons why they continue working in such a terrible environment, with no incentives to perform admirably and effectively. In all cases, incentives emerged, even if not exactly the same ones found in for-profit situations. Recognition for one's work, professional pride, customer or client feedback, standing in the community, choice of cases or assignments, even pay and promotion were mentioned by the supposedly beleaguered professionals. Identification of incentives came only after professionals and administrators openly discussed the goals of the nonprofit organization and the roles of different players in attaining those goals. In the final analysis, after a concerted effort, the professionals in these not-for-profit agencies agreed that incentives did indeed exist, even if they didn't look like those in the investment banking industry.

The interactive setting and communication-heavy group process of Figure 12.1 came into play in these sessions with not-for-profit personnel. Professionals and others in these organizations or agencies admittedly must work hard to define effective incentives, but the task is doable and necessary. Professionals cannot hide behind a cloak of nonmeasurability of performance metrics and an aversion to developing incentives that support those metrics. This evasive behavior can only result in not-for-profit organizations' inability to justify what they do and explain why they deserve funding and budget extensions.

THE VERDICT: EXECUTION IN PEOPLE-BASED, PROFESSIONAL SERVICE ORGANIZATIONS

The people-based professional service organizations of Figure 12.1 do present challenges for effective strategy execution. They are staffed in whole or in part by professionals—lawyers, physicians, professors, scientists, engineers—who rely on knowledge or expertise in decision-making. These employees opt for professional self-control and eschew the controls imposed by hierarchical or bureaucratic systems of authority. Professionals often avoid the search for the development of performance metrics, especially when measurements are demanded or provided by "outsiders," managers who are not part of the professional ranks. These employees, in fact, often can be heard to assert that "you can't measure what we do," for only they can assess and judge the value of contribution to the organization or the larger scientific community.

These attitudes about work often clash with managers' or administrators' perceptions of what's needed to formulate and execute strategy. Professional-bureaucratic conflict has long existed and plagued decision-making in complex organizations, including decisions about strategy making and making strategy work.

Still, in the final analysis, the people-based, professional service organization can make intelligent decisions about execution, much like their service and for-profit counterparts. The organizations and agencies on the far right of Figure 12.1, especially the not-for-profit ones, can present challenges, but this doesn't relieve professionals from participating in strategy formulation and execution activities.

A helpful approach to making strategy work begins with seeing most people-based professional organizations as characterized by high levels of reciprocal interdependence and, consequently, in need of the decision, communication, and interaction processes outlined above. In these settings, professionals, administrators, and other key stakeholders, including customers, clients, or even government/regulatory personnel, need to interact, realizing that all are essential to execution success. They need to understand that less than full participation of key stakeholders and lack of agreement with chosen action plans can only lead to poor results, including power plays, conflicts, and ineffective performance.

In brief, strategy execution in people-based, professional service organizations, in for-profit and not-for-profit settings alike, is possible and necessary. Attempts to place these organizations into a separate nonperforming category for the various reasons listed previously represent an avoidance of the real facts and rejection of the positive work that can be done in the area of strategy execution.

SUMMARY: STRATEGY EXECUTION IN SERVICE ORGANIZATIONS

There are four key conclusions suggested by the analysis in this chapter:

1. Service organizations or functions in business and government are a huge part of U.S. GDP and the world economy. Service businesses are prevalent and important. This fact cannot be denied. The question consistent with the focus in this book on making strategy work is whether strategy execution in service businesses is similar to, or different from, that in product-based businesses.

2. In most respects, strategy execution is identical to that in product-based businesses. Consideration of the key execution-related factors discussed in this book reveals this similarity. Service businesses need to do industry and competitor analysis and derive a strategy for positioning themselves and competing in an industry or strategic group. Developing a strategy is vital to service organizations, just as it is in product-based firms.

   Service businesses also need to concern themselves with other execution-related decisions or actions. They need to worry about organizational structure, interdependence and coordination requirements, incentives, culture, and change management. Power and control issues come into play, and they must be confronted and dealt with in the service sector. Service organizations, much like their product-based counterparts, must focus on talent and capabilities to support planning and execution activities.

3. One class of service organization does present additional execution challenges: the people-based professional service organization. Equipment- or machine-based organizations reflect the impersonality and the rational decision-making of product-based companies regarding execution, but the people-based professional examples of service providers present additional concerns.

The latter organizations are usually staffed heavily by professional employees. Some are staffed almost exclusively by professionals, while others aren't totally professionally based, but have a large and important professional contingent. Examples include law firms or legal departments or functions in larger organizations; individual physicians' practices or groups of physicians and nurses in hospitals or other health-care settings; scientists and engineers in R&D organizations or units of larger organizations; professional, knowledge-creating staff in consulting firms; professional staff in government agencies; and, of course, professors in universities. These organizations may be profit-oriented; in many cases, they represent not-for-profit organizations or agencies.

Why are these organizations particularly challenging to the effective execution of strategy? A number of issues must be resolved routinely to make strategy work.

One key issue is that of professional versus administrative control over planning, operations, and execution decisions. Professionals desire self-control, based on professional knowledge and ideology. Lawyers, physicians, and professors feel that they know best what's good for customers or clients. A problem exists when the professionals are imbedded in an organization with "nonprofessional" administrators or managers who desire control over administrative matters. The definition of professional versus administrative matters, however, varies among the professionals and bureaucrats, leading to conflicts and other problems. Who rules or reigns creates problems, including those related to effective strategy execution.

Another issue deals with performance metrics and a lack of clarity in cause-effect relations or how to achieve desired ends. Professionals, especially in not-for-profit organizations or government agencies, avoid even eschew the definition of clear performance standards. Arguments that, as professionals, "we know if we're performing well" or "outsiders can't measure and evaluate what we do" are frequently heard. The lack of clarity in how to achieve unclear or underspecified performance goals creates uncertainty and "subjectives," not objectives, a fact that leads to conflict and poor definition of strategy, goals, and execution actions or steps.

The lack of clear, agreed-upon objectives and reliance instead on "subjectives" create additional problems with incentives. In the people-based, professional service organization, incentives can't easily be aligned with subjective, competing measures of performance and unclear execution methods. Poor or nonexistent metrics and unclear cause-effect relationships work against the creation and use of effective incentives. Still, incentives are needed to support strategy execution, despite the difficulties involved.

Again, the basic underlying element is professionals' desire for self-control and the rejection of outside sources of control. This hurts goal definition, strategy formulation, and clear stipulation of execution requirements.

The next question is how these conditions can be overcome in people-based, professional service organizations. If conditions remain as defined, making strategy work is, indeed, problematical.

4. The answer is found, at least in part, by asserting the fact that planning, coordination, and execution decisions reflect the conditions inherent in reciprocal interdependence. This final conclusion is central to effective decision-making in people-based, professional service organizations.

Under the conditions of reciprocal interdependence, all actors or participants are in an all-network decision structure, such as the following:

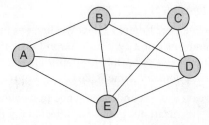

All players, A through E, are equals. All are *necessary* participants in decision-making, but no participant or subset of participants is *sufficient* for decision-making. All have a stake in the decision outcomes, and intense interaction, communication, and discussion are vital to group agreement. Parties left out of the discussion can veto or resist decisions made by the active participants.

This interactive setting can aid decisions about planning and execution in people-based, professional service organizations. Professionals, administrators, clients or customers, unions, and other stakeholders meet in an interactive setting, argue about the merits of plans and possible execution steps, and reach some sort of closure.

This setting and the communication it suggests can go far to define performance metrics and the steps or actions required to achieve those metrics. This approach is far from perfect, but the risks of failure associated with the exclusion in decision-making of key factions or groups are far greater. People-based professional organizations present high challenges to agreement on strategy and the actions required to make strategy work, and this approach can help move the organization forward to address the challenges noted in this chapter.

ENDNOTES

i. Erik Brynjolfsson and Andrew McAfee, *Race Against the Machine*, Digital Frontier Press, October, 2011; also see Andrew McAfee, "The Rebound That Stayed Flat," Moncton Free Press, January, 2012.

ii. Dan Fitzpatrick, Gregory Zuckerman, and Joann Lublin, "J. P. Morgan Knew of Risks," *The Wall Street Journal*, June 2012.

iii. David Reilly, "Did J. P. Morgan Fiddle While Risk Burned?" *The Wall Street Journal*, May 21, 2012.

iv. Atsuko Fukase, "Nomura Finds Weaknesses in Controls," *The Wall Street Journal*, June 29, 2012; Aaron Lucchetti, Mike Spector, and Julie Steinberg, "M F Global Autopsy Flags Risks by Corzine," *The Wall Street Journal*, June 5, 2012.

v. Many years ago, I found a reference to machine- and people-based service organizations, and it has affected my thinking ever since. Try as I might, having instituted all sorts of computer searches, I have not been able to locate the original reference. Much has been written on service organizations, but few pieces have captured their essence as well as the lost article. I, obviously, wish to give credit where it is due, but have been hampered in my ability to do so. Others, I'm sure, have seen the original article, and I would be very happy to be apprised by anyone as to the original publication.

vi. Tom Avril, "Abington-Redeemer Merger Off," *The Philadelphia Inquirer*, July 19, 2012.

vii. See, for example, Sharon Terlep, Suzanne Vranica, and Shayndi Raice, "GM Says Facebook Ads Don't Pay Off," *The Wall Street Journal*, May 16, 2012; see also Sharon Terlep and Shayndi Raice, "Facebook, GM Talk New Friendship," *The Wall Street Journal*, July 3, 2012.

viii. See, for example, Jennifer Smith and Ashby Jones, "Practicing Business," *The Wall Street Journal*, May 7, 2012; and Clifford Winston and Robert Crandall, "The Law Firm Business Model Is Dying," *The Wall Street Journal*, May 29, 2012.

ix. Harold Brubaker, "Profit Margins Up Slightly at Area Hospitals," *The Philadelphia Inquirer*, May 17, 2012.

13

Project Management and Strategy Execution

Introduction

The basic model of strategy execution or implementation presented in Chapter 2 has guided all discussions in subsequent chapters. Chapter 2, however, did add an element to the basic model that did not appear in the original version of this book: namely, the possible contribution of project management to the process of making strategy work. The introduction of project management in no way alters the impact and importance of other variables or decisions in the basic model. Rather, project management is being introduced as a tool or process that can facilitate implementation of parts of the basic model, thereby contributing incrementally to the successful execution of strategy. Project management supports the basic model and approach; it does not change or replace it.

This chapter considers the potential contribution of project management to the successful execution of strategy. It first presents the benefits of project management, showing how it can be a useful weapon in management's arsenal to foster execution success. Emphasis is not on providing a full "how-to" analysis of project management, but to show how some elements of this process or approach can aid strategy execution and help make it successful. This chapter also emphasizes that there are potential problems with the use of project management that must be avoided in applying its concepts to the process of making strategy work.

POSSIBLE BENEFITS OF A PROJECT MANAGEMENT APPROACH

Project management is a process, a standardized approach to planning, organizing, resource allocation, and control dedicated to the achievement of a clearly defined goal—project success. Projects can vary in terms of duration, importance, and cost, and part of the project management task is to focus resources carefully on significant projects, while avoiding excessive investments in less critical areas.

Project management is increasingly being used by companies in many industries and is receiving more and more respect for its contributions.[i] While originally used primarily in IT departments or in certain industries—for example, defense, construction, engineering—its use has spread as organizations such as GE, IBM, NASA, SAP, HP, and Microsoft have workable elements of the project management process. Increasing use of and reliance on this approach suggests clearly that organizations are seeing benefits and positive outcomes that recommend and support use of project management. Let's briefly enumerate what appear to be the benefits of this process in those organizations using it as a management tool.

Project management is a standardized process that provides a path to the success of projects and goals related to those projects. The key words here are "standardized" and "path." Standardization denotes the fact that the process is a tool that can be repeated or used again and again, thereby facilitating learning and the development of expertise that has lasting benefits. Processes or routines allow for the training of people to perform key roles, thereby facilitating the development of talent useful to the organization. Standardization and routine practices are often more efficient than ad-hoc approaches to problem solving and project completion.

Provision of a path to desired results is also touted as a benefit. Having a clear path reduces uncertainty and informs managers of the sequential steps needed to move a project methodically toward the desired outcome. Incremental steps allow for adaptation and refinement of actions or decisions along the path and allow managers to handle changes in small bits, thereby avoiding huge changes that people might resist or not fully comprehend. Clear paths to an end are simply more comfortable and useful than unclear paths.

The discussion of paths suggests a control function, and this point deserves additional mention. Controls represent a feedback mechanism that helps to evaluate performance and allow for successful change and adaptation. Controls allow for the analysis and explanation of obtained results and even the conduct of "autopsies" to explain undesired outcomes, points emphasized in previous chapters. Having various points of evaluation of progress along a project path enables the control function further by allowing personnel to understand progress and problems and provide feedback that leads to change and the improvement of performance along the path. Project management, then, not only moves projects forward, it also provides for learning and corrections along the way.

Managers who espouse the importance of communication usually give high marks to project management. People must discuss and agree with projects and related goals, as well as the evaluation metrics or criteria to measure performance along the path of the project. This discussion and need for agreement, it is argued, can lead to more effective communication across diverse functions or groups, especially on complex projects that demand expertise from multiple sources in an organization. Standardized processes or practices that demand confrontation on key issues often facilitate communication and the airing of divergent, but important, opinions.

The use of clear, agreed-upon, logical, and measurable objectives in the project-management process is also touted as a benefit for management and the organization. The incremental steps and evaluation points along the sequential path of project management simply cannot produce desired outcomes if unclear performance measures or "subjectives" are employed. The entire process benefits from agreement on solid metrics and the performance reviews based on them. The effectiveness of feedback, controls, and change programs is enhanced by the existence and use of these measurable objectives in the project-management process, providing an obvious benefit to an organization.

There are additional benefits that managers have espoused regarding the use of project management as a management tool.[ii] The ones mentioned briefly capture their essence. A standardized process or practice that facilitates performance evaluation, the management of change and adaptation, and provision of a clear path to desired outcomes clearly defines a worthwhile and useful tool for the attainment of desired ends. The applicability and utility of such a process or practice for the execution of strategy is probably obvious, but let's take an additional step and add an important caveat. Let's use an additional example to show how project management can facilitate strategy execution, if certain conditions are met. Let's also identify further some problems that can detract from this success and emphasize ways to eliminate or reduce their negative impact.

AN EXAMPLE: PROJECT MANAGEMENT AND MAKING STRATEGY WORK

Chapter 3 noted the importance of translating strategy into actionable items and metrics. Figure 13.1 builds on this point and suggests that, in the process of execution, strategy can be translated into projects and key objectives that can be inputs to a project management approach. A sequential path to desired outcomes can then be developed, and the steps and benefits noted previously for project management can support the execution process.

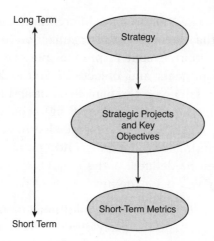

Figure 13.1 Translating Strategy into Projects and Key Objectives

While simple and straightforward, Figure 13.1 does suggest important issues for execution and making strategy work.

DEFINING THE PROJECTS AND KEY OBJECTIVES

Clearly, the definition of key projects and objectives is vital to the project management process. At the highest level, managers must lay out the key projects related to the successful implementation of a strategy. Top management has responsibility for strategy formulation; the argument presently is that upper management also has responsibility for defining the key projects and goals related to making the chosen strategy work.

A cost-leadership strategy, for example, must be translated into major projects related to this competitive approach. Major cost reduction programs in important areas—for example, introducing more efficient, but expensive technologies—are defined by upper management working with key people below the C-level—functional heads or SBU managers. Responsibility for key projects or objectives must be assigned at these levels where managers, in turn, can translate them into goals that cascade down to the next level(s) of responsibility within their functions or SBUs, as Figure 13.1 suggests.

Similarly, a strategy of product differentiation must define the key parameters that distinguish the organization in its chosen market. A desire for improvement in product performance, for example, can lead to projects and objectives at the highest levels with responsibility falling on top management and key corporate (e.g., R&D) and functional (e.g., engineering) people to define required performance levels and the steps needed to achieve those distinguishing performance parameters. Additional projects and objectives can then be defined as the major projects are translated in smaller components for the next levels of responsibility.

A significant point here is worth additional mention and emphasis. C-level managers and their key direct reports are responsible, not only for strategy—how to position the organization and compete effectively—but also for the first critical steps in a project-management approach to execution. Key projects related to strategy implementation are the responsibility of these top managers. Views of execution or implementation that focus only on lower levels doing the nitty-gritty execution work are misleading and incomplete, as top managers clearly must be involved in the execution process. A project management approach emphasizes this top-management inclusion in defining early implementation steps or projects.

Once key projects are defined, the process of project management can come into play.[iii] The path to project completion can be laid out by defining clear metrics of performance and time frames along the chosen paths. Periodic reviews can monitor interim measures of performance and keep the project on track. Corrections can be made as a result of learning and incremental changes and improvements can support the project management approach, which, in turn, is helping to implement the organizational strategies of cost leadership or differentiation mentioned in the previous examples.

It is obvious thus far that project management supports or builds upon steps, actions, needs, or conditions that previous chapters have analyzed and discussed as important for strategy execution. A solid strategy is still the key to success, as is the translation of the strategy into operating objectives (Chapter 3). Project management aids coordination (Chapter 5). The complementarity to the discussion of sequential change in Chapter 7 is clear, as is the similarity to the concept of feedback and controls in Chapter 6. Obviously, the project management process must be supported by incentives and the organizational culture (Chapters 6 and 8). The project management process highlights the importance of these previous discussions, while supporting their relevance for making strategy work.

A caveat is in order, however. Project management is useful and productive, if certain conditions are met. The benefits of the process are not automatic; care must be taken to use project management in a way that fosters execution and doesn't impede its progress. Keys to success for example, include the definition of key projects or objectives and attention to the linking or cascading of projects and objectives across organizational levels. Successful strategy execution—and sound project management—starts at the top and moves down through the organization. A key issue, then, is how not to lose sight of key projects as they are translated down the organization. How does the organization ensure attention to key projects and objectives in this cascading process?

Define few key projects. It often is true that "less is more." Top management must define a couple or few key projects, at most. The number of projects can breed uncontrollably if too many are chosen at the highest levels. The need is to focus on a few project areas related strongly and undeniably to strategic success. Even a single, high-level project—for example, building a 787 dreamliner at Boeing—can breed a host of related projects; having more than a single, huge project can only lead to disaster. Similarly, at one point in the execution of the DaimlerChrysler M&A strategy, the merged companies were pursuing approximately 120 projects, clearly a recipe for confusion and performance problems. Less, indeed, can be more.

Set priorities. Even with a few key projects, priorities must be discussed. Competitive forces change, resources become challenged, and management time and attention become factors in fast-changing environments. Priorities must guide decisions and actions when these challenges occur. As a wise old CEO once told me: "When everything is important, then nothing is important."

Successful strategy execution demands focus and an almost relentless pursuit of details or steps related to success. Setting clear priorities helps to achieve this focus and direct attention to key results. Coupled with few projects, setting priorities enables the project management process and fosters the execution of strategy.

Focus on participation and buy-in. Even with only a few major projects, care must be taken not to lose or disenfranchise people as work moves down the organization. The logic and importance of a major project must be communicated clearly. As project needs move vertically, the relation to strategy and its execution must be clarified and people's roles in making strategy work reinforced. Consider the case of a cost-leadership strategy and the resultant demands on communication and buy-in generated by it (see Figure 13.2).

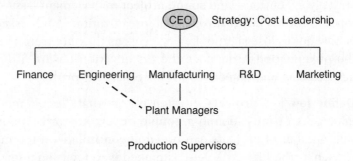

Figure 13.2 Communication and Vertical Connections to Support a Cost-Leadership Strategy

The choice or refinement of a cost-leadership strategy creates a critical project: introduction of a new technology or manufacturing process. The head of manufacturing leads this major project, which generates additional project responsibilities and performance-goal paths for plant managers. In turn, plant managers bring production-line supervisors into the mix, defining their roles in project or subproject completion. In effect, the major project has been broken up into related goals or project pieces to support the major project's needs or requirements. Engineering assists in this process of vertical inclusion by consulting on key technical issues related to the introduction of the new, critical technology.

What's needed to make this case work? Clearly, communication of the project's relation to strategy and its role in strategy execution is absolutely necessary to generate commitment and buy-in down through the organizational levels noted. Plant managers and production supervisors must see the relevance and importance of project and subproject goals. The paths to goal attainment must be clear and marked by measurable performance metrics. Problems, performance glitches, and changes must be communicated clearly, up and down the manufacturing function's hierarchy. Engineering, too, must buy into the project and be seen as facilitating movement toward project goals.

The same vertical linkages, communication, and buy-in would also come into play in a service organization. Strategic programs in banks, for example, move from corporate through regional heads, to branch managers and employees within branch banks. A major project must be supported by goals across these levels in the bank. The relevance and importance of actions and execution of a project must be seen as supporting the bank's strategy and contributing to strategic success. Effective communication and buy-in or commitment are necessary to fuel project performance and strategy execution.

These, admittedly, are simple, straightforward cases. Still, using project management to support the strategy-execution process must follow the guidelines suggested in these examples. Communication and knowledge sharing, project definition, clearly defined goals, a path to desired ends, and an emphasis on change and adaptation are all needed for project and execution success.

Leadership counts. Project management is a tool that can move projects related to strategy execution to desired results. But the process will fail if leadership doesn't espouse and support the process. From the C-level down through corporate functions or centers of excellence through key businesses and functions managers must support the use of all tools and processes the organization employs, including project management. This support is related inextricably to the development of a "culture of execution," a critical point made throughout this book. Leadership can help create and support this culture by focusing on the issues and processes defined in previous chapters, plus the complementary tenets of project management currently being discussed.

These are just a few issues related to the employment of project management in the process of strategy execution. Project management can be a useful and productive tool in the quest for execution success and the attainment of strategic objectives. The present treatment of project management is, of necessity, brief and highlights only key points of this process and how they are related to making strategy work. A great deal of additional literature is available to those interested in pursuing project management in greater detail.

One more point must be stressed about the relevance of project management to making strategy work. As with all tools or standard processes or practices, potential pitfalls often lurk behind the seemingly obvious benefits. It definitely would help if these problems or pitfalls could be identified and eliminated before they harm the execution process. Let's now turn to this important task.

POTENTIAL PITFALLS WITH PROJECT MANAGEMENT

If project management is employed to aid the strategy execution process, a number of issues must be confronted to avoid problems that might arise.

DEGREE OF FORMALITY

One of the first issues to consider is the degree of desired formality in the project management process. This can range from highly informal to a highly formal process, as Figure 13.3 suggests.

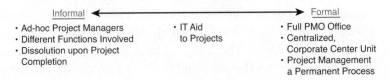

Informal ←――――――――――――――――→ Formal

- Ad-hoc Project Managers
- Different Functions Involved
- Dissolution upon Project Completion

- IT Aid to Projects

- Full PMO Office
- Centralized, Corporate Center Unit
- Project Management a Permanent Process

Figure 13.3 Degree of Formality of Project Management

An informal approach sets up a project team in an ad-hoc way, but not for every project or task. Project managers can come from different functions or areas of expertise depending on the nature of the project. Or the project manager might always come from a particular function—for example, marketing—if major projects typically deal with issues usually handled by the chosen function, such as new product development or customer satisfaction. The project team is dissolved at the completion of its work; no permanent project organization exists.

At the other extreme is the highly formal approach to project management. A permanent project management office (PMO) exists as an organizational unit. Project management is a permanent process, with virtually all tasks and projects led by full-time project managers. This represents a permanent, full-time commitment to project management as a standard management process or practice.

In the middle of the formality continuum is the IT department that occasionally is called upon to move projects along to completion. IT is a permanent function, but project management is not its only responsibility. If requested, IT personnel can help move colleagues along the project path in a consulting, facilitative role.

Potential dangers surround the degree of formality of project management. Informal processes may not be taken seriously because of their ad-hoc, occasional usage. Infrequent use can work against the standardization and repetition required for learning and sound management of the process. Choice of project manager is critical here; experience, leadership, and a positive reputation are needed to gain the respect of followers and ensure that informal processes of influence lead to effective performance against project goals. Top-management support that is clear and unequivocal is also vital to ensure the success of the project-management program.

The most likely dangers derive primarily from the formal approaches to project management. Excessive formality in a standardized, repeated process can be seen as bureaucratic, a routine approach that is foisted upon all projects, regardless of project needs or differences.

A related issue derives from a "means-ends inversion." Rather than functioning as a means to project ends, an aid for goal achievement, highly formalized project management becomes an end in and of itself. Adherence to standardized guidelines and rules becomes the rule. Project reports proliferate. "Paperwork" or requested reports must be filed on schedule, even if they bear little resemblance to actual project progress. The PMO becomes a powerful, bureaucratic force that stifles, rather than supports, project performance and the execution of strategy. If this occurs, if the means to desired ends become ends in and of themselves, the negative implications are obvious and often generate additional problems or points of resistance to project management.

Clearly, a decision regarding the desired formality of project management is important. Where projects are the norm, the usual approach to business, a more formalized program may be desired. Care, then, must be taken to avoid the problems just noted. Where occasional projects support strategy execution, more informal methods of project management make sense.

TENSION BETWEEN ROUTINE AND AUTONOMY

A problem related to the formality of project management is the tension or outright conflict between routine and autonomy in decision-making. Managerial autonomy is a desired commodity, especially when dealing with nonroutine problems and issues. If routines are seen as attacking and thwarting the desired autonomy, this can lead to poor problem solving.

The routine versus autonomy issue is especially salient and problematical in professional service organizations. The previous chapter discussed professional-bureaucratic conflict. Professionals, it was argued, desire autonomy and some flexibility in using their expertise and judgment when solving problems. Professionals are trained to use their knowledge in confronting nonroutine problems as they occur, including those that arise under strategy execution. Routine and overly standardized processes are often seen as bureaucratic, an affront to professional knowledge and integrity.

The logical conclusion is that formal approaches to project management in professional service organizations should seldom be employed, unless the professionals have some influence over goals, project paths, and key decisions. If a PMO, with full-time managers, attempts to exercise formal authority over professionals who believe that they are losing control, the actual results will certainly be problematical. Clashes between routines and autonomy are highly probable in professional service organizations, and this fact must be considered in any attempt to employ project management as a tool in the execution of strategy.

MANAGING CULTURE AND CHANGE

The issues of culture clashes and problems in managing change have already been implied in previous discussions, but they deserve separate mention. Different geographical, organizational, or intra-organizational unit cultures can impact the effectiveness of project management as a tool supporting strategy execution. In the DaimlerChrysler merger, culture certainly came into play when managing the postmerger projects. Daimler's more formal, mechanistic culture clashed mightily with the more informal culture of Chrysler. A culture wherein problems were solved by engineers in a hierarchically influenced process was at odds with the less hierarchical, more informal culture at Chrysler based more on marketing influence. Managing too many projects with two very different cultures proved to be a huge problem that negatively affected the execution of the merger strategy.

Project management also implies change as feedback about performance against project-based goals or metrics is collected and analyzed. Many of the factors noted in Chapters 7 and 8 dealing with change come into play, including control over the project management process and resistance to changes that clash with professional, functional, or managerial influence over decision-making. Incentives also come into play (Chapter 6), as managers must buy into the process of project management and the routines and changes it signals. Without skin in the game, a belief in the use of project management and its standardized approach will be weak, at best. This raises another related issue.

EVIDENCE OF VALUE ADDED

For buy-in to occur and commitment to project management to develop, participants in the process must see clear value-added outcomes of the process used to support strategy execution.

Measurable metrics must exist—project goals and outcomes—and performance against them must be seen as important and valuable to the organization or the participants involved. The project management process must produce measurable, positive, and valued results. If it doesn't, its utility as an aid in making strategy work will be diminished and its acceptance negated. If the process isn't seen as a means to a valuable and important end, it will be viewed as a burden and not a valuable tool.

The issue of scarce resources also comes into play. Even if the project management process produces some positive results, the question still will be "is it worth it?" Do the results justify the costs and expenditures laid out for it? Can scarce resources—including management's time—be better employed elsewhere? Are the real and opportunity costs simply too great to support the tool being employed? Again, evidence of value added outcomes is definitely needed.

Figure 13.4 provides an overview and summary of the role of project management. The figure indicates that the critical issues in making strategy work are shown in the basic model developed in Chapter 2 and discussed throughout this book. The contributions of structure, coordination, clear responsibilities, buy-in, and so on to the execution of strategy are critical to making strategy work. Project management can aid, abet, and support these factors or conditions by providing the incremental help or support noted in this chapter.

Figure 13.4 Project Management's Support of Strategy Execution

Project management can be a useful tool in an overall process of strategy execution. It can be an effective "means to an end," certainly not an end in itself.

SUMMARY

This is the final chapter in the Applications section of this book. It has shown how the process of project management can potentially support the execution of strategy. It discussed the benefits of project management but also identified possible pitfalls or problems that must be avoided.

Project management is a standardized process that provides a path to the successful attainment of project goals. Standardized processes can be learned and repeated, and provision of a path to desired ends reduces uncertainty, allows for incremental steps in execution, and provides a natural path for performance evaluation. Additional benefits of project management include improved communication, effective feedback and controls on performance, and learning, benefits derived from the use of clear, agreed-upon metrics of performance, the airing of divergent points of view, and buy-in to the project management approach to management.

These benefits or outcomes can support the approach to strategy execution presented in this book. Project management does not replace the critical steps and decisions the present model lays out for execution success. Rather, it supports the model laid out and discussed in Chapter 2 through Chapter 9 and provides a tool to facilitate some aspects of the strategy execution process.

Keys to the successful use of project management include definition of few projects; setting clear priorities on projects and related goals; a strong focus on participation and buy-in to the process; development of clear performance metrics; sustained efforts to improve communication; and a commitment to incremental changes that improve project performance.

Another key issue for success that deserves separate mention is the critical role of leadership. Definition of key projects and related goals often starts with C-level managers and their key direct reports. Successful project management and successful strategy execution begin at the top and then cascade down the organization. Views of project management or strategy implementation that focus only on lower levels doing the nitty-gritty work are simply misleading and wrong.

Some potential pitfalls or problems associated with the use of project management include excessive formality and bureaucracy in its deployment; means-ends inversions in which project management becomes an end in and of itself, not a means to derived outcomes; creation of conflict between routine and autonomy in decision-making; lack of evidence of value added contributions in the process; excessive real and opportunity costs; and conflicts with culture and the changes required to make project management work.

Project management can be an effective weapon in management's arsenal when trying to make strategy work. As with all tools, knowing the benefits and potential costs of their deployment is the first requisite for success.

ENDNOTES

i. See, for example, Jonathan Feldman, "Project Management Is Finally Getting Real Respect," *Information Week*, October 18, 2010.

ii. For example, see Eric Verzuh, *The Fast Forward MBA in Project Management*, John Wiley and Sons, 2012.

iii. Again, a full analysis of how to do project management is not possible here. There is ample literature on the topic that can provide additional details, including the Fast Forward MBA book referenced above. See, also, James Lewis, *The Project Manager's Desk Reference*, 3rd ed., McGraw-Hill, 2006; *The Project Management Institute, A Guide to the Project Management Body of Knowledge*, 4th ed., PMI, 2008.

Welcome to the survey on strategy execution mentioned in Chapter 1.

Executive Business Panel Questionnaire
GartnerG2 and The Wharton School

PUTTING STRATEGY INTO PRACTICE

INTRODUCTION

Welcome to our survey on strategy execution. The Wharton School of the University of Pennsylvania and GartnerG2, a research service for business strategists, are seeking to understand challenges faced by managers as they make decisions and take actions to execute strategic plans to improve their company's competitive advantage.

The survey should take about 5 minutes to complete (Responses to open-ended questions may take longer). You are part of a carefully selected group that has been asked to participate in this survey, and we appreciate your assistance. As with all surveys we conduct, your responses are confidential. Should you have any difficulties in responding, please contact us at websupport3@gar.com or call our panel support line at +1-800-xxx-xxxx.

To start, click on "Start Questionnaire." Thank you for your participation!

QUESTIONNAIRE

Q01)   We've identified 12 obstacles or hurdles to successful strategy execution. In your experience, how big a problem for execution is each of the following for your company? Use a 7-point scale, where a 1 means *not at all a problem* and a 7 means *a major problem*.

		Not at all a problem						A major problem	Don't know
1.	Poor or vague strategy	1	2	3	4	5	6	7	DK
2.	Not having guidelines or a model to guide strategy execution efforts	1	2	3	4	5	6	7	DK
3.	Insufficient financial resources to execute the strategy	1	2	3	4	5	6	7	DK
4.	Trying to execute a strategy that conflicts with the existing power structure	1	2	3	4	5	6	7	DK
5.	Inability to generate "buy in" or agreement on critical execution steps or actions	1	2	3	4	5	6	7	DK
6.	Lack of upper management support of strategy execution	1	2	3	4	5	6	7	DK
7.	Lack of feelings of "ownership" of a strategy or execution plans among key employees	1	2	3	4	5	6	7	DK
8.	Lack of incentives or inappropriate incentives to support execution objectives	1	2	3	4	5	6	7	DK
9.	Poor or inadequate information sharing between individuals or business units responsible for strategy execution	1	2	3	4	5	6	7	DK
10.	Unclear communication of responsibility and/or accountability for execution decisions or actions	1	2	3	4	5	6	7	DK
11.	Lack of understanding of the role of organizational structure and design in the execution process	1	2	3	4	5	6	7	DK
12.	Inability to manage change effectively or to overcome internal resistance to change	1	2	3	4	5	6	7	DK

Executive Business Panel Questionnaire
GartnerG2 and The Wharton School

Q02) Strategy execution requires information sharing and coordination. Please rate the effectiveness of the following coordination methods for strategy execution between functions, business units, and key personnel within your company. Use a 7-point scale, where a 1 means *highly ineffective* and a 7 means *highly effective*.

		Highly ineffective						Highly effective	Not applicable	Don't know
1.	Use of teams or cross-functional groups	1	2	3	4	5	6	7	NA	DK
2.	Use of informal communication (i.e. person-to-person contact)	1	2	3	4	5	6	7	NA	DK
3.	Use of formal integrators (e.g., a project management or quality assurance organization)	1	2	3	4	5	6	7	NA	DK
4.	Use of a matrix organization or a "grid" structure to share resources or knowledge	1	2	3	4	5	6	7	NA	DK

Q03) Based on your perceptions of knowledge and information sharing within your company during strategy execution, please indicate the extent to which you agree or disagree with the following statements. Use a 7-point scale, where a 1 means *strongly disagree* and a 7 means *strongly agree*.

		Strongly disagree						Strongly agree	Not applicable	Don't know
1.	Employees are reluctant to share important information or knowledge with others	1	2	3	4	5	6	7	NA	DK
2.	Some sources of information are unreliable	1	2	3	4	5	6	7	NA	DK
3.	Managers are reluctant to trust information generated from sources outside their own departments	1	2	3	4	5	6	7	NA	DK
4.	Information fails to reach people who need it	1	2	3	4	5	6	7	NA	DK
5.	Employees fail to understand or evaluate the usefulness of available information	1	2	3	4	5	6	7	NA	DK

Executive Business Panel Questionnaire
GartnerG2 and The Wharton School

Q04)   I know there are problems with strategy execution in my company when....

		Strongly disagree						Strongly agree	Not applicable	Don't know
1.	Execution decisions take too long to make	1	2	3	4	5	6	7	NA	DK
2.	Employees don't understand how their jobs contribute to important execution outcomes	1	2	3	4	5	6	7	NA	DK
3.	Responses to customer problems or complaints take too long to execute	1	2	3	4	5	6	7	NA	DK
4.	The company reacts slowly or inappropriately to competitive pressures while executing strategy	1	2	3	4	5	6	7	NA	DK
5.	Time or money is wasted because of inefficiency or bureaucracy in the execution process	1	2	3	4	5	6	7	NA	DK
6.	"Playing politics" is more important than performance against strategy execution goals for gaining individual recognition	1	2	3	4	5	6	7	NA	DK
7.	Important information "falls through the cracks" during execution and doesn't get acted on	1	2	3	4	5	6	7	NA	DK
8.	We spend lots of time reorganizing or restructuring, but we don't seem to know why this is important for strategy execution	1	2	3	4	5	6	7	NA	DK
9.	We're unsure whether the strategy we're executing is worthwhile, effective, or logical, given the competitive forces we face in our industry	1	2	3	4	5	6	7	NA	DK

Q05)   Managers have told us that *executing* strategy is more challenging than *formulating* strategy.
         Please tell us whether you agree with this view and briefly explain your answer.

Q06)   Finally, what other factors not mentioned in this survey make the execution process challenging
         or difficult in your company?

INDEX